MONEY OVER TWO CENTURIES

Money Over Two Centuries

Selected Topics in British Monetary History

BY
FORREST CAPIE AND GEOFFREY WOOD

OXFORD
UNIVERSITY PRESS

OXFORD
UNIVERSITY PRESS

Great Clarendon Street, Oxford, OX2 6DP,
United Kingdom

Oxford University Press is a department of the University of Oxford.
It furthers the University's objective of excellence in research, scholarship,
and education by publishing worldwide. Oxford is a registered trade mark of
Oxford University Press in the UK and in certain other countries

First Edition published 2012

Impression: 1

British Library Cataloguing in Publication Data
Data available

Library of Congress Cataloging in Publication Data
Data available

ISBN 978–0–19–965512–0

Printed in Great Britain by
MPG Books Group, Bodmin and King's Lynn

Acknowledgements

Over the years that we have worked on monetary history we have had the benefit of collaborating with a range of co-authors, and of receiving assistance and advice from numerous economists and economic historians, as well as help from the assistants on our projects. We are grateful to them all.

We have a particular debt to four others. First, to Professor Terence Mills and Dr Dimitrios Tsomocos, who have co-authored with us respectively three and one of the papers in this volume. This co-authorship reflects neither the full extent of our joint work over the years, nor the full extent of what we have learned from them. And finally, we wish particularly to thank Katherine Begley and Christopher Thomas of the Bank of England. They were of the greatest possible assistance in finding data and other sources that we wished to consult, and most valuable of all, guiding us to important sources and references that we did not know existed until they showed them to us.

Forrest Capie
Geoffrey Wood

17 October 2011

Contents

List of Figures

List of Tables

1

Introduction

We started out a long time ago with an ambition to produce a monetary history of the United Kingdom along similar lines to that of Friedman and Schwartz's Monetary History of the U.S. We recognized that it was a considerable ambition and were not unaware of some of the hazards. A great deal was achieved and we published a substantial volume of monetary data for the British economy from 1870 to 1982. This was a major archival project, the results of which were published in 1985 (Capie and Webber, *A Monetary History of the United Kingdom, 1870–1982*; and reprinted twice thereafter). Until that point there were no long-run consistent series for monetary data over this period. That provided a solid statistical basis for future work by ourselves and others.

However, more serious problems than originally anticipated arose when it came to writing an analytical account of British monetary experience. With an open economy such as Britain's was over the entire period, these difficulties were not readily resolved. The US on the other hand was not nearly as open in the international trade sense and could be approximated as a closed economy for the period covered by Friedman and Schwartz, as indeed Friedman and Schwartz did treat it. The treatment of the American economy as closed is important, and in part accounts for the fact that American macro-economic models of the economy for a long time have entirely left aside external aspects. Given the dominance of American economics it is not surprising that the rest of the world tends to import and employ these models without adaptation, and often with unhelpful results. The difficulty arose particularly with extensions of the Phillips Curve analysis.

Treating that relationship as a 'menu of policy choice' (Samuelson and Solow, 1960) had led to unsatisfactory outcomes in many countries. Inflation tended to fluctuate, sometimes significantly, about a rising trend as policy lurched from the unemployment to the inflation objective. But despite the original specification of the curve not being consistent with how it was often used, it took some years, and the arguments of Friedman (1968) and Phelps (1968) to teach that the approach was not just unworkable in practice but theoretically ill thought out. Attention then shifted to the 'inflation-augmented

Phillips Curve', in recognition that people were really concerned with real rather than nominal earnings and labour costs. In practical terms, this tended to be interpreted as monetary policy's being guided by the output gap, subject to attention being paid to measures of inflation expectations. In the years 2010 and 2011 in the UK, for example, the minutes of the Bank of England's Monetary Policy Committee consistently display claims that inflation would fall back to target because there was substantial spare capacity in the economy, and inflation expectations and wage awards were not rising with inflation. There was none of what was termed by some 'domestically generated inflation'.

There are two types of difficulty with this approach. The first, which we do not discuss in detail at this point, is that it is inconsistent with the reasons for central bank independence. The primary purpose of that was not to take policy away from the politicians who had manipulated it to electoral advantage—there is little evidence of such systematic behaviour—but rather to give it a clear and long-term focus, to have it unbuffeted by current events and focused consistently on stability in the longer term.

The second type of criticism is that the approach described above is unhelpful for an open economy. Britain has something of the order of 30 per cent of national income engaged in foreign trade. British wages, therefore, are substantially affected by wage costs overseas. The claim that because wage awards are moderate there are no inflation dangers fails to recognize that. Similarly, inferring from below-inflation wage settlements that there are no significant long-term inflation expectations is simply unjustifiable in an economy as open as the UK—and even in the US now, with its expanding foreign trade share of GNP, is much more dubious than it used to be. And finally, what is the 'output gap'? In principle it is the gap between the economy's supply potential and aggregate demand. All acknowledge that to be hard to measure. But even more important, is it a meaningful concept? Do we in the UK talk of the 'supply potential' of a particular geographical area? Where are the estimates of the 'supply potential' of Milton Keynes? They do not exist, and for the excellent reason that Milton Keynes has as its source of potential supply the rest of the UK. And in turn, the UK has as its source of potential supply the entire world. In other words, the output gap is in principle a meaningless concept for any economy that is open to the rest of the world; and for an economy as open as the UK that principle is of practical importance.

Recognizing the fundamental difference between open and closed economies did as we have remarked make writing a complete monetary history distinctly intractable. Nevertheless, we did produce a substantial amount of work on many aspects of the monetary economy across the whole period. These mark many of the key points in the story. The papers presented in this volume were written over a long time period. But motivation remained the same throughout and we believe that the results have held and have a chance of continuing to do so. Further, we believe that, while a more complete account still has to be written, a consistent story can be told and that the papers that follow here point the way to such a story.

We have divided the papers into three groups, and presented them in chronological order as all good history should. The first part covers the period of the classical gold standard from 1870 until the First World War and focuses on the key issues of that time. The second part deals with the troublesome inter-war years, when there was a breakdown in the international economy, and it goes further, into the War and immediate post-war years. And part three brings together papers on some post-war international questions. It also adds a new paper and some conjectures on the outlook for central banking given what has happened more recently and drawing on historical experience.

PART 1: THE YEARS 1870–1914/39

For a long time the common perception of this period was that it marked the beginning of British economic decline and that the 'great depression' and deflation dominated the period. It is perhaps easy to see how this view emerged but it has long been recognized as a distorted picture. Several features are related and quite often one was used to support another without there being a sound reason. Economic growth was slowing from what it had been. There was a long period when prices were falling (1873–96) albeit at a very low rate. Neither of these features is difficult to explain but the scale is in need of revision before the explanation is given.

At the same time it should also be remembered that this was a period of great stability with macro-economic stability resting on monetary stability, which in turn was supported by financial stability. The banking system had evolved in the course of the nineteenth century to the point where banks had learned prudence, worked out what the shape of their balance sheets should be, and carried the appropriate liquidity and capital to guard against financial uncertainty. This was also a time before there was any suggestion of a cartel being in operation in banking. The Bank of England had also learned how to behave as a lender of last resort to provide liquidity in times of unexpected need. Although the gold standard was in place it had become accepted that temporary suspension would be required in times of crisis as had happened on several occasions before 1870. That recognition was in part responsible for the lack of need to suspend. It was also a lightly regulated world. All these elements contributed to the remarkable stability that prevailed across this period and indeed lasted until well after the Second World War.

Nevertheless, it is not surprising to find that come the latter part of the nineteenth century Britain was doing less well in terms of output growth than it had been doing. With the American Civil War and the Franco-Prussian War behind them, more and more countries were industrializing at faster rates and provided considerable competition for Britain, where no doubt a certain complacency had crept in. This is to put it at its simplest. There are many explanations offered for the comparative slowdown in British performance that is sometimes called decline, ranging over everything from the class system through the education system, the price paid for being the first to industrialize, the costs of Empire, the overly conservative banking system, and so on. This was certainly a period of clearly failing agricultural performance and gently falling prices, most clearly in the years 1873–96. All this added up for some to the conclusion that the country was in decline and in the grip of a great depression. However, agriculture was suffering from intense foreign competition as transport costs tumbled and grain flowed in from around the world. Agricultural interests, particularly the grain-growing part, were disproportionately represented in Parliament, and the parliamentary inquiry into the observed distress arrived at the gloomiest of views. But it was agriculture rather than the wider economy that was in decline.

Economic performance generally was less bad than was implied. The most recent views depending on the work of Matthews, Feinstein, and Odling-Smee (1982), and of Greasley (1986), and Crafts (1991), and others show that average annual growth rates fell from a high in the middle of the nineteenth century of around 2.5 per cent to a low point of around 1 per cent, but that was not reached until the first decade of the twentieth century.

One of the reasons for the gloomy perspective was the fact that prices were falling. The theories of the business or trade cycle that were prevalent at that time suggested that all series moved together. In the upswing when things were good prices, employment, incomes, and so forth were all moving up. While in the downswing prices were falling along with employment and incomes. So falling prices went with depression. It is clear that the general price index—not that there was one available at the time—was falling from 1873 to 1896. (This incidentally was true for many countries.) But prices were falling at a very gentle rate, something less than 1 per cent per annum. That must have been barely perceptible to contemporaries. After a period of years it would have become clearer but it was a very gentle decline. It is possibly the only occasion in recent British history—say after 1790—that qualifies as a period of deflation, though the 1920s might on some measures. (Occasional years of falling prices are not deflation.) The principal cause of the fall was the worldwide adoption of the gold standard. As more and more countries were building gold stocks to participate in the system, that put pressure on gold supply and hence on base money, and that squeezed money growth. Interestingly, for Britain, money growth over these falling-price years was about 1 per cent below output growth. After the gold discoveries of the mid 1890s gold was sufficiently plentiful and British money growth picked up again and grew at around 1 per cent more than output growth and there were rising prices of close to 1 per cent per annum.

But how serious for the economy was the experience of deflation? Our papers on the subject examined the theories of Maynard Keynes (1930) and Irving Fisher (1933). For Keynes's theory the key is to see whether there is any evidence that price change was expected; while for Fisher it was to see whether unexpected price change produced problems through some specified channels. Our conclusions were that deflation transmitted no adverse effects to the real economy through the channels suggested by these models. This evidence is supported by the behaviour of bond rate spreads. So the period of falling prices does not appear to have brought the calamitous effects that are sometimes thought of as inevitable consequences.

More generally, our investigation of the effects of money in the economy was guided by basic monetary theory. That tells us that, under the gold standard, determination of the quantity of money lies outside the control of the authorities, although that must be modified for a large or dominant economy in the system, such as Britain was. But there is still interest in examining the relationship between broad money and the monetary base. In this system money should move after a change in income. If the authorities did expand the money supply and lowered short-term interest rates then, in the absence of exchange-rate risk, money would flow abroad in search of higher interest rates, and the monetary expansion would be negated. Against that, if real incomes grew the demand for money would increase and there would be an inflow of money. And yet money moving after income does not mean that money is unimportant for movements in income. We examine these questions in several papers.

As far as the demand for money goes our findings were that the demand for money was stable in this period, with the income elasticity very close to unity and the price elasticity also close to unity.

Our interest in economic fluctuations was guided in the first instance by the traditional theory of the impact of monetary fluctuations on a range of variables. The fluctuations would eventually dissipate themselves in price movements. One puzzling result of this investigation was a positive effect of money growth on interest rates. Money growth should ultimately leave interest rates unchanged unless it is overly rapid and produces expectations of inflation. But there was also clear confirmation of the Gibson Paradox, the relationship between the level of prices and that of interest rates. We provide an explanation in our paper written jointly with Professor Terry Mills, 'Money, Interest Rates, and the Great Depression: Britain from 1870 to 1913' (Chapter 2 of this collection.)

Although there was remarkable stability in this period there is still much of interest for investigation. But we have provided a sounder base for the conclusions that have been reached by different means.

PART 2: INTER-WAR/WAR AND IMMEDIATELY AFTER

The world of stability and comparative prosperity for the world at large that had prevailed for forty years or so before the war came to an abrupt end in 1914. For the course of the war and the immediate post-war years of adjustment there was a huge disruption to international trade and finance. Trading patterns were of course immediately affected. That then had a serious impact on domestic production which apart from the switch to production of materials for the war had also to cater for the loss of imports. In the British case, for example, this meant a major switch from pastoral to arable farming. With meat imports severely reduced substitution had to take place.

There was an immediate problem for the financial markets when war broke out. A failure of remittance from continental Europe produced conditions much like those of a typical financial crisis and that led to a large injection of liquidity. That together with the continuous need for more resources led to further monetary expansion, and that in turn produced inflation that eventually reached 20 per cent per annum. Different countries suffered to differing degrees and the consequences for exchange rates further complicated international exchange.

In addition to monetary expansion most countries borrowed on a huge scale from whatever sources were available. The repayment of these debts plus the reparation payments imposed by the victors on the losers produced another set of problems for the world economy for the next ten and even twenty years.

Exchange rate

The first obvious problem on the international front after the war was how to restore stability, and attention focused quickly on international trade and the exchange rate. Britain had been at the centre of the international gold standard before the war and so most of the attention centred on what Britain was going to do about restoring the system. Difficulties were increased because not only were price levels greatly out of kilter but they had risen so much that the available supply of gold was insufficient to support the value of prevailing incomes.

As far as Britain was concerned the ambition quickly became the desire to return to the gold standard at the pre-war parity (of $4.86). That entailed a certain amount of deflationary pressure and the support of the United States who were keen to see a restoration of the pre-war arrangements. The shortage of gold was overcome by allowing countries to hold foreign exchange in addition to gold in their reserves in the new system, hence the new name 'gold exchange standard'.

Argument continues about whether or not this was the correct approach to the problems of the time. For example, should another rate have been chosen? Or might something entirely different have been constructed? But there was almost unanimous agreement at the time that it was the appropriate course. Britain then led the way, but it was impossible to know what other countries would do and at what rate they would return to the standard. As it happened the French, the most important economy and holder of gold after the US and Britain, went back at a rate that placed them at an advantage to the others. The Soviet Union had been born in these troubled years, hyperinflation was raging in much of Central and Eastern Europe, debt repayment was being argued about and German reparation payments were a source of continuing difficulty. These all combined to frustrate attempts at international agreement.

For Britain, then, the 1920s were dominated by the question of the exchange rate. For the first five years efforts were concentrated on getting the price level in line with the US. This was more or less achieved and the standard was restored in its new form in April 1925. In the following few years the efforts were aimed at keeping to the restored rate. Although there were these deflationary pressures British growth in these years was surprisingly good—something in excess of 2 per cent per annum and the best that had been achieved for more than forty years.

Financial crisis

At the end of the 1920s and beginning of the 1930s there was the biggest ever collapse of the world economy in the Great Depression. The worst of that was in the United States and parts of continental Europe. But interestingly, Britain remained remarkably unscathed. There was certainly a recession. Output fell by around 5 per cent across the period 1929–32. Unemployment rose sharply but that is better explained by real wages (see Beenstock, Capie, and Griffiths, 1984). But while there were financial crises around the world there was none in Britain.

We use Schwartz's (1986) definition of a financial crisis as something that threatens the payments system. There was no sign of that in Britain. There were none of the common conditions for a crisis. There was no monetary expansion, no easy credit, no surge in asset prices, and none of the euphoria that commonly accompanies the build-up to a crisis. The banking system was entirely sound. There was barely a threat to the level of profits of the banks through these years. There were problems for the merchant banks which were directly exposed to the crises in continental Europe. But these did not seriously impinge on the commercial banking system and, to the extent that they did, were easily contained. Solutions were found in the German standstill agreements and other means.[1]

We argue that what happened in 1931 is better understood as an exchange-rate crisis. That certainly can be seen in big part as an immediate consequence of the continental European crises. But it should be stressed that in the world of the time it was no longer possible to hold to the parity of pre-war days. The system had come to the end of its useful life. As we argue in our paper on 1931, it was not simply a question of overvaluation of the pound. The system was abandoned as a consequence of its internal inconsistencies.

Debt conversion

Apart from the problems of international debt Britain's domestic debt was a burden carried across the inter-war years. Where the debt ratio had fallen to a low of 27 per cent immediately before the First World War, after the war it was 200 per cent. With interest rates of roughly 5 per cent, that came to annual debt-servicing payments of £400m. Anything that could be done to ease that burden was desirable.

Attention fell on War Loan 1917. That carried a coupon rate of 5 per cent. It had been issued in 1917 and had a final redemption date of 1947. The scale of the issue was staggering: £2,553m had been issued, and this one stock was equal to roughly half of GDP. By the beginning of 1932 there was still £2,100m outstanding and at that stage equal in value to around 30 per cent of GDP. The ambition then was to carry out a conversion into a stock with a 3.5 per cent coupon with a redemption date of '1952 or after'.

It was a complicated exercise. All manner of enticements and penalties were employed alongside a major propaganda exercise. And the conversion was generally felt to have been a big success in terms of replacing the existing stock with the new stock without damage to the markets or producing monetary expansion. So one immediate objective was achieved, that of reducing the current debt-servicing burden.

But a bigger ambition was to reduce the whole structure of interest rates and whether that was achieved is more difficult to establish. According to some it did. For example, Kaldor said just that: it 'brought down the whole structure of long-term interest rates . . . which led to the fastest rate of economic growth in British history' (Kaldor, 1982, p. 1) Among other things our paper sets out to test that. The short rate is more easily explained by what was happening to sterling. That rate was rising with the pressure on sterling in 1930/31 and it eased after the break with gold in 1932. As for the long rate as captured in the

[1] Arguments are being put that link the difficulties of the merchant banks to financial stability. (See for example Accominotti, 2011.)

consol yield the conversion lengthened the maturity of the debt, and so long rates would be expected to rise relative to short rates. That is what happened. But there was some drop in the yield that coincided with the conversion. A possible explanation for that is that the reduction of debt-servicing costs produced an immediate expectation of reduced taxes. So the successful operation could have produced the observed fall in the yield at the time of the conversion. But there is no evidence of a dramatic fall in the consol yield brought about by the conversion, and it was not that that brought about the era of 'cheap money'.

Leaving the gold standard allowed interest rates to fall and monetary expansion to follow, and paved the way for the economic expansion that took place across the rest of the 1930s. Prices rose gently from 1932 to 1939 and output grew rapidly at around 4 per cent per annum.

Price controls

On the outbreak of war in September 1939 there were fears of inflation (partly from the memory of the First World War), but also because in war resources are used by government on a scale much greater than peacetime. And there is a quickening in the pace of resource mobilization. Governments have almost invariably resorted to controls to enable them to carry this out. The fears of inflation were soon realized as prices rose sharply in the first eighteen months of the war. Government aimed to win the war with as little inflation as possible, and in the budget of 1941 it was forecast that prices would be held at their then current level for the duration of the war. The available price indexes suggest that this was achieved. How was it done?

Fiscal policy was implemented for the first time in a Keynesian fashion. An estimate of the inflationary gap was made and taxes altered to close as much of the gap as possible. Borrowing made up another tranche. There was, nevertheless, monetary growth in excess of 'normal' times. We estimate the extent of that and its impact on the price level and then show that the other measures taken must be responsible for the success in holding prices fairly steady across the following four years. These measures were rationing and subsidies and price controls.

Containing inflation was a major objective of policy and must be considered a considerable success. Increased taxes and bond finance contributed to the success and reduced the need to print money. Subsidies simply altered relative prices. Price controls played a significant part, supported by rationing; indeed, we argue that rationing was crucial to the success. And there was more than patriotism involved—there were severe penalties for violation of the controls. We accept that it is impossible to allow properly for the quality changes that undoubtedly took place.

However, it remains to ask if prices then return to where they would have been in the absence of the controls. That is more difficult to answer, but the indications are that they do. The controls work in the sense that they keep the lid on prices for the duration of the war and inflation then has to be coped with in the calmer times of peace.

PART 3: POST-WWII, THE INTERNATIONAL DIMENSION, AND THE FUTURE

Will money as we currently know it, fiat money, survive, or will it be displaced by electronic barter? The first paper in this section addresses that question from a transactions costs perspective, the argument that money evolved to reduce the costs of transacting via barter. The approach is a very traditional one, and follows on the work of many scholars, most recently Karl Brunner and Alan Meltzer. (See particularly Meltzer (1998) for an overview of their work and its predecessors.) In the first chapter of this section after setting out that approach we develop a formal model which, utilizing transactions costs arguments leads to the conclusion that money will survive, and thus to the further conclusion that central banking in a form we would recognize today has a future.

But central banks have evolved over the years. This is particularly emphasized in the final paper in this section, which traces the evolution of the objective of central banks from their early origins, reaching the conclusion that the ultimate objective has always been, in the current terminology, the preservation of monetary and financial stability. Vital to that evolution, though, particularly in Britain but in fact worldwide, has been the changing international dimension. Two issues particularly bearing on this have been European Monetary Union, and the development of the International Monetary Fund into a body which some have claimed serves, or in weaker versions of the claim can serve, as a central bank for the world.

Monetary unions

In our work on European Monetary Union we have consistently maintained that there are important lessons from past monetary unions, and that these lessons have been neglected in most discussions of the subject. Reviewing analytical work on EMU leads inescapably to the conclusion that the literature cannot guide one to any conclusion on whether EMU is an optimal currency area or even a feasible currency area. Rather one can consider whether EMU satisfies the conditions under which previous unions have survived. As numerous previous authors have shown, these conditions are quite demanding: for example, Balassa observed (1973) 'reserve flows[2] are not solely responsible for the equilibrium of regional balances of payments and that short-term as well as long-term capital movements, income changes, government transfers as well as labour migration all contribute to it.'

Our examination of previous monetary unions in the nineteenth and the twentieth centuries fully supports this conclusion; it showed that institutional change well beyond the simple establishment of a union was necessary for it to survive. In particular, there needed to be the political cohesion that would allow all the factors Balassa listed to be acceptable. Most notably, there was need of labour mobility and of fiscal transfers in response to regional difficulties, and these needed to be arranged by a permanent and generally accepted institution and mechanism, not produced on an ad hoc emergency basis.

An international lender of last resort?

As has, regrettably, often been the case in recent years, discussion of the institutions of the international monetary order has taken place entirely ahistorically. There has been no consideration of the conditions under which these institutions were designed and established, or of the problems they were designed to address.

The IMF grew out of the years of dirty floating, trade barriers, and competitive devaluations of the 1930s. But the main protagonists in its design were the United States and the United Kingdom, and that was undoubtedly reflected in its design. The US was concerned mainly to stabilize exchange rates, while the UK's goals were both to safeguard its balance of payments position if the inter-war system of imperial preference were abandoned, and to restore sterling's international position. This led to two proposals, the White plan and the Keynes plan. The latter seemed to seek to deal with all possible international financial problems including postwar reconstruction and development finance. The White plan focused on exchange stabilization, and the fund to achieve that would not have the new international currency Keynes envisaged, but have as its reserves existing national currencies and gold. The plan adopted was much closer to that of White than that of Keynes, in particular involving little interference with domestic policies. The IMF was the institution designed to run the system, and the main obligation of IMF members was to allow free current account convertibility. Restrictions on the capital account were allowed. Many, notably Ronald McKinnon (e.g. 1979),

[2] These he mentioned because of the stress laid on them in a prior paper by Mundell (1973).

have argued that the system never really functioned as intended. But be that as it may, it is clear that the IMF was primarily designed to deal with exchange rate stabilization in a pegged exchange rate system. Its evolution from that has been considerable.

It survived into the era of floating exchange rates by reinventing itself as a 'crisis manager'. Or so it has been claimed. But the evidence for the existence of *international* crises, analogous to domestic ones by, for example, being spread by contagion, is slight. Argentina's 1995 problems followed those of Mexico in 1994—but the problems of Argentina were genuine, and the biggest effect Mexico may have had is to lead people to look more carefully at Argentina than they had done heretofore. And as for the spread of problems across South East Asia in the late 1990s, the problems of all countries involved were the same—imprudent bank lending combined with inflation resulting from currency pegs. In sum, the Fund's role as crisis manager requires international crises—and these are hard to find.

And of course the IMF cannot lend as an international lender of last resort, analogous to the last resort lending of a central bank, for it cannot supply national currencies to any but a trivial extent. On the occasions when it is claimed to have done so it has, rather, simply lent to one government funds it has borrowed from others at times when no lender was willing to lend his or her own funds on as easy terms. Perhaps a supplier of risk capital of last resort, but not a lender of last resort.

In sum, while the IMF has undoubtedly evolved, its self-interested evolution has not led to its supplanting domestic central banks in their last resort role.

That role is, of course, relevant in the crisis at the end of the first decade of the twenty-first century. Or was it? In fact, a remarkable feature of that episode was that there was little consideration of whether appropriate lender of last resort action would have prevented panic turning to crisis, or, at the least, diminished the consequences of the crisis. Yet again, for all the talk of the lessons of history, when a problem suddenly arose the lessons seemed to be forgotten.

In the past lender of last resort action served to stabilize the system even when individual banks failed. And it was seen as important that individual banks fail, lest, to use the modern term, moral hazard should be allowed to flourish. One reason that lender of last resort was not used in the recent episode was that there was not in most countries provision for orderly closure of banks, and even in countries which had such legislation there were doubts over whether it could handle large or international banks; and it was acknowledged that nowhere could it handle investment banks.

The consequence of that neglect has been a sustained increase in moral hazard. And from that follows a clear lesson. It is essential that banks—banks of all sizes and types—be capable of being allowed to fail, and occasionally actually do so, and in an orderly way. A large grocery chain can fail without causing economy-wide disruption. The legal framework has to be developed so that the same can be true of banks. Without that, panic responses to failures and calls upon taxpayers will be an inevitable feature of our future.

Independence and inflation

Towards the end of the period we had sought to cover, the Bank of England, as part of a worldwide trend, was granted 'independence'. That term was generally left undefined, but as with the Reserve Bank of New Zealand, which the new-model Bank of England closely resembled, the independence took the form discussed in a curiously neglected study by Milton Friedman. In that 1962 paper, which ultimately concluded by arguing that a monetary rule was the best approach to conducting monetary policy, he carefully discussed the meaning of the term 'independence'. He suggested that it could usefully be interpreted as similar to the independence of the judiciary—being free to carry out laws passed by the government, and free of interference from the government, until the law was changed (if it was).

There have been various studies which claimed to show that lack of independence on the part of central banks was the root cause of the endemic inflation of the post-Second World War years (e.g. Barro and Gordon, 1983).

It is far from clear that the deliberate manipulation of monetary policy for electoral advantage described in that analysis was behind most inflations, but, be that as it may, there was a large amount of work which, almost regardless of country and of how independence was measured, claimed to demonstrate that independence was favourably associated with low inflation. But a problem with this result was that every study drew on a good part of the same rather short period—the years of exchange rate flexibility after about 1973. That was understandable in that only with floating exchange rates can most countries have monetary independence, but it did open up the possibility that the result was a chance feature of a particular period.

Accordingly we examined a rather longer period, on the grounds that it was important to distinguish the form of monetary regimes from the substance, and that many regimes—even the gold standard—were not as constricting as a literal interpretation of the rules suggested. We also used as determinants of independence a variety of criteria.

The results were not completely straightforward. Some countries achieved persistent low inflation despite the status of their central bank; changes in that status were entirely unconnected with the central bank's inflation performance. And some countries had rather different inflationary performance despite having identical central bank constitutions. Nevertheless, our longer run study was undoubtedly in general terms supportive of the relationship's existing. Independence did seem to help.

Of course, independence meant that the central bank needed an objective—what it became fashionable to call a mandate. In the final essay of this section, one written for this collection, we argue first that mandate is not the best term, and second and more important, the objectives of central banks have been unchanging since their inception, albeit described in different terms at different times.

Notable in the discussions of independence was the neglect of one of the central bank's key responsibilities—the maintenance of the stability of the banking system, what is called in current terminology financial stability; that being the counterpart to monetary stability. There was no such neglect in the earlier discussions and periods we consider. Rather there was continuity, with objectives unchanging, albeit sometimes described in different terms. How might this dual objective be better obtained in the future than it has in recent years?

One of the remarkable aspects of the recent crisis was the revelation that monetary economists were inclined to downplay, if not actually ignore, the part that the financial system played in the economy: 'the 2007–09 financial crisis made it clear that the adverse effects of financial disruption on economic activity could be far worse than originally anticipated for advanced economies' (Mishkin, 2010, p. 83). Financial frictions 'should be front and centre in macroeconomic analysis; they could no longer be ignored in macroeconometric models that central banks used for forecasting and policy analysis' (ibid.). Mishkin goes on to say that before the crisis the view amongst most economists in academia and in central banks was that price and output stability promoted financial stability. Familiarity with the nineteenth-century gold standard would have raised their eyebrows at that. It seems that a lesson learned from the financial crisis is that monetary policy and financial stability policy are intrinsically linked; some better grasp of history would have served policymakers better.

Central banking in future

Central banks have in recent years come, not altogether successfully, through turbulent times. In the UK, inflation targeting, having at least so far as inflation control was concerned worked well in its early years, has in the years of turbulence been a failure. The Bank of England has not achieved its mandate. There are dangers here for the Bank's credibility, and thus in turn dangers of inflationary spirals and sharply rising bond yields. The stability of prices and long-term interest rates which contributed so much to the nineteenth century's prosperity seems far away. But what to do about it? One reason behind the failure obvious to outsiders is the failure of the Bank's inflation forecasting. While we explain above one reason that we think lay behind that failure, we do not claim remedy is easy. In view of that, it would surely make sense for the Bank, and any central bank in similar difficulties, to target, not the inflation forecast, but rather actual inflation, responding to deviations from the desired rate in a damped manner, an approach akin to that of the Taylor (1993) (or the less well-known McCallum (1988)) rule, but focusing on inflation not on an amalgam of that and real growth.

As for financial stability, when there is, as there is now, an opportunity to clean the slate and begin again, we believe that the following principles, or perhaps we had better call them guidelines based on historical experience, should be adopted. Failure must be possible. Regulation should be light and characterized by simplicity and clarity. Transparency must be full. The payments system must be protected. Competition should be encouraged. In other words, the framework must be clear and uncertainty reduced as far as possible. The latter must be aided by credibility—conviction by the participants that the rules will be followed.

The payments system should be protected. Competition within the payments system should be encouraged. The failure of any one institution should not matter greatly for the system. The rest of the financial system can be left to do what it chooses with the proviso that suitable closure procedures are available. The Bank of England should behave as lender of last resort within the payments system. There is no moral hazard involved in that. Banks within the payments system can and should fail if they do not have the liquid assets appropriate to the occasion.

For the system, but particularly the non-payments sector, there should be light regulation and full transparency. Light, clear, and simple regulatory rules aid the process of market discipline. Transparency means that balance sheets need to be understood by directors, auditors, shareholders, and other interested parties.

CONCLUSION

This introductory chapter has sought to summarize and draw together the large body of work in this collection, a body of work itself a sample of a larger body.

A further summary is therefore unnecessary. What we would say in conclusion is that we think we have learned a great deal from the study of history. We think all economists would learn from such study, and we hope that our efforts will both help and encourage them to do so.

REFERENCES

Accominotti, Olivier (2011) 'The London Merchant Banks, the Central European Panic, and the Sterling Crisis of 1931', *Journal of Economic History*.

Balassa, B. (1973) *The Theory of Economic Integration*, London: Allen and Unwin.

Barro R. J. and Gordon, D. B. (1983) 'A Positive Theory of Monetary Policy in a Natural Rate Model', *Journal of Political Economy*, 91(4), 589–610.

Beenstock, Michael, Capie, Forrest, and Griffiths, Brian (1984) 'Economic Recovery in the United Kingdom in the 1930s', Bank of England Academic Panel Paper No. 23.

Capie, Forrest and Webber Alan (1995) *A Monetary History of the United Kingdom, 1870–1982*, London: Allen and Unwin.

Crafts, N. F. R. (1991) 'Economic Growth in Nineteenth Century Britain: Comparisons with Europe in the Context of Gerschenkron's Hypothesis', in R. Sylla and G. Toniolo (eds.), *Patterns of European Industrialization in the XIX Century*, Oxford: OUP.

Fisher, I. (1933) 'Booms and Depressions', *Econometrica*, 1(1).

Friedman, M. (1962) 'Should there be an Independent Monetary Authority?' in Leland B. Yeager, (ed.), *In Search of a Monetary Constitution*, Boston, MA: Harvard University Press.

——(1968) 'The Role of Monetary Policy', *American Economic Review*, 58 (March), 1–17.

——and Schwartz, A. J. (1963) *Monetary History of the US, 1867–1960*, Princeton: Princeton University Press for NBER.

Greasley, D. (1986) 'British Economic Growth: The Paradox of the 1880s and the Timing of the Climacteric', *Explorations in Economic History*, 23(4), 416–44.

Kaldor, N. (1982) *The Scourge of Monetarism*, London: Blackwell.

Keynes, J. M. (1930) *A Treatise on Money*, London: Macmillan.

McCallum, Bennett T. (1988) 'Robustness Properties of a Rule for Monetary Policy', Carnegie Rochester Conference Series for Public Policy, 29 (Autumn), 173–202.

McKinnon, Ronald (1979) *Money in International Exchange: The Convertible Currency System*, New York: Oxford University Press.

Matthews, R., Feinstein, C. H., and Oddling-Smee, J. C. (1982) *British Economic Growth*, Oxford: Clarendon.

Meltzer, Allan H. (1998) 'What is Money?', in Geoffrey Wood, (ed.), *Money, Prices, and the Real Economy*, Cheltenham: Edward Elgar.

Mishkin, Frederic S. (2010) 'Monetary Policy Flexibility, Risk Management, and Financial Disruptions', *Journal of Asian Economics* 23 (June), 242–46.

Mundell, Robert A. (1973) 'Uncommon Arguments for Common Currencies', in H. G. Johnson and A. K. Swoboda (eds), *The Economics of Common Currencies*, London: Allen and Unwin.

Phelps, Edmund S. (1968) 'Money Wage Dynamics and Labor Market Equilibrium', *Journal of Political Economy*, 76(S4), 678–711.

Samuelson, P. A. and Solow, R. (1960) 'Analytical Aspects of Anti-inflation Policy', *American Economic Review*, 50(2), 177–94.

Schwartz, A. J. (1986) 'Real and Pseudo Financial Crises', in F. H. Capie and G. E. Wood (eds), *Financial Crises and the World Banking System*, London: Macmillan.

Taylor, John B. (1993) 'Discretion Versus Policy Rules in Practice', Carnegie-Rochester Conference Series on Public Policy, 39, 195–214.

Part One

2

Money, Interest Rates, and the Great Depression: Britain from 1870 to 1913*

INTRODUCTION

In this chapter we examine the impact of changes in the quantity of money on aggregate economic variables in Britain over the years 1870 to 1913. This subject has been examined by two of the present authors (Capie and Wood, 1984) but the statistical techniques used were fairly rudimentary, and the analytical framework within which hypotheses were tested was set out rather sparsely. This chapter sets out to remedy these deficiencies. Its structure is as follows. The first section outlines the historical background of the period; it gives an account of what is currently the conventional view of macroeconomic developments in this era. The second section sets out the analytical framework we use to organize the empirical work. This analytical framework is the traditional model of the impact of money on real and nominal interest rates. This framework has two advantages for the present purpose. It provides a most detailed account of the effect of money on key macroeconomic variables and, second, it lets us consider various explanations of the Gibson Paradox, a phenomenon which, although certainly noted and discussed before this period, was named and came to prominence as a result of examination of data from the years examined here. The data themselves are then described. This prepares the way for the statistical work. The chapter then concludes with a discussion of the results of that work, focusing first on the Gibson Paradox and then on how the results contribute to an understanding of the role of money in Britain in the late nineteenth and early twentieth centuries.

* Originally published as Forrest H. Capie, Terence C. Mills, and Geoffrey E. Wood (1991). 'Money, Interest Rates, the Great Depression: Britain from 1870 to 1913', pp. 251–284, in James Foreman-Peck (ed.), *New Perspectives on the Late Victorian Economy: Essays Quantitative Economic History, 1860–1914*.

HISTORICAL OVERVIEW

The view that is most widely held on Britain during this period is of an economy increasingly under pressure and beginning to struggle for position in the income per capita league: a tough competitive climate was developing, as a result of the United States, Germany, and others emerging as major industrial powers. Many recent accounts of Britain's poor economic performance have dated the origins of relative decline from the 1870s: see, for example, Kirby (1981), Elbaum and Lazonick (1986), and Sked (1987).

Much of this account of decline did, however, rest on a less than robust database and this is reflected in the long debate over if, and when, a climacteric occurred. Some placed the climacteric in the 1870s, Coppock (1956), for example; others, notably Phelps Brown and Handfield Jones (1952), set it in the 1890s. Feinstein's (1972) aggregate output data helped clarify some issues and the publication of Matthews et al. (1982) and the companion paper, Feinstein et al. (1982), presented a picture of growth in slight but steady decline from the 1850s through to a nadir in the Edwardian era. Annual average growth rates fell from around 2.5 per cent in the 1850s to around 1 per cent in the 1900s. Questions have been raised, however, about the reliability of even these data. Greasley (1986) suggested that Feinstein's income series was mismeasured because of the poor quality of the underlying wage data, and proposed a revised estimate of aggregate output based upon a corrected income series. Although Greasley's criticisms appear to have considerable merit, his revised series has been itself the subject of a severe and apparently damning attack by Feinstein (1987) who, nevertheless, accepts that his original data are in need of revision.

The empirical work on estimating trend rates of output growth reported by Feinstein et al. and Greasley has recently been superseded by the research of Crafts et al. (1989a and b), who use structural time series models to isolate and estimate both the trend and cycle components of a variety of output and production series for this period. Their finding for aggregate output is of only a slight fall in trend growth during the years 1899 to 1913, the period favoured by Feinstein et al. for exhibiting the climacteric, and no evidence at all of a climacteric in the 1870s. Indeed, when industrial production is considered, a steady decline in trend growth is found to start in the mid nineteenth century and to continue through most of the third quarter of the century before levelling off, that is, the decline began *before* the so-called 'Great Depression' and well before the dates usually assigned to the climacteric.

This changes substantially what needs to be explained. Where once it was accepted that the period 1873 to 1896 was one long period of stagnation, the 'Great Depression', this would now appear not to be the case: there was no great depression and neither was there any climacteric.

Interestingly, histories of almost all the developed, and some of the developing, world have accounts of a long depression in this period. Whether these accounts will hold up when the database is strengthened is not clear, but the suspicion is that they will not. It seems that, at least for several cases, while there was a long downswing in prices, or a long deflation as it tended to be called, there was little setback to output. These falling prices were thought to indicate a long-lasting depression because in the business cycle all macroeconomic variables moved together, and falling prices meant contraction. But did this hold for a secular trend?

There was some evidence apparently confirming that it did. First, agriculture was still important in many countries and certainly suffered in this period. The agricultural interest was politically vocal and still powerful. It promoted the idea that there was a depression and sought help, often in the form of tariff protection. Second, there was a severe and longer lasting cyclical downturn in either the 1870s or 1880s in many countries. But that apart, depression was being read from price behaviour. Even Kondratieff's cycle was essentially a price cycle.

There was certainly a clear, long downswing in prices. Prices in Britain fell from the 1870s to the mid 1890s and rose from then until 1914. The extent of the fall and rise, though, has been considerably modified from that thought at the time. While between 1873 and 1896 wholesale prices (the original indicator used) fell by 39 per cent and rose by 40 per cent from then until 1914, Feinstein's deflator fell by only 20 per cent and rose by 17.6 per cent.

Two strands developed in the literature to explain this long swing in prices, one real and the other monetary. The real explanation rests essentially on the extension of arable farming in the new world and on the transport revolution. These conjoined to produce tumbling prices of agricultural goods in Britain—an important part of the world market—and in the rest of Europe. This, the argument goes, lowered prices because in any index these were highly significant. Note, however, that the argument rests on prices falling more and more each year for many years. Bordo and Schwartz (1981) cast considerable doubt on this line of argument in a specific and rigorous test of the hypothesis.

The real explanation, say its opponents, confuses relative prices with the general price level. Those advancing the monetary explanation do not dispute the fall in agricultural prices. There is nothing to dispute; that there was a fall in agricultural prices and in the general price index is a well-established fact. What they reject is the idea that agricultural prices brought the price index down, that is, lowered the general level of prices. Only a scarcity of money in relation to output could do that. Had there not been such a scarcity, falling agricultural prices would have been offset in their effect on the general level of prices by rising prices elsewhere. Proponents of the monetary explanation argue that there was a scarcity of money relative to output and that it resulted from the fact that from 1870 onwards the world economy was developing rapidly while at the same time the main industrial countries were adopting the gold standard. There was therefore a shortage of gold base money per unit of output as these countries acquired reserves of gold. Prices thus fell steadily until the scarcity was corrected by the gold discoveries of the early and mid 1890s in Australia, South Africa, and the Klondike, Cagan (1965) pointed out that, whereas in the 1850s the world's monetary stock was growing at 8 per cent per annum, in the critical years 1875–87 the rate of growth dropped to 1 per cent per annum. And since Cagan demonstrated that money determined prices in the United States, he argued 'the same explanation must hold for all countries, including England, that were on the gold standard and had close commercial ties with the United States' (p. 250). From the gold discoveries onwards there was actually a small surfeit of gold in relation to output, and prices thus crept steadily upwards.

As is now well established, deficient monetary data led to a confused picture for Britain, but the deficiencies are now in good part removed. A detailed account is given in Capie and Webber (1985) of the deficiencies of the old data, and of how the series used in this paper (and also in Capie and Wood (1984)) were constructed. We return to these data below. It is now necessary to set out the analytical framework of the present paper.

ANALYTICAL FRAMEWORK

Money, interest rates and prices In this section we set out the traditional analysis of the effects of a once and for all shift from one steady rate of money growth to another. We are, because of data limitations, particularly concerned with the effects of such a shift on the nominal yield of a nominal asset, but we do at points note also the behaviour of certain other yields. The monetary change is unanticipated, but, when it occurs, it is fully perceived. For expository simplicity, it is assumed that the price level is initially constant, and is expected to remain so.

On the assumption that the general level of prices is slower to change than both nominal interest rates and real income, the effects of such a monetary change can be divided into four stages. First there may be a loanable funds effect. This is succeeded by a liquidity effect. Real income then starts to move; this affects interest rates. And then there is an effect on the general level of prices, and on price level expectations; this latter in turn produces the ultimate impact of the monetary change on the nominal yield on nominal assets. These various stages are described in order.

Loanable funds effect This comes about because revenue accrues to the issuers of new money. This revenue may be spent on consumption goods, in which case the first impact of the money growth is on the prices of these goods. To use the example given by J. S. Mill (1848), if the money growth were the result of a gold discovery, the initial effects would be on the wages of gold-miners and on the prices of what these miners buy. But, if the revenue is used to augment wealth, there is an increase in the supply of loanable funds. This affects *all* yield—real and nominal, *ex post* and *ex ante*, on real and on nominal assets—because it is so far being assumed that inflation expectations do not change, and that the money growth was unanticipated.

Liquidity preference effect This effect is also an initial effect of the changed rate of money growth but, unlike the loanable funds effect, does not depend on choices concerning the disposition of the revenue from money creation, and produces a sustained decline rather than an immediate drop in rates (again, because of the above noted assumptions, rates however defined). Rates behave in this way because we have moved to a higher growth rate of money. So long as no variable except interest rates can change, there is a continually rising ratio of real (and nominal) money to real income. To induce this to be held, the opportunity cost of holding real cash balances (the nominal rate of interest) has to fall and it keeps on falling until the third effect comes into play.

The income effect We now have lower real and nominal interest rates on all types of asset. The prices of the services of assets have therefore risen relative to the prices of the assets which supply these services. Nominal expenditure rises, and as prices (including money wages) have not yet changed, so does nominal output. This increases the quantity of real cash balances demanded at every opportunity cost, and, hence, as income rises the nominal yield on nominal assets also rises, gradually reversing the liquidity effect. (As price expectations have by assumption not yet changed, real yields on real assets, and real yields on nominal assets, *ex post* and *ex ante*, also rise.) All these rates rise until they are back at their pre-monetary expansion level, for only then is the stimulus to expenditure dissipated. But the process does not end there.

Price expectations A higher rate of money growth has been superimposed on an unchanged real economy. Hence, the only way, since no real variable changes, that the increased nominal money stock will be held is if prices rise. They rise eventually at the same rate as the growth of money.[1] When

[1] There must at some point be a jump in the price level, or a rise at faster than its equilibrium growth rate, as individuals adjust to the higher cost of holding real cash balances. This implies that there is in fact a real change, since the total utility yield on money falls. But the above discussion refers to conventional measures of real income, which exclude that yield; and it looks beyond that price level transition to its equilibrium inflationary path.

prices are rising at this rate, if price expectations have not changed, realized real rates of interest on all assets fall again. Price expectations must change.

Ultimately the inflation is fully anticipated. At this point, nominal yields on nominal assets (both *ex ante* and *ex post*) have risen by an amount equal to the inflation rate; while real yields, *ex ante* and *ex post*, on real and nominal assets, are unchanged.

Our empirical work is in part addressed to considering whether this full process can be observed in the UK from 1870 to 1913. As it is also, however, concerned with the existence (sometimes challenged), and possible explanation, of the Gibson Paradox, it is necessary next to survey the principal literature on this phenomenon, so as to summarize the questions it raises.

The Gibson Paradox Over the period 1870–1913 there appears to be a positive association between the nominal interest rate and the level of prices—an association which Keynes (1930) called the Gibson Paradox, after A. H. Gibson, who first drew attention to the relationship.[2]

This association between the price level and some measure of the nominal interest rate is clearly not deducible from any standard classical model. Double the money supply (and thus the price level), and all real variables, including the rate of interest—which is a variable having the dimension £ per £ per time—are homogenous of degree zero with respect to such a comparative static change in the nominal variables. What, then, can explain the association between the price level and the interest rate? The answer most in accordance with the theory outlined above was first advanced by Irving Fisher (1907, 1930) and later given qualified support by Friedman and Schwartz (1982). They argued that because a move from one fully anticipated inflation rate to another would (even with the real return on physical capital unchanged) alter the nominal yield on nominal assets, the *appearance* of a relationship between nominal yields and the *level* (as opposed to the rate of change) of prices could be produced. This relationship would appear if inflation expectations adjusted to inflation with a lag, so that the longer inflation persisted (and thus the higher the price level rose), the higher would the nominal yield rise, until it stabilized when the inflation became fully anticipated. The correlation between nominal interest rates and the price level is close if the period it takes people to adjust their expectations is about as long as the swings in prices.

That is not, however, the only explanation that has been offered. Wicksell, and later Keynes, offered an explanation which was also within the traditional framework, but posited a movement in the real rate of return on physical assets. According to both Wicksell (1907) and Keynes (1930), nominal rates on nominal assets were pulled down by a downward drift in the natural rate of

[2] An admirable, and brief, survey of explanations of the paradox can be found in Cagan (1984).

interest, the real return on real assets, reflecting a decline in the marginal physical productivity of capital. This occurred in the first half of the period, and was replaced in the second half by a rise as the American mid and far west were opened up. Price level movements were in turn induced because the market rate lagged behind the actual rate.

Although different from the Fisher explanation, that is within the same analytical framework. Some explanations, however, entirely reject the framework by denying the influence of money on prices. Mathias (1983, p. 367) wrote as follows:

> Many vital factors do not fit the thesis. Bullion dealers reported no shortage of gold: the reserves of the Bank of England stayed high. Furthermore—a key fact—interest rates on Lombard Street stayed low—consols were under 3 per cent per annum yield and the discount rate between 2 and 3.5 per cent per annum. These depressed interest rates . . . suggest an exactly contrary thesis to the monetary one—that excess savings were seeking investment outlets; that money was over-plentiful in relation to investment opportunities of every sort.

Throughout that quotation there is a confusion, made explicit in the last sentence, between money and credit. But what seems to be implied is that there was a persistent abundance of money (an excess supply?), but that *nominal* interest rates stayed low because of *real* factors, with money not affecting prices. What then did determine prices? Phelps Brown and Ozga (1955) advanced an explanation, which was taken up by Coppock (1961). Phelps Brown and Ozga argued that, when industrial production grew more slowly than production of primary goods, primary goods prices fell, and exerted a downward cost-push on prices; and the converse happened when the growth rate of industrial production exceeded that of primary production. Coppock adopted this view, and explained the co-movement of prices and interest rates as the result of a slowing of Britain's growth in the 1870s not being offset in its impact on world industrial production until the German and American growth of the 1890s. These explanations have no role for money. If money enters at all, it is passive, and interest rates and the price level behave as they did because of real factors.

Subsequent to these explanations, monetary forces came back into favour. Hughes (1968) supported the Keynes-Wicksell view. Paish (1966) and Hicks (1967) advance an explanation which is, if not monetary, certainly financial; they ascribe the fall in long rates to a shortage of high quality long assets in the market.

Three comparatively recent studies take the view that money growth determined the trend of prices, and that the behaviour of interest rates has to be reconciled with that. These are Sargent (1973), Harley (1977), and Friedman and Schwartz (1982). These all start from Irving Fisher (1907, 1930), who argued that the underlying relationship was between interest rates and inflation, and the observed relationship the result of inflationary expectations (which Fisher argued depended on past inflation) changing very slowly. But, as Sargent put it, this explanation of the Gibson Paradox may be 'really only a redefinition of it'; for Cagan had earlier (1972) pointed out that the mean adjustment lags estimated by Fisher do seem remarkably long—ten to thirty *years* (Shiller and Siegel (1977) advance this same criticism of the Fisher explanation). After an extensive and complex analysis, and like empirical work, Sargent reached the following main conclusions:

> within the context of bivariate models, interest and inflation appear mutually to influence one another. One implication of this finding is that Irving Fisher's explanation of the Gibson Paradox, which posits an unidirectional influence flowing from inflation to interest, is inadequate.
>
> (Sargent, 1973, p. 447)

The next, and penultimate, study to be examined is that by Knick Harley (1977). Harley robustly supports a 'Fisherian' explanation. He argues that 'the money market adjusted to price expectations, and there was little effect on real interest rates' (p. 73). And again, 'the decline in the market rate of interest in the 1870s can be fully accounted for by price expectations and is fully consistent with a monetary explanation of the price trends' (p. 73).

He supports this by an equation which relates interest rates to the ratio of money to income, gold reserves at the Bank of England (published weekly and an indicator of near term market conditions widely used by contemporary observers), price expectations, and unemployment (as an indicator of the business cycle phase which, he argued, was an influence on price expectations).[3] Turning to the long rate (that on consols), he finds this to be well predicted by 'assuming that the long rate was dependent on the expected short rate and that the expectations of the short rate were generated by a geometrically weighted distributed lag of past short interest rates' (p. 83).

Finally in this section we come to Friedman and Schwartz (1982). Here we simply summarize their findings on the Gibson Paradox; their work is turned to again below. At the beginning of their chapter (chapter 10) on money and interest rates, they remark, 'we are left with no single satisfactory interpretation of that supposedly well-documented empirical phenomenon' (p. 479).

Fair, but there is more than that to what they find. First, they deduce *analytically* the length of lag for Fisher's explanation to be correct. 'A close correlation between rising prices and rising interest rates requires that the time it takes for people to adjust their anticipations must be roughly comparable to the duration of long swings in prices' (p. 547). They go on to observe that the Gibson Paradox seems to be a phenomenon of particular periods (a point

[3] The conditions under which the cycle phase adds information are discussed in Neftci (1986).

reinforced by Dwyer's (1984) study). Following a suggestion of Klein (1975), they remark that Fisher effects had reason to emerge more quickly in recent years, as in fact they had; for as the price level became more volatile, so did the reward to forecasting it increase.

Friedman and Schwartz remark that reliance on past prices to forecast future prices is far from always sensible. They do nevertheless tend to support Fisher's explanation for the Gibson Paradox—partly by noting that the studies which rejected the explanation actually included in their data sets periods when the paradox did not occur; partly by rejecting (on Cagan's grounds[4] and also by use of their own series for the real rate) the Wicksell explanation; and partly by finding shorter lags than Fisher on price expectations. Their explanation of the end of the Gibson Paradox is consistent with this—a change in the monetary standard, which produced greater incentives to forecast future price movements. In other words, 'Gibson' was replaced by 'Fisher' as lags shortened, and lags shortened because there was an incentive for them to do so.

That brief survey of the literature points to four questions, answers to which would help discriminate among these explanations of the paradox. Did money affect prices? (as Mathias and others denied). Can we confirm Sargent's finding on the relationship between prices and the rate of interest? Does money growth affect interest rates as Harley found? And does it lead to a Fisher effect on the nominal rate?

And there is one final question on the issue of the Gibson Paradox. Benjamin and Kochin (1984) have denied its existence; they claim it is the chance product of wars producing both high interest rates and high prices.

It is clear that the above list of questions corresponds rather closely to the effects which the traditional theory of the effect of money on interest rates leads one to seek in the wake of a monetary impulse. The empirical work can thus readily address both issues. The next stage, therefore, is to describe the data. The way is then clear for the empirical work.

THE DATA

The previous studies which have been mentioned used a variety of money supply definitions, each of which has a number of important defects. With the publication of Capie and Webber (1985), however, many of these defects were removed; this volume (tables I.1 and I.3) was the source of our money stock

[4] Wicksell had attributed the decline in the real rate in the first part of the period to an expansion in bank-created money increasing the supply of savings. But Cagan (1965) found that, at any rate in the US, changes in the monetary base dominated money growth.

data. Because the relationships between money and the other variables could perhaps be influenced by the definition of money used, two series are considered here: the narrow, money base, definition, denoted M0, and the broader series, M3. For exact definitions of these two series, see Capie and Webber (1985).

The interest rate employed is the yield on Consols. This has almost exclusively been used as the measure of the long-term rate of interest in this period. Series for short rates of course also exist, but these are not well suited to the examination of hypotheses about, or depending on, the Fisher effect. The usual Consol yield series, denoted here as *RC*, is that given in Capie and Webber (1985, table III.10). However, as Harley (1976) points out (see also Capie and Webber (1985, pp. 316–20)), this series has traditionally been miscalculated for the years 1880 to 1903. It overestimates the true yield on Consols for two reasons. The price of Consols in this period rose above par, thus increasing the possibility of redemption at par and decreasing the true yield; and the details of Goschen's conversion of the National Debt in 1889 affected the way in which Consol yields were calculated. We therefore also use a revised Consol yield series, that given in the appendix to Harley (1977) and denoted here as RH.

The real output series that is used is, as has become traditional, that of Feinstein (1972); and hence his implicit GDP deflator is used as the price series. These series are denoted QF and PF, and were taken from Capie and Webber (1985, table III.12).

Annual observations for all series are available from 1870 to 1913, except for M3, whose initial (1870) observation is missing. The two monetary series, M0 and M3, are graphed in Figures 2.1 and 2.2; the two interest rates, RC and RH,

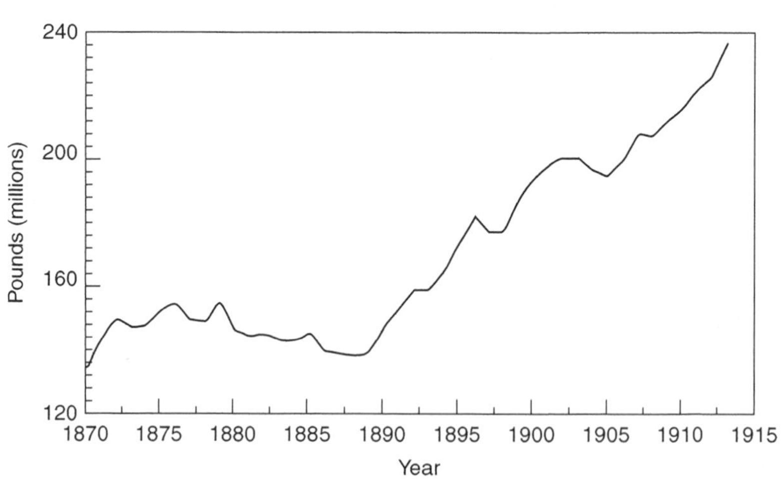

Figure 2.1. Narrow money: M0

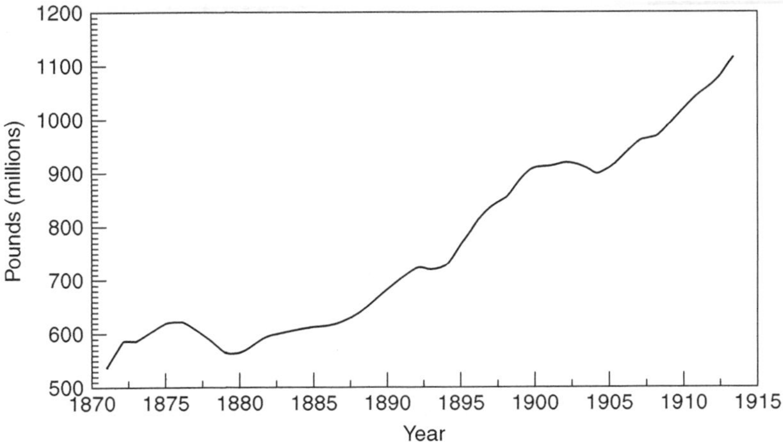

Figure 2.2. Broad money: M3

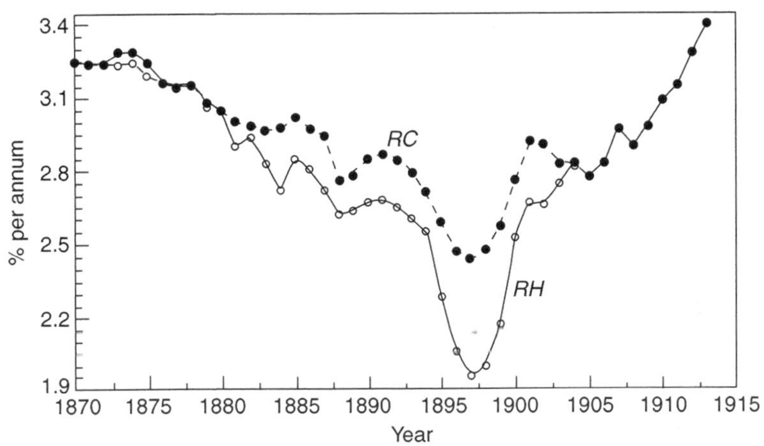

Figure 2.3. Interest rates

are graphed in Figure 2.3; the output series, QF, is shown in Figure 2.4 and the price series, PF, in Figure 2.5.

M0 and M3 display roughly similar evolutions over the data period, with both series increasing in level from 1889, although pronounced cyclical movements do occur. Before 1889 the levels of the series are both roughly constant. The Consol yield traces out a distinct 'U' shape, with the trough occurring in 1897. (Harley's recalculated series has a much steeper decline than the conventional series, the 1897 minimum values being 1.96 per cent and 2.45 per cent respectively.) The output series displays a marked upward movement

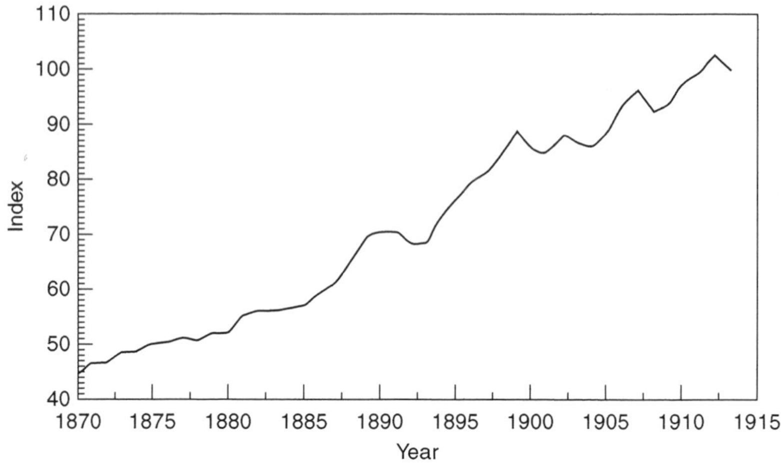

Figure 2.4. Output

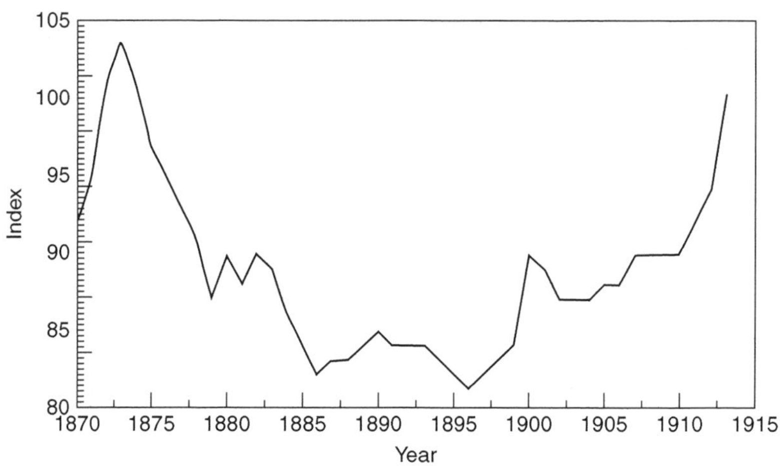

Figure 2.5. Price level

with variability around trend appearing to increase with level. The price deflator traces out an approximation to a 'U' shape.

It is useful at this point to set out more formally some of the statistical characteristics of these series. They all display non-stationarity of mean; the money and output series having a predominantly increasing mean level, the interest rate and price series having mean levels that are non-constant, but without any overall trend. Moreover, for both money and output, and possibly prices, variability tends to be roughly proportional to level, suggesting non-stationarity in variance. This implies that univariate models fitted to these series (an essential starting point for multivariate modelling) would require both logarithmic transformation and first differencing, so that (continuous) growth rates were modelled. For interest rates, however, only first differences, without any logarithmic transformation, would seem to be necessary. The need for first differencing of all series is confirmed by a number of criteria: by inspection of the sample autocorrelation functions for the levels, first and second differences of the logarithmically transformed series (except interest rates), by using the conventional Box and Jenkins (1976) identification approach, by the minimum sample variance criterion (Anderson 1976), and by formal tests for unit roots (Dickey et al. 1986). The univariate ARIMA models chosen for each series are shown in Table 2.1, where lower-case letters denote logarithms of upper-case variables, for example $m0 = \log(M0)$.

The money series, M0 and M3, follow ARIMA(0,1,I) and ARIMA(1,1,0) processes respectively, with average growth rates of 1.4 and 1.97 per cent per annum and residual standard errors of 2.86 per cent and 2.16 per cent respectively. Both interest rate series are ARIMA(1,1,0) processes with almost identical autoregressive parameters, but the residual standard error of RH, at 0.096 percentage points, is considerably larger than that of RC, which is 0.069 percentage points, this being a consequence of the far greater variability of the former series. The output series is a random walk, with a drift (growth rate) of 1.9 per cent per annum. The price series follows an ARIMA(1,1,0) process.

Having thus described the series, it is now possible to proceed to the empirical work.

Table 2.1. Univariate ARIMA models

$\Delta m0_t$	=	$0.014 + a_t + 0.329a_{t-1}$, (0.006) (0.150)	$\hat{\sigma} = 0.0286$	$Q_6(4) = 4.07$
$\Delta m3_t$	=	$0.011 + 0.446\Delta m3_{t-1} + a_t$, (0.001) ǀ (0.144)	$\hat{\sigma} = 0.0216$	$Q_6(4) = 41.15$
ΔRC_t	=	$0.489\Delta RC_{t-1} + a_t$, (0.139)	$\hat{\sigma} = 0.0688$	$Q_6(5) = 44.11$
ΔRH_t	=	$0.500\Delta RH_{t-1} + a_t$, (0.136)	$\hat{\sigma} = 0.0961$	$Q_6(5) = 44.77$
Δqf_t	=	$0.019 + a_t$, (0.004)	$\hat{\sigma} = 0.0284$	$Q_6(5c) = 44.77$
Δpf_t	=	$0.317\Delta p_{t-1} + a_t$, (0.159)	$\hat{\sigma} = 0.0248$	$Q_6(5) = 42.38$

Note: Figures in parentheses are estimated standard errors; $\hat{\sigma}$ is the estimated equation standard error; $Q_k(\nu)$ is the Ljung-Box (1978) portmanteau statistic for testing model adequacy using the first k residual correlations and is distributed as χ^2 with ν degrees of freedom.

THE EMPIRICAL WORK

The natural extension of univariate ARMA modelling, which was undertaken in the previous section for the purposes of data description, is to build a vector ARMA model of the relationship between output (q), money (m), the price level (p), and the interest rate (R). As there are two money and interest rate series available, there are four possible combinations of variables, each of which has been investigated.

The vector ARMA representation of a multivariate process, in our case $y = (q,m,p,R)$, is a very general one and can be used to represent a wide class of data generation processes (see, for example, Hendry et al. (1984)). It has become standard practice to transform the individual series, usually through differencing, to ensure that the vector y is jointly stationary. This is to allow standard identification, estimation, and testing procedures to be applied, for non-stationarity leads to difficult inferential problems, as analysed by Phillips and Durlauf (1986).

We have seen in the previous section that all series are individually non-stationary, each requiring first differencing and all but the interest rates also needing a logarithmic transformation. However, as shown in a pure time series context by Lutkepohl (1982) and Tjostheim and Paulsen (1982), it is not the case that individually differencing component series that are separately non-stationary is necessarily required for the multivariate process to be jointly stationary. Moreover, and of greater relevance for econometric analysis, linear combinations of these series may be stationary without them being differenced. This is the concept of cointegration analysed, for example, in Engle and Granger (1987), and the implications of which for econometric modelling appear to be far reaching. There is strong evidence, however, that differencing of individual series is required. Examination of schematic plots of the sample cross correlation and partial autocorrelation matrices for each four dimensional vector, in the manner proposed by Tiao and Box (1981), suggested very strongly that first differencing is required for each series, even in this multivariate setting. (We did not consider inducing stationarity by detrending using a polynomial in time, as was done by Dwyer (1985), in a related study. This was because the work of Nelson and Kang (1981, 1984), amongst others, has shown the deleterious effects of such a procedure in terms of producing innovations falsely exhibiting pseudo-periodic behaviour and in finding spuriously significant regression relationships.) Furthermore, standard tests for cointegration between the variables in y found little conclusive evidence to reject the hypothesis of non-cointegration (but see footnote 8 below). Additional evidence is also provided by estimating vector ARMA models containing just first differenced series.

The specification, estimation, and testing of such models is still in its infancy, with no general consensus having been reached as to the best modelling procedure to employ. The approach taken here, primarily dictated by computing resources, was to employ the statespace technique of Akaike (1976).[5] As it turns out, no moving average parts were found in any of the models, so that all are pure vector AR processes; in fact, all models are of order one (vector AR(1)). This is additional evidence in favour of non-cointegration, for, if the series were indeed cointegrated, this would be revealed by the presence of (non-invertible) moving average components in the model (Engle and Granger 1987). The models so obtained are set out in Table 2.2, and are reported in the form

$$\begin{bmatrix} q_t \\ m_t \\ p_t \\ R_t \end{bmatrix} = \begin{bmatrix} \varphi_{11} & \cdot & \cdot & \cdot & \varphi_{14} \\ \cdot & \cdot & \cdot & & \cdot \\ \cdot & & & \cdot & \cdot \\ \varphi_{41} & \cdot & \cdot & \cdot & \varphi_{44} \end{bmatrix} \begin{bmatrix} q_{t-1} \\ m_{t-1} \\ p_{t-1} \\ R_{t-1} \end{bmatrix} + \begin{bmatrix} v_{1t} \\ \cdot \\ \cdot \\ v_{4t} \end{bmatrix}$$

$$\Sigma = \begin{bmatrix} \sigma_{11} & & & & \\ \cdot & \cdot & & & \\ \cdot & & \cdot & & \\ \cdot & & & \cdot & \\ \sigma_{41} & \cdot & \cdot & \cdot & \sigma_{44} \end{bmatrix}, P = \begin{bmatrix} 1 & & & & \\ \cdot & \cdot & & & \\ \cdot & & \cdot & & \\ \cdot & & & \cdot & \\ \rho_{41} & \cdot & \cdot & \cdot & 1 \end{bmatrix},$$

where P is the contemporaneous correlation matrix of innovations obtained from Σ, the contemporaneous covariance matrix of $v_t = (v_{1t}, \ldots, v_{4t})$.[6] These multivariate models reduce the residual standard errors of all the variables when compared with the univariate models of Table 2.1: the best fitting models reduce the residual standard errors of the output and price series by approximately 30 per cent, that for M0 is reduced by 15 per cent and that for M3 by 20 per cent, and the residual standard error for the Consol yield as traditionally constructed is reduced by 7 per cent and for Harley's alternative it is reduced by 3 per cent. Moreover, the marginal significance levels attached to the V statistics (see footnote 6), shown in parentheses under the values, reject

[5] This uses the PROC STATESPACE routine in SAS/ETS (SAS, 1985). The procedure begins by fitting a sequence of vector AR models using the Yule-Walker equations and selects the order for which Akaike's Information Criterion is minimized. This criterion is based upon the residual variance of an estimated model, which is then 'corrected' by a penalty factor that is proportional to the number of parameters that have been estimated. This selected order is then taken as the number of past lags to use in a canonical correlation analysis which then determines the form of the model, which may contain a moving average part. Once the form has been decided, the free parameters are then estimated by maximizing a likelihood function based on the sample autocovariance matrix.

[6] Also shown is Anderson's (1984, chapter 9) statistic $V = -K\log|P|$, which is distributed as $\chi^2(f)$ on the null hypothesis that P is the identity matrix, and where $K = T-(2p+11)/6$ and $f = 1/2p(p-1)$, T being the number of observations and p being the dimension of P. Here $T = 43$ and $p = 4$, so $K = 239/6$ and $f = 6$.

Table 2.2. Estimated vector AR(1) models

(i) *(QF, M0, PF, RC)*

$$\begin{bmatrix} \Delta qf_t \\ \\ \Delta m0_t \\ \\ \Delta pf_t \\ \\ \Delta RC_t \\ \\ \end{bmatrix} = \begin{bmatrix} 0.060 & 0.273 & 0.224 & 0.130 \\ (0.138) & (0.130) & (0.155) & (0.054) \\ 0.303 & 0.100 & 0.113 & 0.085 \\ (0.156) & (0.147) & (0.176) & (0.061) \\ 0.385 & 0.274 & 0.308 & -0.000 \\ (0.122) & (0.115) & (0.137) & (0.047) \\ 0.383 & -0.104 & 0.541 & 0.432 \\ (0.391) & (0.368) & (0.441) & (0.152) \end{bmatrix} \begin{bmatrix} \Delta qf_{t-1} \\ \\ \Delta m0_{t-1} \\ \\ \Delta pf_{t-1} \\ \\ \Delta RC_{t-1} \\ \\ \end{bmatrix} + \begin{bmatrix} v_{1t} \\ \\ v_{2t} \\ \\ v_{3t} \\ \\ v_{4t} \\ \\ \end{bmatrix}$$

$$\Sigma = 10^{-3}\begin{bmatrix} 0.565 & & & \\ 0.087 & 0.727 & & \\ -0.087 & -0.003 & 0.441 & \\ -0.233 & 0.275 & 0.591 & 4.555 \end{bmatrix} \quad P = \begin{bmatrix} 1 & & & \\ 0.15 & 1 & & \\ -0.17 & -0.01 & 1 & \\ -0.15 & 0.15 & 0.42 & 1 \end{bmatrix}$$

$$V = \underset{(0.073)}{11.53}$$

(ii) *(QF, M3, PF, RC)*

$$\begin{bmatrix} \Delta qf_t \\ \\ \Delta m3_t \\ \\ \Delta pf_t \\ \\ \Delta RC_t \\ \\ \end{bmatrix} = \begin{bmatrix} 0.088 & -0.132 & 0.303 & -0.164 \\ (0.152) & (0.188) & (0.186) & (0.054) \\ 0.343 & 0.301 & 0.111 & -0.022 \\ (0.120) & (0.148) & (0.146) & (0.043) \\ 0.338 & 0.143 & 0.192 & 0.037 \\ (0.142) & (0.175) & (0.173) & (0.050) \\ 0.342 & 0.184 & 0.482 & 0.420 \\ (0.420) & (0.519) & (0.514) & (0.150) \end{bmatrix} \begin{bmatrix} \Delta qf_{t-1} \\ \\ \Delta m3_{t-1} \\ \\ \Delta pf_{t-1} \\ \\ \Delta RC_{t-1} \\ \\ \end{bmatrix} + \begin{bmatrix} v_{1t} \\ \\ v_{2t} \\ \\ v_{3t} \\ \\ v_{4t} \\ \\ \end{bmatrix}$$

$$\Sigma = 10^{-3}\begin{bmatrix} 0.606 & & & \\ 0.088 & 0.375 & & \\ -0.155 & 0.122 & 0.527 & \\ -0.208 & 0.096 & 0.605 & 4.645 \end{bmatrix} \quad P = \begin{bmatrix} 1 & & & \\ 0.18 & 1 & & \\ -0.27 & 0.25 & 1 & \\ -0.12 & 0.07 & 0.39 & 1 \end{bmatrix}$$

$$V = \underset{(0.019)}{15.11}$$

(iii) *(QF, M0, PF, RH)*

$$\begin{bmatrix} \Delta qf_t \\ \\ \Delta m0_t \\ \\ \Delta pf_t \\ \\ \Delta RH_t \\ \\ \end{bmatrix} = \begin{bmatrix} 0.040 & -0.301 & 0.263 & -0.100 \\ (0.138) & (0.126) & (0.159) & (0.039) \\ 0.282 & 0.138 & 0.157 & 0.026 \\ (0.161) & (0.147) & (0.185) & (0.045) \\ 0.401 & 0.265 & 0.277 & 0.017 \\ (0.122) & (0.112) & (0.141) & (0.034) \\ 0.502 & 0.096 & -0.003 & 0.519 \\ (0.558) & (0.511) & (0.643) & (0.156) \end{bmatrix} \begin{bmatrix} \Delta qf_{t-1} \\ \\ \Delta m0_{t-1} \\ \\ \Delta pf_{t-1} \\ \\ \Delta RH_{t-1} \\ \\ \end{bmatrix} + \begin{bmatrix} v_{1t} \\ \\ v_{2t} \\ \\ v_{3t} \\ \\ v_{4t} \\ \\ \end{bmatrix}$$

$$\Sigma = 10^{-3}\begin{bmatrix} 0.555 & & & \\ 0.069 & 0.754 & & \\ -0.071 & -0.004 & 0.438 & \\ -0.340 & 0.300 & 1.012 & 9.122 \end{bmatrix}$$

$$P = \begin{bmatrix} 1 & & & \\ 0.11 & 1 & & \\ -0.14 & -0.01 & 1 & \\ -0.15 & 0.11 & 0.51 & 1 \end{bmatrix}$$

$$V = \underset{(0.025)}{14.47}$$

(iv) *(QF, M3, PF, RH)*

$$\begin{bmatrix} \Delta qf_t \\ \Delta m3_t \\ \Delta pf_t \\ \Delta RH_t \end{bmatrix} = \begin{bmatrix} \underset{(0.149)}{0.097} & \underset{(0.193)}{-0.299} & \underset{(0.199)}{0.438} & \underset{(0.041)}{-0.136} \\ \underset{(0.119)}{0.341} & \underset{(0.153)}{0.269} & \underset{(0.159)}{0.148} & \underset{(0.033)}{-0.026} \\ \underset{(0.139)}{0.343} & \underset{(0.180)}{0.204} & \underset{(0.186)}{0.118} & \underset{(0.038)}{0.048} \\ \underset{(0.585)}{0.337} & \underset{(0.757)}{0.843} & \underset{(0.782)}{-0.452} & \underset{(0.161)}{0.574} \end{bmatrix} \begin{bmatrix} \Delta qf_{t-1} \\ \Delta m3_{t-1} \\ \Delta pf_{t-1} \\ \Delta RH_{t-1} \end{bmatrix} + \begin{bmatrix} v_{1t} \\ v_{2t} \\ v_{3t} \\ v_{4t} \end{bmatrix}$$

$$\Sigma = 10^{-3}\begin{bmatrix} 0.586 & & & \\ 0.077 & 0.372 & & \\ -0.131 & 0.118 & 0.514 & \\ -0.273 & -0.168 & 1.009 & 9.078 \end{bmatrix}$$

$$P = \begin{bmatrix} 1 & & & \\ 0.16 & 1 & & \\ -0.24 & 0.27 & 1 & \\ -0.12 & -0.09 & 0.47 & 1 \end{bmatrix}$$

$$V = \underset{(0.002)}{20.50}$$

---

the null hypothesis of zero contemporaneous correlation between the innovations v_{it} in all models.

Interpretation of the vector AR(1) models is hampered by the individual coefficients often being correlated and imprecisely estimated, for even in systems of this relatively small size, twenty-six parameters (sixteen autoregressive coefficients plus ten contemporaneous covariances) are being estimated from forty-three observations. We therefore follow Sims (1980) in analysing the properties of each model by supplementing direct interpretation with the examination of innovation accounting decompositions and impulse response functions. These measure the proportion of the k-step ahead forecast variance of a variable explained by innovations in other variables, and the dynamic response of a variable to an innovation in the others, respectively. To undertake such analysis, orthogonalizing triangularizations have to be performed if the Σ matrices are non-diagonal, that is if the model innovations are contemporaneously cross-correlated. Such transformations provide a reordering of the variables so that the (transformed) innovations are contemporaneously uncorrelated and thus ensure that the influence of an innovation on a variable can be uniquely identified.

That this is the case has been shown above by the significant V statistics for each model. In particular, every model has a large, positive contemporaneous correlation between the price level and interest rate innovations. Hence triangularization is required. One theme of Leamer's (1985) criticisms of vector autoregressive model building is that any such triangularization should not be arbitrarily chosen but should be based on considerations of economic theory. Dwyer (1985) suggests two hypotheses concerning the behaviour of the United Kingdom during this period that are of help here. The United Kingdom had a fixed exchange rate relative to gold, and, if an economy is small relative to the rest of the world, events within the economy will not have any discernible effect on the price level or on the interest rate in that part of the rest of the world which is on the gold standard. If shocks within the economy are also uncorrelated with those in the rest of the world, then neither the price level nor interest rate will show any influence of these domestic shocks. Hence, under this 'small country' hypothesis, the price level and the interest rate may be regarded as 'predetermined', in the terminology of Cooley and Leroy (1985), with respect to money stock and output. The alternative hypothesis suggested by Dwyer is that of the 'representative economy', which has the money stock predetermined with respect to output, the price level, and the interest rate.

These alternative hypotheses lead us to consider two triangularizations: the 'small country' ordering of (P,R,Q,M), which also embodies the 'Gibson Paradox' relationship between the price level and the interest rate plus the exogeneity assumptions used by Mills and Wood (1982) in analysing the demand for money during this period; and the 'representative economy' ordering of (M,Q,P,R). Table 2.3 presents innovation accounting decompositions (see Sims (1980) and Doan et al. (1984)) for both orderings. We find that the majority of decompositions are robust, in the sense of remaining reasonably stable, to the alternative orderings and in all cases responses are virtually complete within five years. Where differences do occur, it is in the response of interest rates to output and monetary innovations, although even here the orderings give broadly consistent results. The distinctive features of these decompositions are threefold: (i) there is virtually no feedback from interest rates to the other variables, although more detailed analysis, to be discussed below, has isolated a feedback into output, (ii) price innovations initially explain a large proportion of the variance of interest rates, but this proportion decreases over time as output and monetary innovations become more

Table 2.3. Proportions of forecast error *k* years ahead accounted by each innovation

(i) *(QF, MO, PF, RC)*

Forecast error in	k	'Small country' ('representative economy') Triangularized innovation in			
		PF	RC	QF	MO
PF	1	1(0.98)	0(0)	0(0)	0(0.02)
	5	0.87(0.82)	0(0)	0.10(0.16)	0.03(0.02)
RC	1	0.64(0.57)	0.36(0.33)	0(0.03)	0(0.07)
	5	0.61(0.47)	0.12(0.11)	0.26(0.37)	0.01(0.05)
QF	1	0.02(0)	0(0)	0.98(0.98)	0(0.02)
	5	0.09(0.09)	0(0)	0.86(0.85)	0.05(0.06)
MO	1	0.02(0)	0.01(0)	0.03(0)	0.94(1)
	5	0.08(0.05)	0.01(0)	0.13(15)	0.78(80)

(ii) *(QF, M3, PF, RC)*

Forecast error in	k	'Small country' ('representative economy') Triangularized innovation in			
		PF	RC	QF	M3
PF	1	1(0.81)	0(0)	0(0.07)	0(0.11)
	5	0.88(0.72)	0(0)	0.09(0.18)	0.03(0.10)
RC	1	0.57(0.57)	0.43(0.43)	0(0)	0(0)
	5	0.53(0.41)	0.14(0.11)	0.24(0.47)	0.09(0.01)
QF	1	0.08(0)	0(0)	0.92(0.95)	0(0.05)
	5	0.22(0.13)	0(0)	0.75(0.75)	0.03(0.12)
M3	1	0.07(0)	0(0)	0.04(0)	0.89(1)
	5	0.09(0.04)	0(0)	0.08(0.10)	0.83(0.86)

(iii) *(QF, MO, PF, RH)*

Forecast error in	k	'Small country' ('representative economy') Triangularized innovation in			
		PF	RH	QF	MO
PF	1	1(0.98)	0(0)	0(0.02)	0(0)
	5	0.86(0.82)	0(0)	0.11(0.16)	0.03(0.02)
RH	1	0.84(0.78)	0.16(0.15)	0(0.02)	0(0.04)
	5	0.50(0.47)	0.11(0.09)	0.37(0.40)	0.02(0.04)
QF	1	0.01(0)	0(0)	0.99(0.99)	0(0.01)
	5	0.09(0.12)	0(0)	0.85(0.83)	0.06(0.05)
MO	1	0.04(0)	0(0)	0.02(0)	0.94(1)
	5	0.11(0.07)	0(0)	0.11(0.13)	0.78(0.80)

(iv) *(QF, M3, PF, RH)*

Forecast error in	k	'Small country' ('representative economy') Triangularized innovation in			
		PF	RH	QF	M3
PF	1	1(0.82)	0(0)	0(0.06)	0(0.12)
	5	0.86(0.72)	0(0)	0.08(0.16)	0.06(0.12)
RH	1	0.79(0.67)	0.21(0.13)	0(0.01)	0(0.19)
	5	0.45(0.31)	0.04(0.03)	0.03(0.07)	0.48(0.59)
QF	1	0.06(0)	0(0)	0.94(0.96)	0(0.04)
	5	0.33(0.20)	0(0)	0.55(0.54)	0.12(0.26)
M3	1	0.13(0)	0(0)	0.03(0)	0.84(1)
	5	0.17(0.08)	0(0)	0.07(0.11)	0.76(0.81)

important, and (iii) there appear to be important feedbacks from money and output innovations to price innovations, but price innovations have a somewhat weaker effect on output and money.

These innovation accounting decompositions, when allied with analysis of the accompanying impulse response functions (not shown here) and the coefficient estimates of the vector AR(1) models, led us to specify and estimate two classes of structural models, distinguished by which definition of money is employed. The form of the structural model for the M0 definition of money is

$$\begin{aligned} \Delta q_t &= \alpha_0 + \alpha_{21}\Delta m0_{t-1} + \alpha_{31}\Delta p_{t-1} + \alpha_{41}\Delta R_{t-1} + \varepsilon_{1t} \\ \Delta m0_t &= \beta_{11}\Delta q_{t-1} + \varepsilon_{2t} \\ \Delta p_t &= \gamma_0 + \gamma_{11}\Delta q_{t-1} + \gamma_{21}\Delta m0_{t-1} + \varepsilon_{3t} \\ \Delta R_t &= \delta_{30}\Delta p_t + \Delta_{41}\Delta R_{t-1} + \varepsilon_{4t}. \end{aligned} \tag{2.1}$$

For the M3 definition of money the structural model is

$$\begin{aligned} \Delta q_t &= \alpha_0 + \alpha_{41}\Delta R_{t-1} + \varepsilon_{1t} \\ \Delta m3_t &= \beta_{10}\Delta q_t + \beta_{11}\Delta q_{t-1} + \beta_{21}\Delta m3_{r-1} + \varepsilon_{2t} \\ \Delta p_t &= \gamma_{10}\Delta q_t + \gamma_{11}\Delta q_{t-1} + \gamma_{31}\Delta p_{t-1} + \varepsilon_{3t} \\ \Delta R_t &= \delta_{30}\Delta p_t + \delta_{41}\Delta R_{t-1} + \varepsilon_{4t}, \end{aligned} \tag{2.2}$$

where, in both models, the ϵ_{it} are both serially and contemporaneously uncorrelated.

The specific models estimated for each combination of variables are shown as Table 2.4. No variable is strongly exogenous in either system; and in the M0 models only the interest rate cannot be assumed to be predetermined (see Cooley and Leroy (1985) for the distinction between strong exogeneity and predeterminedness and the importance of this distinction in models of this type). A greater degree of simultaneity exists in the M3 system, where only output can be assumed to be predetermined. Identical models are obtained for the two interest rate series, which have a direct feedback only on output. The structural parameters in all models are fairly precisely estimated, but, because of the considerable feedback present in each system, detailed analysis is again best performed using impulse response functions. However, now that we have been able to make identifying assumptions of predeterminedness, the ϵ_t's in models (2.1) and (2.2) can be regarded as exogenous shocks and hence impulse response functions do have precise structural interpretations. Figures 2.6 and 2.7 show the impulse response functions for the two models containing the RC interest rate: virtually identical response functions, apart from scaling, were obtained for the models containing RH.

The four systems are distinguished by important differences in the response to monetary shocks. M0 shocks have an initial once-for-all negative impact on output, a similar but positive effect on the price level, and a positive impact, that is spread over a number of years, on interest rates. Note that the

Table 2.4. Selected structural models

(i) *(QF, MO, PF, RC)*						
Δqf_t	=	0.022	$-\ 0.272\Delta m0_{t-1}$	$-\ 0.113\Delta \mathrm{RC}_{t-1}$		$\hat{\sigma} = 0.0247$
		(0.004)	(0.137)	(0.052)		
$\Delta m0_t$	=	$0.371\Delta qf_{t-1}$				$\hat{\sigma} = 0.0279$
		(0.130)				
Δpf_t	=	-0.010	$+\ 0.373\Delta qf_{t-1}$	$+\ 0.280\Delta m0_{t-1}$	$+0.327\Delta pf_{t-1}$	$\hat{\sigma} = 0.0215$
		(0.004)	(0.126)	(0.116)	(0.139)	
$\Delta \mathrm{RC}_t$	=	$1.188\Delta pf_t$	$+\ 0.442\Delta \mathrm{RC}_{t-1}$			$\hat{\sigma} = 0.0634$
		(0.386)	(0.129)			
(ii) *(QF, M3, PF, RC)*						
Δqf_t	=	0.019	$-\ 0.139\Delta \mathrm{RC}_{t-1}$		$\hat{\sigma} = 0.0259$	
		(0.004)	(0.052)			
$\Delta m3_t$	=	$0.180\Delta qf_t$	$+\ 0.322\Delta qf_{t-1}$	$+\ 0.351\Delta m3_{t-1}$	$\hat{\sigma} = 0.0163$	
		(0.085)	(0.094)	(0.103)		
Δpf_t	=	$-0.270\Delta qf_t$	$+\ 0.344\Delta qf_{t-1}$	$+\ 0.305\Delta pf_{t-1}$	$\hat{\sigma} = 0.0212$	
		(0.110)	(0.112)	(0.140)		
$\Delta \mathrm{RC}_{t-1}$	=	$1.359\Delta pf_t$	$+\ 0.432\Delta \mathrm{RC}_{t-1}$		$\hat{\sigma} = 0.0632$	
		(0.416)	(0.129)			
(iii) *(QF, M0, PF, RH)*						
Δqf_t	=	0.022	$-\ 0.297\Delta m0_{t-1}$	$-\ 0.078\Delta \mathrm{RH}_{t-1},$		$\hat{\sigma} = 0.0247$
		(0.004)	(0.134)	(0.035)		
$\Delta m0_t$	=	$0.371\Delta qf_{t-1}$				$\hat{\sigma} = 0.0279$
		(0.130)				
Δpf_t	=	-0.010	$+\ 0.373\Delta qf_{t-1}$	$+\ 0.280\Delta m0_{t-1}$	$+0.327\Delta pf_{t-1},$	$\hat{\sigma} = 0.0215$
		(0.004)	(0.126)	(0.116)	(0.139)	
$\Delta \mathrm{RH}_t$	=	$1.863\Delta pf_t$	$+\ 0.439\Delta \mathrm{RH}_{t-1}$	,		$\hat{\sigma} = 0.0859$
		(0.525)	(0.123)			
(iv) *(QF, M3, PF, RH)*						
Δqf_t	=	0.019	$-\ 0.091\Delta \mathrm{RH}_{t-1}$	,	$\hat{\sigma} = 0.0261$	
		(0.004)	(0.037)			
$\Delta m3_t$	=	$0.180\Delta qf_t$	$+\ 0.322\Delta qf_{t-1}$	$+\ 0.351\Delta m3_{t-1},$	$\hat{\sigma} = 0.0163$	
		(0.085)	(0.094)	(0.103)		
Δpf_t	=	$-0.270\Delta qf_t$	$+\ 0.344\Delta qf_{t-1}$	$+\ 0.306\Delta pf_{t-1},$	$\hat{\sigma} = 0.0212$	
		(0.110)	(0.112)	(0.140)		
$\Delta \mathrm{RH}_t$	=	$2.156\Delta pf_t$	$+\ 0.426\Delta \mathrm{RH}_{t-1}$	,	$\hat{\sigma} = 0.0859$	
		(0.560)	(0.122)			

interest rate response to a monetary shock is an indirect one, with the effect running from money, through output and prices, to interest rates. M3, on the other hand, is purely passive, with no feedback to other variables in the system.

The impacts of output and price shocks are crucially dependent on the monetary series used. The output series, QF, has a positive impact on both M0 and M3, but for the former series the response is quick, being virtually completed within two years, while for the latter it is both stronger and longer lasting, taking about five years to complete. Shocks to QF have an overall

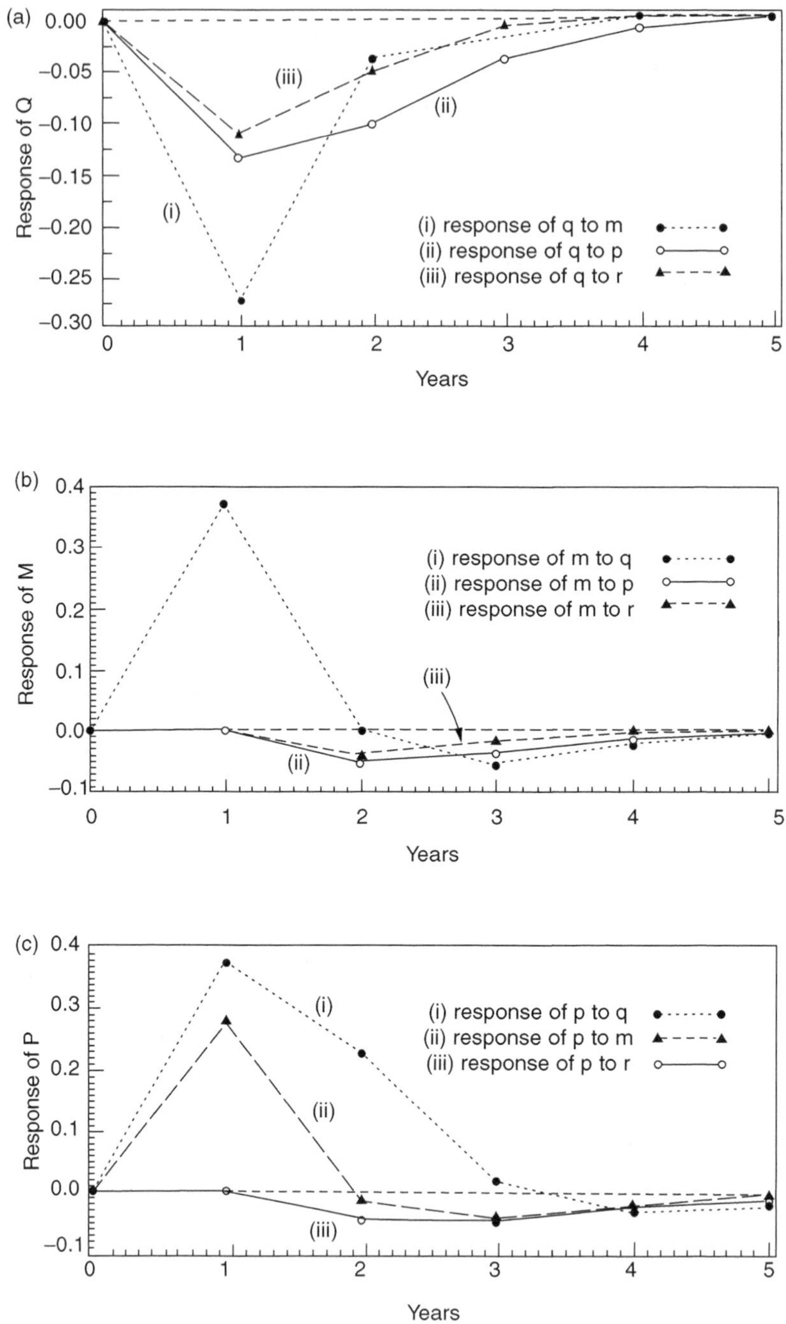
(a)
Response of Q
0.00
−0.05
−0.10
−0.15
−0.20
−0.25
−0.30
(i)
(ii)
(iii)
(i) response of q to m
(ii) response of q to p
(iii) response of q to r
0
1
2
3
4
5
Years
(b)
Response of M
0.4
0.3
0.2
0.1
0.0
−0.1
(i) response of m to q
(ii) response of m to p
(iii) response of m to r
(ii)
(iii)
0
1
2
3
4
5
Years
(c)
Response of P
0.4
0.3
0.2
0.1
0.0
−0.1
(i)
(ii)
(iii)
(i) response of p to q
(ii) response of p to m
(iii) response of p to r
0
1
2
3
4
5
Years

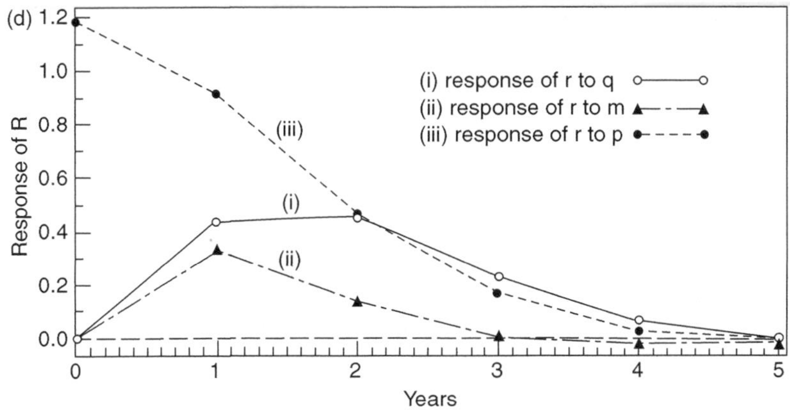

Figure 2.6. Impulse response functions for (QF, MO, PF, RC)

(a) Output responses
(b) Money responses
(c) Price responses
(d) Interest rate responses

positive effect on the price level, PF, which takes roughly four years to work out, but when the M3 definition of the money supply is used, a QF shock has a contemporaneous, negative impact on PF, whereas with M0 there is no such effect. A similar response is found with the interest rate: when M3 is used as the monetary variable, QF shocks have little effect, apart from a contemporaneous negative one, whereas with M0 the response of interest rates is large and positive, taking about five years to complete. Interest rates respond immediately and positively to a price shock, the response being powerful, roughly exponential in decline, and with much of the response being completed within four years. PF also has a negative effect on output and both definitions of money. All responses are basically completed within a maximum of five years, with the most powerful effects being observed in the first two years.

THE FINDINGS

This chapter started by briefly setting out the traditional theory of the impact monetary fluctuations have on various variables before dissipating themselves in rising prices, and then linked this analysis with a series of questions prompted by the substantial body of work on the Gibson Paradox. It is convenient to follow that order in summarizing the results.

First, and worthy of emphasis, there is no initial negative effect of either definition of money on the observed nominal yield on nominal assets. This

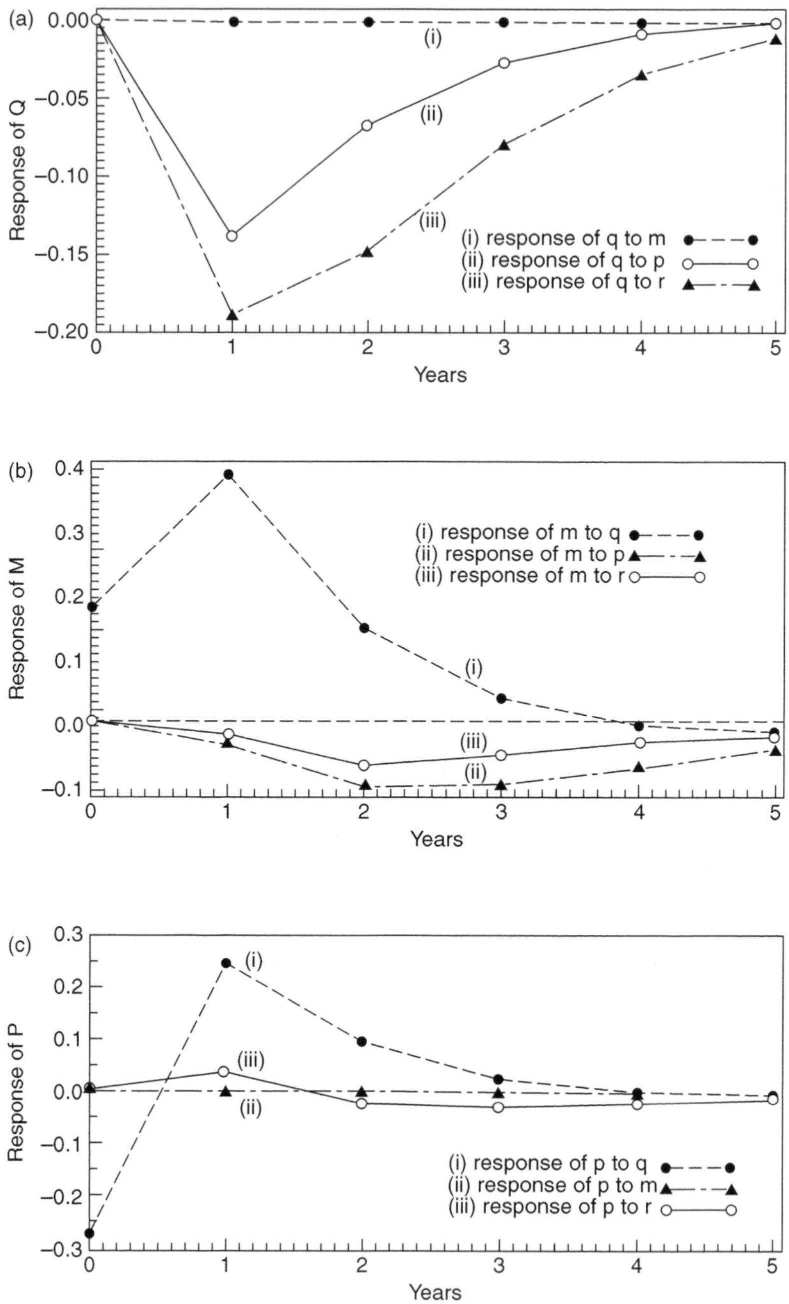
(a)
Response of Q
0.00
−0.05
−0.10
−0.15
−0.20
(i)
(ii)
(iii)
(i) response of q to m
(ii) response of q to p
(iii) response of q to r
0
1
2
3
4
5
Years
(b)
Response of M
0.4
0.3
0.2
0.1
0.0
−0.1
(i) response of m to q
(ii) response of m to p
(iii) response of m to r
(i)
(iii)
(ii)
0
1
2
3
4
5
Years
(c)
Response of P
0.3
0.2
0.1
0.0
−0.1
−0.2
−0.3
(i)
(iii)
(ii)
(i) response of p to q
(ii) response of p to m
(iii) response of p to r
0
1
2
3
4
5
Years

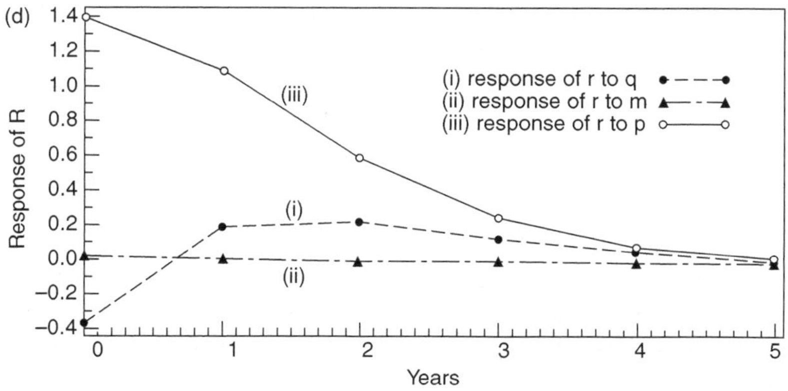

Figure 2.7. Impulse response functions for (QF, M3, PF, RC)

(a) Output responses
(b) Money responses
(c) Price responses
(d) Interest rate responses

does not mean there is no such effect, but it does mean that, if there is, it is over within our unit of observation, one year. (Data limitations preclude using a shorter period of observation.) This result has the most interesting implication that any deviations from the aggregate supply curve produced by monetary disturbances were, within this period, completed within one year.[7]

Second, there is a positive effect of money growth on interest rates. At first glance this seems puzzling. Money growth should ultimately leave interest rates unchanged, unless it produces expectations of inflation. Why should it produce such expectations under a commodity money standard?

Benjamin and Kochin (1984) accept this, and argue that there were no price trends under the gold standard. In a sense this is true; the price level in Britain stood in 1914 where it had been in 1870. But this does not mean that there were not long swings in prices. In his comment on Benjamin and Kochin, Cagan (1984) noted the presence of such swings in the US, and suggested that the gold standard delivered price level stability only over half-centuries. It took that long for a price swing to end and reverse. And in the UK a Royal Commission was established to look into the causes of the price level decline from 1870: the trend in prices was clear to contemporaries, notwithstanding its

[7] Whether this is quick or slow depends on one's prior expectations. But it is striking support for the finding of Friedman and Schwartz (1982) of no effect of money on output in the UK. This latter finding was of such great surprise to two of the book's reviewers, Charles Goodhart and David Laidler, that the former replicated the econometrics before accepting the result (1982), while the latter argued that it was a chance product of carrying out estimation over a period combining different exchange rate regimes (1982). For a further discussion of these arguments, see Capie and Wood (1989).

subsequent reversal. So, although an individual with a fifty-year time horizon might not have displayed a Fisher effect in his capital market transactions, it is perhaps not surprising that others did. This has a bearing on the questions prompted by the study of the Gibson Paradox, so we turn next to these.

First, and most important, a positive relationship between the level of prices and that of interest rates remains. There is a clear confirmation of the Gibson Paradox—its existence does not depend, as Benjamin and Kochin (1984) claim, on the eye being fooled.

Second, M0 affects prices (M3 responds purely passively to nominal income, according to these results).[8] Third, we reject Sargent's (1973) claim that prices are affected by interest rate shocks, and so remove one of his principal objections to Fisher's explanation of the Gibson Paradox. Fourth, in confirmation of Harley (1977), money growth does affect interest rates.

To what explanation, if any, of the Gibson Paradox does that pattern of results point? Crucial to the Fisher explanation is that money affects prices, which it does.[9] Crucial too is that interest rates display a Fisher effect in response to monetary change—which they do. That M0 be exogenous to the system is inconsistent with the Keynes-Wicksell explanation. Accordingly, then, we conclude that our results are more consistent with Fisher's explanation than with any other.

Turning now to a broader question, where do these results leave us in relation to what is known about the British economy in the late nineteenth century? How is our understanding of the role and behaviour of money affected?

In an open economy under a gold standard, traditional monetary theory predicts that income should influence money. We find it does; it has a positive effect on broad money and the effects are worked out over a period of five years. Output also has an effect on the monetary base, although here the effects have worked out inside two years. But the causality runs both ways, for the monetary base has a clear positive impact on prices and so of course on

[8] That M3 is purely passive may seem puzzling. It may, indeed, be an accidental by-product of the statistical manipulation; see Wood (1984) for an examination of this possibility in a similar context. It may well, however, be the product of the openness of the British economy combined with the exchange rate regime. In such a setting, the result is fully consistent with a monetary explanation of price level trends: see Mills and Wood (1978), and the discussion of that paper in Friedman and Schwartz (1982). However, recent work by Mills and Wood (1989) has now isolated a feedback effect running from M3 to the other variables. This comes via error correction terms in the system containing M3, these appearing as a consequence of cointegration being detected by very recently developed maximum likelihood techniques. Nevertheless, the impact of M3 is still only small and does not alter the basic conclusions of this chapter.

[9] It should be noted that the above quoted views of Mathias, which this finding decisively rejects, are from the most widely used textbook of the past twenty years on British economic history, and, it should be added, from the latest (1983) edition.

nominal income. In addition, we note that shocks to output have an effect on prices and that they work through within four years.

No part of monetary theory suggests that money affects real output in the long run, and it is the long-run behaviour of the British economy that has been traditionally debated. The findings of this chapter on the causes and consequences of monetary fluctuations lend support to a monetary interpretation of the long price deflation.

The 'depression' of the first half of this period was, so far as Britain as a whole was concerned, confined to nominal variables. Real depression was essentially confined to agriculture.

One problem that has stood in the way of widespread acceptance of this monetary explanation has been the 'Gibson Paradox'. If the fall in the general price level was a consequence of deficient monetary growth then, the argument went, there should have been a rise in interest rates. But in fact interest rates fell with prices.

The explanation of the Gibson Paradox that our results support is therefore crucial in underpinning the monetary explanation of the price decline. Our explanation of the paradox is consistent with a monetary explanation of prices; indeed, it depends on it, and it depends also on there being long swings in prices, as in fact there were.

We therefore conclude that the long decline followed by a long rise in prices in the period 1870–1913 is, for the UK as for the US, a result first of a scarcity of and then a small surfeit of money, not of an abundance of agricultural products. The results of this study fully support the traditional view of the role of money in the economy. The behaviour of the general level of prices over a long period was a monetary phenomenon in this period, and the behaviour of nominal interest rates was exactly as such a conclusion would lead one to expect.

REFERENCES

Akaike, H. (1976) 'Canonical Correlations Analysis of Time Series and the Use of an Information Criterion', in R. Mehra and D. G. Lainiotis (eds.), *Advances and Case Studies in System Identification*, New York: Academic Press.

Anderson, O. D. (1976) *Time Series Analysis and Forecasting: The Box-Jenkins Approach*, London: Butterworths.

Anderson, T. W. (1984) *An Introduction to Multivariate Statistical Analysis*, second edn, New York: Wiley.

Benjamin, D. K. and Kochin, L. A. (1984) 'War, Prices and Interest Rates: A Martial Solution to Gibson's Paradox', in M. D. Bordo and A. J. Schwartz (eds.), *A*

Retrospective on the Classical Gold Standard, 1821–1931, University of Chicago Press for NBER, 587–604.

Bordo, M. D. and Schwartz, A. J. (1981) 'Money and Prices in the Nineteenth Century: Was Thomas Tooke Right?', *Explorations in Economic History*, 18, 97–127.

Box, G. E. P. and Jenkins, G. M. (1976) *Time Series Analysis: Forecasting and Control*, revised edn, San Francisco: Holden-Day.

Cagan, P. (1965) *Determinants and Effects of Changes in the Stock of Money 1875–1960*, New York: Columbia University Press for NBER.

——(1972) *The Channels of Monetary Effects on Interest Rates*, New York: NBER.

——(1984) 'Mr. Gibson's Paradox: Was it There?', in M. D. Bordo and A. J. Schwartz (eds.), *A Retrospective on the Classical Gold Standard, 1821–1931*, University of Chicago Press for NBER, 604–10.

Capie, F. H. and Webber, A. (1985) *A Monetary History of the United Kingdom*, Volume 1: *Data, Sources, Methods*, London: George Allen and Unwin.

——and Wood, G. E. (1984) 'Gold, Empire, and Crises: Some Explorations in U. K. Monetary History', Centre for the Study of Monetary History, Discussion Paper 13, City University Business School.

————(1989) 'Anna Schwartz's Perspective on British Economic History', in M. D. Bordo (ed.), *Money, History, and International Finance: Essays in Honor of Anna Schwartz*, University of Chicago Press for NBER.

Cooley, T. F. and LeRoy, S. F. (1985) 'Atheoretical Macroeconometrics: A Critique', *Journal of Monetary Economics*, 16, 283–308.

Coppock, D. J. (1956) 'The Climacteric of the 1890s: A Critical Note', *Manchester School*, 24, 1–31.

——(1961) 'The Causes of the Great Depression', *Manchester School*, 29, 205–32.

Crafts, N. F. R., Leybourne, S. J., and Mills, T. C. (1989a) 'The Climacteric in Late Victorian Britain and France: A Reappraisal of the Evidence', *Journal of Applied Econometrics*, 4, 103–17.

——————(1989b) 'Trends and Cycles in British Industrial Production 1700–1913', *Journal of the Royal Statistical Society*, Series A, 152, 43–60.

Dickey, D. A., Bell, W. R., and Miller, R. B. (1986) 'Unit Roots in Time Series Models: Tests and Implications', *American Statistician*, 40, 12–26.

Doan, T. A., Litterman, R. B., and Sims, C. A. (1984) 'Forecasting and Conditional Projection Using Realistic Prior Distributions', *Econometric Reviews*, 3, 1–100.

Dwyer, G. P., Jr. (1984) 'The Gibson Paradox: A Cross-Country Analysis', *Economica*, 51, 109–27.

——(1985) 'Money, Income and Prices in the United Kingdom: 1870–1913', *Economic Inquiry*, 23, 415–35.

Elbaum, B. and Lazonick, W. (eds.) (1986) *The Decline of the British Economy*, Oxford: Clarendon Press.

Engle, R. F. and Granger, C. W. J. (1987) 'Cointegration and Error Correction: Representation, Estimation and Testing', *Econometrica*, 55, 251–76.

Feinstein, C. H. (1972) *National Income, Expenditure and Output in the United Kingdom*, Cambridge University Press.

——(1987), 'Wages and British Economic Growth: A Comment', Harvard University, mimeo.

——Matthews, R. C. O. and Odling-Smee, J. C. (1982) 'The Timing of the Climacteric and its Sectoral Incidence in the UK', in C. P. Kindleberger and G. di Tella (eds.), *Economics of the Long View*, Volume 2, Part 1, Oxford: Clarendon Press, 168–85.

Fisher, I. (1907) *The Rate of Interest*, New York: Macmillan.

——(1930) *The Theory of Interest*, New York: Macmillan.

Friedman, M. and Schwartz, A. J. (1982) *Monetary Trends in the United States and the United Kingdom*, University of Chicago Press.

Goodhart, C. A. E. (1982) 'Monetary Trends in the United States and the United Kingdom: A British Review', *Journal of Economic Literature*, 20, 1540–51.

Greasley, D. (1986) 'British Economic Growth: the Paradox of the 1880s and the Timing of the Climacteric', *Explorations in Economic History*, 23, 416–44.

Harley, C. K. (1976) 'Goschen's Conversion of the National Debt and the Yield on Consols', *Economic History Review*, 2nd Series, 29, 101–6.

——(1977) 'The Interest Rate and Prices in Britain, 1873–1913: A Study of the Gibson Paradox', *Explorations in Economic History*, 14, 69–89.

Hendry, D. F., Pagan, A. R., and Sargan, J. D. (1984) 'Dynamic Specification', in Z. Griliches and M. D. Intrilligator (eds.), *Handbook of Econometrics*, Volume 2, Amsterdam: North-Holland, 1023–100.

Hicks, J. R. (1967) *Critical Essays in Monetary Theory*, Oxford: Clarendon Press.

Hughes, J. R. T. (1968) 'Wicksell on the Facts: Prices and Interest Rates, 1844 to 1914', in J. N. Wolfe (ed.), *Value, Capital and Growth: Papers in Honour of Sir John Hicks*, Edinburgh University Press, 215–55.

Keynes, J. M. (1930) *A Treatise on Money*, London: Macmillan.

Kirby, M. W. (1981) *The Decline of British Economic Power Since 1870*. London: George Allen and Unwin.

Klein, B. (1975) 'Our New Monetary Standard: The Measurement and Effects of Price Uncertainty, 1880–1973', *Economic Inquiry*, 13, 461–83.

Laidler, D. (1982) 'Friedman and Schwartz on Monetary Trends: A Review Article', *Journal of International Money and Finance*, 1, 293–305.

Leamer, E. E. (1985) 'Vector Autoregressions for Causal Inference?', *Carnegie-Rochester Conference Series on Public Policy*, 22, 255–304.

Ljung, G. M. and Box, G. E. P. (1978) 'A Measure of Lack of Fit in Time Series', *Biometrika*, 65, 297–303.

Lutkepohl, H. (1982) 'Differencing Multiple Time Series: Another Look at Canadian Money and Income Data', *Journal of Time Series Analysis*, 3, 235–43.

Mathias, P. (1983) *The First Industrial Nation: An Economic History of Britain, 1700–1914*, London: Methuen.

Matthews, R. C. O., Feinstein, C. H., and Odling-Smee, J. C. (1982) *British Economic Growth 1856–1973*, Oxford: Clarendon Press.

Mill, J. S. (1848) *Principles of Political Economy*, London: Parker, Son and Bourn.

Mills, T. C. and Wood, G. E. (1978) 'Money, Income and Causality under the Gold Standard', *Federal Reserve Bank of St. Louis Review*, 60, 22–7.

——(1982) 'Econometric Evaluation of Alternative Money Stock Series, 1880–1913', *Journal of Money, Credit and Banking*, 14, 265–77.

——(1989) 'Money and Interest Rates in Britain from 1870 to 1913', Midland Montagu Centre for Financial Markets, Discussion Paper 9, City University Business School.

Neftci, S. (1986) 'Is There a Cyclical Time Unit?', in K. Brunner and A. H. Meltzer (eds.), *Carnegie-Rochester Conference Series on Public Policy*, 24, 11–48.

Nelson, C. R. and Kang, H. (1981) 'Spurious Periodicity in Inappropriately Detrended Time Series', *Econometrica*, 49, 741–51.

——(1984) 'Pitfalls in the Use of Time as an Explanatory Variable in Regression', *Journal of Business and Economic Statistics*, 2, 73–82.

Paish, F. W. (1966) *Long-Term and Short-Term Interest Rates in the United Kingdom*, Manchester University Press.

Phelps Brown, E. H. and Handfield Jones, S. J. (1952) 'The Climacteric of the 1890s', *Oxford Economic Papers*, 4(3), 266–307.

——and Ozga, S. A. (1955) 'Economic Growth and the Price Level', *Economic Journal*, 65, 1–18.

Phillips, P. C. B. and Durlauf, S. N. (1986) 'Multiple Time Series Regression with Integrated Processes', *Review of Economic Studies*, 53, 473–95.

Sargent, T. J. (1973) 'Interest Rates and Prices in the Long Run', *Journal of Money, Credit and Banking*, 5, 385–449.

Shiller, R. J. and Siegel, J. J. (1977) 'The Gibson Paradox and Historical Movements in Real Interest Rates', *Journal of Political Economy*, 85, 891–907.

Sims, C. A. (1980) 'Macroeconomics and Reality', *Econometrica*, 48, 1–48.

Sked, A. (1987) *Britain's Decline*, Oxford: Blackwell.

SAS (1985) *SAS/ETS User's Guide*, Version 5 Edition, Cary, NC: SAS Institute Inc.

Thornton, H. (1802, 1978) *An Enquiry into the Nature and Effects of the Paper Credit of Great Britain*, Fairfield, NJ: Augustus M. Kelley.

Tiao, G. C. and Box, G. E. P. (1981) 'Modelling Multiple Time Series with Applications', *Journal of the American Statistical Association*, 76, 802–16.

Tjostheim, D. and Paulsen, J. (1982) 'Empirical Identification of Multiple Time Series', *Journal of Time Series Analysis*, 3, 265–82.

Wicksell, K. (1907) 'The Influence of the Rate of Interest on Prices', *Economic Journal*, 17, 213–20.

Wood, G. E. (1984) 'Comment on "Real Output and the Gold Standard Years" by Stephen Easton', in M. D. Bordo and A. J. Schwartz (eds.), *A Retrospective on the Classical Gold Standard 1821–1931*, Chicago University Press for NBER.

3

Money Demand and Supply under the Gold Standard: the United Kingdom, 1870–1914*

INTRODUCTION

This chapter is concerned with the behavior and determination of money demand and money supply in a particular monetary regime, the gold standard, and in a particular country, the United Kingdom. Restriction to one country plainly raises concern over how representative of the regime the results we set out may be. Although such concern is inevitable, it should not be overdone. This is partly because restriction to one country is to an extent forced on us by the data—for the United Kingdom has for this period higher-quality, more consistent and complete, data than exist for other countries under gold standard regimes. But there are more and better reasons than that for accepting the results as representative. First, they are completely unsurprising; they are as theory would lead one to expect. Second, they are from a period of comparative economic tranquillity in the United Kingdom; there is thus little chance that the results are dominated by some extraordinary, important but unique, event. There is every reason to think that the findings are what should be expected qualitatively (and quantitatively in one important respect, homogeneity of money demand with respect to the price level) in every other gold standard country.

Nonetheless, there are some institutional features which are important, and should be set out before the detailed findings are examined. These institutional features relate to the UK banking system, and to the gold standard itself. We discuss them in that order.

In the years covered in this chapter, 1870–1914, the UK banking system was evolving quite rapidly towards the system of a few banks with nation-wide

* Originally published as Forrest H. Capie and Geoffrey E. Wood (1996). 'Money Demand and Supply Under the Gold Standard: The United Kingdom, 1870–1914', pp. 261–283, in Tamin Bayoumi, Barry Eichengreen, and Mark P. Taylor (eds). *Modern Perspectives on the Gold Standard*. © Cambridge University Press, 1996, reproduced with permission.

branching (although some still retained a regional bias) that the United Kingdom has today. There were also changes, first in practice and then in law, regarding the disclosure of information on banks' balance sheets. These features, and the influence of them on the money supply, are captured by the base multiplier framework of analysis. This framework is set out in detail below, but it is necessary here to defend its use as the approach is unfashionable, indeed has often been rejected as inappropriate, in the United Kingdom in recent years.

The criticism commonly encountered is that reserve ratios are not imposed on British banks, and that the Bank of England does not operate by controlling the supply of monetary base. Neither of these criticisms bears on the present issue. First, the approach can be viewed simply as an accounting framework, one which shows how the banks' attitude to reserve holding and the public's to the use of cash, both varying over time, interacted in an accounting sense to determine the money supply supported by a given amount of gold. But we would argue more strongly for the period under review: banks *did* have a clear cut view of the reserves they wished to hold relative to deposits, and the public's cash holding was influenced by economic considerations (see the discussion below).

These factors do, of course, only determine the money supply given the base. Is analysis of the supply of and demand for money of any particular interest in a genuinely fixed exchange rate regime such as the gold standard? After all, in such a regime, monetary conditions are out of the hands of the domestic money authorities. Although that is often taken as meaning that the money supply is unimportant, that extension of the point is incorrect. The exchange rate regime determines the *source* of money base change, but does not render it unimportant. Changes in the quantity of money, however produced, will affect income. While income fluctuations will produce accommodating monetary flows, it is equally true (and important) that monetary flows will produce accommodating income fluctuations; we discuss this further below (pp. 61–3 and 72–3).

The gold standard was different from most other regimes, not only in being a fixed exchange rate system; it was different also in the way in which it influenced expectations. The price level behaved in a very stable and predictable way, moving little from year to year and, over a long period of years, moving in long swings, their length determined by variations in the demand for and supply of gold, about a level trend (see Cagan, 1984, Mills, 1990, Mills and Wood, 1992, for a discussion of this). Prices were, no doubt in part as a result of this experience, expected to be stable. This is suggested by the stability of long-term interest rates relative to short (discussed further below) and is crucial to the explanation of the Gibson Paradox (for a review and examination of all the explanations of this phenomenon, see Mills and Wood, 1992). As will emerge below price expectations play little part in explaining the demand for money under the gold standard, and the short rate is often a more satisfactory explanatory variable than the long rate; the above discussion suggests why.

Finally in this Introduction we briefly outline the structure of the chapter. There is first a discussion of the money supply data. This provides one of the reasons for their being so many estimates of a money demand relationship for this period; for, as will emerge, the data have in recent years changed substantially. Several money demand equations are then surveyed, and their similarity discussed. We then turn to the money supply and examine in turn the base multiplier framework; the determination of the money supply given the base, and how and why these determinants varied over time; and the impact of financial crises and the lender of last resort (LLR) actions to contain them on the behavior of the money supply. The chapter ends with a brief concluding overview of the main findings.

MONEY DEMAND UNDER THE GOLD STANDARD

The demand for money under the gold standard is in principle no different from the demand for money under any other money supply regime. The demand is determined by the convenience yield of money in its various uses, and is a demand for *real money balances*—purchasing power—not for nominal balances. Nevertheless, money demand under the gold standard is a subject both deserving separate study from other periods, and providing a benchmark which can assist interpretation of results from other periods. The reason for this is that 1870–1914, the classic years of the gold standard, is a period particularly well suited to testing the basic theory of money demand. They were years of financial stability in the United Kingdom. The economy grew steadily; prices moved slowly and indeed started and ended the period at almost the same level; and both short and long interest rates moved within a modest range. Table 3.1 and Figures 3.1–3.4 summarize these data.

Further, the financial system was stable. There were no major bank failures or panics; banking spread steadily through the United Kingdom, and the banking system evolved gradually towards the form it was to take very soon after the end of World War I, a few large banks with extensive branch networks. Financial innovation, at least at the retail level, was essentially nonexistent. Hence none of the problems such innovation can cause for money demand studies was present. And finally, the data allow—or perhaps compel—a major simplification. There is little choice over which definition of money to use—one can use notes and coin, or notes and coin *plus* bank deposits. Bank deposits cannot be subdivided into interest bearing and noninterest bearing—the data are not available (see Capie and Webber, 1985).

Table 3.1. Economic performance, United Kingdom, 1870–1914

Year	GNP (1)	DEF (2)	Real GNP (3)	GNP (percent) (4)	RPI (5)	RPI (percent) (6)	Short (7)	Long (8)
1870	1081	92	11.75		108.00		3.276	3.246
1871	1184	95	12.46	6.07	111.00	2.78	2.62	3.235
1872	1244	101	12.32	−1.17	118.00	6.31	3.927	3.239
1873	1285	104	12.36	0.32	120.00	1.69	4.438	3.235
1874	1325	101	13.12	6.18	113.00	−5.83	3.5	3.242
1875	1290	97	13.30	1.37	109.00	−3.54	2.87	3.195
1876	1274	95	13.41	0.84	108.00	−0.92	1.771	3.155
1877	1251	93	13.45	0.31	108.00	0.00	2.427	3.141
1878	1238	91	13.60	1.14	102.00	−5.56	3.683	3.15
1879	1161	87	13.34	−1.91	99.00	−2.94	1.589	3.07
1880	1306	90	14.51	8.74	103.00	4.04	2.328	3.041
1881	1277	88	14.51	0.00	101.00	−1.94	2.875	2.997
1882	1318	90	14.64	0.92	100.00	−0.99	3.396	2.977
1883	1363	89	15.31	4.58	100.00	0.00	3.004	2.962
1884	1315	86	15.29	−0.16	95.00	−5.00	2.38	2.972
1885	1277	84	15.20	−0.58	89.00	−6.32	2.052	3.021
1886	1272	82	15.51	2.04	87.00	−2.25	2.062	2.967
1887	1340	83	16.14	4.08	86.00	−1.15	2.344	2.941
1888	1361	83	16.40	1.57	86.00	0.00	2.37	2.762
1889	1408	84	16.76	2.22	87.00	−1.16	2.752	2.779
1890	1455	85	17.12	2.12	87.00	0.00	3.698	2.849
1891	1498	84	17.83	4.18	87.00	0.00	2.563	2.868
1892	1470	84	17.50	−1.87	88.00	1.15	1.568	2.845
1893	1452	84	17.29	−1.22	87.00	−1.14	2.375	2.793
1894	1504	83	18.12	4.83	83.00	−4.60	1.008	2.716
1895	1530	82	18.66	2.97	81.00	−2.41	0.844	2.588
1896	1596	81	19.70	5.60	81.00	0.00	1.539	2.47
1897	1617	82	19.72	0.08	83.00	2.47	1.885	2.442
1898	1720	83	20.72	5.09	86.00	3.61	2.607	2.474
1899	1842	84	21.93	5.82	84.00	−2.33	3.274	2.574
1900	1926	90	21.40	−2.41	89.00	5.95	3.664	2.764
1901	1989	89	22.35	4.43	88.00	−1.12	3.198	2.921
1902	1964	87	22.57	1.01	88.00	0.00	3.013	2.909
1903	1963	87	22.56	−0.05	89.00	1.14	3.375	2.83
1904	1977	87	22.72	0.71	90.00	1.12	2.646	2.829
1905	2030	88	23.07	1.51	90.00	0.00	2.655	2.775
1906	2095	88	23.81	3.20	91.00	1.11	4.06	2.833
1907	2145	90	23.83	0.11	93.00	2.20	4.49	2.971
1908	2080	90	23.11	−3.03	91.00	−2.15	2.206	2.899
1909	2150	90	23.89	3.37	92.00	1.10	2.304	2.981
1910	2239	90	24.88	4.14	94.00	2.17	3.175	3.087
1911	2326	92	25.28	1.63	95.00	1.06	3.019	3.153
1912	2393	94	25.46	0.69	98.00	3.16	3.618	3.279
1913	2542	100	25.42	−0.15	100.00	2.04	4.365	3.391
1914	2572	95	27.07	6.51	101.00	1.00	2.951	2.991

Sources: Cols. 1, 2, and 5 from Capie and Webber (1985, table III.12); cols. 7 and 8 from Capie and Webber (1985, table III.10).

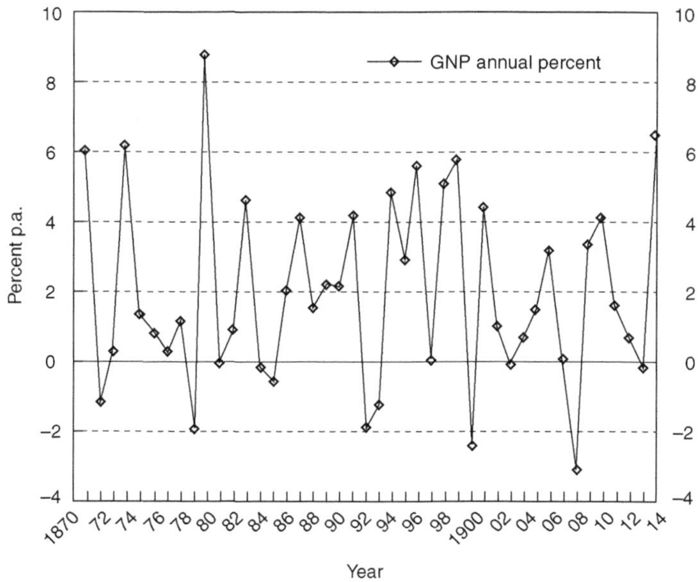

Figure 3.1. UK GNP, annual change, 1870–1914

Source: Capie and Webber (1985), tables III.12 and III.10

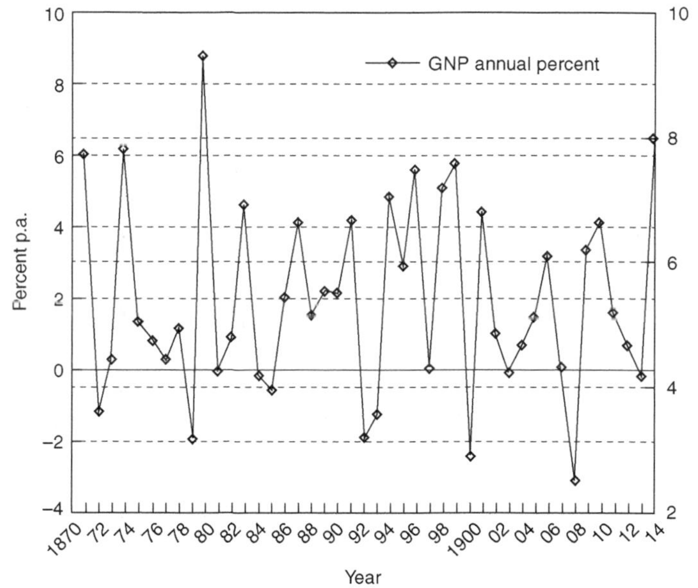

Figure 3.2. UK real GNP, annual change, 1870–1914

Source: Capie and Webber (1985), tables III.12 and III.10

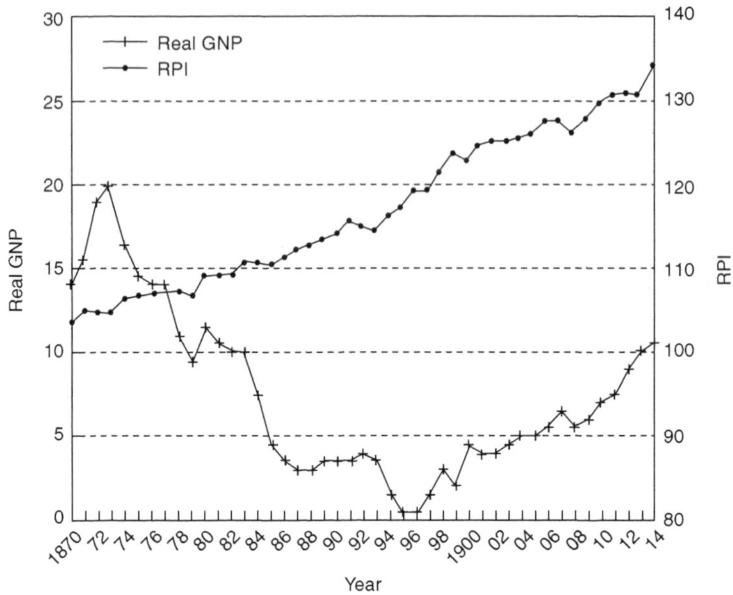

Figure 3.3. UK real GNP and RPI, 1870–1914
Source: Capie and Webber (1985), tables III.12 and III.10

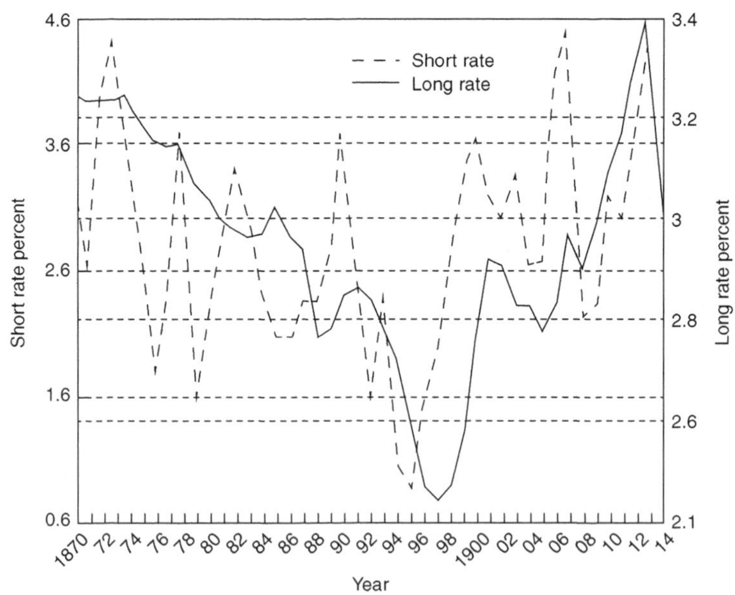

Figure 3.4. UK short and long rates, 1870–1914
Source: Capie and Webber (1985), tables III.12 and III.10

Accordingly, money demand studies of this period test basic money demand theory, with results uncontaminated by many of the factors that have caused problems in recent years. This relative simplicity does not mean there have been few such studies. There have been several, in good part because the data—particularly the measures of the money stock, but also the interest rates—have changed. The next section briefly discusses why these data revisions were made. We then turn to reviewing some of the studies of money demand in this period.

DATA REVISIONS

Monetary series prior to Capie and Webber (1985) were constructed largely on the basis of published data (there was no 'official' series). This reliance on published data introduced two deficiencies. First, the figures which were published were not very informative. Banks were not required to publish complete balance sheets. Only joint stock banks had any obligation—that being to publish information relating to shares, capital, and dividends. All UK bank deposit series for the late nineteenth century used the printed balance sheets of the banks that chose to make their accounts public. These were published both individually and in the aggregate in the half-yearly edition of *The Economist*'s Banking Supplement.

The chief defect this introduced into the monetary series resulted from more and more banks publishing every year. This caused *The Economist*'s series to increase—but the increase resulted not only from growth in the stock of money, but from growth in the part of it which was reported. Not only was there a spurious trend; there was also a spurious step. From 1891 onwards, private banks (i.e. non-joint stock) started to publish their figures. Those figures, too, appeared in *The Economist*. So the series suddenly jumped upwards in 1891.

These were the two major problems. There was also a variety of others. Because different banks published at different times, the figures aggregated in *The Economist* could be for balance sheets months apart. Sometimes when a bank was absorbed by another its figures were (correctly) dropped, but were sometimes not added to those of the other banks. The figures were swollen by double counting—mainly of the interbank deposits the provincial, Scottish, and Irish banks held with their London agents. Finally, most banks 'window dressed' their accounts; this increased the amount of interbank and customers' deposits.

These problems were well-known, and those who constructed UK money data attempted to deal with them. The Capie and Webber (1985) series was, however, produced with the aid of access to previously unpublished balance sheets. It was thus able to solve the problems created by the spurious trend, and the spurious step of 1891. A detailed account of the work of previous scholars, and of Capie and Webber's revisions, can be found in Capie and Webber (1985, chapters 2 and 11).

Harley (1976) revised the consol yield series. The most widely used series (reproduced for example in Sheppard, 1971) is misleading for two reasons. It does not take account of the possibility of conversion (or redemption) on the yield of consols when their price rose above par—as the price of 3 percent consols did in 1881. Harley suggests that 2 1/2 percent consols are a better guide to yields. Second, he argues that the yield on Goschen consols, issued in 1888, was miscalculated in the standard sources (for the years before 1903) because it did not properly allow for the 1903 reduction in the coupon from 2 3/4 percent to 2 1/2 percent. All work subsequent to Harley's paper has (so far as we know) used his data. But as will emerge below, the results seem insensitive to data revision.

THE DEMAND EQUATION

All the studies discussed below follow the same general theoretical framework. The model relates the amount of money demanded to the price level, real income, a short-term interest rate, and a long-term interest rate. The own rate on money should of course also be an argument in the demand function, and one study (Friedman and Schwartz, 1982) reports estimates containing a measure of that own yield. Friedman and Schwartz use the measure proposed in Klein (1970), derived on the assumption of a competitive banking system leading banks to pass on to their customers the net return on bank assets, and calculating this return on the basis of market interest rates. This leads to the return on deposits being a fraction of the market rate, the fraction being equal to

$$1 - \frac{R}{D}$$

where R/D is the reserve/deposit ratio, and reserves are non-interest bearing. Income per unit of money would then be a weighted average of that rate and the zero rate on currency (the weights are determined by the currency/deposit (C/D) ratio).

There can be no doubt that the argument is right in principle. Before proceeding to the results of the empirical work, the variable should therefore be discussed further, so that we can understand its lack of success. Most important, it presumes a competitive banking system. In the British banking system of these years there was some degree of cartelization—in particular, there were agreements which prevented interest being paid on deposits, or restricted it to below the competitive level. These agreements were certainly not all-pervasive, but they did produce deviations from competitive behavior (see Goodhart, 1972, pp. 178–88; Griffiths, 1973). (There are in principle also statistical problems with the measure; but they may well not be problems in practice; see Friedman and Schwartz, 1982, n. 46, pp. 270–74.)

The equations we discuss below broadly fall into two groups—those which examine the demand for money in this period as part of a longer study, and those which consider the period in isolation. We briefly discuss the first group, and then, in more detail, the latter. It is worth noting at the outset, though, how similar the results of the various studies are. Without exception, three features stand out very clearly in every study. First, the function is stable. A change in income, the price level, or the interest rate (or rates) has the same effect on the amount of money demanded at whatever time we are in the period; and at any given level of these variables, the amount of money demanded is the same, regardless of when the observations occur. Second, the income elasticity of demand is very close to unity. Third, the demand is for real balances: double the price level, and the demand for nominal balances doubles; double nominal balances, and the price level doubles.

This stability and simplicity of the money demand function is of the greatest importance for interpreting the behavior of the British economy in those years, for it means that there can be no doubt when there was an excess supply of or excess demand for money. Clarification of the influence of money on the economy is therefore greatly simplified.

Now to a selection of the studies which have produced this simplification. Two studies not readily comparable with the others are those contained in Friedman and Schwartz (1982), and a commentary on it by Hendry and Ericsson (1991). Friedman and Schwartz estimated a function that was stable, after allowing for some special factors, over a century from 1870. A discussion of these special factors highlights just how stable the function was in the gold standard years, and also suggests why.[1] Apart from that, the special factors allowed for are war and its immediate aftermath, and the depression and associated uncertainty of the inter-war years.[2] Note that *none* of these special factors was important in the United Kingdom before 1914. This reinforces our earlier suggestion that the stability of the estimated function in the gold

[1] For the United States they included a term to allow for increasing financial sophistication before 1903. In the United Kingdom there was as noted above a developed, stable, nationwide banking system by 1870. For detailed discussion of the effect of this on the demand for money, see Bordo and Jonung (1981); Capie and Wood (1986a).

[2] In his discussion of these, Goodhart (1982) suggests that rather than treating these episodes by use of dummy variables it would be worthwhile attempting to explain money holding behaviour during them in more detail. This interesting suggestion has not yet been implemented.

standard period is a reflection of the stability of the period, allowing us to see how the money holding behaves in the absence of shocks.

The Friedman and Schwartz study was examined somewhat critically by Hendry and Ericsson (1991), their criticism being directed at the statistical methods used. Friedman and Schwartz (1991) replied; in part of their reply, they point out that Hendry and Ericsson's findings were actually the same as theirs. Hence the Friedman–Schwartz study is not inconsistent with our opening general summary of how money demand behaved in this period in the United Kingdom.

Turning now to studies which concentrate exclusively on the gold standard years, we note first the study by Mills and Wood (1982), and then turn to Klovland's (1987) paper, which comprehensively reviewed previous work on the subject. The Mills and Wood study was an attempt to discriminate statistically between various measures of the money stock then available. That aspect of the paper is now superseded, as all the series they examined have been displaced by Capie and Webber (1985). What is now notable about the paper's results is that all *four* measures of money used (Sheppard's, 1971, series for UK bank deposits and UK money supply; Nishimura's, 1973, measure of bank deposits; and a measure comprising Nishimura's bank deposits *plus* Sheppard's net coin and currency outside banks) yielded results for all purposes identical in the important aspects of income, interest rate, and price elasticities (see Mills and Wood, 1982, p. 272.) In view of the differences in the series, this is perhaps somewhat surprising; but no explanation has as yet been given.

Another paper worthy of note before we turn to a general review is Capie and Rodrik-Bali (1985). This paper followed the method suggested in Hendry (1979) 'intended over-parameterisation with data-based simplification.' The resulting specification was in general consistent with the other studies surveyed here. But there are some interesting minor differences. The demand for money was affected by permanent income—not surprising, although not generally examined in this period. But what the authors did note as a puzzle was that the demand for money depended negatively (*ceteris paribus*) on the real growth rate. This has been found elsewhere (Hendry and Mizon, 1978) but it is not common. Otherwise the results display the robustness to changes in econometric techniques and minor data changes that we have already noted as characterizing this period—the income elasticity of demand was unity, the demand was homogeneous in the general level of prices, and the interest elasticity of demand was negative, albeit low.

Now to Klovland's study. As well as presenting his own work, he gathered the results of four previous papers. These, together with his preferred equation, comprise Table 3.2. (The equations differ slightly from the original versions, as for the sake of consistency Klovland re-estimated them all using his preferred money stock data.) The long-run price level homogeneity with

Table 3.2. Alternative demand for money equations, 1878–1913

A Coefficient estimates (MW) Mills and Wood (1982, (9))

$$
\begin{array}{llllll}
\Delta_1(m-p)_t & = 0.209\Delta_1 y_t & -0.434-\Delta_1 p_t & -0.032 r_t^{TB} & -0.103(m-p-y)_{t-1} \\
 & (0.159) & (0.226) & (0.013) & (0.083) \\
 & +0.027 & & & \\
 & (0.013) & & &
\end{array}
$$

(*HE*) Hendry and Ericsson (1983, Table VIII (i))

$$
\begin{array}{llllll}
\Delta_1(m-p)_t & = -4.94\Delta_2 RL_t & +0.880 — \Delta_4 y^t & -0.692\Delta_1^2 P_t & -0.196\Delta_1^2 P_{t-2} \\
 & (3.52) & (0.138) & (0.074) & (0.091) \\
 & +0.467\Delta_1^2(m-p)_{t-1} & -0.093\Delta_1^2(m-p)_{t-2} & -0.708 RS_t & \\
 & (0.046) & (0.080) & (0.230) & \\
 & -0.149(m-p-y)_{t-4} & -0.069 & & \\
 & (0.048) & (0.032) & &
\end{array}
$$

(*LH*) Longbottom and Holly (1985, (7))

$$
\begin{array}{llllll}
\Delta_1(m-p)_t & = -0.042\Delta_2 r_t^L & -0.708\Delta_1^2 P_t & -0.260\Delta_1 P_{t-1} & +0.512\Delta_1(m-p)_{t-1} \\
 & (0.034) & (0.065) & (0.097) & (0.083) \\
 & -0.124\Delta_1^2(m-p)_{t-2} & -0.018 r_t^N & +0.261 y_1 & -0.281(m-p)_{t-1} \\
 & (0.037) & (0.006) & (0.034) & (0.042) \\
 & -0.012 & & & \\
 & (0.061) & & &
\end{array}
$$

(*CRB*) Capie and Rodrik-Bali (1985)

$$
\begin{array}{llll}
\Delta_1(m-p)_t & = -0.195\Delta_1 \ \ln(1+RS/100)_t & +0.082(\Delta_1 y_t + \Delta_1 y_{t-3}) & -0.627\Delta_1^2 p_t \\
 & (0.524) & (0.082) & (0.196) \\
 & -0.515\Delta_1 p_{t-1} & -0.904 \ \ln(1+RS/100)_{t-2} & -0.123(m-p-y)_{t-1} \\
 & (0.231) & (0.482) & (0.087) \\
 & +0.025 & & \\
 & (0.013) & &
\end{array}
$$

(*k*) Klovland (6)

$$
\begin{array}{llllll}
\Delta_1(m-p)_t & = 0.007(\Delta_1 r_t^D - \Delta_2 r_t^S) & +0.613 — \Delta_2 y_t & -0.702_1^2 p_t & -0.421\Delta_t p_{t-1} \\
 & (0.004) & (0.057) & (0.039) & (0.053) \\
 & -0.113\Delta_1^2(m-p)_{t-2} & -0.035(r^{S*} + r^{L*}) & +0.040(r^D - r^S)_{t-3} & \\
 & (0.023) & (0.004) & (0.011) & \\
 & -0.425(m-p-y)_{t-2} & -0.173 & & \\
 & (0.033) & (0.022) & &
\end{array}
$$

B Summary statistics	*MW*	*HE*	*LH*	*CBR*	*K*
T	36	36	36	36	36
k	5	9	9	7	9
s	0.0182	0.0103	0.0097	0.0194	0.0063
R^2	0.445	0.844	0.411	0.943	
$LA(4,T-k-4)$ 1.58	0.30	0.74	3.49	0.67	
ARCH	3.75	0.21	2.83	1.62	
NORM	3.37	0.95	0.02	1.04	0.24
CHOW $(8,T-k-8)$	0.30	0.95	0.29	0.17	
Long-run elasticities					
Short rate	−0.305	−0.134	−0.063	−0.187	−0.177
Consol rate				−0.082	
Own rate			0.063	0.095	

respect to nominal money is rejected for Mills and Wood (1982), and Capie and Rodrik-Bali (1985) (it is not rejected on the data those authors use) but retained in all other equations. Longbottom and Holly (1985) have the long-run income elasticity different from unity, but not significantly so. As Klovland notes, the short-run dynamics differ between the models—perhaps not surprisingly, as each uses a different opportunity cost variable. Every one of these, though, was a short rate. The consol yield appeared (and then insignificantly) in only two equations—*HE* and *LH*. This insignificance is highly likely (as Mills and Wood, 1982, suggested) to be the result of the stability of the long rate over these years as a result of the low actual and expected inflation produced by the gold standard regime.

Klovland concludes his survey by noting that despite the data changes all the main results that we noted in the opening of the section were reproduced. He, too, contrasts the stability of the function and its robustness to data changes with evidence from later periods, but offers no explanation.[3]

To conclude this section, the result seems to be that the money demand function in the gold standard years was stable and well behaved. Interpretation of the role of money in these years should therefore be relatively straightforward. Furthermore, this stability helps interpret the apparent instability of the demand function in later periods.[4]

MONEY SUPPLY

Under the gold standard the quantity of money lies outside the control of the monetary authorities, though some modification to this statement is required in the case of the large or dominant economy in the system. The relationship of the money stock to real income is complex. There is nevertheless still interest in examining the relationship between the broad money stock and the monetary base. This part of the chapter outlines the basic theoretical framework and then considers the second part of this question, the role of the public and the banks in the process. As a starting point take a fixed exchange rate system and leave aside that it was commodity based. In such a system, money would move *after* changes in (real or nominal) income, and not before. The explanation is straightforward. Assume the monetary

[3] In his concluding paragraph Klovland remarks, erroneously, that, because money was endogenous 'the evidence from this time period does not fit well into a framework which assigns a major causal role to the stock of money under a fixed exchange rate regime.' His confusion is that he does not distinguish between the causes of money growth and the consequences of that growth. See Friedman and Schwartz (1982, p. 325).

[4] A most interesting discussion of this apparent instability can be found in Christ (1993). These issues are also discussed in a most useful paper by Taylor (1993).

authorities expand the money supply by lowering short-term interest rates. Since there is no concern about exchange rate risk, money flows abroad to obtain a higher interest rate there, and the monetary expansion is negated.[5] Conversely, an expansion of *real* income in a country increases the amount of money demanded.

By various channels,[6] including a rise in interest rates as there is initially excess demand for money, money is attracted into the economy until the excess demand is eliminated and interest rates are again at the world level. In such a setting, then, money can *follow* fluctuations in real income, but does not lead them. Money *following* income does not mean that money is unimportant for movements in income. As Friedman and Schwartz (1982, 325, n. 14) put it:

> in a fixed exchange rate regime the quantity of money is endogenous, and cannot be determined, except for brief periods, by the monetary authorities. Monetary policy cannot affect the quantity of money except temporarily; nonetheless changes in the quantity of money, however produced, will affect income. Indeed, it is precisely because they do that a gold standard or other fixed exchange rate regime is self-adjusting . . .
>
> The exchange rate regime does not affect the existence of a 'causal' link from money to income; it affects the forces determining the quantity of money and thereby whether the situation is one of largely unidirectional influence from money to income or of simultaneous determination and interaction.

The full force of this argument can be understood by moving from a fixed exchange rate to a gold standard. In such a system the money supply in Britain could expand (for more than a brief period) for *two* reasons: income expansion in Britain, producing a monetary inflow as described above; or a gold discovery (outside Britain). This gold is spent on goods, services, and assets, and thus finds its way into circulation in every country of the world. Some flows into Britain, and produces effects so in this case, the money flow precedes changes rather than follows them. And even if the money flow followed rather than initiated a change, this need not mean it has no subsequent effects; for the ratio of nominal money to income will be higher if the money flows than if it does not, and this in turn will have consequences.

A third should be added to these two possible money income relationships. If the economy is sufficiently large then monetary fluctuations originating there, although spilling over to the rest of the world, nevertheless affect that country's money stock by having a significant effect on the *world's* money stock. While Britain was not a gold producer, this last possibility is not ruled out, if the banking system evolved so as to support a larger money stock on an unchanged gold base. It has also been argued that the size of the British

[5] In fact some of the monetary expansion will remain; the proportion will depend on the share of the originating country in the world economy.

[6] See McCloskey and Zecher (1984) for a detailed discussion of these.

economy and the fact that sterling was a key currency meant the Bank of England was in a position to use its discount rate and influence the world distribution of gold.

MONEY SUPPLY PROCESS

The useful framework referred to above for examining the money supply process is that of the money multiplier that places the behavior of the banks alongside the monetary authorities and the public. The simplest expression of this is the following:

$$M = mB,$$

where m is the money multiplier, B is the monetary base, and M is the money stock. The money multiplier can be shown as:

$$\frac{\frac{C}{D}+1}{\frac{R}{D}+\frac{C}{D}}$$

and this brings out the fact that the public who hold currency (C) in relation to deposits (D) can influence the size of the money stock if they change the ratio in which they hold cash as against deposits. Equally, the banks choose to hold cash reserves (R) as cover for their deposit liabilities. When they feel the need to raise that cover, they dampen down the total money stock. This way of examining the money supply process brings out that there are three parties influencing the total money stock—the monetary authorities, the banks, and the public. There are generally good reasons for believing that the behavior of the banks and the public is relatively stable, leaving the outcome of the money stock largely in the hands of the monetary authorities or at least as the product of the monetary base, however that is determined. But although the behavior of the banks and public was stable and predictable, it could vary.

In Britain in this period there were no legal restrictions on the reserve-deposit (R/D) ratio and the variation from bank to bank could be quite considerable. Indeed, the idea of a reserve ratio was not clearly articulated at the beginning of this period, though obviously banks worked with some idea of requisite cover or they were in danger of going out of business. There is evidence that the first consciously stated reserve ratio was self-imposed by the Lincoln Bank in 1872 and that in the course of the next twenty years or so most English banks came to employ an announced minimum ratio. Contemporary estimates of the size of the ratio lend support to our own estimates.

According to one survey of seventy-five nonclearing banks the range was 9–17 percent. An estimate of twelve London clearing banks gave a range of 10.4–16.8 percent. Our own estimates for the system as a whole show that it fluctuated between 8.5 percent and 12.5 percent (with a mean of 10.4 percent and standard deviation of 1.1 percent)(Capie and Webber, 1985). After some initial erratic behavior in the 1870s, from the early 1880s onwards the *R*/*D* ratio was on a gently upward trend. That is, the banks held a growing quantity of reserves in relation to deposits. This must therefore have been a factor holding down the growth of the broad money stock. This growth of the *R*/*D* ratio is on the face of things slightly perplexing. A jump in the proportion of reserves could indicate fears of instability or financial uncertainty. It is not a jump, but rather a slow steady growth, that has to be explained and, in any case all the evidence for the period, particularly from the 1880s onwards, would seem to be against crises and instability. The last major financial crisis was in 1866 and economic stability, however measured, generally improved towards the end of the century.

It might be hypothesized that small banks would have held higher reserves than large banks since the latter acquired a certain soundness by virtue of size. But if this were the case the trend in *R*/*D* would have been *downwards* since small banks shrank as a proportion of total bank population. However, the rising ratio can be explained, and the explanation we offer would be as follows. Small banks in fact held smaller reserves than large banks. Turner (1972) found in his investigations that the lowest ratios of all were amongst the nonclearers. The reason for this is that private banks were not obliged to publish their accounts. As more and more banks published accounts there was therefore an increase in the ratio; the need to publish in itself provided a pressure to keep a higher ratio of reserves. And this move to publish coincided in time with the Baring crisis (of 1890), when it became accepted that the banks should hold a higher ratio.

One method (Friedman and Schwartz, 1963) of examining the contribution of each proximate determinant of the money supply gives the fraction of monetary change which was produced by each of the determinants between the beginning and the end of any selected period. Over the period as a whole it was high-powered money (the base) that explained by far the greatest part of the change in the broad money stock—some 70 percent. As already shown, *R*/*D* was acting to slow monetary expansion; the cash/deposit ratio (*C*/*D*) was acting to offset this. The effect of *C*/*D* was considerably stronger than that of *R*/*D* over the whole period, although within some periods the respective contribution of each of these factors was more or less the same. For the period 1897–1913 monetary base is the powerful explanation, *R*/*D* is strong and *C*/*D* has lost a little of its importance. In summary, in spite of the considerable changes that took place in this period, the monetary base was the prime determinant of money supply in this period.

What also stands out in this period is the considerable growth and changing structure of the banking system. This deserves some comment, for not only was it an important element in the relative stability of the financial system and in producing an environment in which there were no banking panics or financial crises, but it clearly had enormous potential for changing the money stock.

We have already hinted at how the structure was important in reducing monetary volatility and hence played a part in reducing the likelihood of monetary shocks affecting output. Some further comment on the changing structure may be useful. By 1870 British banking had already evolved to close to its modern form with a number of commercial banks, the largest of which had many branches across the country. Table 3.3 shows how this form developed over the next fifty years.

As early as 1870 there were 2,728 bank offices in the country (0.87 offices per 10,000 population). Although the total number of banks in all categories fell fairly steadily throughout the period there were still over 100 banks in 1914 and there were around 8,000 bank offices at that point (1.63 per 10,000 population). The fall in the total number of banks was in part the result of a growing concern for size, associated as it was with greater reserves, security and prestige; hence came the mergers/acquisitions that took place at an accelerating pace in the 1890s. But the main point to make is that there was a great growth, from an already substantial base in 1870, of this branching network. This meant that any one bank, usually with headquarters in London, had loans and sources of funds in most if not all parts of the country covering the whole spectrum of industry, agriculture, and services. This branch network meant that if a branch, or even several branches, were in trouble in an area adversely affected by a fall in demand for its product, the resources of the bank could readily be diverted to ease the pressure. This could be done without any indication being given to a wider public and so could remove an important potential source of apprehension for the depositor.

Table 3.3. Bank branching, United Kingdom, 1870–1920

	London banks		Provincial banks		All UK banks		Bank branches per 10,000 population
Year	Banks	Branches	Banks	Branches	Banks	Branches	
1870	56	84	299	1092	387	2728	0.87
1880	65	109	258	1396	358	3454	1.00
1890	65	149	200	1795	303	4347	1.16
1900	39	135	108	1875	188	5822	1.44
1910	27	36	47	1516	112	7565	1.68
1920	29	31	21	949	75	9668	2.08

Source: Capie and Webber (1985).

There were nonetheless still many banks in Britain without branches and there were fairly frequent bank failures; and there were also regular new entrants to the system every year. The failures did not result in runs; they were simply accepted as part of the normal pattern of business enterprise. There were even occasionally quite large bank failures such as that of the City of Glasgow Bank in 1878. This was a badly managed bank, with corrupt practices, which was clearly insolvent and was allowed to fail. It had close connections with a number of other banks, all of which were affected. But there was no run on banks, no banking panic, no financial crisis (although it may have been a near miss), no significant rise in C/D or R/D ratios.

SHORT-RUN PROBLEMS

The gold standard was demonstrably a provider of long-run stability. But what happened in the short run? What happened when, for example, the financial system was threatened and there was the prospect of a consequent collapse in the stock of money? This should be differentiated from 'financial distress' or 'pseudo-crises' which may threaten the wealth of one group in society, but does not threaten the prosperity of the entire economy. For example, in Britain there was undoubtedly financial distress when the City of Glasgow Bank failed. Shareholders suffered, but there was no run on the banking *system*. (For a discussion of the distinction between real and pseudo-crises, see Schwartz, 1986.)

A financial crises is a run to cash by depositors nationwide. The switching of funds from one institution to another undoubtedly causes distress to the first institution, and could cause it to fail, but does not threaten the financial *system* or the economy as a whole. What is notable about this aspect of British monetary experience in the years studied in this chapter is the absence of a crisis. There was none. This is a quite different experience from that of either continental Europe or the United States. In both of these, genuine crises on the above definition occurred. This contrast of experience suggests that an explanation for the absence of crises in Britain must be sought not in a claim that the whole world was stable, but in something unique to British experience.

Two features of the British financial system provide much of the explanation: the structure of banking and the Bank of England acting as lender of last resort. We consider them in turn. A classic cause of a bank's failing is a problem affecting local industry. Suppose, for example, there is a crop failure in one area of the country, or some manufacturing industry suddenly loses its market because of an exogenous shock such as a foreign war or a tariff. Loans cannot be repaid, or even serviced. The bank's assets deteriorate, while liabilities remain unchanged; and some depositors lose their wealth. If this is recognized as being a purely local event, it may not spread to other banks. But in the absence of good information it could spread— even if thought to be due to a local event people elsewhere might still run for cash to be absolutely safe.

Such an episode could occur under unitary banking, but was unlikely under branch banking. Branching allows diversification (as does the scale usually associated with branched but not with unitary systems). Hence these shocks are unlikely to affect the entire branch network simultaneously. A shock to one branch is withstood with the help of others not adversely affected. Depositors at the branch which suffered loan defaults do not lose their deposits, so no bank run starts. The structure of British banking in the years before World War I was such as to reduce the likelihood of a banking crisis.

The attitude and action of the Bank of England constitute the second feature. The Bank of England acted as *lender of last resort.* It had acted in this way before 1870, and it is worth looking at the outcome of these actions, for this will highlight both what the Bank did and the reasons why it never needed to do so in subsequent years. A financial crisis occurs because an event has triggered a run from bank deposits to cash. The way to curtail such a run is to supply the cash. The central bank supplies it to banks in exchange for securities, and the banks then supply it to their customers. The central bank has lent 'to the market'—that is to say, to any institution which offers securities at the discount window. The ready availability of cash reassures the public, the run ends, and the crisis comes to an end. That was how the Bank acted in the crises of 1847, 1857, and 1866. The market got nervous, panic broke out, and there was an immense demand for cash. The Bank was allowed to suspend the 1844 Act, allowing an expansion of the fiduciary issue, and more cash was forthcoming. From then on the knowledge that the Act could be suspended prevented panic, for people knew they could get cash.

Walter Bagehot is often credited with convincing the Bank of England of the need to act as lender of last resort.[7] That was plainly unnecessary; what he in fact did was to urge it to commit itself in advance to doing so. This, he argued, would eliminate the fear that cash could not be obtained and so would prevent crises from arising. It appears, then, that we cannot distinguish between the Bank's precommitment and the structure of the banking system as the cause of the absence of banking crises in Britain. Both may have contributed; perhaps either would have been sufficient.

In this period there were three occasions when crises have been identified. The first was 1878, the second the 'Baring crisis,' and the third the panic at the outset of the 1914–18 war.

In 1878 a number of banks got into difficulties following the collapse of the City of Glasgow Bank. Not all were directly or even indirectly connected with

[7] His advice appeared in *The Economist*, which he edited and in 'Lombard Street'. For a detailed discussion of this issue, see Rockoff (1986).

that bank but there were undoubtedly fears in the market of widespread difficulties. As noted above, the City of Glasgow Bank was allowed to fail. There was no bail-out. But neither did a crisis develop. That can be seen from the behavior of the C/D ratio and the R/D ratio.

Baring's difficulties in 1890 derived from involvement in Argentina. The flow of remittance from Argentina stopped. The Bank of England organized a rescue—a lifeboat. In contrast to the Chancellor of the Exchequer (Goschen), who was reluctant to provide government assistance lest Baring prove to be insolvent, the Bank thought that the problem was one of illiquidity. It persuaded other banks to agree, on the basis of a report which concluded that Baring was fundamentally sound but needed some £10 million in liquidity. Baring was put into liquidation and there was a modest rise in the demand for cash. Baring was reconstituted as a limited liability company with a new chairman and the Argentinian debt written off. Although both the Bank and the City were busy, there was no crisis. Note that there was not a classic lender of last resort operation—one was not needed.[8]

Finally, in 1914 the prospect of imminent war caused plunging stock prices and a failure of remittance from overseas. A rush for liquidity began and the banks called in their loans to the Stock Exchange and the discount market, further weakening the former and driving the latter to the Bank of England. Fortunately all this occurred just before a bank holiday—which was extended. Assistance was provided to the stock market under a scheme proposed by the clearing banks, and the Bank of England gave assistance to the discount market. There may have been a subsequent inflation (see Goodhart, 1986) but that was to some extent intertwined with the exigencies of war finance. This episode exemplifies the problem of explaining UK financial stability in these years. The consequences of large well-diversified banks are inextricable from those of having a precommitted lender of last resort.

SUMMARY

The experience of the gold standard in the years 1870–1914 has frequently been cited as a model of exchange rate and price stability. The world economy prospered. Britain was at the center of the system, and her experience, while mixed in terms of output growth (Feinstein, 1972), was nevertheless one of

[8] It may be that, concerned with the dangers of fostering 'moral hazard', the Bank Governor had been determined that financial institutions should not feel that they could always turn for rescue to the Bank. There was therefore, not a classic lender of last resort operation—but the collective guarantee instead. Although the Baring crisis had the effect of permanently enhancing the Bank's authority, the Bank's aim had been to throw the banking system on to its own resources in case of banking crises, rather than on to the Bank: Bagehot upside down?

price and general stability. The British experience could, however, have been unique, since Britain was a large economy in the international trade sense and exercised considerable influence in the world economy over capital flows. In that now well-known phrase, Britain was the 'conductor of the international orchestra'.

As far as the role of money in the British economy goes it is clear that fluctuation in the supply of money relative to income was the long-run determinant of the behavior of the general level of prices. In other words the view that there was serious economic depression, and that collapsing agricultural prices were the cause of the general price level movement, can be rejected. There was of course as is well-known a depression in southern agriculture (in arable farming), and there was a more general prolonged downturn in the economy in the 1880s. But the trend rate of growth of output over the whole period, while declining, was fairly steady.

The general level of prices declined slowly but steadily from 1873 to 1896 (the period formerly referred to in the literature as the Great Depression), and then rose slowly but steadily until 1913 when they were back more or less where they had been in 1870. (Indeed, the whole nineteenth century was a period of when prices were more or less flat, insofar as they can be measured.) A relationship between cyclical fluctuations in money and fluctuations in output is elusive for the United Kingdom in this period, a finding which contrasts with the United States. For the United States, Friedman and Schwartz found a relationship. But it was a case of *major* fluctuations in output being associated with major fluctuations in money. Monetary stability in Britain may in part be explained by the structure and maturity of the banking system—one that had a small number of large banks with country-wide branch networks. The other element in the stability was the acceptance, in this period, by the Bank of England of its responsibility to act as lender of last resort in the classic fashion—that is, lending to the market as a whole rather than bailing-out individual institutions; and it did so in a precommitted way—it indicated in advance its willingness to do so.

The remarkable monetary stability that prevailed in all probability contributed to the stability of the money demand function in this period; while supply and demand have separate determinants, the behavior of demand was influenced by the behavior, and expected behavior, of supply.

REFERENCES

Bordo, M. D. and Jonung, L. (1981) 'The Long Run Behaviour of the Income Velocity of Money in Five Advanced Countries 1870–1975: An Institutional Approach', *Economic Inquiry*, 19.

Bordo, M. D. and Schwartz, A. J. (eds.) (1984) *The Retrospective on the Classical Gold Standard 1821–1931*, University of Chicago Press for NBER.

Cagan, P. (1984) 'War, Prices and Interest Rates: A Martial Solution to Gibson's Paradox', in M. D. Bordo and A. J. Schwartz (eds.), *A Restrospective on the Classical Gold Standard 1821–1931*, University of Chicago Press for NBER.

Capie, F. H. and Rodrik-Bali, G. (1985) 'The Money Adjustment Process in the UK 1870–1914', *Economica*, 52, 117–22.

——and Webber, A. (1985) *A Monetary History of the United Kingdom 1870–1982*, Vol. I: *Data, Sources, Methods*, London: George Allen & Unwin.

——and Wood, G. E. (1986a) 'The Long Run Behaviour of Velocity in the UK', Monetary History Discussion Paper 23, City University Business School.

——(1986b) *Financial Crises and the World Banking System*, London: Macmillan

Christ, C. F. (1993) 'Assessing Applied Econometric Results', *Federal Reserve Bank of St. Louis Review*, 75(2), 71–94.

Eichengreen, B. (1985) *The Gold Standard in Theory and History*, London: Methuen.

Feinstein, C. H. (1972) *National Income, Expenditure and Output of the United Kingdom 1855–1965*, Cambridge University Press.

Friedman, M. and Schwartz, G. E. (1963) *A Monetary History of the United States, 1867–1960*, Princeton University Press for NBER, 119–34.

——(1982) *Monetary Trends in the United States and in the United Kingdom 1870–1970*, University of Chicago Press for NBER.

——(1991) 'Alternative Approaches to Analysing Economic Data', *American Economic Review*, 81, 39–99.

Goodbart, C. A. E. (1972) *The Business of Banking 1891–1914*, London: Weidenfeld & Nicolson.

——(1982) 'Monetary Trends in the UK and the US', *Journal of Economic Literature*, 20, 1540–91.

——(1986) 'Comment on Seabourne', in F. H. Capie and G. E. Wood (eds.), *Financial Crises and the World Banking System*, London: Macmillan.

Griffiths, B. (1973) 'The Development of Restrictive Practices in the UK Monetary System', *Manchester School*, 4 (March), 3–13.

Harley, C. K. (1976) 'Goschen's Conversion of the National Debt and the Yield on Consols', *Economic History Review*, 34(1) (February), 101–6.

Hendry, D. F. (1979) 'Predictive Failure and Econometric Modelling in Macro Economics: The Transaction Demand for Money', in P. Ormerod (ed.), *Economic Modelling*, London: Heinemann.

——and Ericsson, N. R. (1991) 'An Econometric Analysis of UK Money Demand in Monetary Trends in the US and UK', *American Economic Review*, 81, 8–38.

————(1983) 'Assertion Without Empirical Basis'. Paper presented to the Bank of England's panel of Academic Consultants, Panel Paper No. 22, October.

——and Mizon, G. E. (1978) 'Serial Correlation as a Convenient Simplification, not as a Nuisance: A Comment on a Study of the Demand for Money by the Bank of England', *Economic Journal*, 88, 549–63.

Klein, B. (1970) 'The Payment of Interest on Commercial Bank Deposits and the Price of Money: A Study of the Demand for Money', Ph.D. dissertation, University of Chicago.

Klovland, J. T. (1987) 'The Demand for Money in the United Kingdom 1875–1913', *Oxford Bulletin of Economics and Statistics*, 49 (August), 251–71.

Longbottom, A. and S. Holly (1985) 'Econometric Methodology and Monetarism: Professor Friedman and Professor Hendry on the Demand for Money', London Business School, Discussion Paper.

McCloskey, D. and Zecher, J. R. (1984) 'The Success of Purchasing-Power Parity: Historical Evidence and its Implications for Macroeconomics', in M. D. Bordo and A. J. Schwartz (eds.), *A Retrospective on the Classical Gold Standard 1821–1931*, University of Chicago Press for NBER, 121–170.

Mills, T. C. (1990) 'A Note on the Gibson Paradox Under the Gold Standard', *Explorations in Economic History*, 27, 277–86.

——and Wood, G. E. (1978) 'Money, Income, and Causality under the Gold Standard', *Federal Reserve Bank of St. Louis Review* (2), 22–27.

————(1982) 'Econometric Evaluation of Alternative UK Money Stock Series, 1870–1913', *Journal of Money, Credit and Banking* (May), 265–77.

————(1992) 'The Gibson Paradox Re-examined', in S. N. Broadberry and N. F. R. Crafts (eds.), *Money, Trade and Business Cycles: Essays in Honour of A. G. Ford*, Cambridge University Press.

Nishimura, S. (1973) 'The Growth of the Stock of Money in the UK 1870–1913', Hosei University, Discussion Paper, unpublished.

Rockoff, H. (1986) 'Walter Bagehot and the Theory of Central Banking', in F. H. Capie and G. E. Wood (eds.), *Financial Crises and the World Banking System*, London: Macmillan.

Schwartz, A. J. (1986) 'Real and Pseudo Financial Crises', in F. H. Capie and G. E. Wood (eds.), *Financial Crises and the World Banking System*, London: Macmillan.

Sheppard, D. K. (1971) *The Growth and Role of UK Financial Institutions 1880–1962*, London: Methuen.

Taylor, M. (1993) 'Modelling the Demand for UK Broad Money, 1871–1913', *Review of Economics and Statistics* 75 (February), 112–17.

Thomas, B. (1984) 'Discussion of S. Easton's Paper', in M. D. Bordo and A. J. Schwartz (eds.), *A Retrospective on the Classical Gold Standard 1821–1931*, University of Chicago Press for NBER, 544–46.

Turner, A. J. (1972) 'The Evolution of Reserve Ratios in English Banking', *National Westminster Bank Quarterly Review* (February), 52–63.

4

Money in the Economy, 1870–1939*

INTRODUCTION

The late nineteenth century and the early twentieth saw striking developments in the financial sector in Britain, and in the monetary system within which the financial sector operated.

At the start Britain had a large number of banks (in January 1870 there were 387), some of them operating nationwide. The numbers soon began to fall, and by the First World War the system was dominated by a few large banks—the 'clearing banks', as they were known. The change occurred through a variety of processes—voluntary amalgamation, amalgamation in the face of failure, takeovers hostile and friendly, outright failure, and occasional simple withdrawal from the industry.

The timing of events in the monetary system was almost the opposite: peace followed by turmoil. The years 1870 to 1914 were years of relative monetary tranquillity, the heyday of the classical gold standard. Britain was on the standard and more and more countries were joining it. Being on the gold standard was regarded as economically prudent, and, indeed, as the discussions before Austria joined in 1892 make clear (see Yeager, 1984), essential for belonging to the civilized community of nations. As Schumpeter (1954) observed, it was 'a symbol of sound practice and badge of honour and decency'. There were, of course, fluctuations in the rate of growth of the supply of gold, and fluctuations in the demand for it as new nations joined the standard. But so far as Britain was concerned the only alteration in the system 1870–1914 was the open acceptance by the Bank of England of the role of lender of last resort.

After 1914 all changed, and for the worse. The gold standard was suspended. Prices rose dramatically during the war. The Armistice brought boom

* Originally published as Forrest Capie and Geoffrey Wood (1994). 'Money in the Economy, 1870–1939', pp. 217–46, in Roderick Floud and D. N. McCloskey (eds), *The Economic History of Britain since 1700*, Second Edition, Volume 2: 1860–1939. © Cambridge University Press, 1994, reproduced with permission.

and then monetary stringency, until the gold standard was resumed at the pre-war parity in 1925. Britain finally abandoned the gold standard in 1931. Floating exchange rates, and domestic monetary autonomy unconstrained by any commodity base, characterized the years down to the Second World War.

MONEY UNDER THE GOLD STANDARD

What is possible under the gold standard? Suppose first of all that the standard was simply a fixed exchange rate system—set aside that it was based on the commodity called 'gold'. If exchange rates were fixed, money would move *after* changes in (real or nominal) income, but would not precede them. The explanation is straightforward. Assume the monetary authorities expand the money supply. Since there is no concern about exchange risk, money flows abroad to obtain a higher interest rate there, and the monetary expansion promptly ceases (in fact some of the monetary expansion will remain; the proportion will depend on the share of the originating country in the world economy). Conversely, consider an expansion of *real* income in a country, increasing the amount of money demanded. By various channels, including a rise in interest rates in view of the initial excess demand for money, money is attracted into the economy until the excess demand is eliminated and interest rates are again the same worldwide. In such a setting, then, money can *follow* fluctuations in real income, but cannot lead them.

It must, however, be emphasized that money following income does not mean that money is unimportant for income. The argument is made by Friedman and Schwartz (1982, p. 325, fn. 14). They wrote:

> In a fixed exchange rate régime the quantity of money is endogenous, and cannot be determined, except for brief periods, by the monetary authorities. Monetary policy cannot affect the quantity of money except temporarily; nonetheless changes in the quantity of money, however produced, will affect income. Indeed, it is precisely because they do that a gold standard or other fixed exchange rate régime is self-adjusting . . . The exchange rate régime does not affect the existence of a 'causal' link from money to income; it affects the forces determining the quantity of money and thereby whether the situation is one of largely unidirectional influence from money to income or of simultaneous determination and interaction.

The full force of the argument can be understood by moving from a fixed exchange rate to a gold standard. In such a system the money supply in Britain could expand (more than temporarily) for *two* reasons: income expansion in Britain, producing a monetary inflow as described above; or a gold discovery (outside Britain). The newly mined gold is spent on goods, services, and assets, and thus finds its way into circulation in every country of the world. Some gold flows into Britain, and produces its usual effects. And so in this case the money flow precedes changes rather than follows them. Even if the money flow followed rather than initiated a change, it may have subsequent effects; for the ratio of nominal money to income will be higher if the money flows than if it does not, which in turn will have consequences.

To these two possible relationships between money and income a third must be added. It occurs if the economy is sufficiently large that monetary fluctuations originating within it, although spilling over to the rest of the world, nevertheless affect that country's money stock by having a significant effect on the *world's* money stock. Of course, Britain was not a gold producer, so the last possibility seems to be ruled out. But the British banking system evolved so as to support a larger and larger money stock on an unchanged gold base. Further, the British economy bulked large in the world, giving some reason to suppose that the Bank of England could influence the world distribution of gold. Whether it actually could and did remains to be seen.

Money demand before the First World War

The connection between income and money is well summarized in the British demand for money, a thoroughly studied function. Friedman and Schwartz (1982) include 1870–1914 as part of a longer study. Others have examined the demand for money 1870–1914 itself (Capie and Rodrik-Bali, 1983; Klovland, 1987 and Mills and Wood, 1988). The crucial statistic is the money supply, the thing to be demanded, estimates of which have recently been revised (Capie and Webber, 1985, pp. 9–51). Three conclusions stand out. First, the demand function is stable. A change in income, the price level, or the interest rate each has the same effect in all years; and at any given level of the variables the amount of money demanded is the same, regardless of when the observations occur. Second, the income elasticity of demand is very close to unity: a 1 per cent rise in income, other things equal, causes a 1 per cent rise in the quantity of money demanded. Third, the demand is best expressed as a demand for real balances, which is to say that the price-level elasticity of demand for money was also unity. A 1 per cent fall in prices causes a 1 per cent fall in the demand for money. In short, one can interpret changes in the ratio of nominal money to nominal income as producing excess supply of or excess demand for money.

MONEY, PRICES, AND THE GREAT DEPRESSION

A widely held view of the British economy in the last quarter of the nineteenth century is that it experienced 'depression'. Other countries were emerging as competing industrial powers, and agriculture suffered as the American Mid-west was opened up. The data, however, do not provide much support for 'depression'. Some students of the period claim there was at least a 'climacteric', but the timing alleged differs widely. For example, D. J. Coppock (1956) places it in the 1870s, while Phelps Brown and Handfield Jones (1952) set it in the 1890s and McCloskey (1970) in the 1900s, if at all. Matthews, Feinstein and Odling-Smee (1982) present a picture of slow and steady deceleration of growth from 2.5 per cent per year in the 1850s to around 1 per cent per year in the 1900s. Still later Crafts, Leybourne and Mills (1989a and b) find only a slight fall in trend growth over the period 1870–1913, and no evidence at all of a climacteric in the 1870s (the evidence has been refined further by Feinstein, 1990b). The years 1873–96 were not a sustained period of depression.

Why, then, were there so many reports of depression by contemporaries and later historians (Saul, 1969)? The reports were not confined to Britain. Histories of almost all the developed and some of the developing world claim the period as 'depression'. The answer is that prices fell. Prices drifted down worldwide from 1873 to 1896. British wholesale prices fell by 39 per cent from 1873 to 1896, and then rose by 40 per cent to 1914; and Feinstein's GDP deflator, broader based with less emphasis on agriculture, fell by 20 per cent and then rose by 17.6 per cent.

There are two contrasting explanations of the fall. One is real. Prices fell, it is said, because the extension of arable farming in the New World and the revolution in transport drove agricultural prices down; similarly, technological change was bringing down the price of manufactured goods. Such events, however, would cause a change only in relative prices: agricultural and manufactured prices would fall; but without something driving down prices as a whole the prices of, say, services and rents would rise (their relative prices were going up, not down).

The second explanation is monetary. Prices were lowered by a scarcity of money relative to output in the first half of the period, and the opposite in the second. Money in Britain grew by 33 per cent in the downswing 1873–96 while real output grew by 53 per cent; in the upswing 1896–1914, in contrast, the money stock grew by 40 per cent and real output by 36 per cent. The different patterns of money growth were produced by a combination of rapid economic development world-wide and the main industrial countries joining the gold standard. The demand for gold increased, and there was no rise in supply until the gold discoveries in the early and mid-1890s in Australia, South Africa, and the Klondike (Rockoff, 1984, and Barro, 1984, argue that the discoveries were in fact induced by the earlier rise in demand).

The monetary explanation is consistent with the behaviour of wholesale prices in relation to the GDP deflator in Britain; and it is also consistent with the international character of the price decline. More elaborate empirical work (Capie et al., 1991; Mills and Wood, 1992) lends further support. The authors constructed a statistical model of money, prices, output, and interest rates. The conclusion was that output in Britain influenced money, and that money and output both influenced prices, but that money had no effect on output. Recognizing, of course, the dangers of using such delicate techniques on the data of these years (see Wood, 1984) the results nevertheless support the interpretation of the period as one of price decline, not real output depression, produced by the demonstrable shortage of money relative to output (Cagan, 1965). The shortage was reflected in the popular pressure at the time for an increase in the money supply (in the United States through the coinage of silver).

There was undoubtedly a depression in agriculture. The prices of agricultural goods fell on average by 42 per cent—in other words a substantial relative price decline against the general index. But the 'Great Depression' from the 1870s to the 1890s was a two-part phenomenon: overall prices fell and agricultural prices fell further. The first was a monetary phenomenon, the second a real one produced by changing supply conditions in agriculture.

THE BUSINESS CYCLE

If there is a relationship between money and real output it exists only in the short run. In the long run money is neutral with respect to output. It affects only the price level. But in the short run there is at least the possibility that excess money stimulates output growth, or conversely that monetary stringency brings about a contraction in real economic activity. Different approaches to this question are found in, for example, the work of Friedman and Schwartz (1963) and of Lucas (1972, reprinted 1981).

In Friedman and Schwartz the source of cycles is the slippage between the 'monetary base' (gold or other moneys that can be used as reserves in the vault) and 'money', money being all means of payment including cheques. It is the tendency to overshoot that produces a cycle. Any discrepancy between desired and actual money balances results in excess spending, stimulating output.

The discrepancy does not appear if markets clear perfectly, as they do in the new classical models (nor does it occur if the interest rate takes all the slack, as it does in Keynesian models). For the new classicals (among them Lucas) the cycle comes about from a confusion on the producer's part between relative and general prices. A small change in price can bring about a large change in output, reinforced perhaps by the difference between transitory and permanent changes in price (Brunner and Meltzer, 1989). A change in the general price level that was mistaken by the producer for a change in the price of his own product, and also thought to be a transitory change, would set cyclical forces in motion.

Friedman and Schwartz found that there was a link between money and real output for the United States in their classic study of 1963. Their cautious conclusion was that changes in the money stock conformed to the *major* movements in the business cycle chronology, with a long lead. The statistical evidence they presented was supported by detailed study of particular historical episodes.

But no such analysis of the British experience has been carried out. There were fluctuations in the British economy long before industrialization. In the eighteenth century and before, spilling into the early nineteenth century, harvests have been taken as the initiators of the cycle (Rostow, 1948; Ashton, 1955). But for the nineteenth century the dominant explanation has been exports, as for example for 1790–1850 by Gayer, Rostow and Schwartz (1953) and for 1870–1914 by Ford (1963).

The export model leaves little room for money. Ford (1981) stated that 'monetary influences were not a significant internal cyclical factor in the United Kingdom'. Pre-Keynesian writers such as Hawtrey (1913) on the contrary regarded the cycle as 'a purely monetary phenomenon' and there have been some recent studies that have brought money into the picture. Walters (1969) for instance found that the monetary model outperformed the Keynesian model over the years 1880–1914. And Eichengreen (1983) found that for the late Victorian period the fluctuations in the monetary base were the single most important determinant of the trade cycle.

Recently it has been possible to examine the relationship more rigorously. In addition to Feinstein's output data, new monetary data became available (Capie and Webber, 1985). When the techniques of Friedman and Schwartz were replicated for Britain, however, no strong conclusions were possible. The links between money and output were ambiguous. Further, using an approach of Barro (1987) to investigate specifically the response to unanticipated as against anticipated changes in monetary series, no useful results were found (Capie, 1990). With the help of the latest time series techniques it was possible to carry out a more detailed examination (Capie and Mills, 1990). The techniques allow a more reliable decomposition of the observed monetary and output series into the unobserved trend and the cyclical component. It is then possible to test the relationship between the two cyclical series. But again in the British case the results showed that the causal link between money and output was weak and ambiguous.

Why the contrast with the strong findings for the United States? The most obvious difference is that output and money were less volatile in Britain than in America. Recall that Friedman and Schwartz stressed that money caused output changes only at major turning points. If there were no comparable major turning points in Britain (as the evidence suggests) then neither should there be the strong money/output link. Britain experienced no major banking crises between 1870 and 1913. This undoubtedly contributed to the less volatile monetary series. The sound banking structure, with large banks with head offices in London and branches scattered across the whole country, appears to have allowed diversified portfolios for each bank. In the United States, by contrast, banks were confined by law to one state, and were therefore undiversified, vulnerable to local shocks. Banks failed readily and panics often followed (Bernanke, 1983, suggests that the American failures produced recession through the contraction of credit in the area served by the bank, a local effect impossible in Britain). And the Bank of England acted as a lender of last resort, at a time when the United States had no central bank at all.

INTEREST RATES

Figure 4.1 shows two interest rates, a short-term rate on bank bills and a long-term rate on Consols ('consolidated government stock': that is, government bonds with no fixed redemption date). They are adjusted for Goschen's conversion of 1888 (Harley, 1976). In 1888 the Chancellor of the Exchequer, Goschen, sought to take advantage of low and falling rates of interest in order to reduce the rate of interest paid on the national debt (that is, the bonds of the government). From 1889 to 1903 Goschen's conversion scheme lowered the nominal rate of interest on Consols to 2.75 per cent per year (£2 15s) and thereafter to 2.5 per cent (£2 10s). Harley (1976) argues that it is incorrect,

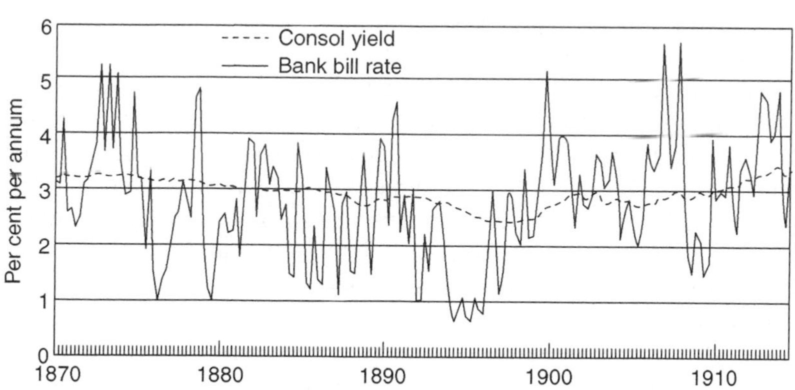

Figure 4.1. UK Consol yield and bank bill rate, 1870–1915
Source: Capie and Webber (1985).

however, to assume that these were the true yields on the Consols. The markets had fully discounted the 3 per cent Consols in anticipation of a conversion. And the new Goschen Consols could not be considered as long-term securities and therefore it was incorrect to calculate their yield by dividing 2.75 per cent by the price of the Consol. Furthermore, in the mid 1890s the market expected the low short-term rates to rise, resulting in a higher yield for longer-term maturities. The series allows for Harley's corrections.

Note the sluggish movements in the long-term rate. The interest rate in the ordinary sense is a merely *nominal* rate—which is to say, it is the rate of return before any adjustment for inflation. The nominal rate therefore has two components. It is the 'real' rate plus the expected rate of inflation (or, what is relevant for the period before 1896, minus the expected rate of deflation). An interest rate of 2 per cent per year would actually be worth 4.6 per cent per year if prices were falling, as they were from 1873 to 1896, at 2.6 per cent per year on average: a £100 investment would earn 2 per cent from the bond and 2.6 per cent from being able to buy more with each pound sterling, for a total 'real' return of 4.6 per cent. Dividing the nominal interest rate into these two components is important because different forces affect them. The real part is determined by the balance of supply and demand between saving and investment; the inflation part is determined by expected inflation.

The money supply did not grow exactly as demand required. Therefore the price of holding money—the nominal interest rate—had to fluctuate, to induce the changed supplies to be held. But notice the stability of the long-term rate. The monetary fluctuations would have fed through to the long rate only if they led to expectations of inflation or disinflation. They did not do so—because they were expected to be transitory. It was sensible, albeit perhaps not rational in the technical sense, to form expectations from past inflation experience. The stability of the long rate relative to the short is therefore a product of the money supply regime, under which sustained inflation had been modest in pace and very slow to change.

The above argument requires that the real rate also be stable. It apparently was. The observed stability of the nominal rate would require an implausible offset in expectations if the underlying real rate was in fact moving around. Friedman and Schwartz (1982; summarized in Schwartz (1982) and Mills and Wood (1992)) have by quite different statistical techniques found that the real rate was stable. The observed stability of the long rate relative to the short rate should be interpreted as the result of the stability of inflationary expectations.

Notice also in the figure that the long-term rates were low. Here too the distinction between real and nominal rates is crucial. Over the first part of the period (1873–96) the price level fell as we have seen at 2.6 per cent per year on average; and over the second part (1896–1913) it rose 2.24 per cent per year on average. (The inflation was gradual by later standards: even in the stable 1950s it was 4 per cent per year, in the 1960s 5 per cent, in the 1970s fully 15 per cent, and in the 1980s 6.5 per cent.) The low level of the long rate as compared with rates typical recently was, therefore, a second product of the money supply regime.

And note finally that the rise and fall of the long-term interest rate paralleled the fall and rise of prices. The fact is known (from Keynes 1930) as the Gibson Paradox, after the writer who first drew attention to it. It is 'paradoxical' because a change in the price level should leave interest rates unchanged, being a mere change in the unit of account.

Keynes and the Swedish economist Knut Wicksell saw nominal rates as being pulled down by a decline in real rates in the first half of the period —the notion of a Great Depression again—and then rising after 1896 with the boom of investment worldwide. Prices followed, they argued, because market rates lagged the decline and produced monetary stringency. But we have seen that there is little evidence of a decline in the real rate. And the Keynes–Wicksell arguments suppose that monetary stringency was produced by interest rates contracting bank lending; as argued above (and in Capie and Webber, 1985) it was in fact produced by a relative shortage of gold.

The American economist Irving Fisher (1867–1947) argued that inflationary expectations would adjust, with a lag, to actual inflation. In consequence the deflation of 1873–96 would produce a gradual realization that inflation was going to continue, and a gradual lowering of nominal interest rates to reflect the expectation. In 1896 the financial markets expected deflation to continue. They were wrong, but it took a similarly long lag for them to realize it: during which realization the nominal interest rates gradually rose. Friedman and Schwartz (1982) note that the Gibson pattern disappeared when inflation rates had become so volatile that it was unreasonable to forecast inflation by simple extrapolation, slowly adjusting.

In short, the peculiarities of the late nineteenth century in the matter of money were the product of a peculiarly stable monetary environment (reinforced, it may be, by the way gold production responded (Barsky and Summers, 1988)).

FINANCIAL INTERMEDIATION

The bulk of all financial intermediation, taking the savings of depositors and transforming it into investment, was done by the banking system. A useful framework for examining the contribution of the banking system is one that places it in the money supply process alongside the monetary authorities and the public. The simplest expression of this is:

$$M = mb$$

where m is the money multiplier, B is the monetary base (the gold in a strict gold standard, for example), and M is the money stock. The money multiplier can be shown as:

$$\frac{C/D + 1}{R/D + C + D}$$

The public, who decide how much currency (C) to hold in relation to deposits (D), can influence the size of the money stock if they change the ratio. Equally the banks, who decide how much cash reserves (R) to hold in relation to their deposit liabilities (namely, as cover for the chequing accounts they owe to the public), can also influence it. When they feel the need to raise the cover they dampen down the total money stock. This way of examining the money supply emphasizes that there are three parties influencing the total money stock—the monetary authorities (who set B), the banks, and the public.

There were no legal restrictions on the reserve/deposit ratio, and the variation from bank to bank could be quite considerable. Indeed the idea of a reserve ratio had not yet been articulated at the beginning of the period, though obviously banks worked with some idea of requisite cover or they went out of business. The first consciously stated reserve ratio appears to have been self-imposed by the Lincoln Bank in 1872; in the course of the next twenty years or so most English banks had come to employ an announced minimum ratio. Contemporary estimates of the size of the ratio lend support to our own estimates. According to one survey of seventy-five non-clearing banks the ratio of reserves to deposits ranged from 9 to 17 per cent. Twelve London clearing banks ranged from 10.4 to 16.8 per cent. Our own estimates for the system as a whole show that it fluctuated between 8.5 per cent and 12.5 per cent (with a mean of 10.4 per cent and standard deviation of 1.1 per cent; Capie and Webber, 1985).

After some initial erratic behaviour in the 1870s, the reserve to deposit ratio (R/D) trended upward. That is to say, the banks held a rising quantity of reserves in relation to deposits. The rise held down the growth of the money supply. The growth of the reserve/deposit ratio is on the face of things perplexing. A jump in the proportion of reserves is generally associated with fears of instability or financial uncertainty. It was not a jump, however, but a slow and steady growth. Furthermore, small banks should hold higher reserves than large banks, since the large banks acquire a certain soundness by their size. But if this were the case the trend in R/D would have been *downwards*, since small banks shrank as a proportion of total bank population.

The solution to the puzzle may be as follows: small banks in fact held smaller reserves than large banks. Turner (1972) found that the lowest ratios of all were amongst the non-clearers. The private banks were not obliged to publish their accounts. As more and more banks published accounts there was therefore an increase in the ratio: the need to publish in itself provided a pressure to keep a higher ratio of reserves. And the move to publish coincided in time with the Baring crisis of 1890, when it became accepted that the banks should hold a higher ratio.

Friedman and Schwartz (1963) used a method of determining the contribution of each proximate determinant of the money supply for the US. Table 4.1 gives the results of our application of the method to the UK, giving the fraction of monetary change produced by each of the determinants between the beginning and the end of the period.

The sub-periods selected are chosen to allow comparisons with other studies. Over the period as a whole it was high-powered money (the base, B) that explained by far the greatest part of the change in M3—some 70 per cent. As already shown, R/D was acting to reduce the monetary expansion; C/D was acting in the other direction, and was considerably stronger taken over the whole period. In the sub-periods 1870–9, 1880–96, and 1880–1913 the respective contribution of each of these factors was more or less the same. For the period 1897–1913 the monetary base is the most powerful explanation, R/D is strong, and C/D has lost a little of its importance. In summary, whichever way we look at it the monetary base is the prime determinant of money supply in the period. Table 4.1 shows the effect over a variety of sub-periods.

What catches the eye is the growth and changing structure of the banking system. By 1870 British banking had already begun to resemble its modern form, with a number of commercial banks the largest of which had many branches across the country. Table 4.2 shows how the form developed over the next fifty years. As early as 1870 there were 2,728 bank offices in the country (0.87 offices per 10,000 of the population). Although the total number of banks in all categories fell fairly steadily throughout the period there were still over 100 banks in 1914 and there were around 8,000 bank offices at that point (1.63 per 10,000 of the population). The fall in the total number of banks was in part the result of an advantage of large size, associated as it was with greater

Table 4.1. The proximate determinants of changes in the UK money supply, 1870–1913

Fraction of the change in £M3 attributable to	1870–1913	1880–1913	1870–79	1880–96	1897–1913
B	0.692	0.72	1.16	0.32	1.21
C/D	0.38	0.35	0.16	0.5	0.24
R/D	−0.084	−0.039	−0.315	+0.15	−0.43
Interaction	+0.012	−0.03	0.00	0.03	−0.02

Notes: B = 'high-powered money' (the base); C/D = the currency–deposit ratio; and R/D = the reserve–deposit ratio.
Source: Capie and Rodrik-Bali (1983).

Table 4.2. Banks and bank branches, 1870–1920

	London banks		Provincial banks		All United Kingdom banks		Bank branches per 10,000 of population
	A	B	A	B	A	B	
1870	56	84	299	1,093	386	2,728	0.87
1880	65	109	258	1,396	358	3,454	1.0
1890	65	149	200	1,795	303	4,347	1.16
1900	39	134	108	1,875	188	5,922	1.44
1910	27	36	47	1,516	112	7,564	1.68
1920	29	31	21	949	75	9,668	2.08

Notes: Columns A = number of banks; columns B = number of branches.
Source: Capie and Webber (1985).

reserves, security, and prestige; hence the accelerating mergers of the 1890s. But the pattern was older. Any one bank, usually with headquarters in London, had loans and sources of funds in most if not all parts of the country covering the whole spectrum of industry, agriculture, and services. The branch pattern, as we have noted, meant that if a branch (or even several branches) were in trouble in an area adversely affected by a fall in demand for its product the resources of the bank could readily be diverted to ease the pressure.

Many banks in Britain continued without branches, and there were fairly frequent bank failures (Figure 4.2) and corresponding entry to the places left open. But failures, as has been noted, did not result in runs. They were accepted as part of the normal pattern of business enterprise. The City of Glasgow Bank failure in 1878 is a case in point. Although a considerable bank,

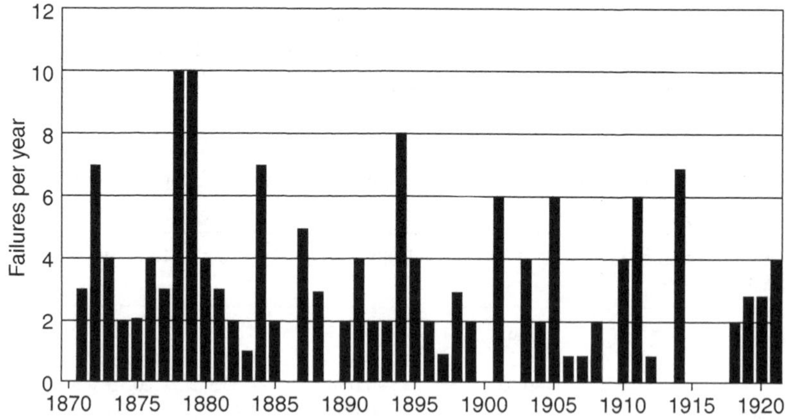

Figure 4.2. UK bank failures, 1870–1921
Source: Capie and Webber (1985).

it was badly managed and corrupt. It was allowed to fail, which caused difficulties for other banks. Yet there was no run on banks in general, no banking panic, no financial crisis, no significant rise in C/D or R/D ratios, those indicators of caution.

THE BANKS AND INDUSTRY

A considerable literature contrasts 'banking' and 'market' orientated economies. Large European banks, for instance, are said to have helped industry develop, while British banks are said to have failed in this role. A long list of allegations has been made against the banks: that London-based deposit banks were averse to industrial finance; that amalgamation contributed by increasing the extent of 'London' practices; that British banks held portfolios radically different from their continental counterparts, being biased to liquid assets.

The indictment comes with an explanation: the banks, it is said, grew up in the Industrial Revolution, when their function was to provide short-term credit for small businesses. The alleged aversion to long-term commitments seems to be instanced by the experience of the 1860s, when several investment banks were formed on the continental model but then spectacularly crashed, in the Overend Gurney crisis of 1866. Liquidity conscious banks with short-term loans and safe readily saleable investments seemed to become the norm from 1870 onward.

But an indictment is not a conviction. We know little in fact about the relationship between banks and industry, and more research needs to be done before the banking industry can be convicted of failure to serve industry's needs. It is quite possible, for example, that industry demanded little finance from the banks: other financial institutions, such as the active British stock market, provided the required capital (Collins, 1990).

FINANCIAL CRISES AND THE LENDER OF LAST RESORT

A financial crisis threatens the stability of the entire system, and causes therefore a collapse in the stock of money, as people and banks rush for liquidity. Such events should be distinguished from 'financial distress' or 'pseudo crises' (Schwartz, 1986), which may threaten someone's wealth but do not threaten the prosperity of the entire economy. The United States undoubtedly experienced a genuine financial crisis in worsening waves from 1929 to 1933. By contrast, the City of Glasgow Bank failure in 1878 caused shareholders to suffer loss, but without threat to the banking system as a whole.

Branch banking was one insurance against crisis. The other was the attitude and action of the Bank of England, as lender of last resort—which is to say, the bank of banks, issuing money when the banks ran out. On 10 May 1866 Overend, Gurney & Co. shut down. The market was nervous, and panic broke out the next day. There was an immense demand for cash, and the Bank, for fear of breaking the legal limit on the amount of paper money it could issue, hesitated. The Bank Charter Act was then suspended, allowing an expansion of paper money unbacked by gold, and more cash was forthcoming: the Bank bought Consols with the new cash on the open market, putting cash into the hands of the investors seeking it. The panic ended abruptly, for people knew they could get cash. Although a small drain of notes continued for about a week the crisis ended without the Bank in the end having to issue more paper money than the suspended law allowed (Batchelor, 1986).

Similar behaviour by the Bank in the still earlier crisis of 1825 was described by Jeremiah Harman, a director of the Bank:

> We lent it by every possible means and in modes we have never adopted before; we took in stock on security, we purchased Exchequer bills, we not only discounted outright, but we made advances on the deposit of bills of exchange to an immense amount, in short by every possible means consistent with the safety of the Bank, and we were not on some occasions over nice. Seeing the dreadful state in which the public were, we rendered every assistance in our power. (quoted in Bagehot 1873: 73)

The crisis of 1825, too, ended within days.

The Victorian essayist and editor of *The Economist* Walter Bagehot is often credited with convincing the Bank of England of the need to act as lender of last resort. That was plainly unnecessary. What he in fact did was to urge it to commit itself in advance to doing so (see Rockoff, 1986).

This, he argued, would eliminate the fear that cash could not be obtained and so would prevent crises from arising in the first place. As Meltzer (1986, p. 33) puts it, Bagehot's 'main recommendation is that the Bank should announce in advance that, although it is privately owned, it accepts the responsibility of a bank of issue to protect the money stock'.

It is difficult to distinguish between the Bank's pre-commitment to the lending in a crisis and the branched structure of the banking system as the cause of the absence of banking crises in Britain. Both may have contributed; perhaps either would have been sufficient.

An instance is the so-called Baring crisis. The Baring bank got into difficulties in 1890, as a result of involvement in Argentina. The flow of remittance from Argentina stopped. The Bank of England organized a rescue—a lifeboat.

Against the thinking of the Chancellor of the Exchequer, Goschen, who was reluctant to provide government assistance lest Baring prove to be insolvent, the Bank decided that the problem was one of illiquidity. It persuaded other banks to agree, on the basis of a report concluding that Baring was fundamentally sound but needed some £10 million in liquidity. Baring was liquidated and there was a modest rise in the demand for cash. The bank was reconstituted as a limited liability company with a new chairman and the Argentinian debt written off (which is to say accepted as a loss). Although both the Bank of England and the rest of the City were very active there was no crisis. Note that there was not a classic lender-of-last-resort operation—one was not needed.

Another illuminating crisis was that of 1914 (Seabourne, 1986). The problem had two aspects. The prospect of imminent war caused plunging stock prices and a failure of remittance from overseas. A rush for liquidity began and the banks called in their loans to the stock exchange (which dealt in stock certificates) and the discount market (which dealt in bills), further weakening the stock exchange and driving the discount market to the Bank of England. Fortunately all this occurred just before a bank holiday—which was extended. Assistance was provided to the stock market under a scheme proposed by the clearing banks, and the Bank of England gave assistance to the discount market. There may have been a subsequent inflation (see below; and Goodhart, 1986) but it was to some extent intertwined with the exigencies of war finance, not the crisis. Again the episode exemplifies the problem of explaining UK financial stability in these years. The consequences of large well-diversified banks are inextricable from those of having a pre-committed lender of last resort.

WAR FINANCE

The First World War was to last much longer, and to cost more in lives and other resources, than anyone expected. There was therefore no advance planning to raise funds for the war on the scale required.

Governments can raise funds by three means—taxation, borrowing, and inflation. The last of these is possible under a fixed exchange rate system only if all countries inflate. During the First World War Britain, as was conventional at times of war, suspended the gold standard. Sterling floated, interest rates were raised to defend it, and a variety of exchange controls were adopted (Pollard, 1983). The floating of sterling meant that all three sources of finance were available. This is not to imply that inflation was necessarily a deliberate policy choice, but when it happened it helped the government's finances: the government issued paper money that depreciated in value.

In August 1914 the stock of government debt stood at just over £700 million; by August 1919 it had risen to roughly £7,500 million. Over the same period the monetary base (M0: gold, currency and other promises by the Bank of England to pay) grew by around 119 per cent and broad money M3 (including chequing and savings deposits) by around 114 per cent. There was also a fiduciary issue of currency notes (that is, paper money unbacked by gold) totalling £320 million in issue by the end of the war. Prices therefore rose from 100 in 1913 to 211 in 1919. In the last year of peace, tax revenue from income and other taxes (except inflation) was £198 million. In the last year of war it was £889 million. National income in wartime is peculiar, much of it being waste by the standards of peacetime. A large but short-lived boom occurred after the war. Table 4.3 below makes two comparisons, setting bounds (upper for the war years, lower for the first year of peace) on the true ratio. The ratios are to be compared with the values in 1913.

In November 1914 the income tax and super tax rates were doubled to 2s 4d (12 per cent) and 1s (5 per cent) and duties on beer and tea were raised. It was not enough. Tax rates were raised again during the second half of 1915 and still again later—income tax by a further 40 per cent and super tax to 2s 6d and then to 5s in 1916–17 and 6s in 1918–19. The exemption limit was reduced from £160 to £130 in 1915 (£100 was the rough equivalent of £1,500 in purchasing power of 1990). Indirect taxation continued to rely primarily on its traditional bases of alcohol and tobacco. Customs, excise, estate, land, and house duties rose from £115.8 million in 1913 to £169.2 million in 1916–17 and £208.8 million in 1919–20. On an index basis there was a rise from 100 to 114.7 followed by a fall to 94.80. There was also a profits tax (Kirkaldy, 1921; Morgan, 1952).

All this was not nearly enough to finance the war. So the government borrowed, as it had done in time of war for two centuries, at high rates. In November 1914 £350 million of 3.5 per cent bonds were issued at a price of £95 against a face value of £100, repayable in 1925–8. An unlimited loan was announced in June 1915 of 4.5 per cent bonds issued at par. By March 1916 £900 million had been raised. Conversion rights—into 3.5 per cent war

Table 4.3. Revenue and debt in the First World War, 1913–20

Year	Total revenue (£bn)	GNP (£bn)	National debt (£bn)	Rev./GNP	Debt/GNP
1913	0.198	2.322	0.6	0.0853	0.258
1914	0.227	2.347	1.105	0.0967	0.471
1915	0.337	2.676	2.133	0.1259	0.797
1916	0.573	3.176	4.011	0.1804	1.263
1917	0.707	3.951	5.872	0.1789	1.486
1918	0.889	4.77	7.435	0.1864	1.559
1919	1.34	4.992	7.832	0.2684	1.569
1920	1.426	5.688	7.585	0.2507	1.334

Sources: Capie and Webber (1985); and Liesner (1989).

bonds 1925–8, 2.5 per cent Consols and 2.75 per cent and 2.5 per cent annuities were attached. By 1917 only £100 million of the first type of bonds were outstanding. The third and last big issue of war loan offered two types of security, a 5 per cent bond (issued at 95) repayable 1929–47 and a 4 per cent bond repayable 1929–42, free of income but not of super tax. Then in 1917 the government began issuing war bonds in a steady stream. Floating debt (that is, short-term debt) also rose substantially. In March 1919 the total of Treasury Bills and Ways and Means Advances had reached £1,400 million, as compared with £16 million just before the outbreak of the war.

INFLATION AND THE 1914 CRISIS

As was remarked above, one symptom of the 1914 panic was an 'internal drain'—a run to cash by UK residents. Provision of currency notes was therefore an essential part of the scheme to deal with the panic. But was the injection too large or too prolonged? Goodhart (1986) suggests that it was both, and that it contributed substantially to wartime inflation. The monetary base certainly expanded very fast over the first few months of the war.

While the initial injection of notes was certainly desirable, it is far from clear it was desirable for it to remain. The financial panic was expected to end fairly quickly, and indeed did so. Why, then, was the cash injection allowed to remain in the system? It may have been deliberate—a resort to the inflation tax because nothing else could be levied so quickly. In any event, a substantial part (approaching one half) of the wartime monetary expansion took place by November 1914, three months into a war that was to last four years. The monetary base then fell back below the November 1914 level for a year and a half. The monetary expansion was certainly triggered by the 1914 panic—but it is likely that it went on too long. Just why it did remains obscure.

MONEY IN THE ECONOMY: 1918–39

After the war, from 1919 to April 1925, sterling floated, with the objectives of returning eventually to gold at the pre-war parity. From 1925 to September 1931 Britain was back on gold. From the end of September 1931 to 1939 there was a managed float; the Exchange Equalisation Account (EEA) was established in 1932. The question is what the effect of all this was on money.

In the first, floating period, so long as there was no intervention in the foreign exchanges the stock of money was entirely determined by domestic factors. This is, of course, in sharp contrast with the gold standard. To get back

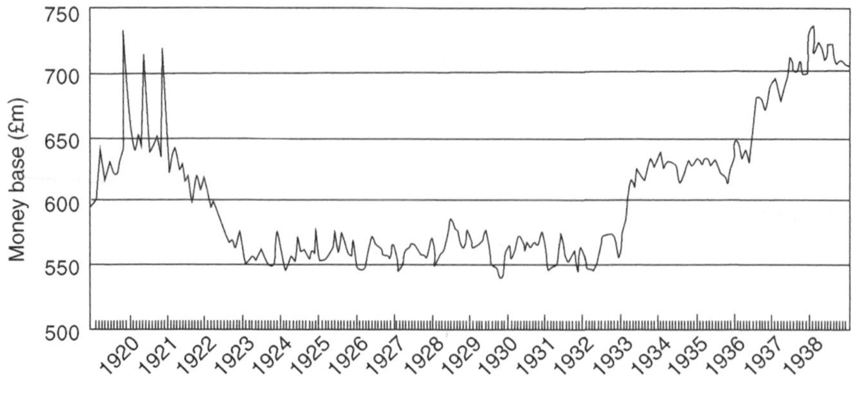

Figure 4.3. UK money base, 1919–39

Source: Capie and Webber (1985).

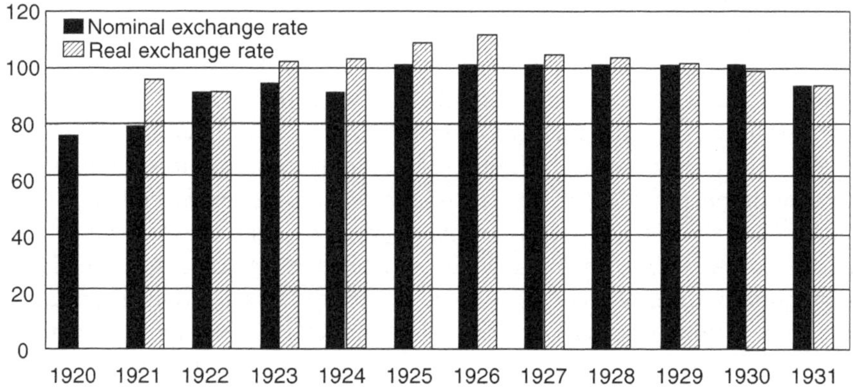

Figure 4.4. Real and nominal exchange rate, 1920–31

Source: Dimsdale (1981b).

to gold, however, money was kept tight. Figure 4.3 shows growth in the money base; Figure 4.4 shows the nominal price of dollars in terms of sterling, the £/$ ratio; Figure 4.5 shows bank rate, the bill rate, and the Consol yield. The policy was 'successful', in that sterling managed to attain its old parity.

Exchange rates, being prices determined in asset markets, can move much more quickly than national price levels. Consequently there can be a gap between the *nominal* and the *real* exchange rate. The nominal rate is that quoted on the exchanges; the real exchange rate is the nominal rate adjusted for actual changes in the price level, relative to some base. For example, suppose the nominal rate of the pound against the dollar in the exchange market depreciated by 10 per cent during some year. If the two national price levels did not change there would also be a 10 per cent real depreciation. But if

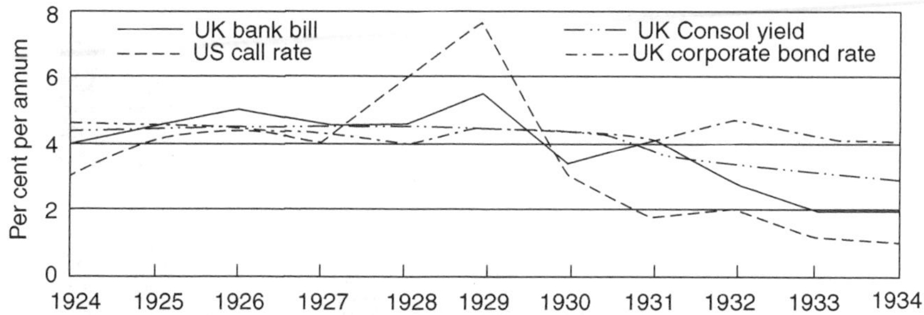

Figure 4.5. UK and US interest rates, 1924–34

Source: Capie and Webber (1985) for UK; Friedman and Schwartz (1982) for US.

the British price level had in the meantime risen by 10 per cent the real rate would not have changed at all; for the price of British relative to American goods would not have changed.

Figure 4.4 shows the behaviour of sterling in *real* terms and the nominal exchange rate against the dollar (for a detailed discussion of the real series see Dimsdale (1981a)). It can be seen that there was a real appreciation of sterling, from 94.7 to 111.1(17 per cent); between 1921 and 1926. Of course the calculations are uncertain; but it would be hard to argue that there was no real appreciation at all. It produced a squeeze felt particularly by the traded goods sector and therefore helps explain the boom in house building and the recession in traditional exports.

During the late 1920s the influences on the money stock were once again primarily external. Britain was linked again to the United States through a now-fixed exchange rate. Figure 4.5 shows the extent of the linkage in UK and US short and long rates. Figures 4.6 and 4.7 show the behaviour of monetary aggregates. The US monetary collapse of 1930 can be seen vividly, but Britain dodged it by going off gold.

The years down to the Second World War were years of 'managed float'. The authorities intervened on the exchanges to dampen fluctuations in the rate, but not to keep it artificially high or low. External influences on the economy, therefore, were felt entirely in the rate of exchange.

INTER-WAR BACKGROUND

The British economy emerged from the war in a condition vastly altered. Wartime disruption led foreigners to substitute their own for Britain's goods, and Britain being a particularly open economy, dependent on trade, was therefore exposed to current account deficits. Before 1914 the visible trade

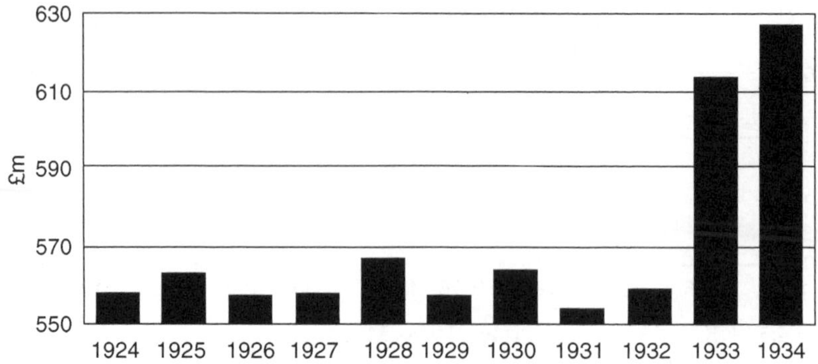

Figure 4.6. UK monetary aggregate (M0), 1924–34
Source: Capie and Webber (1985).

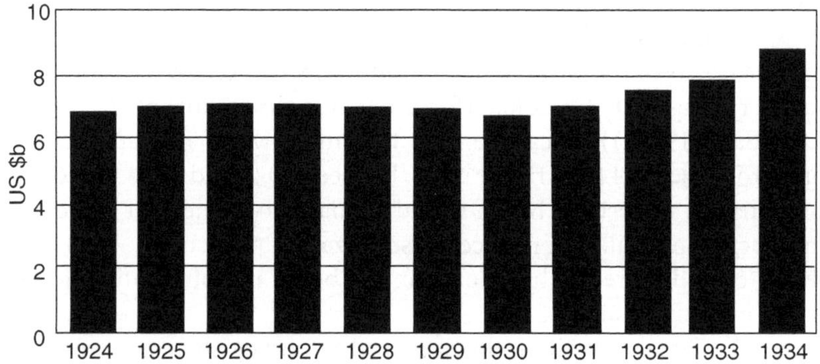

Figure 4.7. US high-powered money, 1924–34
Source: Friedman and Schwartz (1982).

deficit was amply offset by earnings on invisibles—not least the interest earned on foreign securities. During the war Britain had been obliged to run down her holdings of foreign assets, and the consequent loss of wealth was a weakening factor; shipping services, too, were reduced with the contraction in trade, and other invisibles were similarly affected adversely. The deficit on current account made it harder to drive the pound back to its pre-war parity.

More strictly domestic was a problem that derived directly from the war effort, the huge quantity of government debt. In 1913 government debt was approximately £600m—that is, around 35 per cent of national income. After the war it was approximately £8,000m—that is, more than 200 per cent of national income. (The ratio was similar after the Napoleonic Wars and again after the Second World War; much higher, it should be noted, than the ratios that have recently alarmed the United States.) The burden which servicing the debt placed on the Exchequer was substantial, particularly since the debt had been issued in wartime at historically high interest rates.

THE MONETARY AND MACRO-ECONOMIC VARIABLES

Figure 4.8 shows the movement of the main monetary and macroeconomic variables in the economy in the inter-war years. There was considerable economic growth, with prices tending to fall at first, then rise. Across the whole period real GNP grew by on average over 2 per cent per annum—perfectly healthy by British historical standards. The monetary variables did not grow as fast as output and thus overall prices fell. In accord with the quantity equation, the real output growth of 2 per cent per annum was matched by monetary growth of 1 per cent per annum and a price fall on average of 1 per cent per annum. It was again the case that the money multipliers were relatively stable and that the monetary base provided most of the explanation for the way 'broad money' moved.

The currency/deposit ratio (a measure among other things of the caution of bank customers) exhibits a pronounced cyclical pattern. It rises from 1922 to 1926 then falls to a trough in 1931–32 before turning up and rising for the rest of the decade. The range, however, is not great, lying between 12.5 and 16 per cent. The stability dispels any notion of a British financial crisis in 1931. The competing forces of financial sophistication (the tendency to get out of money and into financial assets) and monetization (the extension of the monetary economy by increasing use of money) were probably weak and certainly more or less equal. The widespread belief that low points in the currency/deposit ratio coincide with peaks in the business cycle and vice versa is derived in the main from US data, bank panics there beginning close to the business cycle peaks (Gorton 1988). But Britain in the inter-war years shows no such relationship (nor did it from 1870 to 1914), since it had no panics. A sharp rise in the ratio did occur in 1931, though never to panic levels—in view of the

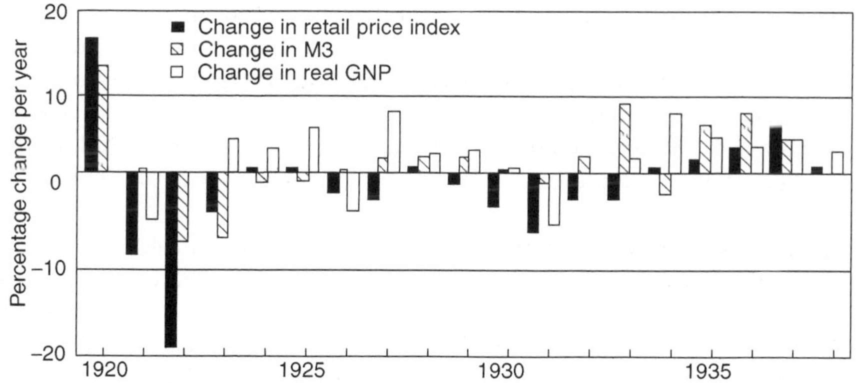

Figure 4.8. Annual changes in the retail price index, M3 and real GNP, 1920–39

Source: Capie and Webber (1985).

fears about liquidity spreading through Europe at the time the surprise would have been if people had not attempted to get out of bank deposits and into currency. But the fear was dispelled quickly and the ratio quickly reverted to normal. The threats of war in the late 1930s were more potent in this respect than the collapse of the international monetary system in 1931.

The reserve/deposit ratio (under the control, recall, of bankers, and reflecting their attitudes) showed very little variation across the whole period, and averaged 11 per cent. Even through the depression years in Britain 1929–32 there is nothing exciting to report—itself a startling fact in comparison with events in Germany and the United States. The ratio jumps in 1933, readily explained by the huge inflow of funds from abroad, drawn by the attractiveness of sterling (the dollar was devaluing; cf. McCloskey and Zecher, 1984). After the link with gold was severed in September 1931 the pound depreciated by 24 per cent in three months, and in 1932 it still looked cheap to foreigners. The Exchange Equalisation Account, established in 1932, was unable to sterilize these inflows completely and they therefore found their way into the banks. Bank reserves remained high partly because the Bank of England, alarmed by world banking failures in the early 1930s, pressed bankers to keep them high. There is no evidence of what used to be asserted, namely, that in the 1920s when a tight money policy was being pursued it was offset by the banks lowering their reserve/deposit ratios. The famous Macmillan Committee (1931) stressed the need for the banks to maintain fixed cash ratios.

BANKING

Some of the bigger bank mergers took place during the First World War. Ever-bigger banks seemed reasonable in view of German competition—Germany being notorious for enormous investment banks—a point made especially by the Chairman of Midland Bank. Before the First World War there were no legal constraints on mergers. The heavily concentrated system that resulted by 1918 persisted through the inter-war years and beyond: in 1919 the five largest clearing banks held around 80 per cent of current account deposits in England and Wales. They were prevented from further mergers only by the Treasury's opposition.

In the late nineteenth century, bank profits had been healthy and grew steadily, though the greater fluctuations in interest rates between the wars resulted in somewhat more pronounced fluctuations. Even in the depression of 1929–32 no losses were reported by the commercial banks, at the same time that thousands upon thousands of banks around the world were collapsing. The British banks remained highly liquid and very cautious in investment. After the highly liquid assets of cash and Treasury bills, the banks invested largely in UK government securities. The only illiquid part of the balance sheet were so-called 'advances', that is, short loans to businesses and individuals: fixed period loans, overdrafts and commercial bills. Thus the banks continued their role of offering short-term credit to industry.

The Macmillan Committee (J. M. Keynes was a major influence on it) wanted the banks to behave more like German investment banks, lending long to industry allegedly 'starved' of such funds. The British banks defended themselves by pointing out that around 50 per cent of their assets were tied up in loans of one kind or another to industry, a high degree of commitment to industry, leaving industry free to seek somewhat longer loans elsewhere. As Collins (1990) puts it, 'in effect [the banks] claimed they were prepared to meet all legitimate demands for credit from industrial and other customers within the established guide lines governing the granting of such loans'. The 'starving' of British industry of long-term finance from banks continues to fascinate historians; yet industry floated loans in the City and locally with cease. Collins argues, however, that the banks did exercise some oligopoly power to constrain the advances to the private sector. Strict price-fixing ruled; a minimum rate of 5 per cent was set for advances for any customer, no matter how good.

BOOM AND SLUMP

Immediately after the war there was a considerable boom and then a dramatic end to the boom and the deepest and steepest of economic recessions in British economic history, that of 1920–21. The usual story is that during the war the public built up liquidity, since there were few consumer goods available and non-war investment was low. At the end of the war the liquidity was released for consumption. The authorities could have dampened spending as a precaution against overheating, but the political climate (a war-weary populace, revolution in Russia and elsewhere, and the need to placate potentially rebellious returning troops) impelled them to permit easy conditions.

Money was important. The monetary base rose sharply between the third quarter of 1918 and the second quarter of 1920—from £540 million to £671 million, 25 per cent in eighteen months. In the next quarter it sharply contracted. Short-term interest rates had in fact been moving up from late 1919, well in advance of the downturn. The movement in interest rates may not have been strictly a policy choice but rather the result of a struggle between Whitehall and Threadneedle Street. The Treasury favoured low interest rates, the better to refinance the war debt; the Bank favoured high interest rates, the better to re-establish sterling at the pre-war parity. The Bank won. The Bank was concerned to choke off inflation, and was also keen to regain the control over rediscount policy that it had surrendered in wartime. The role of money in producing the 1920–21 slump should not, however, be exaggerated. The slump was particularly severe in industries which expanded massively in the war, and again in the 1919–20 inflation, known generally as 'the restocking boom', making up for war damage. Such industry could scarcely escape sharp contraction with the coming of peace.

THE RETURN TO GOLD

Britain returned to the gold standard, at the pre-war parity, in 1925. The exchange rate against the dollar was then once again $4.86/£. The decision has been widely regarded as having been taken without much thought, and is blamed for the persistent unemployment in Britain during the 1920s. Winston Churchill, Chancellor of the Exchequer at the time the decision was taken, came to regard it as the greatest mistake of his life (Grigg, 1948). But recent work shows that the decision was not taken unthinkingly and that it is far from clear that the return did harm.

Britain took the lead and other countries followed. Therefore had Britain chosen another rate the likelihood is that the other countries would have set their rates in proportion: so it is doubtful that choosing, say, $4.40/£—a 10 per cent lower figure, which is what has been contemplated in retrospect—would have made much difference for Britain's international position. Furthermore, the decision to return seemed well founded in experience. Countries which had operated without the restraint of gold had undergone after the war wild swings in both output and prices—the examples of Germany and Austria, with price levels increasing by factors of literally millions, were on the minds of policy makers. And perceptions of how the standard had worked before 1914 were important. Britain had been on the gold standard, at the historic price of sterling for gold, with an interregnum from 1797 to 1819, since 1717 (Ashton, 1955). The years immediately before 1914 were the cumulation of a long and most satisfactory experience. Output fluctuated moderately about a rising level; short-term price movements were, and were seen to be, transitory and insignificant (note in evidence the behaviour of Consol yields); and world trade grew steadily. All of this may have been purely *associated* with gold—there may have been no causal connection. But such a long association was persuasive, and not unreasonably so (Sayers, 1960a). Finally, as a great trading power—perhaps not quite so great as was assumed in 1925, but important nonetheless—Britain, it was thought, could stabilize the conditions of world trade, to its own long-term benefit in larger exports and cheaper imports, by leading a re-establishment of gold.

From 1919 the government had resolved to return eventually to gold at the old parity (useful narratives of the period are Aldcroft, 1970, and Pollard,

1983). By January 1924, the pound was at $4.26, and thereafter it rose steadily towards the pre-war parity. This was convenient, and was still another argument for fixing the parity at its old value. The Gold and Silver Export Embargo Act (1920) expired in 1925, so a decision on exchange rate policy had in any case to be taken. The return at the old parity was announced by Winston Churchill in his budget speech of April 1925.

The decision, in other words, was not precipitate or irrational. The British delegation to the Genoa Conference of 1922, for example, had urged a worldwide return to gold. The Association of Clearing Banks and the Federation of British Industry supported the move. Criticism did not develop until the summer, when John Maynard Keynes published *The Economic Consequences of Mr Churchill*, but even then the criticism was of the rate chosen, not the return to gold itself. On the basis of purchasing power parity calculations—that is, how much British prices had moved relative to other prices since 1914—Keynes argued that sterling was Ten per cent overvalued. Ten per cent is well within the inevitable margin of error in such calculations; and subsequent authors have produced different figures. Gregory (1957) produced a much lower figure, while Redmond (1982) on an effective rate basis (that is, allowing for the importance of particular currencies in British trade) produced an overvaluation of 25 per cent.

This last calculation could, of course, not have been carried out at the time; the data did not exist, and the concept was not well articulated. But setting that aside, does it confirm Churchill's subsequent regret? It is far from clear that it does. There are both analytical and empirical arguments on the other side. In a striking anticipation of concepts subsequently made much use of by economists—credibility and the money supply regime—Kiddy, editor of the 'Bankers Magazine', argued at the time that to change the parity would wreck the standard; it would remove the guarantee of stability. It is a point of some substance. And by 1929, four years after the 'wrong' parity, many industries were exporting more than at their 1913 peak; the industries still in difficulties by 1929 had anyway shown signs of weakness before the war, because of a changed structural pattern of comparative advantage.

CAUSES OF DEPRESSION

Money played at best only a minor role in the economic depression of 1929–32. The main evidence on the role of money in economic cycles is found in Friedman and Schwartz's study of the US (1963). Their conclusions were that money was a prime factor in bringing about *major* cyclical downturns. The main point is that the British depression of 1929–32 was not major. Over the three years output fell by a mere 6 per cent, trivial in relation to the US (35 per cent) or even many European countries, especially Germany. The slump of 1921 had been worse in Britain.

Stock market prices did fall from late 1929 onwards and in 1933 reached a low point of some 30 per cent below their peak of 1929 (again, no disaster by American standards). While a case can be made that the stock market had real effects through a variety of channels the case is not strong. For one thing British consumption and investment both held up through 1930. More importantly, holdings of securities by individuals, even indirectly through pension schemes, were on a small scale at this time. Deflating nominal wealth by prices would reveal little change in real wealth.

The late 1920s, however, show monetary stringency. Money growth and prices were relatively flat from 1924 onwards. In the last quarter of 1928 money base fell, and it fell in three of the four quarters of 1929. The broader definition of money, M3, was also falling in late 1928 and fell in every month in the first half of 1929. Short-term interest rates were rising, consistent with this indication of monetary stringency. The Treasury bill rate was drifting upwards from 4.1 per cent in late 1928 and rose through 1929 to 6.1 per cent. Bank rate was seen as the clearest indicator of the monetary authorities' intentions and it rose steadily from late 1928 when it was 4.5 per cent to 6.5 per cent in September 1929, and this when prices were flat and with price expectations more or less flat, too. But this is not the stuff of major depressions. Our judgement is that factors other than the money supply, most obviously the collapse in exports as world trade fell, were of far greater importance.

THE 1931 CRISIS

In 1931, after a change of government, Britain left gold. This was not as before simply a wartime suspension, an event allowed and, to the extent that war is normal, normal under the rules of the gold standard. Was it the result of the parity chosen in 1925? Or was there some other influence?

Problems with the parity emerged in 1930, when gold losses resumed (having abated since 1928). Although both France and the US supported the pound, in the sense that their central banks were willing to buy and sell pounds at the official rate, French opinion was that the UK's unbalanced budget was the source of the problem. True, the budget was in deficit. But a large part of the deficit was merely cyclical, and therefore transitory. Unemployment in 1931 was 21 per cent of the insured workforce, equivalent on the current definition to an unemployment rate of around 16 per cent. Unemployment relief contributed substantially to the deficit. The underlying budgetary position was not unsustainable, in the sense of being both structural (that is, not a product of the cyclical position) and so large as to be incapable of being financed except by money creation (Sargent and Wallace, 1981). What of the *actual* budgetary position? A case can be constructed for arguing that it did cause problems. A deficit financed by bonds could raise interest rates, which would reduce the demand for money. The resulting excess supply of money could produce a once-for-all depreciation. But bond yields were not rising throughout 1925–31; and short rates only started to rise *after* the exchange rate came under pressure. Furthermore, the supposed chain of events would require an implausibly high sensitivity of money demand to interest rates.

Excess money produced by over-rapid supply growth can also be ruled out. Table 4.4 shows both money and prices from 1920 to 1932; they give no hint of excess supply. Can overvaluation therefore be blamed? The evidence is not compelling. Some export industries were depressed—but as noted above they had been depressed before 1914, and were only sustained by the closing off of foreign competition by the war. Moggridge (1972) focuses on the invisible account, which deteriorated as interest rates fell at home and world trade slowed abroad (reducing Britain's large receipts from shipping and financial services). These no doubt combined to produce weakness.

The weakness was made fatal for the gold pound of 1717, however, by a world-wide scramble for liquidity, having little or nothing to do with British policy. It swept through Europe following the collapse of Kredit Anstalt in May 1931 and in Germany throughout the summer of that year (Kindleberger, 1986). At the same time the Macmillan Report revealed Britain's short-term liabilities to be even greater than previously thought: merely knowing the precarious balance sheet was enough to make it a factor. Balances were withdrawn from London, funds were drained from the Bank, and, in the wake of the Invergordon mutiny on 15 September (the sailors refused a pay cut), Britain left gold, on 21 September 1931.

Table 4.4. Money and prices from 1920 to 1932

Year	Money supply M3 (£m)	Annual change in M3 (proportional)	Retail price index	Annual change in RPI (proportional)
1920	2,890	0.12	244	0.16
1921	2,880	0.00	222	−0.09
1922	2,660	−0.08	179	−0.19
1923	2,470	−0.07	171	−0.04
1924	2,450	−0.01	172	0.01
1925	2,430	−0.01	173	0.01
1926	2,420	0.00	169	−0.02
1927	2,460	0.02	164	−0.03
1928	2,500	0.02	163	−0.01
1929	2,540	0.02	161	−0.01
1930	2,550	0.00	155	−0.04
1931	2,520	−0.01	145	−0.06
1932	2,570	0.02	141	−0.03

Britain's position *was* weak; but it was the kind of weakness that could reverse given time, a kind that had been ridden out before. There were *real* structural adjustments to be made to the pattern of production, which an exchange rate could not prevent. The government deficit and the revelations of a weak liquidity position for the nation required borrowing from abroad. Instead the French gobbled up British gold. What happened in 1931 was not a vindication of claims that 1925 had been catastrophic: it was largely the result of the French failing to play by the rules of the old game.

ECONOMIC RECOVERY

Yet leaving gold was not undesirable. Being off gold meant that Britain did not import the subsequent US monetary squeeze. In fact, the economy recovered smartly. The economic upswing in Britain from mid 1932 was amongst the strongest ever experienced. Many explanations have been offered as to how it started and was sustained and in these accounts money has featured strongly. The 1930s are known as the decade of 'cheap money'. In late 1932 the Bank rate was lowered to 2 per cent and it stayed unchanged until the eve of war. All other short-term interest rates reflected the easy money conditions of the time. One line of argument is that the government brought about a reduction in interest rates in mid 1932 by carrying out a great conversion of the national debt, from the high-interest bonds coming due from the war to low-interest bonds suitable to the conditions of the time (Kaldor, 1985). Since government cannot by decree reduce long-term interest rates the argument is somehow incomplete. The conversion operation was to offer a new dated stock with a coupon rate of 3.5 per cent in exchange for the 5 per cent war loan stock of 1917 of which over £2,000 million was outstanding (in 1932 some 27 per cent of the total national debt). Through a combination of propaganda, cajoling major holders of war loan stock, offering financial incentives and by other means, the authorities were able *in the favourable contemporary conditions* to effect the conversion (Capie et al., 1986).

The principal condition was indeed the abandonment of the gold standard, freeing Britain from concern about attracting funds from abroad. With prices flat or rising only slightly, real interest rates fell. As to whether or not one views the departure from the gold standard as a policy decision or a fait accompli given the state of Britain's reserves there is no unambiguous position. But that only matters if the question is the role of the government. We are interested here in the role of money rather than the means by which monetary magnitudes came to be what they were. In any case, interest rates around the world were falling. British interest rates could fall rather than being used in defence of the exchange rate. The conversion of the national debt to low interest rates—seen as a result rather than a cause of monetary conditions—eased the government's budgetary burden and at the same time fostered expectations of improving monetary conditions. All these developments helped to bring down and hold down money rates of interest. And in any event real interest rates stayed low. They undoubtedly encouraged investment. Interest rates were low at a time when the nation needed such encouragement. Real rates in the long run are not the product of monetary conditions (Mills and Wood, 1988). Money was not therefore central to the recovery, but doubtless it was accommodating.

PREFACE TO WAR: 1937–38

The British economy experienced a strong cyclical upswing in the 1930s and reached a peak late in 1937. It then entered a short but quite sharp contractionary phase, reaching a low point late in 1938. Had war not been on the horizon the contraction might well have been deeper and longer. Industrial output fell by over 10 per cent in a twelve-month period in 1937–38, comparable to the first year of the 1929–32 depression. Strangely, prices were rising sharply in the months leading up to September 1937 and yet unemployment was still substantial.

The US underwent a similar cyclical experience and Friedman and Schwartz (1963) place the blame at the door of the Federal Reserve Bank (the American central bank). But most contemporary commentators did not list monetary stringency among the causes of the 1937 recession in Britain (Capie and Collins, 1980). There was no sharp contraction in the most important bank variables, and more apparent to contemporaries the short-term rates of interest remained low (and with prices rising somewhat, real rates were surely lower). Long rates had been drifting upwards from mid 1935 but short rates remained low. The authorities pursued a 'cheap money' policy, and there is a clear and steep rise in the monetary base in 1936 and 1937. The rise in long rates in 1937 has been attributed to the commercial banks running down holdings of long-term securities in order to maintain cash reserves and to sustain high levels of advances. There was, too, the growing expectation of war, and the shift to a war footing that it augured.

CONCLUSIONS

It appears from the British experience, then, that money is important for real output only in *major* economic fluctuations. Institutions were crucial to the contrast in monetary stability between Britain and the rest of the world, especially the United States. Britain was served well by its clearing banks and even, in most times, by its devotion to gold. Finally, prices moved proportionately with the difference between money and the growth in real income. In the long run the quantity theory held.

REFERENCES

All references to the *Economic History Review* are to the Second Series, unless otherwise stated.

Aldcroft, D. H. (1970) *The Interwar Economy: Britain 1919–1939*, London: Batsford.

Ashton, T. S. (1955) *The Eighteenth Century and Economic Fluctuations 1700–1800*, Oxford: Methuen Co., 49.

Bagehot, W. (1873) *Lombard Street*.

Barro, R. J. (1984) 'Comments on Rockoff', in M. Bordo and A. J. Schwartz (eds), *A Retrospective on the Classical Gold Standard, 1821–1931*, University of Chicago Press.

——(1987) *Macroeconomics*. New York: Wiley.

Barsky, R. B. and Summers, L. H. (1988) 'Gibson's Paradox and the Gold Standard', *Journal of Political Economy*, 96, 528–41.

Batchelor, R. A. (1986) 'The Avoidance of a Catastrophe: Two Nineteenth Century Banking Crises', in Capie et al., 1986.

Bernanke, B. S. (1983) 'Non Monetary Effects of the Financial Crises in the Propagation of the Great Depression', *American Economic Review*, 73, 256–76.

Brunner, K. and Meltzer, A. H. (1989) *Monetary Economics*, Oxford: Blackwell.

Cagan, P. (1965) *Determinants and Effects of Changes in the Stock of Money 1875–1960*, New York: NBER.

Capie, F. H. (1990) 'Money and Business Cycles in Britain 1870–1913', in Velupellai and Thygesen (eds), *Business Cycles, Non Linearities, Disequilibria, and Simulations: Readings in Business Cycles Theory*. London: Macmillan.

——and Collins, M. (1980) 'The Extent of British Economic Recovery in the 1930s', *Economy and History*, 23(1), 40–60.

——and Mills, T. C. (1990) 'Money and Business Cycles in the United States 1870 to 1913: A Reexamination of Friedman and Schwartz', *Explorations in Economic History*, 29(3), 251–73.

——and Rodrik-Bali, G. (1983) *Monetary Growth and Determinants in Britain 1870–1913*, Centre for the Study of Monetary History Discussion Paper No. 6, City University Business School.

——and Webber, A. (1985) *A Monetary History of the United Kingdom 1870–1982*, Vol. I: *Data, Sources, Methods*, London: Allen & Unwin.

——Mills, T. C., and Wood, G. E. (1986) 'Debt Management and Interest Rates: The British Stock Conversion of 1932', *Applied Economics*, 18, 1111–20.

Collins, M. (1990) *British Banks and Industrial Finance before 1939*. London: Macmillan.

Coppock, J. T. (1956) 'The Statistical Assessment of British Agriculture', *Agricultural History Review*, 4, 4–21 and 66–79.

Crafts, N. F. R., Leybourne, S. J., and Mills, T. C. (1989a) 'The Climacteric in Late Victorian Britain and France: A Reappraisal of the Evidence', *Journal of Applied Econometrics*, 4, 103–17.

——(1989b) 'Trends and Cycles in British Industrial Production', *Journal of the Royal Statistical Society*, Series A, 152, 43–60.

Dimsdale, N. H. (1981a) British Monetary Policy and the Exchange Rate 1920–38', in Eltis and Sinclair (eds), *The Money Supply and the Exchange Rate*, Oxford University Press.

——(1981b) 'British Monetary Policy and the Exchange Rate 1920–1938', *Oxford Economic Papers*, 33: 306–49.

Eichengreen, B. J. (1983) 'The Causes of British Business Cycles 1833–1913', *Journal of European Economic History*, 12, 145–61.

Feinstein, C. H. (1990) 'New Estimates of Average Earnings in the United Kingdom, 1880–1913', *Economic History Review*, 43, 595–632.

Ford, A. G. (1963) 'Notes on the Role of Exports in British Economic Fluctuations 1870–1914', *Economic History Review*, 16, 328–37.

——(1981) 'Trade Cycles, 1870–1914', in Floud and McCloskey (eds), *The Economic History of Britain since 1700*, II, Cambridge University Press.

Friedman, M. and Schwartz, A. J. (1963) *A Monetary History of the United States 1867–1960*. Princeton University Press for NBER.

————(1982) *Monetary Trends in the United States and in the United Kingdom, 1870–1970*, University of Chicago Press.

Gayer, A. D., Rostow, W. W., and Schwartz, A. J. (1953) 'The Growth and Fluctuations of the British Economy 1790–1850: An Historical Statistical and Theoretical Study of Britain's Economic Development', Oxford University Press.

Goodhart, C. A. E. (1986) 'Comment on Seabourne', in Capie et al., 1986.

Gorton, G. (1988) 'Banking Panics and Business Cycles', *Oxford Economic Papers*, 40, 751–81.

Gregory, T. E. (1957) 'The Norman Conquest Reconsidered,' *Lloyds Bank Review*.

Grigg, P. J. (1948) *Prejudice and Judgement*, London: Jonathan Cape.

Harley, C. K. (1976) 'Goschen's Conversion of the National Debt and the Gold on Consols', *Economic History Review*, 34, 101–6.

Hawtrey, R. G. (1913) *Good and Bad Trade: An Enquiry into the Causes of Trade Fluctuations*, London: Constable & Co.

Kaldor, N. (1985) *The Scourge of Monetarism*, Oxford University Press.

Keynes, J. M. (1925) *The Economic Consequences of Mr Churchill*, London: Macmillan.

——(1930) *A Treatise on Money*, Macmillan.

Kindleberger, C. P. (1986) *The World in Depression 1929–1939*. Harmondsworth.

Kirkaldy, A. W. (1921) *British Finance during and after the War 1914–21*. London: Sir Isaac Pitman & Sons Ltd.

Klovland, J. T. (1987) 'The Demand for Money in the United Kingdom 1875–1913', *Oxford Bulletin of Economics and Statistics*, 49, 251–71.

Lucas, R. E. (1972) *Studies in Business Cycle Theory*, Oxford. Reprinted 1981, Cambridge, Mass.: MIT Press.

McCloskey, D. N. (1970) 'Did Victorian Britain Fail?' *Economic History Review*, 23, 446–59.

——and Zecher, J. R. (1976) How the Gold Standard Worked', in Frenkel and Johnson (eds), *The Monetary Approach to the Balance of Payments*. Washington, DC: IMF.

Matthews, R. C. O., Feinstein, C. H., and Odling-Smee, J. C. (1982) *British Economic Growth 1856–1973*, Oxford University Press.

Meltzer, A. H. (1986) 'Comment on Anna Schwartz', in Capie et al., 1986.

Mills, T. C, and Wood, G. E. (1988) 'Interest Rates and the Conduct of Monetary Policy', in Eltis and Sinclair (eds), *The Money Supply and the Exchange Rate*, Oxford University Press.

————(1992) 'Money and Interest Rates in Britain from 1870 to 1913', in Broadberry and Crafts (eds), *Britain in the International Economy: Essays in Honour of A. G. Ford*, Cambridge University Press.

Moggridge, D. E. (1972) *British Monetary Policy 1924–1931: The Norman Conquest of $4.86*, Cambridge University Press.

Morgan, E. V. (1952) *Studies in British Financial Policy 1914–1925*, London: Macmillan.

Phelps Brown, E. H., and Handfield Jones, S. J. (1952) 'The Climacteric of the 1890s: A Study in the Expanding Economy', *Oxford Economic Papers*, 14, 266–307.

Pollard, S. (1983) *The Development of the British Economy*, London: Edward Arnold.

Redmond J. (1982) 'The Norman Conquest of 4.86: Was the Pound Overvalued?' Faculty of Commerce and Social Sciences, Discussion Paper No 9, University of Birmingham.

Rockoff, H. (1984) 'Some Evidence on the Real Price of Gold: Its Costs of Production and Commodity Prices', in Bordo and Schwartz (eds), *A Retrospective on the Classical Gold Standard, 1821–1031*, University of Chicago Press.

Rostow, W. W. (1948) *British Economy in the Nineteenth Century*, Oxford: Clarendon Press.

Sargent, T., and Wallace, N. (1981) 'Some Unpleasant Monetarist Arithmetic', *Federal Reserve Bank of Minneapolis Quarterly Review*, 5.

Saul, S. B. (1969) *The Myth of the Great Depression, 1873–1896*, London: Macmillan.

Sayers, R. S. (1960) 'The Return to Gold', in L. S. Pressnell (ed.), *Studies in the Industrial Revolution*, London: Athlone.

Schumpeter, J. A. (1954) *History of Economic Analysis*, Oxford University Press.

Schwartz, A. J. (1982) 'Reflections on the Gold Commission Report', *Journal of Money, Credit and Banking*, 4, 538–51.

——(1986) 'Real and Pseudo Financial Crises', in Capie et al., 1986.

Seabourne, T. (1986) 'The Summer of 1914', in Capie et al., 1986.

Turner, A. J. (1972) 'The Evolution of Reserve Ratios in English Banking', *National Westminster Bank Quarterly Review*, 52–63.

Walters, A. A. (1969) 'Money in Boom and Slump', Hobart Paper 44, Institute of Economic Affairs.

Wood, G. E. (1984) 'Comment on "Real Output and the Gold Standard Years"', in Bordo and Schwartz (eds), *A Retrospective on the Classical Gold Standard, 1821–1931*, Chicago University Press.

5

Deflation in the British Economy, 1870–1939*

INTRODUCTION

For much of the last quarter-century, a principal focus of economists' attention has been inflation and, to some extent, disinflation and the associated costs. More recently, deflation has attracted some interest, although only its possible harmful consequences have been discussed; there has been no mention of deflation as the by-product of increased economic growth interacting with unchanged money growth. This latter is prompted by some sharp rises and falls in asset prices in Japan and more recently the US and to a lesser extent the UK, and the interest taken in the relationship between these and the general price level. But also important were the actual deflations in prices in Japan, China, and Hong Kong, and the near-zero inflation in the US and Europe. An accepted view is that price stability underpins financial stability and that it is unanticipated changes in monetary policy that produces financial distress. What though, do we know about deflation? We need to go back to before World War II to find episodes in almost any OECD country, though there has been some recent experience in Japan and elsewhere. The purpose of this paper is to begin to investigate the effects of deflation in the British economy.

The depression of the 1930s stimulated many developments in economic analysis. But Keynes's ideas on deflation in the *General Theory*, and Irving Fisher's debt-deflation theory, have been at least by comparison neglected. These ideas suggest that 'debt deflation' causes or at the least worsens depressions. Our aim in this chapter is to explore what these ideas can contribute to

* We should like to thank Terry Sithole for research assistance. Paolo di Martino for comments, and participants at seminars at the universities of Buckingham, Nottingham, and Loughborough.

Originally published as Forrest Capie and Geoffrey Wood (2003), 'Deflation in the British Economy, 1870–1939', *The Journal of European Economic History*, Vol. 32 (2003), no. 2, pp. 277–305, reproduced with permission.

understanding the behaviour of the British economy both in the late nineteenth century and in the inter-war years.

We set out the debt deflation ideas of Keynes and Fisher (the models are far from identical) and then see whether any of the key variables in these models moved as the models require for there to be debt deflation at work. We seek to evaluate what contribution the debt-deflation models make to understanding the behaviour of the British economy in the two periods.

The structure of the chapter is as follows. The next section outlines briefly the course of the British economy in the two periods we examine, 1873–96 and 1920–39. Then the debt deflation ideas of Keynes and of Fisher are outlined, and the variables crucial to those 'debt deflation' models identified. As will emerge, price expectations, albeit different aspects of them, are central to both views, so the next section of the chapter considers informally how these might be identified in our two periods. After modelling price expectations we provide differently constructed real interest rates and examine the informational content of the bond market. We then consider the behaviour of bond spreads as a possible route to understanding the role of debt-deflation, before finishing by noting the role of inter-temporal substitution.

THE BRITISH ECONOMY

Our principal focus is on the inter-war years in Britain and the behaviour of the economy during these is outlined first. Following a boom at the end of the First World War there was a period that ran until the early 1930s when prices were either falling or flat. They fell most sharply in the recession at the end of the 1920s. Interestingly, asset prices rose quite consistently throughout, and in the later 1920s were rising quite rapidly. They then fell steeply in the recession years of 1929 to 1932 and beyond. In the closest preceding period of falling prices, the long deflation of the late nineteenth century (1873–96) the economy while continuing to grow, was doing so at an ever slowing pace. In the 1920s and 1930s, in contrast, the economy performed much better than in the nineteenth century deflation—at least from peak to peak, 1924: 29–37. There have been no deflations since then, though there have been several occasions when asset prices have moved in a way dramatically different from the general price level.

Price experience is our key concern. In the inter-war period it followed a pattern that was not greatly out of line with what it had been in the past. But it should not be surprising that to a certain extent it also reflected the attempts at restoring monetary order following war. Thus there were fluctuations but also a slightly downward trend. Using the cost of living index gives the following picture. After considerable inflation in the war, prices continued rising and then rose sharply in the immediate post-war boom. They then collapsed from a peak of 151 in October 1920 to 99 in March 1923 as Britain sought to rejoin the international gold standard at sterling's old parity. They drifted down further until 1925 and were then more or less flat until 1929. They fell still further in the worldwide depression, levelled out in 1933 and from then on drifted up slightly in the upswing of the 1930s. At the end of the period they were a little lower than they had been at the beginning. How much expectation of this general deflationary path there might have been is an important question to which we return later.

The behaviour of the British economy over the years 1873 to 1896, the previous period of deflation was much less dramatic. That period was at one time described as 'the Great Depression'. But that was a misnomer that derived in part from the association of falling prices with relatively declining economic performance, and in part from the deteriorating position of agriculture (in the face of severe competition from the new world) and the voice that landowners had in parliament. In fact the trend rate of growth was not out of line with previous periods. Real output (GDP) rose from 1873 to 1896 of over 50 per cent in a twenty-three year period. There were some falls along the way, the worst of them being in 1879 and the mid 1880s. Unemployment, as captured in the percentage of insured workers unemployed, fluctuated broadly in line with output. Unemployment averaged 5 per cent per year across the whole period. There were three years in which it went above 9 per cent, and four in which it fell below 2.2 per cent.

Prices fell on average from 1873 to 1896. An index of the GDP deflator (with 1913=100) began the period in 1873 at 109.2 (a peak), and finished it in 1896 at 86.2, an average decline of exactly 1 per cent deflation per annum. The decline was of course not smooth, but rather a fluctuating path about a downward trend. Prices did, though, move fairly modestly year by year. The biggest fall in the period was 4.7 per cent in 1879; and the biggest rise was 4.3 per cent in the following year, 1880. Short-term interest rates fluctuated substantially but showed no signs of any trend consistent with US experience and inflation expectations of close to zero (see M. Friedman's *Money Mischief*, 1992), while Consol yields drifted downwards very gently and showed little year-by-year movement.

Financial stability is also at the centre of our interest, for it underpins macro-stability. Financial stability is difficult to measure, perhaps impossible. But if ever there was a country and a period in which financial stability could be said to obtain it would be Britain in the period between 1870 and 1939. We have noted that there were some sharp general price movements (though these were for the most part associated with war). There were, too, some sharp asset price movements. And there were of course fluctuations in the real economy. But financial stability prevailed. There were no banking panics, no financial crises (no threat to the money stock). No single measure can express the degree of financial stability but perhaps a good guide can be found in commercial bank profitability. That remained remarkably stable across the whole period. (Capie, 1988, and Capie and Billings, 2001). The behaviour of components of the money multiplier support that view: there was no example of a rush to cash or a collapse in the multiplier (Capie and Webber).

HYPOTHESES

The two basic approaches are those of Keynes and Irving Fisher. We first set out the approach which originated with Keynes, and then turn to that of Fisher. The first point to be made is that in developing their theories Keynes and Fisher had rather different objectives. The former was primarily concerned to show that wage flexibility (a particular form of price flexibility) would not necessarily stabilize output. Fisher was concerned to show a stronger proposition—that price flexibility would *destabilize* output.

Keynes (*General Theory*, ch. 19) argued that changes in money wages could affect output (and employment) only by changing aggregate demand. He listed several ways by which money wage falls could shift aggregate demand. The first was a transfer of income from workers to rentiers; this would, he conjectured, reduce demand. Then came two which applied to open economies with pegged exchange rates. A fall in wages would boost exports and reduce imports; but against that the resulting fall in real income would cut consumption spending. Fourth was inter-temporal substitution: if money wages fell relative to expected future money wages, current spending would be boosted, while if the fall led to expectations of further falls, spending would itself also fall; investment was the part of total spending Keynes expected to be affected by this channel.

Fifth was a monetary channel; the fall in wages and prices would produce a fall in interest rates, due to a rise in money supply relative to money demand. Sixth was an anticipation of Lucas. Businessmen may mistake a general wage fall for one specific to them, hire more labour in consequence, and thus break the cycle of depression. Last was the effect on indebtedness:

> On the other hand, the depressing influence on entrepreneurs of their burden of debt may partly offset any cheerful reactions from the reduction of wages. Indeed, if the fall of wages and price goes far, the embarrassment of those entrepreneurs who are heavily indebted may soon reach the point of insolvency—with severely adverse effects on investment. (Keynes, 1936, p. 264)

Keynes laid greatest stress on the intertemporal substitution channel, and on interest rates. Keynes thought that effects through interest rates would be weak. Small falls in prices would have small effects and only on short-term interest rates, while large price falls would disturb confidence. He set out in some detail the possibility that a fall in money wages could raise the expected real rate of interest (Keynes, 1936, p. 265).

> The most favourable contingency is that in which money wages are slowly sagging downwards and each reduction in wages serves to diminish confidence in the prospective maintenance in wages. . . . For example, the effect of an expectation that wages are going to sag by say 2 per cent in the coming year will be roughly equivalent to the effect of a rise of 2 per cent in the amount of interest payable for the same period. (G.T., p. 265).

His analysis plainly suggests that wage (price) flexibility cannot cure depressions; but it does not suggest, as Fisher did, that such flexibility can cause depressions.

Fisher's views are set out very clearly in his 1933 *Econometrica* article. For Fisher, debt and deflation were key ingredients in recessions. We have to start from a situation of 'overindebtedness'. Nine factors then come into play. An initial shock causes a change in confidence, and produces distress selling, so bank loans are repaid and the money supply falls. This leads in turn to a fall in prices (a 'swelling of the dollar' in the US case) and a decline in net worth and in profits. These lead in turn to falls in output and employment, followed by increased pessimism, hoarding of money, and decreases in nominal interest rates along with increases in real rates.

The 'overindebtness' which is a key ingredient can, Fisher suggested, arise through a route such as the following. A technological breakthrough fuels borrowing. This leads to speculative enthusiasm, followed by criminality. 'Probably no great crash has every happened without shady transactions' (Fisher, 1932, p. 40). Inflation can lead to similar results, by creating the illusion of easy profits. It is the interaction of debt and deflation which is crucial in Fisher's analysis:

> The very effort of individuals to lessen their burden of debt increases it, because of the mass effect of the stampede to liquidate in swelling each dollar owed. Thus we have the great paradox which, I submit is the chief secret of most, if not all, great depressions; the more debtors pay, the more they owe. (1933, p. 344)

The very process of liquidating debt leads to a fall in bank deposits and thus prices; prices fall faster than debt, real debt rises and 'good risks' are thus exposed to problems. And not only does the real value of debt rise; so does the real interest rate payable on it. In deflations there is a ' . . . fall in the nominal or money, rates, and a rise in the real, or commodity rate of interest' (para 19, p. 341)

A key point distinguishing Keynes from Fisher is that the former saw *expected* real rates as important, while Fisher saw an increase in *realized* real rates as having a damaging effect on *existing* debtors.

Before turning to the data required to examine these propositions, we next set out some thoughts on price expectations.

PRICE EXPECTATIONS

In modern macroeconomics, expectations are recognized as having an important role to play. In modelling, different kinds of expectations, from extrapolative, to adaptive, to rational, have been employed. Currently, though with a range of interpretations, rational behaviour is assumed. This is broadly taken to mean expectations formed on a rational basis using the best information that is freely available, and based on the best economic model of price behaviour. Expectations now focus directly on changes in government policy.

Life was simpler in the nineteenth century in this important respect. Adherence to the gold standard largely removed monetary policy from government control. Thus price expectations were formed differently. In the nineteenth century, at least among the more advanced economies, there developed a respect and admiration for the gold standard. Britain was the strikingly successful economy of the time and had adopted the standard at an early date. Countries that followed that path had stable price experience in accord with the theory of the standard. Prices continued to move with the economic cycle but were flat on trend. More and more countries opted to adopt this regime in the 1870s and it has since been argued that there was a relative shortage of gold, which exerted a downward pressure on prices. In the period from 1873 to 1896 there was a long decline in prices. Gold discoveries and improved technology produced the subsequent reversal in the trend.

Might this deflation have been foreseen? Was it anticipated? That is difficult to establish. There were certainly those at the time who warned that the shrinkage in the supply of high-powered money which would result from abandoning silver and moving to gold would produce deflation. In addition there was the huge extension of primary production in the new world and, via the simultaneous transport revolution, the arrival of these products in north-west Europe. The prices of these primary products fell, and must have been expected to fall further. While these price falls were not the cause of the deflation they did influence some contemporaries and must have contributed to a weakening of pressure on prices. We can conclude that there must have been widespread expectation of price falls in the period. There were, as usual, different explanations for the deflation (real vs monetary again) but there now seems little doubt that gold was the cause. New gold discoveries in the 1890s helped alleviate the gold shortage and prices began to rise again.

During the First World War when the standard was abandoned there were widespread and differential rates of inflation. At the end of the war there was an almost equally widespread desire to restore the monetary order of the late nineteenth century. Since Britain had been at the centre of that system, attention focused heavily on British actions. The story of Britain's return to gold is well-known. From soon after the war price expectations were clearly on a downward course. There was no other possibility. The intention had been clearly announced (Mundell, 2000). All parties were agreed on what was necessary, and the appropriate policies were introduced.

Soon after restoration was achieved in 1925, it became clear that there was still work to be done in Britain and high interest rates persisted over the next few years in order to protect the parity chosen—the one that had held in the nineteenth century. And so price expectations probably continued to have been negative.

Mundell (2000) has recently restated the view that this price expectation must have been much more widely held, indeed held by all those considering a return to gold. The United States had taken over Britain's role of major economy and had experienced inflation during the war. The Federal Reserve had then engineered a recession in 1920/21 that brought the dollar price level '60 percent of the way back to the prewar equilibrium' (p. 328). But that still left prices 40 per cent higher than they had been, and gold reserves correspondingly lower. The increased demand for gold as restoration was pursued would inevitably bring deflation. Mundell argues that this was understood at the time by the leading monetary economists. He cites Cassel, who had been explicit on the point even before Britain had returned to gold in 1925:

> The gold standard, of course, cannot secure a greater stability in the general level of prices than the value gold itself possesses. . . . With the actual state of gold production it can be taken for certain that after a comparatively short time, perhaps within a decade, the present superabundance of gold will be followed, as a consequence of increasing demand, by a marked scarcity of this precious metal tending to cause a fall in prices. (Mundell, 2000, p. 329)

So deflation was already expected in the 1920s. Mundell (p. 329) goes on to say, '. . . that deflation was caused by the return to the gold standard was not only predictable, but was actually, as we have noted above, predicted.' Prices were to fall much more in the depression of the 1930s and Mundell goes on to say that the deflation was a consequence of not returning to the pre-1914 price level in 1920/21. That was not achieved until 1934 when the dollar price level was the same as it had been in 1914.

Further evidence of the mood of deflation can be found in Britain at the turn of the decade. In 1930, when prices had fallen sharply again after a decade of sluggishness, attention focused on measures that might be adopted to raise prices. When, for example, there was discussion of the introduction of a tariff in 1931 (a dramatic proposal given Britain's history as the great upholder of free trade), great play was made of the fact that this was a policy that would raise prices. That on its own was advanced as a powerful recommendation for the policy.

In other words, the whole climate of this period was one in which the expectation of price rises must have been exceptionally low and indeed expectation of price falls was quite likely. There seemed, certainly in Britain at least, little prospect of prices rising before the early 1930s.

THE DATA

Plainly the crucial variables in the Keynes and Fisher models are, respectively, the expected real rate and the realized real rate. The first is defined in the normal way: $Re_t = r_t - Ae_t$ where *Re* is the expected real rate over the expected length of the loan, re the nominal rate over that period, and Ae the expected inflation rate over the same period. The real rate for Fisher is slightly non-standard. In his model, problems emerge because an individual or firm has signed up to a nominal rate contract, expecting a certain inflation rate, but the actual rate of inflation turns out to be lower, even negative. Hence the real rate for Fisher at time *t* is as follows:

> $Rt = r_{t-1} - A_{t1}$ where $A_t < Ae_{t-1}$, Rt is the realized real rate, r_{t-1} the nominal rate when the loan was taken on, A_t the inflation rate, and Ae_{t-1} the expected inflation rate when the loan was taken on.

Some of these variables are, at any rate in principle, observable. These are: r_t, r_{t-1}, and A_t. The others can be calculated from these three observable variables if we can somehow devise a measure for A_e—that is, for expected inflation. Before discussing sources for the other three variables, we consider this problem.

James Hamilton (1987) tackled this problem for the US of the Great Depression. He first looked at pre-depression statements of expectations: indicative, but no quantitative help. Then he used time-series models to predict prices, and compared forecasts with actual price out-turns. Finally, he looked at commodities futures prices. He calculated the difference between one month and seven-month futures prices, and compared this with the difference between two one-month future prices, six months apart.

He found that the variability of the expected series was greater than that of the actual, and that the expected series was an unbiased (though noisy) predictor of the actual. On average, over each six-month period the market expected 9.4 per cent inflation; the comparable out-turn was −39 per cent. This bears on prices in general, for knowledge of commodity prices helps predict the CPI. He concluded that the interaction of nominal rates with expectations of deflation (the Keynes effect) could not have contributed to the depression, for deflation was not expected. It is not clear whether or not this contradicts Mundell for he was discussing the need to restore the 1914 gold price over a fairly long period.

What of the Fisher effect? Fisher (e.g. 1933, pp. 346–47) wanted price rises because he thought they would help recovery. Friedman and Schwartz (1963) and Weinstein (1981) however, reject the claim that the National Industrial Recovery Act (NIRA) was beneficial through its effects on raising prices. As they point out, by raising prices it reduced the *real* increase in the money stock. According to Weinstein (op. cit.), it reduced this real increase to zero, for as he points out from 1933 to 1935 prices rose by 14 per cent in the US and so did the nominal stock of money. Friedman and Schwartz argue likewise for the years 1933–37. Increasing union and monopoly power led to increasing price levels. This restricted the room for real income growth within the money-set constraint to nominal income.

But this does not allow for the harmful effects on the real burden of debt, and on the financial system via deterioration in asset values (Bernanke, 1983) that might have been alleviated by the price rise. There is thus the possibility that the price rises might have been of benefit despite the monetary constraint.

PRICE LEVEL AND PRICE LEVEL CHANGE EXPECTATIONS

Price expectations are important in both Keynes's and Fisher's debt deflation theories. For Keynes, they could both affect interest rates (although he did not expect this channel to be of great significance), and work through intertemporal substitution leading to deferral of spending. Fisher, meanwhile, feared that falsified expectations, price falls being greater than expected, could raise the burden of existing debt. How did price expectations actually behave during this period? We have discussed earlier some qualitative assessments of this. Here we turn to simple quantification.

An efficient forecasting method (provided there is no change in the process generating the series to be modelled) is to use a time series model. We do this, acknowledging the limitation imposed by the modest number of data points, for both the price level (as measured by the GNP deflator) and for the year-on-year change of the price level (measured of course by the year-on-year change in the GNP deflator.) This is done for both our periods. The models are shown in an appendix. As will be seen, they are both simple and fit well; this is to be expected given the small amount of variation in the series to be modelled.

Plots of actual and predicted series track closely together in each period. The level series move so closely together that no comment on them is necessary. The year-on-year change series do, however, merit comment. Looking first at the early period, although the series move along together, the 'actual' series is much more variable. That is of course consistent with the extensively documented observation on the gold (and presumably other commodity) standards that long-run movements are constrained, but there is greater scope for short-run variability. This was known at the time, and thereby influenced expectations, as of course did actual experience of long-run stability. (See, for a comparatively recent discussion, Mills and Wood, 1992.)

In the later period, there are no years when the difference between actual and predicted rates of change is sufficiently large to be statistically significant. But if we look at the larger deviations, we find actual exceeding predicted values in 1924 and 1925; predicted exceeding actual in 1931 and 1932; and spikes of actual above predicted in 1937, and in 1939.

The first of these deviations occurs during the period of monetary squeeze before the return to the gold standard; the second the period of relaxation after leaving gold; the third we cannot explain; and the fourth corresponds to the outbreak of war. The first two are of interest because they go exactly the wrong way for debt deflation! (This point is developed further when we examine real interest rates.)

REAL INTEREST RATES

Price expectations lead on to real interest rates. We consider the behaviour of four different series for real interest rates in each of the two periods: a real short rate and a real long rate, first calculated according to the 'Keynes method', taking account of expected inflation, and then according to Fisher, taking account of actual inflation.

To illustrate, we have an annual observation for interest rates, calculated by averaging monthly data (Capie and Webber). We also have an annual GNP deflator. For the 'Keynes series', for example, a 1900 interest rate is taken, and subtracted from it is the change in the GNP deflator expected from 1900 to 1901. That would give our 1900 'Keynes real rate'. For the Fisher series, the 1900 interest rate is taken, and subtracted from it is the change in the deflator between 1899 and 1900. What was important to Fisher, however, is not so much the behaviour of that series as the behaviour of that series relative to what was expected. To deal with that, we compare the Keynes and Fisher series, and, as what would produce deviations is the behaviour of prices relative to price expectations, also look again at our price expectations series in this fresh context.

In the earlier period, the volatility year by year of the price level produces volatility in real rates by all measures. The key point is that there is no sustained rise in either version of the real rate. It is notable, though, that in the years of deflation, real rates were higher than in the later 1890s, and somewhat higher than in the first decade of the twentieth century. In the inter-war period, however, once the immediate post-war volatility was over, interest rates move little, both measures drifting gently downwards.

The 'Keynes' and 'Fisher' series do not display systematic differences in either period, as is to be expected, for price expectations differ little from price behaviour in either period.

A fair summary would be that there is evidence of the deflation being in the UK systematically associated with unusually high interest rates in our first deflation, but none in our second—in contrast with the US experience; and that there is no evidence of unexpectedly high real interest rates arising from a succession of unexpected price level falls.

EXPECTATIONS AND THE BOND MARKET

It has become common practice when investigating price expectations to examine the long-term bond market. The Fisher equation relating the real rate and expected inflation to the nominal rate is used, and, in the US and the UK, both countries with index-linked long-term government securities, there is now a well-developed set of approaches for calculating inflation expectations over various holding periods.

There were no index-linked bonds in either of the periods we examine; in view of the behaviour of prices to which people were accustomed (and which we have indicated above) it would have been hard to persuade prospective buyers that there were any benefits to be had from purchasing such securities. Nevertheless, it is possible to make some deductions about price expectations—at least those held by participants in bond markets—from the behaviour of bond yields in the two periods we examine, and that task is the focus of this section of the paper.

We first consider the earlier period, and then the inter-war years. The earlier period, 1870–1913, is that for which the Gibson Paradox was first named (by Keynes, 1930) and in which it was first identified, by A. H. Gibson. We summarize our own and some work by others on the paradox to see what can be said about price expectations.

The paradox was that there appeared to be an association between the price level and a nominal interest rate. Various explanations have been advanced. Irving Fisher (1896; 1907; 1930) proposed one based on the Fisher equation relating real and nominal interest rates, and this explanation was later given support by the work of Friedman and Schwartz (1982). They argued that because a move from one fully anticipated inflation rate to another would, even with the real return on physical capital unchanged, alter the nominal yield on nominal assets, the appearance of a relationship between nominal yields and the level (as opposed to the rate of change) of prices could be produced. This relationship would appear if inflation expectations adjusted to inflation with a lag, so that the longer inflation persisted (and thus the higher the price level rose), the higher would the nominal yield rise. Price expectations in this explanation of the paradox thus rise (and fall) with prices.

This is not, however, the only explanation that has been offered. Both Wicksell (1907) and Keynes (1930) suggested a real explanation—nominal rates on nominal assets were pulled down by a downward drift in the natural rate of interest, reflecting a decline in the marginal physical productivity of capital. This occurred in the first half of the period, and was replaced in the second half by a rise as the American west was further developed. Price level movements were in turn induced because the market rate lagged behind the natural rate.

Harley (1977) supports a 'Fisherian' explanation, arguing that 'the money market adjusted to price expectations, and there was little effect on real interest rates'. Further, that 'the decline in the market rate of interest in the 1870s can be fully accounted for by price expectations and is fully consistent with a monetary explanation of price trends' (p. 73).

Next we come to Friedman and Schwartz (1982). They support Fisher's explanation partly by noting that the studies which rejected the explanation actually included in their data set periods when the paradox did not occur. Also they rejected the Wicksell–Keynes explanation (by use of their own series for the real rate of interest), and they found shorter lags than Fisher on price expectations. Their explanation of the end of the Gibson Paradox is derived from the same analytical framework: there was a change in the monetary standard, which produced greater incentive to forecast future price movements.

Finally, on the Gibson Paradox years, we come to Mills and Wood (1992). After an exhaustive survey and testing all of the available explanations of the paradox, they found that while decisive confirmation of Fisher was not possible, decisive rejection of all other explanations was. What is the significance of that in the present context? As noted above, the Fisher explanation requires that price expectations track along with prices. Our simple time-series model (which is inevitably simple in view of data availability) tells us that they did. So this present section confirms that finding, and thus confirms that falling prices were expected in this nineteenth-century period of deflation.

Next we come to the inter-war years. As with the closing decades of the nineteenth century, in the inter-war years our (again simple) model of price expectations tracks the gentle course of the price level. Is this consistent with the behaviour of bond yields? At the time, discussion of the behaviour of yields was not at all concerned with inflationary expectations. Rather, when discussion took place at all, it was mainly in 1932, and was of the effects of the stock conversion expected in that year. We therefore briefly set out the details of that operation, and give a flavour of the discussion surrounding it, before returning to the actual behaviour of yields.

The conversion was of War Loan 1929–47, which bore a 5 per cent coupon, into '3½ per cent 1952 or after'. By March 1932, there was about £2,100m of the stock outstanding. (This was more than a quarter of the whole national debt, or about 50 per cent of 1932 national income.)

Plans for the conversion were first discussed in 1930. By April 1931 yields had been steady for about eight months, and plans for a conversion were drawn up. These were, however, abandoned in the turbulence of first the Austro-German banking crisis, and then of Britain's leaving the gold standard. In 1932 conditions changed rapidly. Bank rate fell from 6 per cent to 3 per cent and Treasury Bill rate to just below 2 per cent. Plans for a conversion into a 3 per cent stock were then made. There was a massive publicity campaign; special incentives were offered to convert; and financial institutions which held the stock were lent on. The conversion was achieved.

That, then, is the background. How did interest rates behave? All the movement in the bill series is associated with the defence and subsequent abandoning of the gold standard. In the consol yield, there is almost no action apart from around the time of the stock conversion. Capie, Mills, and Wood (1986) confirm that to be the case. A simple time series model of the Consol yield was constructed, and intervention analysis was used to see if there was any change in the series which required explanation.

There appears to have been a small but statistically significant step in the consol yield at the time of the conversion. What can be said about price expectations from this? Neither inflationary expectations nor the behaviour of the real rate would seem to fit the bill. Not only is neither of these likely to produce a step change, but the Treasury was committed to monetary easing, so expectations of inflation, if affected, should have risen, and 1932 was the trough of the recession (so rising resource use should have raised the real rate). Capie, Mills, and Wood (1986) suggest the step was due to the fact that the successful conversion allowed tax reductions—one objective of the operation—and so allowed a fall in the before-tax rate of return observed in the market.

What does this tell about price expectations? After the step of the stock conversion there was a gentle drift down—again, as was found for our earlier period, consistent with expectations of gently falling prices and, therefore, with our model of expectations. As, too, in the nine century, price expectations moved sluggishly so that interest rates and the price level moved closely together. Yields and prices started to rise again in 1935. So, as in the 1890s, only a little more so, price movements were gentle and, so far as we can tell, were expected.

BOND RATE SPREADS

Some authors have suggested how 'debt-deflation' might by other routes affect the real economy, and have gone on to suggest ways by which the presence of debt deflation might be indicated, and its extent measured.

One route was outlined by Eichengreen and Grossman (1997): 'By "debt-deflation", we mean a fall in the prices of either assets or goods and services that raises the real value of net debt, thereby worsening the net wealth position of non-financial borrowers and discouraging them from consuming and investing' (p. 68). As they go on to point out, 'Measuring the debt burden poses difficulties for historical research' (p. 69). They therefore followed, 'the procedure of Calomiris and Hubbard (1989) and Mishkin (1991) and focus on the information content of interest rate spreads' (p. 69).

There are criticisms of that approach, but before turning to them, how do Eichengreen and Grossman justify it? They base their justification on adverse selection. Lenders reduce this by requiring collateral from borrowers. As the value of collateral falls (in a deflation) required interest spreads will rise, as another way of compensating lenders for the risk they bear. Hence, they argue, widening spreads over a risk-free rate are produced by debt-deflation, and worsen recessions by progressively restricting borrowing and investing.

For the British experience it is well-known that commercial banks lent extensively without security. It is true that in the closing decades of the nineteenth century the banks increasingly required some security. Yet even by 1914 more than one half of all loans were given on the strength of no more than a personal guarantee (Capie and Collins, 1996).

What are the objections to that approach? They were cogently and forcefully set out in Schwartz (1997). The spread, she argues, reflects both liquidity and expectational forces. This yield spread usually varies procyclically. Why? This can be produced simply by the liquidity of lower quality debt falling in recessions, as default is more likely. Hence, widening spreads are a normal cyclical phenomenon, not a symptom of debt deflation. Further, as Crafts (1997) observes, if the debt deflation discussed works through households' balance sheets, then 'I am rather doubtful that the interest rate spread between commercial paper and the discount rate will be closely related to the relevant changes in household debt positions' (1997, p. 97). But, as he admits, data on household balance sheets are not readily available.

We carry out a similar exercise, following several previous authors who, albeit somewhat sceptical of the value of bond spreads as an indicator of a debt-deflation process at work, have nevertheless examined them in view of the difficulties attached to testing debt-deflation theories. (Eichengreen and Grossman, 1997, are an example of this group.) We share their scepticism, but also their willingness to see what, if anything, can be extracted from the measure.

Before doing so, though, there is another problem to be faced when studying the UK—the lack of a significant and active corporate bond market. To what can we relate the government bond yield in the absence of corporate bonds? We have chosen to use the dividend yield on the UK 'top 100' equity index for the comparison. That comparison is, of course, open to the objection that we are comparing a nominal yield (that on consols) with an income stream which can move to compensate for inflation. The comparison is, however, in our view justifiable in this period because of the stability of the price level and of the modesty of the year-on-year rate of change of the price level.

One further point remains to be noted. There is not a suitable index of dividend yields before 1900. Accordingly, we start the comparison at that date, and run it through to 1939.

What does the comparison reveal? First, the spread was *wider* before the First World War than in almost any year after it—and the years running up to 1914 were years of stability. Second, there are two big, short-lived, spikes in the series. The first occurred during the immediate post-war boom of 1919/20, and the second during the not much longer-lived return to gold. Although perhaps surprising in view of the criticism the return to gold has received, we would offer essentially the same explanation for both episodes. The first period was of actual boom, the latter of expected boom—for many welcomed the return to gold as signalling the return of pre-1914 style stability (see, e.g. Capie, Mills, and Wood, 1986). Thereafter the spread is narrow, not even reaching pre-First World War levels in the run-up to the Second World War.

Accordingly we conclude that, to the extent that the spread indicates a debt-deflation process at work (and we have noted our reservations about this) it shows no evidence of such a process working during the inter-war years in Britain.

Another channel is the effect of leverage on firms' investment spending. This has been proposed and tested by Calomiris, Orphanides, and Sharpe (1997), following work by Calomiris and Hubbard (1989) and Hubbard and Keycap (1992). They argue that it is necessary to test the effects at the firm rather than the aggregate level, and that the effects may be asymmetric Their reasons are as follows. First, aggregate debt/assets may not be a good indicator of the representative debt/asset ratio of firms. Leverage may be important only for cyclically sensitive firms, and its effects would thus not show up in aggregate data. And third, (they worked on post Second World War data) there were too few aggregate observations as the US had experienced only six recessions. As for asymmetry, they argue that capital constraints do not bind so long as a firm's sales are growing, but when sales drop debt service becomes a problem, so expenditures—particularly investment spending—are cut back. The approach is interesting, but the data to pursue it in our time periods do not exist.

INTER-TEMPORAL SUBSTITUTION

There is one final channel to explore. According to Keynes, falling prices could lead to further falls in prices if some consumption and investment decisions were deferred. One, albeit casual, way of doing this, is to look at house prices and equity price changes.

The 1930s saw a major house-building boom. Houses were bought not only by prosperous professionals, but by a much wider group, including skilled manual workers. Various house price series are available. None even purports to cover the whole country, or to represent the entire market.

Accordingly we report both a building cost and a house price series. Before doing so, though, we should remark that there were substantial regional price divergences (these are shown subsequently) and also substantial variation within cities. This intra-city variation was a systematic one; prices fell in the 'inner cities' relative to the new suburbs, as not only did the new houses in the suburbs have attractions such as electric light, but the suburbs were seen as healthier and therefore more attractive places to live. There was thus a systematic relative price change. This should be borne in mind, as the price series we report are essentially for newly-built (suburban) houses. These comprised, it should be said, a substantial part of the stock of housing; between 1919 and 1939 the stock of dwellings went up by about 30 per cent. The first series is Maywald's building cost index. After a sharp rise during the War and in the post war boom, costs fell, and then drifted gently from an index level of just above 100 in 1922 to a low point of just above 80 in 1933. They climbed gently thereafter. The average cost of dwelling houses fell from £700 in 1923 to just over £500 in 1932, and was more or less stable thereafter. It must be noted, though, that houses got somewhat smaller over the period; no series which adjusts for this is available. The 'Chamberlain' subsidy of £75 per house was introduced in late 1923; this seems to have produced a fall in the average house price despite a modest rise in building costs that occurred at the same time. Of course, the average price had a range of variation around it; and it showed substantial regional variation.

The inter-temporal substitution effect gets essentially no support from these data. There are no prolonged periods of falling house prices coinciding with years of recession and sluggish house sales. Thus there are few, if any, data here to support the deflation story. And even if there had been, it is hard to see how inter-temporal substitution could account for a prolonged recession; few items of expenditure can be postponed for many years, and if real interest rates drop the incentive to postpone is of course reduced.

CONCLUSIONS

In this chapter we have examined, as much as the data allow, how the debt-deflation theories of Keynes and Fisher contribute to a understanding of the behaviour of the British economy in either the first quarter of the nineteenth century or in the recession of the early 1930s. For Keynes's theory, the key is to see whether there is any evidence that price change was expected; and for Fisher, in contrast, one must see whether *unexpected* price change produced problems through any of the channels he or his followers listed. We also note arguments of Mundell on whether these price changes were anticipated.

After considering some qualitative views on price expectations we use some simple time series modelling techniques to produce price expectation series. (We also draw on some earlier work we did on expectations in the bond market which provided some support for the current work.) These expectations, in turn, are used to construct a variety of short and long-run interest rate series that accord with the views of Keynes and Fisher. On both prices and interest rates the evidence that emerges is that there is little difference between the actual series and the predicted series. We therefore conclude on this basis that deflation transmitted no adverse effects to the real economy through the channels suggested by these models.

Another way of examining the issue is, at least in theory, to consider the changing behaviour of bond rate spreads. This is beset with problems and these are even greater for the British than for the US economy at this time because of data scarcity. Nevertheless improvising, we did the exercise and again found little or no evidence of deflation transmitting adverse effects. Finally, we consider the possible role of inter-temporal substitution and found no support for that hypothesis either.

In summary, these periods of falling prices do not appear to have brought the calamitous effects that are sometimes thought to be the consequence of deflation. The various strands of evidence brought together here suggest also that there was in the UK little disturbance of the financial markets, and no evidence of financial instability. It is true that in the deflation of 1929 to 1932 falling prices and rigid money wages did produce unemployment. Yet even that was relatively short lived, and there followed a great boom from 1932 to 1937/38.

APPENDIX 1

Data

The interest rate employed is the yield on Consols, which has been used almost exclusively as the measure of the long-term rate of interest in this period. Series for short rates also exist, of course, but these are not as well suited to the examination of hypotheses about, or depending upon, the Fisher effect. The usual Consol yield series, given in Capie and Webber (1985: table III.10) for example, has, as both Harley (1976) and Capie and Webber (1985, pp. 316–20) point out, traditionally been miscalculated for the years 1880 to 1903. This miscalculation leads to an overestimation of the true yield for two reasons. The price of Consols in this period rose above par, thus increasing the possibility of redemption at par and decreasing the true yield, and the details of Fisher's conversion of the National Debt in 1889 affected the way in which Consol yields were calculated. We therefore employ a revised Consol yield series, that given in the appendix to Harley (1977), although related work reported in Capie, Mills, and Wood (1986) has used both this and the traditional series in similar exercises and found little difference in the results so obtained.

The output series used is Feinsten's (1972) compromise estimate of GIDP and hence his implicit GDP deflator is used as the price series. While there has been some discussion recently over the reliability of this output series—see the interchange between Greasley (1986; 1989) and Feinstein (1989) and the discussion in Crafts, Leybourne, and Mills (1989a)—it would still seem to be the best that is currently available.

Annual observations for all series are available from 1870 to 1913, except for M3, whose initial (1870) observation is missing. Details and descriptive discussion of the data and univariate analysis of the individual series is to be found in Capie, Mills, and Wood (1986). In particular, it is found, using a variety of methods, that the logarithms of both money series, output, and prices are an integrated processes of order one, that is, I(1), while the interest rate itself is I(1) findings that are confirmed by Taylor (1989).

APPENDIX 2

Level of GNP deflator

The GNP deflator was analysed over the two periods, 1870–1914 and 1919–39 using standard Box-Jenkins time-series procedures and appropriate models for describing the trend determined. Because of the differences in the underlying trends for the two periods, there was no single model suitable for both periods. The appropriate models determined are both autoregressive process, that is, the basic model is of the form:

$$X_t = \alpha_1 X_{t-1} + \alpha_2 X_{t-2} + \ldots + \alpha_p X_{t-p} + Z_t$$

where X_t is the observed GNP deflator in year t, α_t's are unknown parameters and Z_t is an error term assumed to have mean 0. The above expression describes an autoregressive process of order p, that is, an AR(p) process.

The order of the AR processes was determined by Akaike's information criterion (AIC). If k is the order of the current model, then

$$\text{AIC}(k) = -2 \ln \text{(maximized likelihood)} + 2k$$

The value of k that minimizes AIC(k) is chosen as the order of the AR process.

The models derived are as follows:

- Period 1919–39
  $Y_t = 0.99968(0.2408)\ Y_{t-1} - 0.45561(0.3233)Y_{t-2} + 0.11982(0.2408)\ Y_{t-3} + Z$
  where
  $Y_t = X_t - X_{t-1}$,
  implying that:
  $X_t = 1.99968X_{t-1} - 1.45529X_{t-2} + 0.57543X_{t-3} - 0.11982X_{t-4} + Z_t$
- Period 1870–1914
  Again setting: $Y_t = X_t - X_{t-1}$, the actual model fitted is
  $Y_t = 0.09046(0.3008)Y_{t-1} + 0.02707(0.3008)Y_{t-2} + Z_t$
  implying that:
  $X_t = 1.09046X_{t-1} - 0.06339X_{t-2} - 0.02707X_{t-3} + Z_t$

Hence predictions for the period 1919 to 1939 are based on the previous four years' observations while predictions for 1870 to 1914 are based on the previous three years' observations. The standard errors of the parameter estimates are give in parenthesis.

Rate of inflation

The rate of inflation, estimated by year-on-year rates of change in the GN deflator was similarly analysed, resulting in the following time series models:

- Period 1870–1939
  $X_t = 0.60651(0.0958)X_{t-1} + Z_t$

- Period 1870–1913
  $X_t = 0.27316(0.1467)X_{t-1} + Z_t$
- Period 1921–39
  $X_t = 0.46006(0.2093)X_{t-1} + Z_t$

Hence for the rate of inflation, predictions are simply based on the previous year's observation.

APPENDIX 3

A note on the course of some price series

The main features of movements in aggregate prices have been given in the text. It is only the aggregate price level, and the annual rate of change in that, which we model. However, we describe here the course of some individual commodity prices, together with some asset prices as found in residential properties and equities. Commodity prices for the period 1870 to 1914 all reflect the well-known trend of falling in the first part of the period followed by some modest recovery in the second part, though it is clear there was quite a bit of difference in the extent of the fall and rise across commodities. For example, to take just two–coal and metals were relatively flat throughout against the more obviously tumbling grain prices. Between the wars, the trend was generally downwards for most commodities, and they moved more closely together.

On asset prices, there are houses and equities but the limited data allow only much shorter period description. House price data are available for the inter–war years but not before that. These are interesting in that they show a steady if gentle decline for residential housing from 1923 (105 approx.) to 1938 (75 approx.). The sharpest movement came in 1931. Deflated costs show the same pattern. There was considerable regional difference but not always of the kind that might have been expected—see correlation table. Data on equities are also limited. An equity price index for the late nineteenth century was reported in Capie and Mills (1985). Although limited in coverage it showed some cyclical pattern around a flat trend in the first part of the period, followed by a step up to similar fluctuation around another flat trend in the second part of the period. Data are slightly more plentiful for the period after 1920/25. The first few years showed a strong upswing from the base of 100 to over 140 in 1929. But that collapsed after that point and reached a low point in 1933 at 80. There followed a strong recovery to 1937, then a loss of these gains so that the period ended where it began.

Interest rates reflect some of the course in these variables but not entirely. It is long rates that are of particular interest for this exercise. These are given only brief comment here since they are given separate treatment in a discussion of the Gibson Paradox—a topic that has predominated in this area in the late nineteenth century. Short rates for both periods are represented by both bank rate and prime bank bill rate. Bank rate oscillated around a mean of 3.5 per cent in the period 1870–1914. In the inter-war years it began in a higher range and fell to the fixed ('cheap money era') of 2 per cent in the 1930s. A better indicator of the market rate is found in the prime bank bill rate which was much more volatile. In the first period it shows more of the long-term pattern of a gentle U-shape. Between the wars it again shows much more movement but a very similar pattern to that of the bank rate. But as can be seen, it fell to below 1 per cent for most of the 1930s.

Long rates are captured in the yield on Consols. For the first period these show clearly that U-shape with a particularly exaggerated U in the 1890s. After the immediate post-war adjustment period (1919–21), the yield on consols remained at about 4.5 per cent without much deviation from 1922 to 1931. It then fell steeply, reaching a low of less than 3 per cent in the mid 1930s before drifting up to about 3.7 per cent in 1937.

REFERENCES

Bernanke, B. (1983) 'Non-Monetary Effects of the Financial Crisis in the Propagation of the Great Depression', *American Economic Review*, 73, 257–276.

Calomiris, C. W. and Hubbard, R. G. (1989) 'Price Flexibility, Credit Availability and Economic fluctuations', *Quarterly Journal of Economics*, 104 (August), 429–452.

——Orphanides, A, and Sharpe, S. A. (1997) 'Leverage as a State Variable for Employment, Inventory Accumulation and Fixed Investment', in Capie and Wood (eds) *Unregulated Banking*, London: Macmillan.

Capie, F. H. (1988) 'Structure Conduct Performance in British banking', in Cottrell and Moggridge, *Money and Power*, London: Macmillan.

——and Billings M. (2001) 'Profitability in English Banking in the Twentieth Century' *European Review of Economic History*.

——and Collins M. (1996) 'Industrial Bending by English Commercial Banks, 1860–1914', *Business History*, 38(1), 26–44.

——and Mills, T. C. (1985) 'Conservatism in British Banking', *Explorations in Economic History*, 1, 316–20.

——and Webber A. (1985) *A Monetary History of the UK*, Vol I: *Data, Sources, Methods*, London: George Allen & Unwin.

——and Wood G. E. (1991) *Unregulated Banking: Chaos or Order?* London: Macmillan.

——Mills, T. C. and Wood, G. E. (eds.) (1986) 'What Happened in 1931?' in *Financial Crises and the World Banking System*, London: Macmillan.

Crafts, N. F. R. (1997) 'Comment on Eichengreen and Grossman', in Capie and Wood, *Financial Crises and the World Banking System*, London: Macmillan.'

——Leybourne, S. J., and Mills, T. C. (1989a) 'The Climacteric in Late Victorian Britain and France: A Reappraisal of the Evidence', *Journal of Applied Econometrics*, 4, 103–17.

————(1989b) 'Trends and Cycles in British Industrial production 1700–1913', *Journal of the Royal Statistical Society*, Series A, 152, 43–60.

De Long, J. B. and Summers, L (1986) 'Is Increased Price Flexibility Stabilising?' American Economic Review, 76, 1031–44.

Eichengreen, B. (1992) *Golden Fetters: the Gold Standard and the Great Depression 1919–1939*, Oxford University Press.

——and Grossman, R. S. (1997) 'Debt-Deflation and Financial Instability: Two Historical Explorations', in F. H. Capie and G. E. Wood (eds.), *Asset Prices and the Real Economy*, London: Macmillan.

Feinstein, C. H. (1972) *National Income, Expenditure and Output of the United Kingdom, 1855–1965*, Cambridge University Press.

——(1989) 'Wages and the Paradox of the 1880s: A Comment; *Explorations in Economic History* 26 (April), 227–42.

Fisher, I. (1896) *Appreciation and Interest*, New York: Macmillan.

——(1907) *The Rate of Interest*, New York: Macmillan.

——(1930) *The Theory of Interest*, New York: Macmillan.

——(1933) 'Booms and Depressions', *Econometrica*, 1(1).

Friedman, M. (1992) *Money Mischief*, New York: Harcourt Brace.

——and Schwartz, A. J. (1963) *A Monetary History of the United States*, New York: NBER.

————(1982) *Monetary Trends in the United States and the United Kingdom*, New York: NBER.

Greaseley, D. (1986) 'British Ecomoic Growth: The Paradox of the 1880s and the Timing of the Climacteric', *Explorations in Economic History*, 23, 416–44.

Hamilton, J. (1987) 'Monetary Factors in the Great Depression', *Journal of Monetary Economics*, 19, 145–170.

——(1997) 'Measuring the Liquidity Effect', *American Economic Review*, 87(1) (March), 80–97.

Harley, C. K. (1976) 'Goschen's Conversion of the National Debt and the Yield on Consols', *Economic History Review*, XXIX, 101–5.

——(1977) 'The Interest Rate and Prices in Britain, 1873–1913: A Study of the Gibson Paradox', *Explorations in Economic History*, 14(1), 69–89.

Hubbard, R. G. and Kashyap, A (1992) 'Internet Net Worth and the Investment Process: An Application to US Agriculture', *Journal of Political Economy*, 100, 506–34.

Keynes, J. M. (1936) *The General Theory*, London: Macmillan.

——(1930) *A Treatise on Money*, London: Macmillan.

Lucas, R. E. (1972) 'Expectations and the Neutrality of Money', *Journal of Economic Theory*, 4, 103–124.

Mills, T. C. and Wood, G. E. (1992) 'Money and Interest Rates in Britain from 1870 to 1913', in S. R. Broadberry and N. E. Crafts (eds.), *Britain in the International Economy*, Cambridge University Press.

Mundell, R. A. (2000) 'A Reconsideration of the 20th Century', *American Economic Review*, 90, 327–40.

Schwartz, A. J. (1997) 'Comment on Eichengreen and Grossman', in Capie and Wood, *Financial Crises and the World Banking System*, London: Macmillan.

Tobin, J. (1975) 'Keynesian Models of Recession and Depression', *American Economic Review Proceedings*, 65, 195–202.

Weinstein, M. (1981) 'Some Macroeconomic Impacts of the National Recovery Act, 1933–35', in K. Bruner (ed.), *The Great Depression Revisited*, Boston: Martin Nijhoff.

Wicksell, K. (1907) 'The Influence of the Rate of Interest on Prices', *Economic Journal*, 17 (66) (June), 213–20.

6

Did Velocity Look U-Shaped? Britain in the Nineteenth Century

A particular aspect of the behaviour of the velocity of circulation of money in the UK over the period 1870 to 1980 is the subject of this paper. Our aim is not to fit a money demand function to the data and thus to explain velocity. Rather, we seek to examine the influence of variables that are generally omitted from such functions, perhaps because they have acted only once, or because they act in a slow fashion over a period of years. They are the kind of variables that would produce shifts in a conventional function, either gradually over the years or at a particular time. Various conjectures have in the past been offered as to which variables might exert such influences, and what the direction of influence would be. Irving Fisher (1911) predicted a secular rise in velocity as a result of technical progress such as the invention of aeroplanes and the telegraph. Wicksell (1936) also seemed to expect that.

> It is at once clear that the purely physical conditions under which money can be paid and transported set a definit limit to the magnitude of the velocity of circulation. Money cannot circulate faster—at any rate in a pure cash economy—than a messenger boy can run; its speed cannot exceed that of a mail van, train, or steamer to which is consigned the cash for making payment. (1936, pp. 54–55)

Garvy and Blyn (1969) elaborated this theory of institutional influences, suggesting that velocity followed the U-shaped path it did in the US from 1880 to 1960 as a result of institutional influences, such as the spread of banking, being in later years offset by the development of institutions whose deposits were to some degree substitutes for money. Bordo and Jonung (1981) elaborated the hypothesis of Garvey and Blyn, terming the spread of money 'monetization' and the spread of money substitutes 'financial sophistication', and arguing that the one following the other would produce a U-shape for the long-run behaviour of velocity. They then tested this hypothesis for five countries, and confirmed it, except for the UK.

In a study of the behaviour of velocity over the long term, various possibilities have to be kept in mind. One is that any apparent path may be chance—the accidental by-product of changes in tastes. A second is that the 'trend' is the result of movements in the variables which normally enter the demand function—income and interest rates. Third is that institutional factors have exerted a systematic long-run influence. This paper explores the third possibility. We first describe the data, and then review the contribution of Bordo and Jonung. Then we consider various developments which may have affected velocity in the UK.

THE DATA

For the years before 1922 it is not possible to separate time deposits from demand deposits (see Capie and Webber, 1985); therefore the velocity of M3 is examined before that date. After 1922, both M1 and M3 are examined. Figures 6.1 and 6.2 show the GNP/money series for both definitions of money.

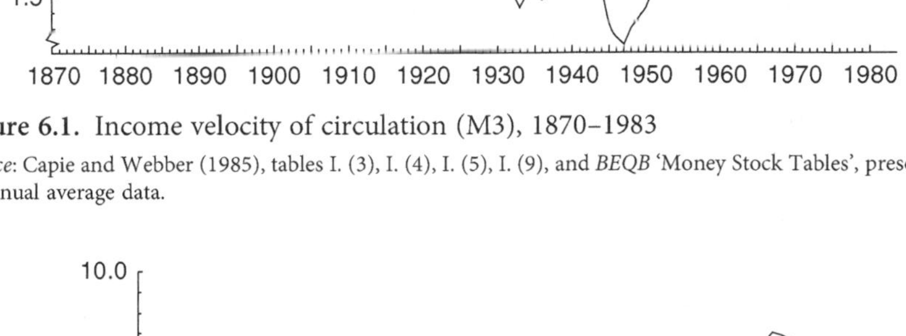

Figure 6.1. Income velocity of circulation (M3), 1870–1983

Source: Capie and Webber (1985), tables I. (3), I. (4), I. (5), I. (9), and *BEQB* 'Money Stock Tables', presented as annual average data.

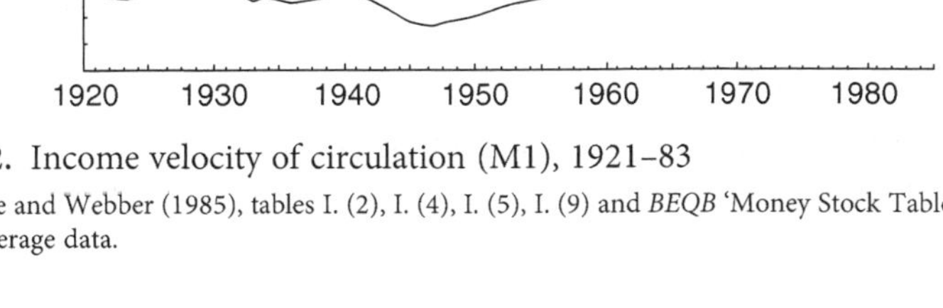

Figure 6.2. Income velocity of circulation (M1), 1921–83

Source: Capie and Webber (1985), tables I. (2), I. (4), I. (5), I. (9) and *BEQB* 'Money Stock Tables', presented as annual average data.

Consider first the behaviour of M3's velocity (V3). It is immediately clear that no distinct trend is apparent, until an approximation to a rather flat U shape emerges from 1918, touches bottom by 1947, and climbs to a peak in 1980.

M1's behaviour is rather similar. Again there is a U-shape, or perhaps more of a V-shape, with its trough in 1948 and its peak in 1980.

BORDO AND JONUNG

Bordo and Jonung developed in some detail a theory to underpin the finding that over a long period velocity followed a U-shaped path. Initially, they argued, an economy becomes 'monetized'. That is to say, the economy moves from barter or primitive money to using money for more and more transactions. Monetization both facilitates the increased division of labour and is promoted by it. (It is promoted by it as increased specialization requires more frequent exchanges.) As monetization proceeds, the ratio of money to income rises—velocity falls, the first part of the U.

The second stage, when 'financial sophistication' dominates, is characterized by the emergence of substitutes for money. These lower the desired money/income ratio. It should be noted that the effect of this process may be different on the narrow and on the broad aggregates. If both the substitutes and the broad aggregates bear interest, the emergence of the substitutes is likely to impinge rather more sharply on the velocity of the narrow aggregate. (The new financial instruments should also, by virtue of being substitutes for money, depress the velocity of the broad aggregate, but it is quite possible that this effect may be too small to be seen.)

Bordo and Jonung discuss various possible proxies for the processes of monetization and financial sophistication. Monetization is associated with the expansion of industrialization and with increased ease of access to banks. To capture the growth of industrialization they suggest as proxies the proportion of the labour force in non-agricultural pursuits, the ratio of cash wages to non-cash wages, the ratio of taxes paid in money to taxes paid in kind, and the proportion of the population living in towns. As indications of the spread of access to banks, they suggest the currency/money ratio, the number of bank branches, and the number of bank accounts per head. However, because of limited data availability and problems of comparability, they used only two proxies–the proportion of the labour force in non-agricultural production to represent industrialization, and the ratio of currency to the total money stock to capture monetization as the banking habit spread. As a measure of financial sophistication, Bordo and Jonung deployed the ratio of non-bank financial assets to bank financial assets. (It should be noted that among non-bank financial assets they included trust company deposits, bonds, and equities. This definition is discussed further below.)

Using this approach, they found they could explain the long-run behaviour of velocity for four countries in their study, but not for the UK. It was conjectured that this was due to industrialization and banking being well advanced in the UK before their data period stated.

THE PROXIES OF THIS CHAPTER

To test this conjecture further, we developed and used several additional proxies for monetization and financial sophistication. As an alternative to the share of labour in non-agricultural production, we used urbanization. This was done because of the possibility that industries in rural areas were slower to monetize than those in cities, so the share of labour in non-agricultural activities might give a misleading impression of the trend of monetization. Instead of the currency/money ratio, we used the currency/deposit ratio; reducing the numerator in this way both better captures the intention of the series, and makes it sharper-moving. This was supplemented by the number of bank branches, as these would both follow and encourage the course of monetization; bank deposits per head; and the number of cheque clearings per head. Tables 6.1 and 6.2 show all these series on five-yearly basis.

For financial sophistication, we followed a slightly different approach from that pioneered by Bordo and Jonung. The basic hypothesis is that as money substitutes emerge as a result of financial sophistication, velocity (other things being equal) rises. Bordo and Jonung used the ratio of non-bank financial assets to bank financial assets as a measure of financial sophistication. It is a useful measure of that, but it does suffer from a problem. 'Non-bank financial assets' are a distinctly heterogeneous group. Their growth may have been dominated by assets which are not close substitutes for money. In that case, looking at the behaviour of the aggregates, although revealing what 'financial sophistication' overall did to velocity, would conceal some information. Accordingly, we disaggregated that category somewhat. We looked at the influence of the growth of building society deposits, life assurance premiums, and pension funds, throughout the period as one category—all these being means of saving open to the small saver. We also examined the effect of the growth of the amount of government securities—an index of the total value was constructed—as these are highly marketable. Finally, we also examined the growth of credit finance companies, in an attempt to capture the influence of credit cards and extended credit arrangements more generally. Regrettably we were not able to devise a proxy to test directly Irving Fisher's hypothesis that as technology increased speed of settlement, velocity would rise.

Table 6.1. Monetization

Year	Share of pop. in major towns	Total no. of bank branches	*Currency* deposits	*Currency* M3	Clearings per capita (000s)	
	%				Nominal	Real
1870	27.8	2728			–	–
1875	27.8 (0)	3205 (1 ‘.51)	0.201	0.167	–	–
1880	28.3 (1.8)	3454 (7.77)	0.176 (−12.4)	0.150 (−10.2)	172	167
1885	32.3 (14.1)	3730 (7.99)	0.160 (−9.1)	0.138 (−8.0)	158 (8.14)	178 (6.59)
1890	33.8 (4.6)	4347 (16.54)	0.144 (−10.0)	0.126 (−8.7)	217 (37.34)	249 (39.89)
1895	34.8 (3.0)	4888 (12.45)	0.126 (−12.5)	0.112 (−11.1)	209 (−3.69)	258 (3.61)
1900	36.0 (3.4)	5922 (21.15)	0.125 (−0.79)	0.111 (−1.8)	237 (13.40)	266 (3.10)
1905	45.9 (27.5)	6759 (14.13)	0.109 (−12.8)	0.098 (−11.7)	307 (29.53)	341 (28.20)
1910	47.3 (3.1)	7564 (11.91)	0.106 (−2.8)	0.095 (−3.1)	348 (13.36)	370 (8.50)
1915	51.3 (8.5)	8494 (12.30)	0.093 (−12.3)	0.084 (−11.6)	358 (2.87)	296 (−20)
1920		9668 (13.82)	0.169 (81.7)	0.145 (72.6)	911 976*	373 400*
					(154.47) (172.63)	(26.0) (35.14)
1925		11300+ (16.89)	0.151 (−10.7)	0.131 (−9.7)	952 (−2.46)	550 (37.5)
1930		12716 (12.53)	0.133 (−11.9)	0.118 (−9.9)	991 (4.10)	639 (16.18)
1935		12979 (2.07)	0.132 (−0.8)	0.117 (−0.8)	838 (−15.44)	599 (−6.26)
1940		12458 (−4.01)	0.164 (24.2)	0.141 (20.5)	868 (3.58)	485 (−19.03)
1945		10806 (−13.26)	0.208 (26.8)	0.172 (22.0)	1389 (60.02)	615 (26.80)
1950		12447 (15.19)	0.176 (−15.4)	0.150 (−12.8)	1913 (37.72)	676 (9.92)
1955			0.219 (24.4)	0.180 (20.0)	3054 (59.64)	823 (21.75)
1960			0.248 (13.2)	0.199 (10.6)	4366 (42.96)	1035 (25.76)
1965			0.240 (−3.2)	0.194 (−2.5)	7731 (77.07)	1537 (48.50)
1970			0.241 (0.04)		14135 (83.84)	2247 (46.19)

Note: Population total excluding Southern Ireland.

Sources: Column 1: Weekly & Quarterly Returns, 1870–1915, Census office, 76th Report of Registrar General, Census office.

Column 2: Capie and Webber (1985); Sheppard (1971). Data adjusted by a factor of 1.06 to match Capie and Webber (1985) data.

Columns 3, 4, 5: Capie and Webber (1985).

Table 6.2. Bank deposits

Year	Demand deposits p.c.		Total deposits p.c.	
	Nominal	Real	Nominal	Real
	(000s)	(000s)	(000s)	(000s)
1875	–	–	15.54	14.26
1880	–	–	13.49 (−13.19)	13.10 (−8.13)
1885	–	–	14.34 (6.30)	16.28 (24.27)
1890	–	–	15.67 (9.27)	18.01 (10.63)
1895	–	–	16.91 (7.91)	20.88 (15.94)
1900	–	–	19 37 (14.55)	21.76 (4.21)
1905	–	–	18.79 (−2.99)	20.88 (−4.04)
1910	–	–	20.23 (7.66)	21.52 (3.07)
1915	–	–	26.25 (29.76)	21.69 (0.79)
1920	–	–	(97,94) 51.96	21.30 (−1.80)
			(111.89)* 55.62*	22.80* 15.12*
1925	24.30	14.05	45.96 (−17.37)	26.57 (16.54)
1930	23.49 (−3.33)	15.15 (7.83)	48.25 (4.98)	31.13 (17.91)
1935	26.94 (14.69)	19.24 (27.0)	53.37 (16.61)	38.12 (22.13).
1940	34.83 (29.29)	19.46 (1.14)	61.61 (15.44)	34.42 (−9.71)
1945	72.09 (106.98)	31.90 (63.93)	111.85 (81.55)	49.49 (43.78)
1950	88.36 (22.57)	31.22 (−2.13)	137.59 (23.01)	48.62 (−1.76)
1955	88.67 (0.35)	23.90 (−23.45)	144.80 (5.24)	39.03 (−19.72)
1960	87.18 (−1.13)	20.66 (−13.56)	157.75 (8.94)	37.38 (−4.23)
1965	95.38 (9.40)	18.96 (−8.23)	184.06 (16.68)	36.52 (−2.30)
1970	09.62 (4.50)	15.85 (−16.40)	212.02 (15.19)	33.7 (−9.84)

Sources: Capie and Webber (1985); Feinstein (1972).

Another conjecture of Bordo and Jonung's was that increased economic stability would diminish the demand for money, by reducing the emergencies for which individuals (and presumably also companies) would suddenly want cash. In addition, these emergencies may be reduced in some countries—among them the UK—by the growth of the welfare state. We examined the first influence via the same measure as that of Bordo and Jonung—a six-yearly moving average standard deviation of the annual percentage change in national income per head. For the second, we used the percentage of GNP spent on social services.

These, then, are the proxies used. We set out how they were used in the next section.

INFLUENCES ON VELOCITY

In this section, we proceed by examining whether monetization, as measured by any of our proxies, is going on while velocity is declining, and then whether financial sophistication is proceeding as velocity is rising. This section of the analysis is in two stages. We first consider monetization and financial sophistication separately, and trace their respective paths along with that of velocity. Second, to ascertain the combined influences of monetization and financial sophistication we look at them jointly, over years when the trend of velocity seems to change—these being 1870–1917, 1918–47, and 1948–70. The data for our monetization proxies are in Table 6.1; they are plotted in Figure 6.3. We consider first urbanization. The share of population

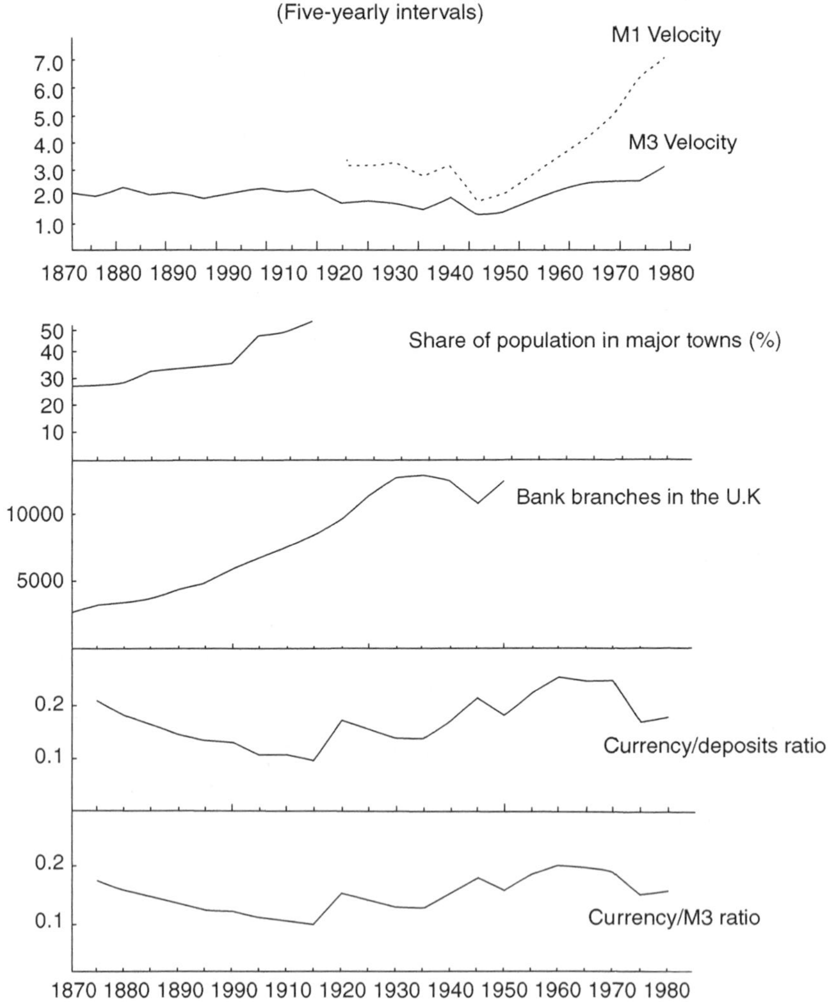

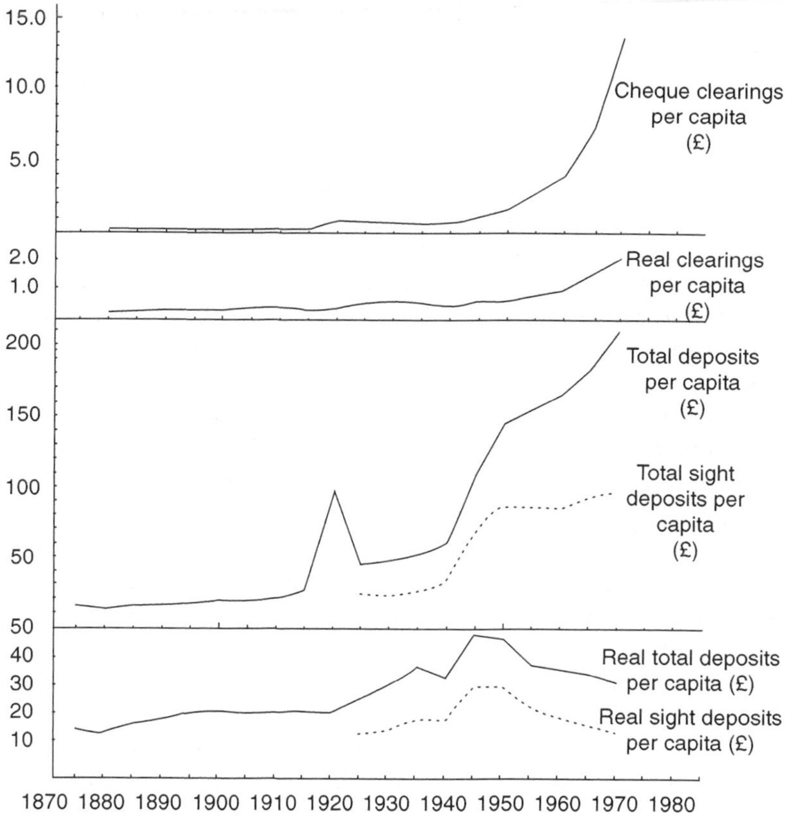

Figure 6.3. Velocity and monetization measures, 1870–1980

in major towns was growing steadily over the period 1870–1915. Over the same period, velocity increased, albeit very slightly. By this measure, then monetization does not seem to have imparted (as has been conjectured in the past) a downward trend to velocity.

This most certainly does not reject the hypothesis, however. In principle, the entire population could be living in towns, all using money, while no one was in what was under the census definition a major town. A further problem is that the census definition of a major town changed several times, and the data are not available to construct a complete series from 1870 to 1970. The series is, however, consistent from 1870 to 1914, and, as noted above, seems not to affect velocity in the hypothesized direction.

We turn next to the spread of banking services. As the table shows, with the exception of 1935–45, the number of bank branches in the UK has increased continually. This does not help to explain the observed behaviour of velocity. What of the rate of change of the rate of increased in bank branches? This series is more variable. In addition, it can be argued that it is the better way to use the series, as an acceleration may reflect an increase in demand to use banking services. This transformation of the series does not help however. From 1870 to 1920 (a period of a slight rise in velocity) the number of bank branches was rising rapidly. Then, looking at a period of decreasing velocity, 1920–35, the rate of spread of banking is also falling.

We next looked at the currency to deposit ratio, and the currency to money ratio. (The two series of course move fairly closely together.) A fall in the ratio of currency to deposits reflects increased use of banks-monetization—and hence should be accompanied by a fall in velocity. In fact from 1870–1920 the opposite of this relationship is observed—a *rise* in velocity (albeit modest) goes with a fall in the ratio.

From 1920 to 1945, when velocity is declining, so is the currency/deposit ratio, consistent this time with the hypothesis. The behaviour of the currency/deposit ratio thus gives a mixed view of the hypothesis. Even this, however, is complicated further. Both end points of falls in the currency/deposit ratio were at the end of wars, when expenditure was depressed. The fall in the ratio may have been exaggerated by their being little to spend on and may not simply be an indication of monetization. Looking at cheque clearings per head, another measure of the use of bank services, these have generally increased steadily. There are, however, three periods when they decline—and velocity falls, in contradiction to the hypothesis.

Overall, then, none of the measures of monetization (separately or taken together) fits in timing or, except occasionally, direction of movement with the hypothesis that velocity declined in the UK as monetization spread. What of financial sophistication? Bordo and Jonung argue that increasing financial sophistication is a major cause of a secular rise in velocity. They suggest that as non-bank financial intermediaries increase, and also offer a wider range of assets, the demand for money, including bank deposits, will fall relative to income. This of course will increase velocity. Does financial sophistication, by any measure, increase velocity?

We first examine the growth of non-bank financial intermediaries—in particular, building societies, life assurance companies, and Trustee Savings Banks (Table 6.3). All these grew, but at different rates at different times. Building Society deposits, for example, have fallen as well as risen. They grew from 1870–85, then fell for thirty-five years, grew rapidly until 1940, declined for ten years, and from 1950 have increased steadily. Deposits at life assurance companies have grown steadily, with the exception of 1910–20 and 1935–45—both periods which included wars. Their growth rate 1880–1965, however (3432 per cent) is just under half that of building societies (6570 per cent). Some of these movements are consistent with the hypothesized effect of financial sophistication, and others are not—clearly the hypothesis can not devise support from this.

Table 6.3. Development of the non-bank financial institutions

Year	Building soc.		Life assurance		Trustee savings		Bonds + savings		NBPA
	Deposits p.c. (£ml)		Funds p.c. (£ml)		Deposits p.c. (£ml)		Certificates p.c. (£ml)		TPA %
	Nom.	Real.	Nom.	Real.	Nom.	Real.	Nom.	Real.	
1870	–	–	–	–	–	–	–	–	–
1875	–	–	–	–	–	–	–	–	–
1880	1.44	1.39	3.58	3.48	2.31	2.24	0.03	0.029	0.31
1885	1.78 (23.61)	2.00 (43.88)	3.97 (10.89)	4.46 (28.16)	2.69 (16.45)	3.02 (34.82)	0.08 (166.67)	0.089 (206.90)	0.333 (7.42)
1890	1.71 (3.93)	1.97 (−1.5)	4.43 (11.59)	5.09 (14.13)	3.09 (14.87)	3.55 (17.55)	0.16 (100.0)	0.18 (102.25)	0.339 (2.73)
1895	1.27 (−25.73)	1.57 (−20.3)	5.07 (14.44)	6.26 (22.99)	3.77 (22.01)	4.65 (30.99)	0.18 (12.5)	0.22 (22.22)	0.344 (1.47)
1900	1.34 (5.51)	1.51 (−3.82)	5.98 (17.95)	6.72 (7.35)	4.67 (23.87)	5.25 (12.90)	0.32 (77.78)	0.36 (63.64)	0.357 (5.31)
1905	1.49 (11.19)	1.66 (9.93)	6.89 (15.22)	7.00 (13.99)	4.89 (4.71)	5.43 (3.43)	0.44 (37.5)	0.49 (36.11)	0.393 (10.08)
1910	1.56 (4.70)	1.66 (0)	7.77 (12.77)	8.27 (7.96)	5.17 (5.73)	5.5 (1.29)	0.56 (27.27)	0.60 (22.45)	0.398 (1.27)
1915	1.29 (−17.31)	1.07 (−3.55)	8.42 (8.37)	6.96 (−15.84)	5.46 (5.60)	4.51 (−18.0)	2.29 (308.93)	1.89 (215)	0.368 (−7.54)
1920	1.71/1.83*	0.75/0.80*	9.35/10.02*	3.83/4.11*	7.65/8.19)*	3.14/3.36	11.32/12.12*	4.64/4.97*	0.327
	(32.56)	(−29.91)	(11.05)	(−44.97)	(40.01)	(−30.4)	(394)	(145.5)	(−11.14)
	(41.86)	(25.23)	(19.0)	(−40.95)	(50.0)	(−25.49)	(429)	(161.38)	
1925	3.44 (87.98)	1.99 (148.75)	12.65 (26.25)	7.31 (77.86)	8.94 (9.16)	5.17 (53.87)	14.65 (20.87)	8.47 (70.42)	0.424 (29.66)
1930	7.57 (120.06)	4.88 (145.23)	16.02 (26.64)	10.34 (41.45)	9.51 (6.38)	6.14 (18.76)	15.00 (2.39)	9.68 (14.29)	0.464 (9.43)
1935	11.99 (58.39)	8.55 (75.41)	19.27 (20.29)	13.76 (33.08)	12.99 (36.59)	9.28 (51.14)	14.36 (−4.27)	10.26 (5.99)	0.489 (5.39)
1940	14.41 (20.18)	8.05 (−5.95)	21.86 (13.44)	12.21 (−11.26)	19.97 (53.73)	11.16 (20.26)	24.88 (73.26)	13.90 (35.48)	0.527 (7.77)
1945	15.45 (7.21)	6.84 (−15.03)	25.29 (15.69)	11.19 (−8.35)	49.88 (149.77)	22.07 (97.76)	52.71 (111.86)	23.32 (67.77)	0.530 (0.57)
1950	23.10 (49.51)	8.16 (19.30)	33.13 (31.0)	11.71 (4.65)	57.95 (16.18)	20.48 (−7.20)	65.08 (23.47)	23.00 (−1.37)	0.522 (−1.51)
1955	38.26 (65.53)	10.31 (26.35)	48.76 (47.18)	13.14 (12.21)	55.75 (−3.46)	15.03 (−26.61)	65.87 (1.21)	17.75 (−22.83)	0.539 (3.26)
1960	56.19 (46.86)	13.32 (29.19)	75.44 (54.72)	17.88 (36.07)	59.38 (6.51)	14.07 (−6.39)	80.08 (21.57)	18.98 (6.93)	0.582 (7.98)
1965	94.61 (68.38)	18.81 (41.22)	122.88 (62.88)	24.43 (35.63)	72.44 (21.99)	14.40 (2.35)	75.76 (−5.41)	16.06 (−20.65)	0.613 (5.33)

Notes: *Population total excluding Southern Ireland.
NBFA = Non-Bank Financial Assets.
TFA = Total Financial Assets.
Total non-bank Financial assets = Building Society Deposits + Life Assurance Fund + Trustee Savings Deposits + Bonds, Savings Certificates.
Sources: UK: Sheppard (1971, pp. 182–83); Capie and Webber (1935).

Deposits at Trustee Savings Banks grew by 3136 per cent over the whole of the period. Their highest rate of increase was over 1924–45, a period when velocity was falling—again an inconsistency with the hypothesis.

Looking at these variables as measures of financial sophistication, it is difficult to conclude that financial sophistication has increased velocity; these measures show no systematic relationship to velocity movements. Looking next at the measure employed by Bordo and Jonung, the ratio of non-bank financial assets to total financial assets, this rises fairly steadily, and shows no sign of acceleration in a period of rising velocity (Table 6.3).

We next, therefore, turned to an examination of increasing economic stability and, important in the UK, the introduction of the welfare state (Table 6.4). Neither of these measures helps. Economic stability, as measured by a fall in the six-year moving average standard deviation of change in increase per head, has been gradually increasing—in periods of falling as well as of rising velocity. The share of income spent on social services (defined as education, health, social security, and unemployment benefits) has generally trended upwards. It fell, however, over 1950–55, when velocity was increasing—again a 'perverse' result.

Table 6.4 Economic stability

Date	6-Year MSD of Y	*Social Serv.* GNP %
1880	1.33	
1885	2.53	
1890	4.93	1.96
1895	4.91	2.72
1900	10.52	2.84
1905	2.53	3.77
1910	11.32	4.36
1915	2.60	3.49
1920	3.35	7.24
1925	3.30	9.18
1930	4.57	11.13
1935	3.17	11.86
1940	1.69	–
1945	3.79	–
1950	2.56	17.80
1955	1.60	16.14
1960	2.14	
1965	2.22	
1970		

Sources: Col. 1: Capie and Webber (1985).
Col. 2: Peacock and Wiseman (1961).

RELATIVE IMPORTANCE OF MONETIZATION AND FINANCIAL SOPHISTICATION

Bordo and Jonung's explanations for decreasing and increasing velocity depend on the *relative* trends in monetization and financial sophistication. Predominence of monetization over financial sophistication causes velocity to decrease, the reverse being the case for increasing velocity. Therefore, to test further the Bordo-Jonung hypothesis it is useful to look simultaneously at the trends in monetization and financial sophistication, and determine whether one is more important then the other.

Over the period 1870–1917, income velocity of circulation slightly increased. Building society deposits decreased slightly over this period, but life assurance funds and trustee savings band deposits are on the increase, with an average growth rate of 3.4 per cent per annum, whereas bank deposits increased at an annual rate of 1.5 per cent. Thus, on the basis of this evidence one could perhaps conclude that financial sophistication dominates monetization, and is the cause of increasing velocity of circulation.

Through the period 1917–47, velocity of circulation has generally decreased; thus one should anticipate that monetization is the stronger force. Total bank deposits per capita are increasing at an annual rate of 4.95 per cent whereas, except for the life assurance funds, the rate of increase of non-bank financial institutions has been much greater, an average rate of 8.3 per cent. Thus, despite the fact that velocity is decreasing, financial sophistication dominates the rate of increase of monetization. The relationship between the relative importance of financial sophistication and monetization breaks down during this period.

The years 1948–80 show a rapid rise in velocity. Thus financial sophistication is expected to predominate. During this period, time and demand deposits increased only slightly, at about 3.2 per cent per annum. However, clearings per capita, which also reflect the demand for banking services, increased rapidly, at an annual rate of 10 per cent. Of the non-bank financial institutions, it is only the building society and life assurance funds which are increasingly rapidly, at an annual rate of 10 per cent and 8.79 per cent respectively. On the basis of this one could therefore again conclude that financial sophistication predominates during this period, and thus explains rising velocity. This conclusion can, however, be reached only by selective reading of the evidence.

CONCLUSIONS

Having devised various proxies for monetization and financial sophistication, we used these to examine a hypothesis associated with, inter alia, Fisher (1911), Wicksell (1936), Garvey and Blyn (1969), and, in its most refined form, Bordo and Jonung (1981). The hypothesis is that, as monetization is followed by financial sophistication, velocity would tend over a long period of years first to fall and then to rise. We found really no evidence to support this for the UK over the years 1870 to 1980. This is the same result Bordo and Jonung (1981) found in their cross-country comparative study. Our first conclusion is therefore in line with theirs: banking was well advanced in the UK before 1870 so the secular forces affecting velocity had in that country largely done their work before the start of the period. Our second conclusion follows from that: explanations of the behaviour of velocity in the UK over this period must be sought along conventional money demand lines, as followed by, for example, Friedman and Schwartz (1982). Monetization and Financial Sophistication seem to have had no systematic effect on the behaviour of the velocity of circulation of money in the UK between 1870 and 1980.

REFERENCES

Bordo, M. D. and Jonung, L. (1981) 'The Long-Run Behaviour of the Income Velocity of Money in Five Advanced Countries, 1870–1975: An Institutional Approach', *Economic Inquiry*, 19 (January), 96–116.

Capie, F. and Webber A. (1985) *A Monetary History of the United Kingdom. 1870–1982*: Vol. 1., London: George Allen & Unwin.

Census Office (1915) 'Weekly and Quarterly Returns, 1870–1915' 76th Report of Registrar General.

Collins, M. (1981) 'The English Banking Sector and Monetary Growth', Discussion paper series, No. 102, January, University of Leeds.

Feinstein, C. H. (1972) *Statistical Tables of National Income, Expenditure and Output of the U.K., 1885–1965*, Cambridge University Press.

Fisher, I. (1911) *The Purchasing Power of Money*. Reprinted 1971, New York: A. M. Kelly.

Friedman, M., and Schwartz A. (1963) *A Monetary History of the United States, 1867–1960*, New York: NBER.

——(1982) *Monetary Trends in the United States and the United Kingdom: Their Relation to Income, Prices and Interest Rates, 1867–1975*, New York: NBER.

Garvey, G. and Blyn, M. R. (1969) 'The Velocity of Money', Federal Reserve Bank of New York.

Holmans, A. E. (1961) 'The Quantity of Money, Gross National Product, and the Price Level: Some International comparisons', *Scottish Journal of Political Economy*, 8(1) (February), 28–44.

Hun, L. T. (1966) 'Substitutability of Non-Bank Intermediary Liabilities for Money: The Empirical Evidence', *The Journal of Finance*, 21 (September), 441–57.

Peacock, A. T. and Wiseman, J. (1961) *The Growth of Public Expenditure in the United Kingdom*, New York: NBER, Unwin University Books.

Rousseau, S. W. (1972) *Monetary Theory*, New York: Alfred Knopf, Books in Economics, 1972.

Sheppard, D. K. (1971) *The Growth and Role of the U.K. Financial Institutions*, 1880–1962, London: Methuen.

Wicksell, K. (1936) 'Interest and Prices', *A Study of the Causes of Regulating the Value of Money*. Reprints of London: Economics Classics.

Part Two

7

What Happened in 1931?*

In 1931 Britain left the gold standard. Why? Was sterling pushed off gold by the backwash of the banking crisis in continental Europe? Was the UK rendered illiquid as a result of the loss of reserves experienced by the primary producers of the Empire as their terms of trade worsened? Or did the cause lie rather in UK policy, in the overvalued sterling exchange rate or the large budget deficit?

These causes are, of course, not mutually exclusive—they all may have played some part. Whether they did, and if so what was their relative importance, is a problem of considerable interest—first in itself, and second in helping to understand why Britain left the gold standard, as opposed to devaluing but staying on gold. If the system were brought down by a crisis, then abandoning gold is readily comprehensible. But if the UK's problem was UK policy, why was sterling not just devalued?

This paper explores these issues, using recently available data and some aspects of economic analysis which, although by no means new, have not previously been brought to bear on this episode.

The argument is in four main sections. First we describe what is usually meant by a financial crisis, and proceed to consider whether there is any evidence that the crisis of continental Europe spread to the UK financial system. We then examine (as far as the data allow) the impact, and timing of this impact, of the worsening terms of trade of primary producers on their London financial assets. That clears the way for consideration of domestic UK policies. Was the budget deficit excessive in any sense? Was the exchange rate the problem Keynes (and many subsequently) made it out to be?

* Originally published as Forrest Capie, Terence Mills, and Geoffrey Wood (1986), 'What Happened in 1931?' pp. 120–48, in Forrest Capie and Geoffrey Wood (eds), *Financial Crises and the World Banking System*. (Palgrave Macmillan), reproduced with the permission of Palgrave Macmillan.

FINANCIAL CRISIS

Is the financial system fragile or robust? Some favour the latter and claim that no crises are possible so long as the money supply is controlled by a set of rules, markets are left to function efficiently, and exchange rates allowed to move to purchasing power parity. On that view, crises are only possible when governments depart from sensible rules. There are those who believe, however, that it is difficult to set the rules and that in the short run financial crises are possible. But what is a financial crisis? One suggestion is that it can be identified when owners of wealth shift quickly out of one type of asset into another. The lender-of-last-resort function consists of 'providing the sought-after liquid assets in abundant amount, and this slows down the stampede'.

Drawing on the work of Minsky (1972), Kindleberger (1982) has elaborated the anatomy of a typical crisis. According to this analysis the crisis starts with an exogenous shock such as a harvest failure; prices rice, new opportunities present themselves and a boom is fed by an expansion of bank credit. Further price rises in turn lead to new profit opportunities and new investment, and a general state of euphoria. There follows speculation on price increases, and as some see others making profits they follow. In other words, a crisis is characterized by a certain amount of irrationality. In the boom, interest rates rise, velocity of circulation of money increases, and prices rise. Then at some point insiders decide to take their profits and get out. There is a hesitation in the market, prices level off, and a race to get out of real assets begins. A specific signal may be the failure of a bank. Finally, prices fall so low that people once more move back from cash into less liquid assets. Certainly many of these features, in that sequence, were present in the financial crises that occurred in the nineteenth century. But does this anatomy of a crisis in any way describe the events in Britain in 1931?

A FORMAL MODEL

Most work by economists (and others) on crises has been verbal rather than mathematical. This in part reflects that until recently most such work has been by writers who were at least as much practical men, men of affairs, as they were scholars. Walter Bagehot is an excellent example. Mathematical techniques, or at any rate their use in print, were confined largely to scholars. The above typology of a crisis continues that tradition, drawing as it does on the work of economists whose studies are rooted in economic history—and often particular episodes in history—rather than in formal economic analysis.

In this section a rudimentary formalization of these ideas is set out. Doing so inevitably loses the richness of detail which characterizes the work of these scholars—and also the vividness of narratives. But that loss can bring gain; the main, the central, and essential features of a crisis can be laid bare.

This will enable a test to be developed which will separate 'crises' from other events—it will lead to a formal definition of a crisis. Whether the test can be applied to the problem of the current chapter will then be considered.

THE APPROACH

It is the characteristic of a crisis that it be unexpected. It strikes suddenly, and cannot be anticipated—it can be prepared against only by being continually in readiness. In Frank Knight's terminology, it is associated with uncertainly, *not* with risk. There is no probability distribution, whether known a priori or from experience, on the basis of which the likelihood of a crisis occurring on any one day, or at any one time in the future, can be calculated. It is an unexpected change in the model which generates events.

As is now fairly well established the 'best' (defined below) way to model any process which generates a series of future events is to construct a statistical model of the time series. This may not supply a behavioural explanation, but strictly in terms of forecasting it is the 'best'—that is, most accurate—approach. Such time-series models use all the information which went into generating the series. A crisis can then be viewed as unpredictable change in the time series.

THE MODEL

A very straightforward example can be found in Meltzer (1982).

Suppose that a variable X is generated by a process such that X at any time (i.e. X_t), is $A_t e^{a(t)t} u_t(1)$ where A, a, and u are random walks, with (for example) $\ln u_t \sim N(o, \sigma_u^2)$.

If A_t and $a(t)$ are constants $\ln X_t$ is expected to change at a constant rate through time. Hence X (whatever it is—share price, national income) will deviate randomly from a constant, stationary trend. In any one period there is risk of departure from trend, but the trend is constant and the expected value at any one time (or an average over time) is known. So far, there is *risk*, but not *uncertainty*.

Uncertainty can now be introduced.

The expected value of $\log X$ at $t + j$ is not just a random walk around a trend.

$$E\ \ln X_{t+j} = E\ \ln A_{t+j} + E\ a_{t+J}(j - t)$$

A and a are assumed to be random walks.

$$E\Delta\ \ln X_{t+n} = E\Delta\ \ln A_{t+n} + E(\Delta a_{t+n}(n - t) + a_{t+n})$$

Changes in A change the level of X, but not the trend. Changes in a alter the trend rate of growth. X_t therefore changes in three ways—transitory random deviations about the trend line, given by u_t; permanent changes in level, given by $\Delta\ \ln A_t$; and permanent changes in growth rate, Δa. The diagram summarizes the three effects.

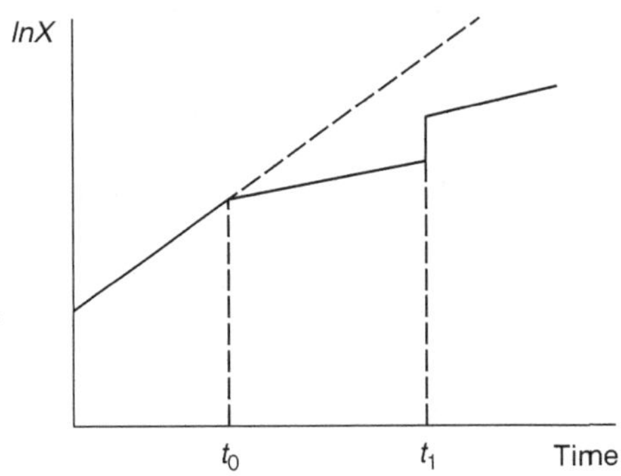

The solid line is the actual path of X. Should neither A nor a change, it would continue beyond t_0 along the dashed line. But a fell at t_0, and A changed (increased) at t_1.

Neither of the events could be anticipated before t_0, because they had not been observed, and we had assumed they could not be deduced a priori. Only the actual values of A, a, and ln u_t were known. A sudden change in A or a is, in the definition above, a *crisis*—although whether large or small depends on the size of the change (inter alia).

APPLICATION

In the present chapter, part of the question addressed is whether there was a crisis in any part of the UK financial system. Series examined for this are prices and various interest rates. We do not formally apply the above test, looking for changes in A or a, because of the small number of observations in each time series. Rather they are examined informally for evidence of such change. This is admittedly non-rigorous, but the non-rigorous application of the above analysis is forced on us by data limitations. If (as turns out to be the case) we reject the hypothesis of a crisis in the financial system on this informal basis, and are incorrect to do so in the sense that a formal test, had it been possible, would have supported the hypothesis, the probability is that the 'crisis' was so small as to be one only in the above, statistical, sense, and not in any practical sense.

The above analysis is also applied formally (modelling *A* and *a* as potential crisis in a time series) to the behaviour of prices and a proxy for price expectations. Was the abandoning of gold preceded, or followed, by a 'crisis' in either of these series?

FINANCIAL MARKETS

The crisis came in the summer of 1931 in the shape of a loss of Bank of England reserves and culminated in the abandonment of the gold standard in

Table 7.1. Money, prices, and interest rates, 1930–31

	Total bank deposits £m	Prices & cost of living (1924=100)	3-month bank bill rate	Consol yield
1930				
January	2230.7	94.0	3.938	4.329
February	2162.1	92.0	3.438	4.630
March	2126.0	90.0	2.344	4.386
April	2162.3	89.0	2.422	4.567
May	2196.7	88.0	2.125	4.454
June	2252.4	88.5	2.219	4.525
July	2253.2	89.5	2.282	4.525
August	2224.0	89.5	2.047	4.494
September	2225.2	89.0	2.125	4.484
October	2257.4	89.5	2.063	4.348
November	2266.6	88.5	2.173	4.283
December	2306.0	87.5	2.297	4.340
1931				
January	2304.8	87.0	2.469	4.310
February	2242.3	86.0	2.672	4.425
March	2177.3	84.0	2.594	4.386
April	2145.7	84.0	2.563	4.274
May	2150.2	83.0	2.079	4.158
June	2204.2	84.0	2.063	4.132
July	2211.6	83.0	4.344	4.310
August	2160.9	83.0	4.251	4.348
September	2121.6	83.0	5.813	4.717
October	2136.7	83.5	5.594	4.425
November	2116.1	84.5	5.844	4.739
December	2153.4	84.0	5.625	4.545

Sources: Capie and Collins (1983); Capie and Webber (1985).

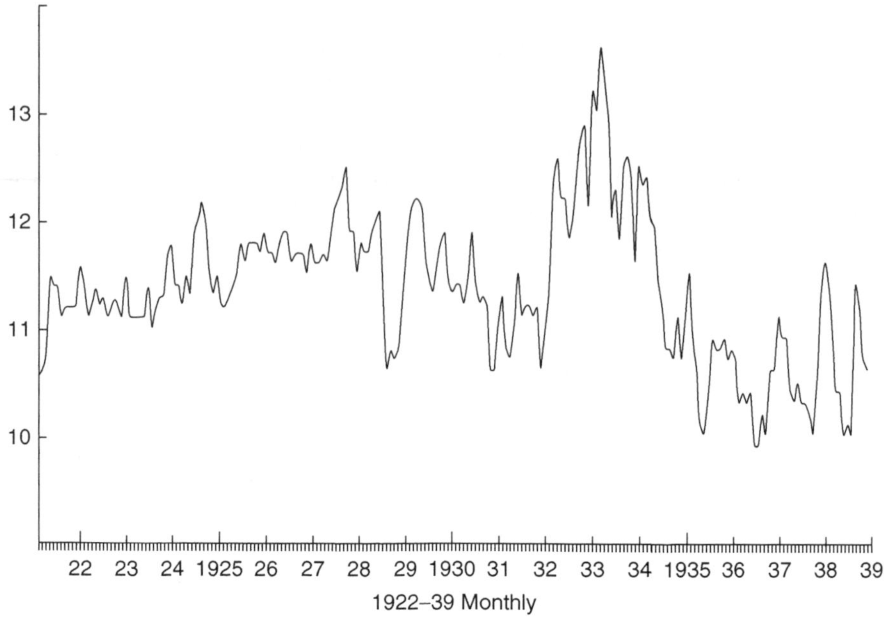

Figure 7.1. Total reserves/total deposits seasonally unadjusted

Figure 7.2. Reserve/deposit ratio of the London clearing banks

September 1931. Table 7.1 and Figures 7.1 and 7.2 present some of the relevant variables in monthly form over the course of the two years, 1930 and 1931.

We begin with the question of an exogenous shock. There does not appear to have been any such shock in Britain within reasonable distance of a 'crisis'. For example, there was no stock market experience comparable to that of the United States. An index of ninety-two industrial security prices shows that these had risen from the base of 100 in 1924 to a peak of 149 in January 1929, but drifted downwards in the course of the rest of that year. There was a major case of fraud that broke on the market in September 1929. The Committee of the Stock Exchange suspended dealings in the shares of the Hatry group of companies. Spurious scrip and duplication and triplication of shares was discovered and the initial impact was to curb activity in almost all securities. The collapse of the Hatry group was regarded by some as the expected sequel to the speculative 'boom' in new company flotations in 1928. (A similar case erupted in France in November—the Oustiric scandal—ruining many banks and scaring investors.) But the markets were quiet in 1930.

Stock market prices drifted downwards that year (from 129 to 99 between January and December); this hardly spells panic or doom, but it is rather a reflection of the generally pessimistic mood of the first full year of economic depression.

So there was no exogenous shock such as would have led on from the 'peak' year 1929 to a boom-panic-crisis sequence. Neither was there any unusual expansion of bank credit nor rise in prices such as would have characterized a typical crisis. Bank deposits did rise from £2250 m at the beginning of 1930 of £2300 m at the end, but that hardly constitutes an expansion of bank credit on the scale suggested by Kindleberger. In the course of 1931 bank deposits were on a downward trend. Similarly with prices, Prices (as measured by the cost of living index) had been stable or slipping down for some years and slid down throughout 1930 and 1931. The index fell from its highest point of these two years, in January 1930(94) to a trough of 83 in late 1931. In short, there is neither the expansion of bank credit nor the rise in prices that are associated with a 'normal' financial crisis.

There was a rise in short-term interest rates in mid to late 1931 but that was associated with the defence of sterling, rather than any internal problems (see Capie, Mills, and Wood, 1983). In midsummer (July), the first increase of the year in interest rates is observed, and rates kept rising through to a peak in September–November of 1931. This rise was not associated with expanding bank credit arising out of new profit opportunities and a rise in the demand for money. Unfortunately, there are no sub-annual income figures to allow a calculation of velocity but there is no evidence that it rose. There was certainly no euphoria in any marker—quite the contrary, for the climate was one of gloom.

Finally, there were no bank failures in Britain either. This is perhaps not surprising for the British banking system was by this time dominated by the 'Big Five' and there were only a few other banks. There does not even seem to have been any pressure on the Banks. Figure 7.1 shows that reserve/deposit ratio for the British banking system was fairly stable throughout the inter-war period and although the greatest movement is, as we would expect, in the years 1931–33, even here the ratio did not move outside the range of 11 per cent to 13 per cent.

In this connection it is interesting to look also at bank profits. Table 7.2 shows commercial bank profits for several countries for selected years from 1925 to 1932. The interesting point is that British banks experienced only the

Table 7.2. Commercial bank profits*

	Profit or loss as percentage of capital and reserves				
	1925	1929	1930	1931	1932
Austria	8.2	5.5	5.0	L 34.4	L136.0
Germany	7.5	7.0	4.5	L118.1	L 15.0
France	10.1	8.8	8.4	L 7.0	6.3
England/Wales	8.5	8.2	7.3	7.9	6.9
Scotland	7.5	7.7	7.4	7.2	7.2
United States	9.0	9.7	7.4	1.7	L 4.9
Australia/New Zealand	7.5	6.8	5.3	3.6	2.7

* These are not intended to be in any sense precise but simply an indication of the broad outline of the movements in profits.
Source: League of Nations.

mildest of falls in their rate of profit, whereas Europeans suffered substantial losses, and there were losses in the Untied States.[1]

RESERVE LOSS

It seems clear that there was no financial crisis in the Kindleberger/Minsky sense within the UK. That particular problem was not transmitted directly from continental Europe. There were, however, other countries, further afield, which experienced great economic problems. Some of these countries had intimate financial ties with the UK. Did the UK import problems from them?

Many of the world's primary producers were at this time still part of the British Empire, and maintained, originally for historical reasons but by this time for convenience, substantial holdings of financial assets in London. These countries did in some cases suffer substantial falls in real income in this period. Their terms of trade worsened sharply, and trade volumes were sluggish. This decline in income would, one would expect, lead to a running down of financial assets, for it would be quite rational for primary producers to anticipate that the decline in income was a cyclical phenomenon; there had been many cycles in the past. Such a run-down could have drained assets from the British banking system, and put financial markets generally under strain as assets were liquidated in large amounts. This could have left British financial markets nervous, exposed to speculative panics, and highly illiquid. Did it?

[1] It has been drawn to our attention by Michael Wagner that the losses shown by the Austrian banks in 1931 and 1932 in fact occurred before 1925, but only appeared in their accounts in 1931 and 1932. The losses of these two years are spurious, in the sense that they were carried forward from earlier years. Why the banks did not show them earlier or why they showed them when they did is not clear.

There is only a small amount of data on reserve holdings in London by primary producers of the Empire. These data are shown in Table 7.3, below. (Ideally a set of balance of payments accounts for the sterling/non-sterling area should be drawn up but so far this has proved too difficult.)

This table suggests that whatever difficulties these countries experienced had a trivial impact on their London reserve holdings. Indeed, the fluctuation of 1931 was no larger than fluctuations that had occurred in the past without causing any problems for the financial system.

Further, even if some countries had withdrawn reserves from London on a significant scale, there is nothing to show that these reserves may not have been redeposited in London, changing ownership but remaining at a leading financial centre.

Accordingly, therefore, it cannot be shown that the difficulties of the primary producers at this time caused problems for the UK via the financial connections between primary producers and the UK. That position can still be maintained—but doing so would entail neglecting what evidence there is (how representative that evidence is, it should be stressed, we have no way of knowing), and would also involve arguing that the funds withdrawn from London were largely deposited elsewhere by their recipients.

The defence of that position must therefore rest entirely on conjecture. The balance of available evidence and of argument is in our view tilted to rejection of that position; the problems of the primary producers did not push the UK off gold.

This finding has implications for the hypothesis that the UK was pushed off gold by the drain of reserves from the sterling area as a whole. If reserves were not drained through the Empire's primary producers, the strain must have been directly on the UK. By ruling out, as far as the data allow, a drain through the primary producers, one is thrown back to examining the UK itself. Ruling out the primary producers also rules out the broader, but related, sterling area hypothesis.

Table 7.3. Gold reserves of Empire primary producers ($m)

	Australia	New Zealand	South Africa	India
1925	162	38	44	109
1926	110	38	37	109
1927	106	38	40	119
1928	109	35	39	124
1929	89	28	37	128
1930	75	32	33	128
1931	51	28	43	162
1932	41	21	36	162

Sources: Nurkse (1944): 233–40; Gregory (1932): 112–15.

UK INTERNAL POLICIES

Two aspects of UK domestic policy have been considered candidates for the role of having pushed the UK off gold. These are budgetary policy, and the choice of exchange rate in 1925.

(a) Budgetary policy

The government of the day was concerned by the size of their deficit. Efforts, including cuts in unemployment benefit, were made to reduce it. Can the UK's problems be ascribed to the budgetary position? There are two interrelated grounds for saying that they cannot.

First, the budget deficit was not growing at a rate so rapid that monetization with eventual inflation, was inevitable. (For a detailed description of this process, see, for example, Sargent and Wallace, 1984.) Indeed, a good part of the deficit was cyclical, and therefore transitory.

Unemployment stood in 1931 at about 3 million, 21 per cent of the insured workforce—equivalent on the definition of unemployment now in use to an unemployment rate of around 16 per cent. This manifestly contributed to the deficit. *Ideally*, to ascertain whether the budgetary position was transitory or permanent—permanent in the sense that it required policy action rather than economic recovery to correct—one should calculate the constant employment budgetary position. Only that can really reveal whether a surge in the deficit in any one year is an economy-induced fluctuation, or a shift of policy to a new, and conceivably unsustainable, course. Budgetary calculations of that nature are not straightforward and results can differ widely. There are in existence, however, two independent calculations of the constant employment budgetary position of the UK in the 1920s and 1930s—the work of T. Thomas (1979) and Roger Middleton (1981). Fortunately, these studies produce similar results. The main focus of these studies was to consider whether fiscal policy was operated in what is generally viewed as a stabilizing way—deficits varying counter-cyclically. As a preliminary to that both authors calculate constant employment deficits. Both find that, on a constant employment basis, the deficit was low—indeed, in 1931 the budget on that definition was in small surplus.

This indicates fairly clearly that the *underlying* budgetary position was not at fault in pushing the UK off gold.

What of the *actual* budgetary position? Could that be responsible? There are strong analytical grounds for arguing that it could not. Under a fixed exchange rate system, a budget deficit financed by the issue of interest-bearing debt attracts rather than repels funds. Interest rates are driven up (perhaps only very briefly, if capital markets are sufficiently responsive) and capital attracted from the rest of the world. A budgetary deficit, so long as it is not so large as to presage monetization and subsequent inflation, cannot lead to pressure to abandon or devalue a pegged exchange rate. The UK's budgetary position cannot be blamed for the abandoning of gold.[2]

(b) A sterling overvaluation

One version of the exchange rate story runs as follows: the proximate source of the financial pressure is found in Central Europe where first the Austrian banks were unable to meet the demands on them and the Credit-Anstalt closed in May. Pressure moved to Germany where the Danatbank closed temporarily in June. There followed a scramble for liquidity throughout Europe. London had short liabilities greatly in excess of gold and foreign exchange reserves in the Bank, a situation known in international financial circles at the time. The same had been true prior to 1914 when the international system seemed to work smoothly, but this time several factors shook the confidence of foreigners. There was the growing feeling that sterling was overvalued. (As early as October 1929, Norman voiced fears that sterling would be forced off gold.) Then the Macmillan Report (13 July) was published, which brought out the damage done to London and revealed the extent of the short-term liabilities. Further, there were growing fears abroad over the extent of the budget deficit. Although this was not large by recent standards, and as argued above fears were not objectively justifiable, it nonetheless worried foreigners and permeated the atmosphere in all financial markets at the time. Foreigners began withdrawing balances from London, and in spite of American and French credits the Bank was left with insufficient reserves with which to defend the exchange rate. A final straw is said to have been the Invergordon Mutiny on 15 September, and Britain left gold on 21 September 1931.

An alternative explanation of the exchange rate crisis is that sterling would have been under extreme pressure anyway because of the weakening balance of payments position, deriving specifically from the poor performance of invisibles. Moggridge (1970) points out that in 1931 Britain's current account balance moved into deficit as a result of the deterioration in invisibles, in part a product of the contraction of world trade. Falling interest rates reduced

[2] This does lead to two issues. There was clearly a scramble for liquidity on the Continent. Under a fixed rate system, this would tend to push up interest rates in the UK. The deficit would have the same tendency. But the authorities were keen to see rates come down (see Capie, Mills, and Wood, 1983). This may have increased willingness to break financial links with the rest of the world, and thereby alleviate domestic interest rate pressures. Second, markets may have taken fright, irrationally on the above arguments, because of the deficit. There is under the gold standard an appropriate central banking response to such an irrationality. The actions of central banks other than the Bank of England are discussed in the final section of this chapter.

receipts from overseas investments and the contraction of trade reduced income from shipping and financial services. In this account the scramble for liquidity only brought matters to a head.

In an attempt at bringing some rigour to this investigation Cairncross and Eichengreen (1983) recently sought to distinguish between the 'liquidity' cause and the 'balance of payments' cause. To this end they examined the determinants of the official settlements balance, arguing that it was that balance rather than any one of the components that determined the extent of reserve flows. [At the same time they conceded the knowledge that a particular component of that balance (in this case the invisible balance) exhibited the largest swing prior to the crisis may be helpful for interpreting the results.]

There are many difficulties with the approach ranging over the data, the econometrics, and the theory of the balance of payments; and in the end the exercise yielded no unambiguous advance on our understanding of the episode.

Some insights can, however, be gained by examining certain consequences of the exchange rate movement after the gold standard was abandoned.

EXCHANGE RATE BEHAVIOUR

Over the three months from September 1931, sterling fell by some 25 per cent against the US dollar, and by somewhat less on a trade-weighted basis. There is a widely accepted view of the effects such a move is likely to have.

Some domestic prices will rise almost mechanically, as tradable goods are marked up in home currency terms to keep their foreign currency prices unchanged. This impact on prices affects inflationary expectations, and in turn affects long-term interest rates and wage claims. This widely accepted view does seem to capture the 'stylized facts' of, for example, the post 1945 UK experience. (See Williamson and Wood, 1976, for a discussion of the model underlying that view and how well it fitted in the UK between 1945 and 1975.) Simple examination of the data on prices and interest rates (see tables) suggests that view does not match the stylized facts of the 1930s. Is this traditional description of devaluation experience still incorrect when the data of the 1930s are examined rigorously? If so what is the explanation?

To investigate whether there was actually anything to be explained, we analysed the time-series behaviour of prices and of interest rates—the latter begin both long bond yields, and, for completeness, short-term, interest rates, to see whether the abandoning of gold (or any of the precursive events) affected any of the series. (Using interest rates in this way does not, of course, commit us to the full Fisher hypothesis; all we need assume is that a change in inflationary expectations has some effect on interest rates.)

The two interest rates examined were the Consol Yield (*RC*) and the rate on three month bank bills (*RB*). The price series employed was the Ministry of Labour Retail Price Index (Cost of Living) (*P*). ARIMA models were built for each series, using the techniques popularized by Box and Jenkins (1976), over the period January 1927 to December 1937 with a total of 132 observations—a period considered to provide an adequate number of observations before and after the period in question, while avoiding other periods of economic upheaval. Charts. a–d show the behaviour of certain key series:

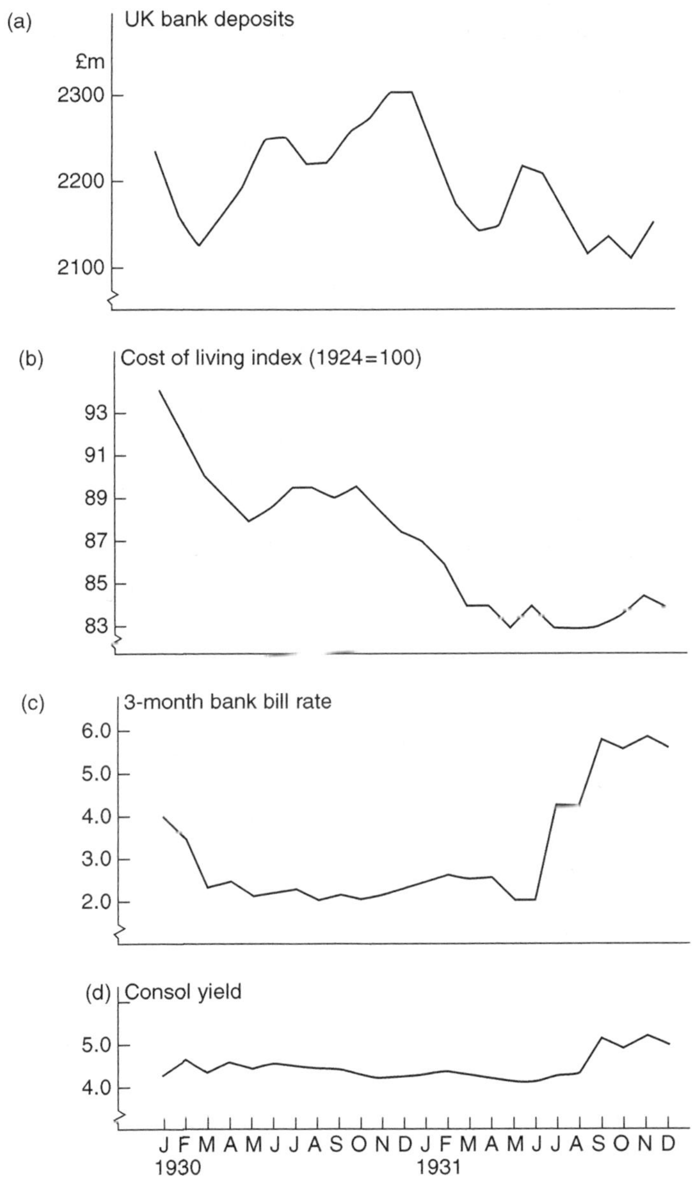

Thus a monthly series $x_t = (1 - B)^d (1 - B^{12})^D Y_p$ transformed to stationarity, is modelled as:

$$\varphi_p(B)\varphi_p(B^{12})x_t = \Theta_q(B)\Theta_Q(B^{12})a_t \qquad (1)$$

where B is the lag operator, a_t is a sequence of independently distributed normal variables having mean zero and variance σ^2, and the $\varphi(B)$'s are polynominals in B of degrees p, P, q, and Q respectively, all of whose roots lie outside the unit circle. The series Y_t is then said to be modelled as an ARIMA (p, d, q) $(P, D, Q)_{12}$ process.

Both interest rate series were adequately fitted by (non-seasonal) ARIMA (0, 1, 2) processes, the estimated models being

$$(1 - B)RC_t = \underset{(.08)}{(1 - .16B} + \underset{(.08)}{.29B^2})a_t \; \hat{\sigma}, = .102 \qquad (2)$$

$$(1 - B)RB_t = \underset{(.08)}{(1 - .09B} + \underset{(.08)}{.27B^2})a_t \; \hat{\sigma}, = .382 \qquad (3)$$

standard errors being shown in parentheses.

The price series displayed a seasonal pattern and required an ARIMA (0, 1, 0) $(0, 1, 1)_{12}$ model, the estimate being

$$(1 - B)(1 - B^{12})P_t = (1 - \underset{(.07)}{.74B^{12}})a_p \; \hat{\sigma}, = .673 \qquad (4)$$

The economic events occurring during 1931 and 1932 may be regarded as non-repetitive exogenous interventions. When the exact timing of such interventions are known their effects can often be accounted for by using the intervention analysis techniques proposed by Box and Tiao (1975).[3]

[3] As an illustration, suppose that an intervention occurs at time t_0. Then its effect can often be modelled as

$$x_t = \frac{\omega(B)}{\delta(B)} I_t + \frac{\theta(B)}{\varphi(B)} a_t \qquad (5)$$

where $\theta(B) = \theta q(B)\theta Q(B)$, $\varphi(B) = \varphi^p(B)$ and $\omega(B)$ and $\delta(B)$ are polynominals in B, their ratio describing the dynamic behaviour of the intervention I_p which can usually take one of three forms (i) a 'step' at t_0 defined as

$$I_t = \eta_t^{(t0)} = \begin{matrix} 0 \text{ for } t < t_0 \\ 1 \text{for } t \geq t_0 \end{matrix} \qquad (6)$$

(ii) a 'pulse' at t_0, defined as

$$I_t = \xi_t^{(t0)} = \begin{matrix} 0 \text{ for } t \neq t_0 \\ 1 \text{ for } t = t_0 \end{matrix} \qquad (7)$$

or (iii) an 'extended pulse' between t_0 to t_1

$$I_t = \varepsilon_1^{(t0,t1)} = \sum_{t = t_0} \xi^{(t)} = \begin{matrix} 0 \text{ for } t < t_0 \text{ and } t > t_1 \\ 1 \text{ for } t_0 \leq t \leq t_1 \end{matrix} \qquad (8)$$

In the present circumstances, however, the exact timing and influence of the interventions are uncertain and the sequence of such shocks may make it difficult to identify correctly the separate dynamic responses. As a consequence, analysis based on the residuals from the fitted models (2) to (4) was first undertaken to identify possible outliers and isolate significant interventions.

Following Hillmer, Bell, and Tiao (1981), we define two types of outliers, additive and innovational. An additive outlier (*AO*) is defined as

$$x_t = \frac{\theta(B)}{\varphi(B)} a_t + \omega_A \xi_t(t_0) \tag{9}$$

and only affects the level of the t_0th observation. An innovational outlier is defined as

$$x_t = \frac{\theta(B)}{\varphi(B)} (a_t + \omega_1 \xi_t) \tag{10}$$

and hence represents an extraordinary shock at t_0 influencing x_{to}, $x_{t_{0+1}}$, . . . through the memory of the system described by $\theta(B)/\varphi(B)$.

If t_0 and all the time-series parameters of the model (1) are known, then, by defining the residuals

$$e_t = \frac{\varphi(B)}{\theta(B)} x_t = \pi(B) x_t \tag{11}$$

we have, for an *AO*

$$e_t = \omega_A \pi(B) \xi_t^{(t_0)} + a_t \tag{12}$$

and for an IO

$$e_t = \omega_1 \xi_t^{(t_0)} + a_t \tag{13}$$

From least squares theory, estimators of the impact, ω, of the intervention and the variances of these estimators are

$$\hat{\omega}_A = \pi^2(F) e_{t_0} \text{Var.}(\dot{\omega}_A) = p^2 \sigma^2 \tag{14}$$

$$\omega_1 = e_{t_0} \text{Var}(\hat{\omega}_1) = \sigma^2 \tag{15}$$

where $\rho^2 = (1 + \pi_1{}^2 + \pi_2{}^2 + \ldots)^{-1}$ and $F = B^{-1}$. Thus the best estimate of the effect of an IO at time t_0 is the residual e_{t_0}, while the best estimate of the effect of an *AO* is a linear combination of e_{t_0}, e_{t_0-t}, . . . with weight depending on the structure of the time-series model. Likelihood ratio test statistics for these outliers are straightforward to construct. If the null hypothesis is that x_{t_0} is not an outlier, then a test that it is an IO is given by $\lambda_1 = \hat{\omega}_1/\sigma$, while a test that it is an *AO* is given by $\lambda_2 = \hat{\omega}_A/(p\sigma)$, both statistics being distributed as $N(0,1)$.

In practice, of course, t_0 and the time-series parameters are unknown. If only t_0 is unknown, we may proceed by calculating λ_1 and λ_2 for each t, making decisions based on the sampling properties of the test statistics given above. However, the time-series parameters (φ's, θ's and σ) are also unknown and estimates of these parameters, particularly σ can be seriously biased by the existence of outliers. This would suggest that decisions should be made more informally on the basis of size and patterns of the statistics.

Table 7.4 lists these statistics for the three series over the years 1931 and 1932. For the *RC* series there is a suggestion of two outliers, the first an *AO*, the second an IO, during the summer of 1931. There is also a pattern of negative statistics in the first half of 1932, culminating in large *AO*'s in May and June and large IO in July. This provides confirmation of the significant stock conversion intervention found in Capie, Mills and Wood (1983). Indeed, on estimation only this intervention was found to be significant, the finally chosen model being

Table 7.4. Outlier test statistics

	RC		RB		P	
	λ_1	λ_2	λ_1	λ_2	λ_1	λ_2
Jan. 1931	−.01	.76	.36	.55	.77	1.54
Feb.	.87	.32	.42	.62	−.36	.34
Mar.	−.24	−1.43	−.34	−.49	−.16	1.68
Apr.	−1.38	−2.08	−.16	−1.22	.83	.26
May	−1.29	−.67	−1.16	.12	−.89	.32
June	−.07	1.24	.11	4.58	.48	.98
July	2.11	3.06	6.28	3.89	−2.05	−1.57
Aug.	.73	1.39	−.84	1.07	−.21	.25
Sep.	2.14	1.41	2.46	1.08	−.71	.06
Oct.	−2.57	−.66	−.57	−.24	−.39	−1.45
Nov.	1.77	.42	.04	.49	1.71	1.26
Dec.	−.88	−2.08	.42	−1.21	.24	.42
Jan. 1932	−1.82	−2.52	−1.28	−4.21	1.32	1.37
Feb.	−1.34	−1.64	−4.02	−4.12	.47	.58
Mar.	−1.26	−.96	−2.72	−1.24	1.39	2.40
Apr.	−.23	−.96	.93	−.71	−.87	−.40
May	−1.18	−2.94	−1.88	1.37	.08	1.23
June	−1.59	−2.99	−.16	−.26	−.39	.88
July	−3.48	−2.09	−.29	−.31	−1.53	−.25
Aug.	.35	−.26	.07	−.36	−.16	.46
Sept.	.35	−.21	−.25	.43	.96	.72
Oct.	−1.62	−.09	.49	.46	1.03	−.03
Nov.	1.67	1.20	1.09	.26	−.22	.14
Dec.	.04	−.21	.48	1.07	.18	.35

$$(1 - B)RC_t = -.22(1 - B)1_t + (1 - .20B + .30B^2)a_t, \sigma = .100$$
$$\quad\quad(.10)\quad\quad\quad\quad(.09)$$

where $1_t = \eta_t^{66)}$, *a* 'step' intervention at June 1932. Thus the shock conversion had an immediate permanent effect on the *RC* series, reducing the level of the series by 0.22 percentage points. No shock in 1931 produced a significant effect on the time-series behaviour of the series, either permanent or transitory.

For the *RB* series, patterns of large statistics are found in the middle of 1931 and the first three months of 1932. Large *AO*s are found at June and July 1931, the second month having an even larger IO. These outliers correspond to the Austrian banking crisis and the May Committee. There is also a suggestion of an IO in September 1931, the month when the UK came off the gold standard. Large AO's are found in January and February 1932, and large 10's in February and March 1932. These outliers have been interpreted in Capie, Mills, and Wood (1983) as a reaction to exchange rate pressures.

On estimation of an intervention model for *RB* the sequence of shocks in 1931 was found to be most adequately modelled by an 'extended pulse' intervention between July and November. The intervention in early 1932 was modelled as a step at February, with the response spread over two months. Thus the model finally selected was

$$(1 - B)RB_t = 1.14(1 - B)I_{1t} - (1.80 + 1.00B)(1 - B)I_{2t}$$
$$\quad(.23)\quad\quad\quad\quad(.33)(.32)$$
$$+(1+.22B^2)a_t\sigma = .316$$
$$(.09)$$

where $I_{1t} = \varepsilon_t^{(55,59)}$ and $I_{2t} = \eta_t^{(62)}$. Thus the sequence of shocks during 1931 had a net effect of increasing the level of *RB* by 1.14 percentage points between July and November, while the shocks in early 1932 permanently reduced the level of the series by 2.80 percentage points.

For the price series no strong evidence of outliers of either type was found for the period and hence the shocks of 1931 and 1932 had no impact on the general level of prices. These results are puzzling at first glance, being quite plainly at variance with what is generally accepted as post 1945 experience. They suggest that the abandoning of the gold standard was not significant for any aspect of the UK financial system; there was no consequent or associated fundamental crisis for the UK banking system, financial markets, or the price level.[4]

[1] This is certainly not to say that the move was of no consequence for the UK economy. Indeed, it was soon to prove of great importance, for it ensured that the severely contractionary monetary policies pursued in the USA were not imported into the UK.

They also raise the question of why this result was found, and before concluding it is useful to consider why the devaluation had such an insignificant effect on prices.

POSSIBLE EXPLANATIONS

There are five explanations of interest, four of one type and one of another. The devaluation may have been fully anticipated; it may have been expected to be transitory; some other movement may have occurred to offset it; or, the return to gold in 1925 was thought even at that time to be transitory. These four are considered in order, before we consider the fifth, which rejects the above described connection between exchange rate changes and price level changes.

(i) Anticipated

There were undoubtedly forebodings before the event. But did they affect any objective indicators? As discussed above, we tested for the existence of outliers in the series of prices and interest rates, so as to allow for the possibility that one or other item of news affected the series before the abandoning of gold. No outliers were found which could be related to the publication of any report, or to any other item of news which would have led to anticipations of the UK leaving gold. Accordingly, whatever forebodings were expressed, they were not acted on to an extent sufficient to affect significantly any financial markets, and they did not affect either the general level of prices.

(ii) Permanent vs transitory

Was the devaluation expected to persist? Had the abandoning of gold been widely believed to be temporary, it is quite possible that it would not have affected either prices or inflationary expectations.

The very strenuousness of the efforts made to remain on gold indicate that the authorities feared leaving it to be an irrevocable step. Two participants were quite explicit in stating that they believed a fall in the rate would last. Siegman (of the Bank) accepted that $4.86 was gone forever, and Niemeyer rejected the idea of pegging at a new rate. There were also discussions of future policy. By December, Norman had formulated plans. Howson says:

> We should eventually return to gold, not necessarily at the former parity but we could not decide the rate until we had
>
> (a) an active trade balance
> (b) a settlement of reparations and war debts
> (c) a budget balanced now and in the future, and
> (d) a competitive price level.
>
> The Governor was not in agreement with those who thought that we must wait until there was an agreement on the part of other countries to 'play the gold standard game according to the rules', whatever this exactly might mean. Foreign lending would begin when confidence was restored.... It would be dangerous to make any statement as to the time or rate of stabilization.... It must be recognised that we have not the means to peg exchange.
>
> As for liaison between the Bank and the Treasury, 'the Government entirely agreed with this proposal and arrangements will be made accordingly'. (Howson, 1975)

From then on, the problem was seen as that of 'managing the sterling exchange so as to give more benefit to British industry than had been possible under the gold standard' (Howson, 1975).

These views all indicated recognition that a fundamental and irrevocable step had been taken. Belief in the transitoriness of the new rate and any expectation of return to the old level can certainly not be invoked to explain the behaviour of prices and interest rates.

(iii) Offsetting events

There are two events which could have offset the effects of the exchange rate movement—a sharp monetary contraction, or a sharp fall in the price of imports.

The first can be rapidly dismissed. Money growth accelerated soon after the abandoning of gold—initially not by much, but even in 1931 manifestly a movement in the wrong direction.

What did the reduction in the price of imports do? Table 7.5 shows the behaviour of a price index for UK imports. This index was falling but the fall of 1931 to 1932 was, while large, certainly not large enough to offset the effects of the devaluation of sterling (on a trade weighted basis) on the level of prices. Further, it should be recollected that the proxy we have used for inflationary expectations also did not respond; even, then, if the terms of trade effect *had* been substantial it would be necessary to explain why it was expected to have a persistent effect on the inflation rate, as opposed to a once-for-all effect on the price level. The behaviour of the index may help explain the behaviour of the price level, but it does not explain *all* of the behaviour of the price level and explains *none* of the behaviour of interest rates.

Table 7.5. Price index for UK imports (1963 = 100)

1925	155
1926	138
1929	134
1930	118
1931	96
1932	89

Source: Key Statistics 1900–1970.

(iv) Was 1925 transitory?

A fourth explanation for the abandoning of gold and subsequent devaluation having no apparent effect is that it was fully anticipated—fully in that when the UK returned to gold, this return was not expected to last, so that the new parity and new commitment had no effect on any economic time series. (We adopt this definition of anticipation since we found no evidence of anticipation of devaluation between 1925 and 1931.)

It is not possible to test statistically for this possibility, for the return to gold was in effect implemented gradually. There had been much discussion in advance (for example, by the Cunliffe Committee), and the exchange rate gradually drifted towards its pre-war parity, the final step on repegging being a small one. A study of contemporary opinion is therefore necessary. The two main opponents of the return to gold, both in their evidence to the Bradbury Committee and elsewhere, were Keynes and McKenna.

Despite their criticism of the decision, that a return to the gold standard would persist was clearly the view of them both; indeed to some extent that was the basis of their criticism. When the decision was taken Keynes immediately switched to advocating policies based on the presumption that the system would persist. We had gone back at too high a parity; that parity would persist; measures, for example protectionism, should be taken to alleviate the consequences. Not only was Keynes critical of the short-term effects of overvaluation: he was fearful also of the long-term consequences. He feared there would be inflation in the US, which would lead to an inflow of gold to the UK, and subsequently to inflation (Pigou papers, evidence of J. M. Keynes to the Chamberlain-Bradbury Committee). In his evidence to the same committee, McKenna was less clear cut. He appeared to differ from some of the proponents, unlike them thinking that the City would prosper without it. He resisted deflation to achieve parity with the US; but, like Keynes, expected US prices to rise until the UK could safely peg. Underlying that position must be the belief that, once restored, the system would last. One of the main protagonists, Montague Norman, clearly expected the system to last, and indeed ascribed its collapse to policy failures *after* 1925:

> Yes, I have made mistakes also. I am now accused for having gone back to the Gold Standard. It was probably a mistake. And still in those circumstances I should do the same thing again. It is easy to see it afterwards. *But a great deal of what has happened in the meantime was not necessary but depended on policy.* It might have been different. (Jucker-Fleetwood, 1968, emphasis added)

Certainly there seem to have been no doubts about the desirability of the gold standard *system*. There were doubts in advance, but only about the parity. The durability of the system was taken for granted—sometimes with trepidation for the inflationary consequences—even by the critics of the system. There is no evidence in the historical record for arguing that the 1925 return was expected to be transitory.

A RESOLUTION

There appears to be a paradox—a major devaluation which affects neither prices nor price expectations, and yet not accompanied by any offsetting factors. There is, however, a resolution of the paradox, and one which sheds light on why the gold standard was abandoned by the UK. The resolution involves rejecting the existence of a link between exchange rate changes and subsequent price level movements.

The view of the relationship set out above is essentially a description of what happens when a country moves from one pegged rate to another. At the second peg, just as at the first, monetary policy has to be *accommodative* to the rest of the world's inflation. Consequences for the rate of inflation arise not from the devaluation but from the necessity to conduct monetary policy so as to make the new exchange rate sustainable.

In contrast, when, as the UK did in 1931, a country moves from a peg to a float, the behaviour of the exchange rate is in the long run irrelevant, and the behaviour of the price level determined in the long run by the behaviour of the stock of money.

As noted above, monetary policy eased after 1931, but very modestly. Hence the apparent paradox can be resolved. After 1931 monetary policy was domestically determined and the exchange rate in the long run irrelevant. Domestic monetary policy clearly was not inflationary in 1931, so neither prices nor inflationary expectations surged on the abandoning of gold. But it should be observed that the theory relates to the long-run, equilibrium, result. The theory does *not* say that there is no transitory effect, some prices rising sharply as a result of devaluation and others falling only slowly so that there is a transitory upward boost to the domestic price level. Indeed, this transitory boost to the price level is inevitable unless domestic prices respond within the period of observation to the monetary squeeze, the fall in the *real* stock of money, created by devaluation.

There seems to have been no such transitory effect on prices in the UK. Taken at face value, this suggests considerable—indeed, rather surprising—price flexibility. It would make 'sticky price' explanation of the Great Depression difficult to accept, and, important for the present purpose, it undermines the notion of a *sustained overvaluation*. After all, if prices responded within a quarter in 1931, a 10 per cent overvaluation which existed in 1925 is unlikely to still be around in 1931 (as Sayers (1976) implicitly assumed).

There must, however, be two qualifications. Just as Cairncross and Eichengreen's (1983) study was undermined by, among other factors, the scarcity of data, so the above finding is 'softened' by the composition of the price index, and by currency invoicing practices.

The index was composed to a much greater extent than its present-day contemporary counterpart of primary commodities—notably food. These goods are flex-price goods, whose price responds very quickly to clear markets. (See Carse, Williamson, and Wood, 1930; McKinnon, 1979.) Hence our results are not so clear cut in their implications as the same results on, say, a present-day CPI would be.

A second qualification arises from currency invoicing practices. If most primary products were invoiced in sterling, then the impact effect of a sterling devaluation on the UK price index would be diminished, changes in the prices of these goods feeding through not mechanically as a result of the changed exchange rate, but only as these prices responded to the changed balance of supply and demand. It is the conventional wisdom that a good part of primary product trade was invoiced in sterling in the 1920s and 1930s. There is, however, no evidence; and it was, until the publication of Grassman (1973) and Carse, Wiliamson, and Wood (1980), conventional wisdom that in the 1960s and 1970s the bulk of world trade was invoiced in US dollars.

The second 'softening' must be noted as a possibility, but one not supported—or refuted—by the data.

All that said, the finding does add weight to the rejection of overvaluation as a cause of Britain's leaving gold.[5] In this it supports studies that have gradually reduced the estimate of the overvaluation—from the 10 per cent suggested by Keynes in 1925, to around 8 per cent now. The last is still an 'overvaluation'

[5] This is aside from the problem that overvaluation can explain devaluation but is not enough by itself to explain the collapse of the system. Consider the Bretton Woods system. There were, as Triffin frequently observed, fundamental flaws in the Bretton Woods system which gradually destroyed it. That system was not wrecked by a set of misaligned parities (although parity misalignment certainly affected the timing and probably the manner of its end).

but not so large as to be conclusive, given the margin of error associated with PPP calculations.

A SUMMING UP

The banking crisis of continental Europe did not impose strains on the internal financial system of the UK. The impoverishment of some gold holders in the Empire may have led to increasing illiquidity of the UK financial system, but what data there are do not suggest this is important. UK budgetary policy was certainly not inconsistent with a fixed exchange rate. It appears that UK prices were sufficiently flexible that any overvaluation there may have been in 1925 could not have persisted until 1931.

When then was the gold standard abandoned? Partly by elimination of other arguments, we are driven back to the view that the cause was the continental European banking crisis. This, as a result of national central bankers failing to act as lenders-of-last-resort followed as individual bankruptcies turned into a national banking crisis and then an international banking crisis. There was a scramble for gold; the Bank of England, because of its low level of reserves, and because of the attention drawn to the low level, was caught up in this scramble; and the two major *national* gold holders, France and the US, failed to follow Bagehot's guidance on how a central bank should act at a time of crisis. The abandoning of the gold standard was the result.

The argument has the appeal of explaining why parities were not just adjusted; that would not have worked in a crisis of the international system. It has the appeal of showing France behaving consistently with its behaviour in the 1920s (see Clarke, 1967), building up its gold holdings without regard to the effect of this on the gold standard system as a whole. And it has the appeal, too, of showing the Federal Reserve acting internationally in the same, deficient, way as Friedman and Schwartz (1963) showed it to have acted domestically. It failed to act as lender-of-last-resort.

But that does prompt a question, one which has troubled many commentators on the gold standard. In principle, the system does not need a dominant central bank to act as Bagehot required—but in practice it appears to, for the system seemed to work best when the Bank of England did fill that role (1870-1914). There is plainly an issue for further research here, but at this point we would offer a conjecture. Just as a domestic banking system can work well without a lender-of-last-resort when there are no strains, so can an international fixed rate system. But when there are pressures, when small lenders are no longer ready to respond in their thousands to small movements in interest rates, a lender-of-last-resort is necessary. Bagehot may have international as well as domestic implications. But to develop that argument is for a separate paper.

We would summarize the conclusions of this chapter as follows.

What happened in 1931 was a crisis, not just the result of overvaluation. That is why the system was abandoned, rather than restructured at different parities. What happened in 1931 was that world saw the consequences of central bankers not understanding central banking.

REFERENCES

Blinder, A. and Solow, R. M. 'The Analytical Foundations of Fiscal Policy', in G. F. Break (ed.), *The Economies of Public Finance'*, Washington, DC: The Brookings Institution, pp. 3–115.

Box, G. E. P. and Tiao, G. C. (1975) 'Intervention Analysis with Applications to Economic and Environmental Problems', *Journal of the American Statistical Association*, (70), 70–9.

——and Jenkins, G. M. (1976) *Time Series Analysis: Forecasting and Control*, Revised edn, San Francisco: Holden Day.

Break, G. F. and Peachman, J. A. (1974) *The Economics of Public Finance*, Studies of Government Finance, Washington, DC: The Brookings Institution.

Cairncross, A. and Eichengreen, B. (1983) *Sterling in Decline*, Oxford: Basil Blackwell.

Capie, Forrest and Collins, Michael (1983) *The Inter-war British Economy: A Statistical Abstract*, Manchester University Press.

——and Webber, Alan (1985) *A Monetary History of the UK, 1870–1982, Data Sources Methods*, London: George Allen & Unwin.

——Mills, T. C. and Wood, G. E. (1983) 'Was the War Loan Conversion Operation a Success', The City University, Centre for Banking and International Finance, *Monetary History Discussion Paper 5*.

Carse, S., Williamson, J. and Wood, G.E. (1980) *The Financing Procedures of British Foreign Trade*, Cambridge University Press.

Clarke, S. V. O. (1967) *Central Bank Cooperation 1924–31*, New York: Federal Reserve Bank of New York.

Friedman, M. And Schwartz A. J. (1963) *A Monetary History of the United States*, Princeton University Press, for the NBER.

Grassman, S. (1973) *Exchange Reserves and the Financial Structure of Foreign Trade*, Farnborough: Saxon House.

Gregory, T. E. (1932) *The Gold Standard and its Future*, London: Methuen & Co.

Hillmer, S. C., Bell, W. R., and Tiao, G. C. (1983) 'Modelling Considerations in the Seasonal Adjustment of Economic Time Series', in A. Zellner (ed.), *Proceedings of the Conference on Applied Time Series Analysis of Economic Data*, Washington, DC: US Bureau of the Census.

Howson, S. (1975) *Domestic Monetary Management in Britain 1919–1938*, Cambridge University Press.

Jucker-Fleetwood, E. E. (1968) 'Montagu Norman in the Per Jacobson Diaries', *National Westminister Bank Quarterly Review*, November.

Keynes, J. M. (1925) *The Economic Consequences of Mr Churchill*, London: Hogarth Press.

Kindleberger, C.P. (1978) *Manias, Panics and Crashes,* London: Macmillan.

——and Laffargue, J. (1982) *Financial Crises: Theory, History, and Policy,* Cambridge University Press.

McKinnon, R. J. (1979) *Money in International Exchange: The Convertible Currency System*, New York: Oxford University Press.

Meltzer, A. H. (1982) 'Rational Expectations, Risk, Uncertainty, and Market Responses' in Wachtel, P. (ed.), *Crises in the Economic and Financial Structure,* Lexington: D. C. Health.

Middleton, R. (1981) 'The Constant Employment Budget Balance and British Budgetary Policy, 1929–39', *Economic History Review*, 34, (2)(May), 266–86.

Minsky, H. P. (1972) 'Financial Stability Revisited: The Economics of Disaster', in Board of Governors of the Federal Reserve System (ed.), *Reappraisal of the Federal Reserve Discount Mechanism*, Vol. 3, Washington, DC: Federal Reserve.

Moggridge, D. (1970) 'The 1931 Financial Crisis—A New View', *The Banker*, 120 (August), 120.

——(1972) *British Monetary Policy 1924–1931* Cambridge University Press.

Nurkse, R. (1944) *International Currency Experience*, Geneva: League of Nations.

Sargent, T. J. and Wallace, N. (1984) 'Some Unpleasant Monetarist Arithmetic', in B. Griffiths and G. E. Wood (eds), *Monetarism in the United Kingdom,* London: Macmillan.

Sayers, R. S. (1976) *The Bank of England 1891–1944*, Cambridge University Press.

Thomas, T. (1979) 'Aggregate Demand in the United Kingdom 1918–1945', in R. Floud and D. McCloskey (eds), *The Economic History of Britain Since 1700*, Vol. 2, Cambridge University Press.

Williamson, J. and Wood, G. E. (1976) 'The British Inflation: Indigenous or Imported?', *American Economic Review*, 66, 520–31.

8

Debt Management and Interest Rates: The British Stock Conversion of 1932*

INTRODUCTION

In 1932 the British Government executed a stock conversion. This conversion has a central role in the monetary history of Britain in that period. A succinct and forceful statement of the conventional view of this role is provided by Nicholas Kaldor, who in 1982 wrote as follows:

> With its [the Gold Standard's] abandonment, on 18th September, 1931, the rule of monetarism came to an abrupt end. The Bank Rate was reduced almost overnight from 6 per cent to 2 per cent, the new Chancellor, Neville Chamberlain, carried out the greatest conversion operation in history (the reduction of the interest on War Loan from 5 per cent to 3 per cent) which brought down the whole structure of long-term interest rates, and introduced a protective tariff on all manufactured goods which led to the fastest rate of economic growth in British history.[1] (Kaldor, 1982, p. 1)

The contemporary assessment was similar. Several countries in the British Commonwealth carried out stock conversions in the 1930s, in emulation of the British operation; and in 1958 Canada, citing this precedent and with the same objective—the lowering of interest rates—also completed a stock conversion.

It is not surprising that contemporaries were impressed by the operation, for it was enormous in scale. The conversion was of War Loan Stock 1929–47 into '3½ per cent 1952 or after'. War Loan Stock was issued in 1917, with 5 per cent coupon. Originally, £2553 m had been issued; by 31 March 1932

* Originally published as Forrest H. Capie, Terry C. Mills, and Geoffrey Wood (1986), 'Debt Management and Interest Rates: The British Stock Conversion of 1932,' *Applied Economics*, Vol. 18 (1986), pp. 1111–26, reproduced with the permission of the Taylor & Francis Group (www.tandfonline.com).

[1] The significance of the tariff has been dealt with elsewhere (Capie, 1978), but it is worth making the point here that Kaldor's 'fastest rate of economic growth in British history' is obtained by measuring from the trough of the Great Depression to the peak of the next cycle: not the usual way of measuring growth rates.

about £2100m was outstanding. (There were 2, 600, 000 separate holdings and it was estimated that only a little over £100m was held by foreigners.) This stock was more than a *quarter* of the whole national debt. (Put another way, it was equal in value to half the national income for 1932.) In contrast, the largest current outstanding stock (Exchequer 12¼ per cent 1999) is £2900m which in 3.2 per cent of the national debt (and is equal in value to just over 1.0 per cent of national income). But aside from confirming the technical skill and market influence of the managers of the UK's national debt, what did the operation achieve?

The aim of this chapter is to answer that question. First, some data on the years before and after the conversion are briefly set out, so as to put the operation into its proper context. There follows an examination of views on the conversion: why it was carried out, and how it was assessed. The details of the operation are then discussed. A statistical test is constructed and used to help reveal any effect on interest rates the operation may have had. Finally the findings are summarized.

ECONOMIC CONDITIONS

Table 8.1 serves to remind us of the sluggish performance of the British economy in the 1920s, and of the steady and noninflationary nature of the 1930s' recovery. Unemployment was persistently high in the 1920s and the

Table 8.1. Inflation, output, and interest rates, 1925–35

	Real GDP 1900 factor cost (£m)	Inflation rate (%)	Unemployment rate (%)	Consol yield (%)[a]	Bill rate(%)	Money growth (%)[a]
1925	4119	0	8.6	4.5	4.8	−0.9
1926	3939	−1.4	9.6	4.7	4.5	0.6
1927	4225	−2.4	7.4	4.6	4.3	1.7
1928	4295	−1.1	8.2	4.5	4.4	1.0
1929	4400	−0.3	8.0	4.4	4.5	−1.2
1930	4395	−0.4	12.3	4.4	2.3	3.3
1931	4153	−2.4	16.4	4.6	5.6	−4.7
1932	4154	−3.6	17.0	3.4	1.1	10.3
1933	4229	−1.4	15.4	3.4	1.1	0.4
1934	4526	−0.7	12.9	2.7	0.5	1.6
1935	4702	0.9	12.0	2.9	0.7	5.5

Note: [a]End of year figures.
Sources: Column 1: Feinstein (1972), table 5. T.16
Column 2: Feinstein (1972), table 61, T.133
Column 3: Feinstein (1972), table 58, T.128
Columns 4 and 6: Capie and Webber (1984).

rate doubled in the depression years. Prices had fallen more or less steadily throughout the 1920s and dropped more steeply in the worst depression years. Interest rates were fluctuating little, and were at the historically high levels associated with defence of the exchange rate. After Britain abandoned the gold standard in 1931, there was an abrupt change in interest rates, and recovery, albeit seen more clearly in Gross National Product (GNP) than in unemployment, got under way. At the same time, prices stopped falling, but there is no hint of any substantial and sustained rise in prices.

VIEWS ON THE CONVERSION

Two aspects of discussion of the operation should be considered: what did it achieve, and how did it achieve it? Some fifty years before him *The Economist* was no less enthusiastic than Kaldor.

> The result of the conversion operation which the Treasury announced on Monday night is more than a success—it is a triumph for the Government and the Nation . . . The prestige of British credit has been enhanced, and an inspiration has been given to other countries with debt-laden budgets to go and do likewise. (*The Economist*, 20 August 1932, p. 339).

Subsequent scholars have, in the main, agreed with this view.

According to Howson (1975), in the 1920s the Treasury was in favour of stimulating the economy and one method was lower interest rates. They therefore planned the conversion in order to bring down interest rates, and in 1931 and 1932, together with the Bank, they successfully achieved this. There were, in Howson's view, several factors behind the success but appeal to patriotism looms large, as does an increase in high-powered money in 1932. The importance of patriotism for the success of the operation is also implied by Sayers (1976), for in his account he talks of great sacrifices of income being made. Like Howson, he believes the Bank facilitated the operation by an expansion of the money supply, 'packing the market with an extra score of millions' (Sayers, 1976, Vol. II, p. 437).

Scepticism over the patriotic explanation was expressed by Nevin (1955) in the first substantial analysis of the operation. He believed that a variety of forces were at work and that the most important of these were outside the control of the authorities. The economy was in depression after 1929 and the low levels of income resulted in a decline in demand for transaction balances. Moreover, there was a growth of confidence in the government late in 1931, following which, and with the knowledge that there was an interest in conversion, there developed an expectation of conversion. This led to purchases of gilts in anticipation of falling interest rates and capital gains. These actions themselves helped bring about the anticipated outcome. All Nevin really allows the authorities is an augmentation of these forces by their 'substantial creation of credit' (a belief not really consistent with the behaviour of the base unless Nevin assigned great importance to the transitory upward fluctuation of the base in 1932); the institution of the Exchange Equalization Account (EEA; designed to smooth sterling fluctuations and so pave the way for a lower bank rate without external factors being allowed to intrude); and the careful design of the conversion offer itself. Nevin, then, differs from other scholars, both in playing down patriotism as a motive for accepting the conversion offer and in his view that the operation was of little significance for the course of interest rates.

How did those who thought the operation had a major effect on rates explain their belief? What model of rate determination had they in mind? Discussion of this scarce. Sayers (1976) addresses the question, but not in a fully satisfactory way:

> On this basis, implying a risk but not probability that the stock would be payable at 100 in 1929 or soon thereafter, the price could never rise far above 100, giving a running yield that was to an extraordinary extent subject to the pull of the five per cent coupon. With the price of the biggest and most freely traded stock in the market governed in this way, the long-term interest rates did not fall as much as they might have done in the first post-war decade. Maybe there was some irrational exaggeration of this influence, but people certainly believed it to be there. When in 1930–32 it became public policy to get long-term rates down, one argument for the drastic conversion operation was that the existence of the 5 per cent War Loan had kept the interest on all British securities 'at an unnecessarily high level'. (Sayers, 1976, p. 437)

The problem with that argument is that while the price was, indeed, kept close to par in expectation of conversion, *because* there was expectation of conversion the stock should have become effectively 'short', and have been treated as such in the market. Its existence may have kept up bill rates, and even short gilt rates, on this argument, but *not* the yield on consols. The effect of the expectation, in other words, should on this argument have been on short rates rather than on long, just, indeed, as conversion expectations had affected rates prior to Goschen's conversion of 1888 (Harley, 1976). Scepticism is reinforced by Tobin (1961) who explicitly addressed the effects of changes in the relative amounts of different kinds of debt:

> the *structure* will depend on relative supplies. In general, an increase in the supply of an asset—e.g. long-term government bonds—will cause its rate to rise relative to other rates. (Tobin, 1961, p. 33; emphasis added).

Tobin is writing about relative real rates, whereas Sayers' argument is about nominal yields. But, nonetheless, both the experience of Goschen's conversion and the argument of Tobin do tend to suggest that whatever effect the stock had, it was more likely to be on the shape of the yield curve, raising short rates relative to long, than on rates in general. Some scepticism about the general view of the operation would seem to be in order.

THE OPERATION IN DETAIL

The run-up to conversion

The stock's final redemption date was 1947, but the government had the right to give three months' notice of repayment at any time after 1 June 1929. The case for conversion was first seriously discussed in 1930, but as yields on gilts were expected to fall, it was decided that the terms on which a conversion could be achieved were sure to improve. Accordingly, nothing was done in 1930. In April 1931, when rates had been steady for about eight months (see Figure 8.1), planning began in earnest. Plans were drawn up to offer holders a twenty-year stock with a 4 per cent coupon (4 per cent would have been just below the then prevailing yield on consols). However, conditions deteriorated from the summer. First there came the Austro-German banking crisis, and then the abandoning by Britain of the gold standard. Amid this turbulence, the conversion plan was shelved.

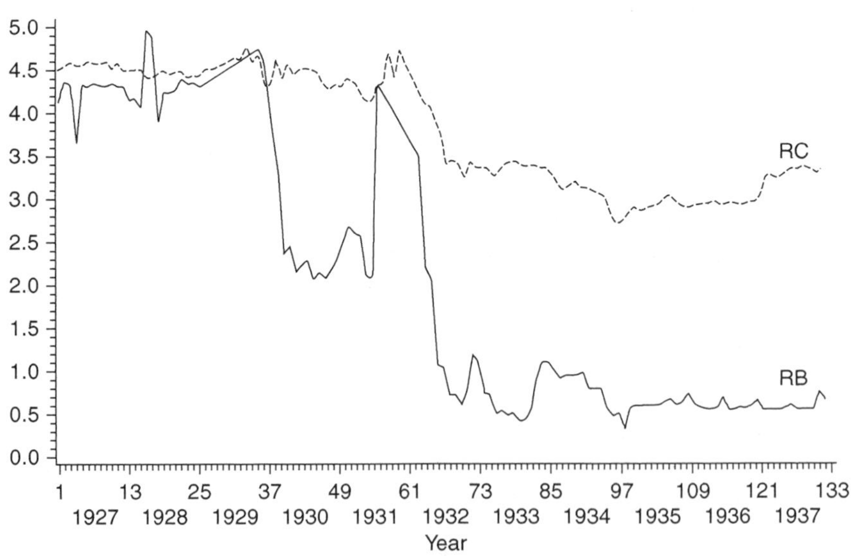

Figure 8.1. The effect of the Stock Conversion on Consol yield (RC) and three month bank bills (RB)

However, circumstances changed rapidly in 1932. Between February and April, the bank rate fell from 6 per cent to 3 per cent, and the Treasury Bill rate fell below 2 per cent. By June, a plan for conversion, offering a stock yielding 3 per cent was being drawn up. These plans were revealed very shortly before the operation took place, and in two stages.

The announcement and execution

On Tuesday, 28 June 1932 it was announced, without any reason being given, that the Stock Exchange would be open on Saturday 2 July.[2] Meanwhile, the Bank of England was active in the money markets. Conditions were very easy for an end quarter; indeed, it was the first time in ten years that at the end of a half-year the market did not seek help from the Discount Office of the Bank of England. Not surprisingly, this had an effect on the money stock. In the course of 1932 to the end of May, the monetary base had fallen at a rate of almost 10 per cent per annum. Between the end of May and the end of June, it grew at an annual rate of 14 per cent. This, in turn, had its expected short-term effect on interest rates, and on Thursday 30 June the bank rate was cut to 2 per cent for the first time since 1900. Also on 30 June, the Chancellor of the Exchequer (Neville Chamberlain) announced the conversion to the House of Commons. In that announcement, the chancellor laid particular emphasis on two points. First, the budgetary strains imposed by the existence of the stock (he pointed out that every ½ per cent off the coupon would lower debt service costs by £10m per annum; and second, that the existence of this stock, according to the 'great consensus of opinion', had 'kept the interest on all British securities at an unnecessary high level' (*Hansard*, 1932, Vol. 267, col. 2122; Sayers, 1976, p. 432). The Chancellor then appealed to patriotism for the acceptance of the conversion.

Further, he offered more tangible incentives to convert, and deterrents to delaying acceptance. Those who gave notice of acceptance within the first month were to be offered a cash bonus of 1 per cent of stock converted. Stockbrokers, banks, and solicitors who handled these acceptances were to be paid ¼ per cent commission during the first month, but only ⅛ per cent (the normal rate of commission) on stock converted in August and September. There was also a provision that holders who did not request cash repayment by 30 September would be deemed to have converted. Thus there were substantial financial inducements to holders to make an early decision, and to financial intermediaries to press their facilities on hundreds of

[2] The announcement was made by the Chairman of the Stock Exchange, presumably on the prompting of the Governor of the Bank of England. There seems to be no record of their meeting, or of what was discussed between them.

thousands of small holders. Two steps were also taken to deter holders from thoughts of alternative investments. An informal embargo was placed on new capital issues and the existing issue of National Savings Certificates was withdrawn.

A massive publicity campaign was launched, which was directed by the newly formed War Loan Conversion Publicity Bureau. The press was thoroughly briefed and the radio was used to support the conversion. In addition, the small holder was assailed from all sides by posters and newspaper advertisements. Each day, a list of institutions which had agreed to convert their holdings was also published as a means of giving holders added justification for converting.

On 1 July all papers carried large spreads with heavily typed headlines outlining the scheme and reporting on the enthusiastic reception in Parliament and the City. Reports followed of the favourable reactions of several foreign countries, particularly those of the Commonwealth where many hoped to follow Britain's lead. Emphasis was given to the favourable response of the big institutions as an example to the rest of the country. By the middle of the month all papers were reporting on the rush to convert in order to benefit from the cash bonus and tax exemptions. Advertisements were placed by many of the big institutions. The Midland Bank offered free services to War Loan Stock holders, the Eagle Star Insurance Company's advertisement talked of 'a scheme by which everyone who wishes to be patriotic can purchase'. Only occasionally was there a report that dampened a little of the euphoria. For example, the *Morning Post* warned that the net return was not as high as it might as first have seemed (12 July 1932).

Response of Institutions

The clearing banks were considered important allies. If they accepted the conversion, their example would help in influencing their customers all over the country. It would be a powerful argument for their branch managers to use when seeking their customers' assent forms. Therefore on 5 July 1932 the Deputy Governor met the clearing bank chairmen and asked them to convert their holdings as a public service. All agreed except one, Midland Bank. The Midland Bank maintained that their first duty was to their depositors. That bank would therefore not accept an 'irredeemable', as any stock which does not have to be redeemed by a given date is considered, in exchange for their War Loan 5 per cent holding, but would accept cash on 1 December. The Chairman of Midland Bank (R. McKenna, a former chancellor of the exchequer) was invited to meet with the Governor the following morning. The Governor tried to persuade him to convert the whole of his £30m holding, but the Chairman would only convert £5m and remained obstinate about the remaining £25m. The Governor then said, 'I'll buy the lot', and this was done, though we do not know at what price.[3]

There is, however, a clue in Clay's biography of Norman. From that account it seems that McKenna was prepared to sell 'at the price of the day' (Clay, 1957, p. 458). Sayers identifies 6 July as the occasion of the interview. The price that day was £101.00, which in view of the £1 cash bonus on conversion would have given the Midland neither an immediate profit nor loss. However, McKenna may have feared that the stock into which he was expected to convert would depreciate, and there may have been further elements influencing his behaviour, such as his desire to resist the power of the Bank of England. Midland Bank then converted their remaining £5m and the bankers' committee was able to say, not with complete honesty, that all the London clearing banks had converted their own holdings.[4]

Finally, attempts were made to stigmatize nonassented stock. Most importantly, it was indicated to the discount houses that nonassented stock, which immediately on announcement of the conversion became a bill of known (and short) maturity, would not be eligible for rediscount at the Bank of England. This ensured that the discount houses, who even then were the major buyers of short-term, eligible paper, had in effect no interest in taking any unassented stock on their books. (Indeed, this also prompted them to assent to the conversion of any stock they already possessed.) By this action the marketability of the unassented stock was much diminished.

As has already been noted, there was also more conventional action by the Bank: the expansion of the monetary base. The expansion was, however, no greater than had occurred on several occasions over a similar period of time in previous years, and was soon removed. The expansion may have played a part but it is difficult to attach to it the importance ascribed by Sayers and Howson.

3 Quoted by Sayers (1976, p. 444). The original source is the Governor's diary. It should be noted that the new stock was in bearer form, and interest was paid gross, rather than net, of UK income tax. Both of these factors supposedly made stocks more attractive to foreigners, and were probably incorporated to help boost the reserves after the strains of 1931.

4 There has been no record found as yet in Midland Bank's archives of their position, or of the price at which the stock was bought by the Bank of England. Midland Bank's Archivist (Dr Edwin Green) has carried out a full search. The board minutes show that the Bank's directors were advised of all purchases and sales of government stock throughout the period. For the months between June and December 1932, despite records of numerous other transactions in government stock, there is no mention of the sale/conversion undertaken with Norman. The assumption must be that McKenna received verbal, non-minuted approval.

QUESTIONS

From this account of the details of the operation, two features stand out. The first is the acceptance, from the very beginning that it would lower *all* UK interest rates. This is discussed in the next section. The other is the extensive use of not always entirely honest advertising (for example, the report of the behaviour of the clearing banks). How important was the barrage of propaganda? The answer to that question depends on whether acceptance of the conversion was profitable.

Investors were being invited to switch to a longer and lower yielding stock—to accept more potential price volatility for less return. Unless the terms of that offer were more favourable than those under which investors would have made that switch without the offer, it would appear that some degree of extra inducement—the propaganda—was indeed necessary.[5] At what price did the stock stand in the market, and what could it buy? The answer to these questions does of course vary according to the date when the data are gathered, and the choice of data requires a little consideration. The opportunities should be calculated in a period of calm as near before the conversion as possible, a period when no major events were disturbing interest rates or interest rate prospects, and when the next major event was the conversion, so that 'nothing' happens between the date used for the calculations and the conversion. This suggests that calculations should be made in May 1932, for the sharp fall in rates after the abandoning of the gold standard was over by April, and the conversion was being planned in June. In May, the price of 5 per cent War Loan ranged from $100\frac{15}{16}$ to $101\frac{9}{16}$ and was at its highest on 13 May.

There was not a wide range of stocks into which to switch; there were only eleven stocks in the market of over five years to redemption, and of these, eight were small issues. Had a holder of the stock switched into Consols, for £100 face value of the stock he would have received £159.60 of Consols, and thus an income of £4.80 per annum in perpetuity had he switched when the stock was at its average price in that month. These figures compared with £3 per annum for at least twenty years. Comparison cannot be precise, for expectations of when the new stock would be redeemed are relevant. Its earliest redemption date was 1952, and it had no final redemption date; but as it was the practice then (as it is now) to view stocks without a final redemption date as perpetuities, comparing the new stock with Consols with no adjustment for prospective redemption is not too misleading.[6] This comparison suggests that the

[5] This assumes that announcement of the offer had no dramatic effect on expectations. Whether, in fact, it had is discussed in the next section of the chapter.

[6] Consols are of course potentially redeemable, on three months' notice. See Harley (1976) for the importance of this from time to time.

conversion offer was rather different from what was available in the market before the operation. The bonus which was offered narrowed the difference, but did not completely eliminate it.

Nevertheless, the operation was in at least one sense a success. By the end of July, when the cash bonus offer expired and the commission rate was halved, assents had been received for 88½ per cent of the total outstanding. On 1 December when cash repayment was to be made only £151m had to be found by the Bank of England. That in itself was important. For had the operation failed, necessitating cash repayment of stock, the monetary base would have jumped by 400 per cent of its level at the end of 1931, as compared to an annual growth rate of around 1 per cent between 1923 and 1931.[7] But did the operation affect long-term interest rates?

INTEREST RATES AND THE CONVERSION

Choice of technique

In estimating the effect of an event such as the stock conversion on the behaviour of a variable, the usual procedure would be to construct and estimate a model to determine the behaviour of the variable and either include the event which is likely to affect it in that model, or ascribe an abnormally large error (if any) which occurred at the appropriate time to the occurrence of that event. What the present context requires is a model of interest rate determination. Such a model would start from the Fisher identity, that the nominal rate equals the real rate plus the expected rate of inflation, and model the two components of the nominal rate, the rate of concern here. Examples of such models can be found, specified in great detail, in, for example, Cagan (1972) or Friedman and Schwartz (1983). The data required include, inter alia, income—possibly corrected to a permanent income series—consumption and investment functions, a money demand function, and a series for expected inflation. The last of these is not available and would in any event be particularly unreliable in 1932, the year after the collapse of a monetary standard which had been used with only wartime

[7] Observing that the dangers were substantial, 'should the operation fail' does prompt a further question, albeit one a little aside from the objective of this study. Nowadays, 'conversions' in the form of the gradual replacement of stocks as their redemption date gets nearer, are going on all the time, and generally a range of stocks is being sold by the authorities. Why was only one stock offered in 1932? So far searches of archives and other written sources have not made it possible to conjecture with a reasonable degree of confidence as to the answer. This requires further investigation.

suspensions since 1717. Quarterly data on income, savings, and investment are not available, whilst an annual model of such an episode is unlikely to be illuminating.

In view of these problems, another statistical approach is chosen, one which is second best in principle, but in this particular case the best available. The technique used is time-series intervention analysis. The conversion is modelled as an intervention which may induce a change in the time path of interest rates. It is possible by this technique to discover whether there is any statistically significant change in the series around the time of the conversion. The technique does not involve an economic model of the effect, but it shows whether there is an effect to model. It is, in other words, identical in principle to the use of a dummy variable to capture the impact of a one-off event. Some details of the technique are set out in the Appendix; for further discussion see Box and Jenkins (1970); Box and Tiao (1975); and Jenkins (1979).[8]

Tests

Two interest rate series were employed to investigate the possible effect of the Stock Conversion. These were the Consol yield, used as the representative long rate and denoted RC, and the rate on three month bank bills, the representative short rate, denoted RB. End month values were used, the data period being January 1927 to December 1937, a total of 132 observations. The two series are shown in Figure 8.1.

An ARIMA (0,1,2) process was found to fit adequately the RC series;

$$(1 - B)\mathrm{RC}_t = (1 - \theta_1 B - \theta_2 B^2)a_t \qquad (1)$$

with parameter estimates $\underset{(0.09)}{\hat{\theta}_1 = 0.16};\ \underset{(0.09)}{\hat{\theta}_2 = -0.29};\ \hat{\sigma}_a = 0.102.$

(See the Appendix for a discussion of the notation used in this section.)

As with dummy variable techniques in general, the technique being employed is ideally used when the timing of the intervention is known. The timing of the conversion is certainly known, but it was discussed in advance and there is some difference of view as to whether it was anticipated.[9] Accordingly, a selection of interventions, that is a range of

[8] This procedure runs the risk of finding a large yield movement which could perhaps be explained but not modelled. But, as will emerge below, there was no such large movement.

[9] Inspection of the price of the stock does not suggest anticipation of the conversion. But Sayers (1976, p. 431) remarks that 'It [the conversion] had for years been a hackneyed subject of discussion in financial circles'. To the contrary, Ian MacPherson, former senior partner in the stockbroking firm of Buckmaster and Moore, an associate of J. M. Keynes, and a relative by marriage to Montague Norman, still vividly recollected sitting in a client's office in Glasgow

starting dates, was considered. The model finally selected for the Consol yield on the basis of goodness of fit and model adequacy was:

$$(1 - B)\mathrm{RC}_t = w_0(1 - B)\eta_t^{(66)} + (1 - \theta_1 B - \theta_2 B^2)a_t, \tag{2}$$

with $\hat{w}_0 = -0.22; \hat{\theta}_1 = 0.20; \hat{\theta}_2 = -0.30; \hat{\sigma}_a = 0.100.$
$\quad\quad(0.10) \quad\quad (0.09) \quad\quad (0.09)$

The intervention occurs in June 1932 (the month the conversion was announced) and is of the step variety, the response function being depicted in Figure 8.2a. The Stock Conversion therefore had an immediate and permanent effect on the RC series, although the magnitude of the intervention is quite small, reducing the level of the series by 0.22 percentage points. The estimate of the response function is just significant and as a consequence, the error variance of the model is reduced slightly by incorporating the intervention. It can therefore be concluded that at the time of the conversion, the Consol yield series shows a small, but statistically significant, downward shift. Explanations are discussed below.

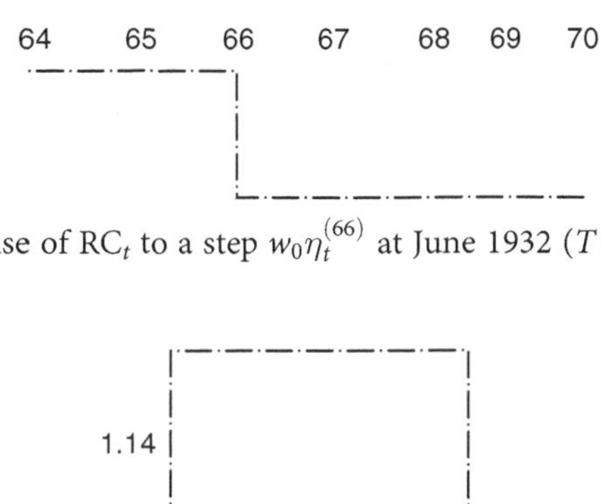

Figure 8.2a. Response of RC_t to a step $w_0\eta_t^{(66)}$ at June 1932 (T = 66; w = –0.22)

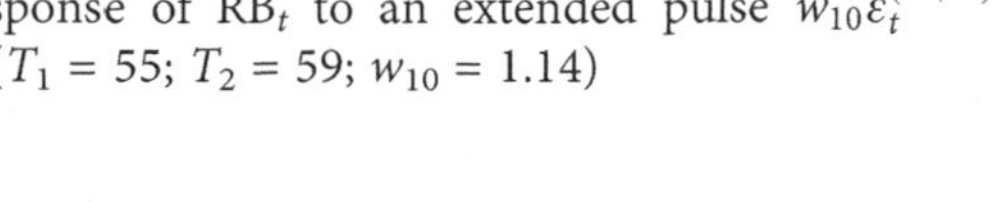

Figure 8.2b. Response of RB_t to an extended pulse $w_{10}\varepsilon_t^{(55,59)}$ between July and November 1931 (T_1 = 55; T_2 = 59; w_{10} = 1.14)

when that client received a telephone call from London telling him of the announcement and described the event as being like a 'bolt from the blue'. (This information was gained through an interview with MacPherson, who, at the time of writing, was still active, albeit on a part-time basis, on the Stock Exchange.)

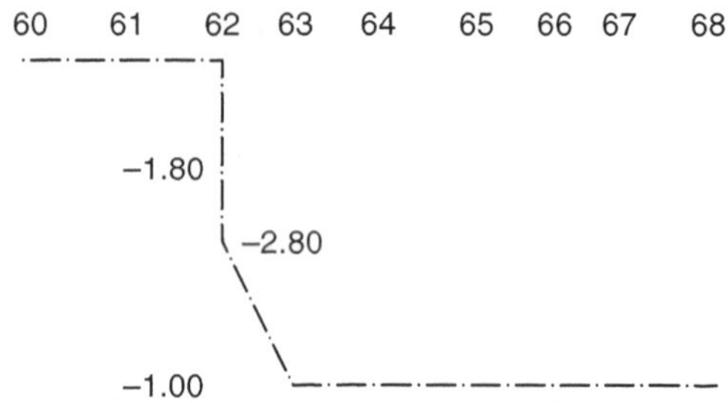

Figure 8.2c. Response of RB_t to a step $(w_{10} + w_{21}B)\eta_t^{(62)}$ at Febraury 1932 ($T = 62$; $w_{10} = -1.80$; $w_{21} = -1.00$)

It is necessary next to consider the effect of the intervention on the yield on three month bank bills (RB). The RB series was also adequately fitted by an ARIMA (0, 1, 2) process:

$$(1 - B)RB_t = (1 - \theta_2 B^2)a_t, \tag{3}$$

with θ_2 =0.32; σ_a =0.405.
(0.09)

By searching for various interventions as described for the long interest rate series, the following model was arrived at:

$$(1 - B)RB_t = (w_0 + w_1 B)(1 - B)\eta_t^{(62)} + (1 - \theta_2 B^2)a_t, \tag{4}$$

with $w_0 = -1.54$; $w_1 = -0.96$; $\theta_2 = -0.25$; $\sigma_a = 0.347$.
(0.34) (0.35) (0.09)

The intervention occurs in February 1932, thus anticipating the conversion by four months. It is again of the step variety, implying that the level of the RB series is permanently reduced by 2.50 percentage points, although this fall is achieved over two months, roughly two-thirds of the fall occurring immediately and the remaining one-third being delayed one month. The parameters of the response function are fairly precisely estimated, and the inclusion of the intervention reduces the error variance by approximately 15 per cent.

Inspection of Figure 18.1 shows this decrease in RB quite clearly, but it is also apparent that this fall was preceded by an equally sharp rise and fall in the latter months of 1931, associated of course with exchange rate problems and consequent upon the abandoning by Britain of the gold standard. Accordingly this whole movement was modelled by an 'extended pulse' intervention, leading to the model.

$$(1 - B)RB_t = W_{10}(1 - B)\xi^{(55,59)} + (w_{20} + w_{21}B)(1 - B)\eta_t^{(62)} + (1 - \theta_2 B^2)a_t \tag{5}$$

with $w_{10} = 1.14$; $w_{20} = -1.80$; $w_{21} = -1.00$; $\theta_2 = -0.22$; $\sigma_a = 0.318$
(0.23) (0.33) (0.32) (0.09)

This earlier intervention increases the level of RB by 1.12 percentage points between July and November 1931 before disappearing. Its inclusion strengthens the Stock Conversion intervention, increasing the permanent reduction in the level of RB to 2.8 percentage points, again spread over two months in a 2:1 ratio. The response functions of these interventions are shown in Figure 8.2b. No other significant interventions occurs. Accordingly the sharp rise and fall in the bill rate is best viewed not as two independent interventions, but as an 'extended pulse'. (See also Figure 8.2c.)

Interpretation

These are the statistical findings. What is their economic significance? First, the bill rate. The sharp rise and fall in that series was best modelled as an extended pulse, rising with pressure on sterling and falling when the defence of sterling was ended at the establishment of the EEA. In terms of timing, exchange rate policy can explain the behaviour of the bill rate. The Consol yield displays two interesting characteristics, one shown by the statistical work in this chapter and one from Figure 8.1. The chart shows that after the conversion, an operation which lengthened the maturity of the debt, long rate rose relative to short rates. This is as would be expected from Tobin's (1961) discussion of the effect of relative supplies of debt on relative yields.

What of the drop in yield that coincided with the conversion? That, at first sight, seems harder to explain. Inflationary expectations may have dropped sharply. But, as noted earlier, the Treasury wanted to ease monetary conditions. It is hard to reconcile the public declaration of that intention with falling inflationary expectations. (Monetary conditions, as measured by growth of the base, in fact did change somewhat; between 1925 and 1931 it fell by about 0.2 per cent p.a. on average and between 1932 and 1938, grew by about 5.3 per cent p.a. on average. But, in any event, no one could anticipate that in 1932.) Could the real rate have fallen? The data are not available to calculate the real rate at all sensibly. But 1932 was the trough of the recession; rising demands for resources thereafter should raise rather than lower the real rate.

There is, however, an explanation available. One of the widely advertised purposes of the conversion was to lower debt service costs, and thereby taxes. This was emphasized by the Chancellor in his speech of 30 June 1932. Marginal tax rates were made lower than they would otherwise have been by the operation. This would lower the *before tax* rate of return—that observed in the market—at which assets would be held. The successful conversion by its effect on expected taxes could thus have produced the observed effect on the Consol yield. (For futher discussion of this type of effect, see Barro, 1974 and 1978.) The behaviour of the time-series of short and long interest rates which the present statistical procedure described is thus capable of economic explanation.

SUMMARY AND CONCLUSIONS

There can be no doubt that the conversion reduced debt service costs. This it did by some £30m p.a., roughly an eighth of the yield of income tax. Thus, it certainly attained one of the Treasury's objectives. The Bank took a chance in offering only one stock—and that with a lower yield and a longer term than the one being redeemed—but the conversion was largely accepted. There can be no doubt that the episode is, in Sayers' (1976, p. 431) words 'illuminating on the ways of the Bank: its determined exercise of all the power derived from its position in financial markets'.

But did it have a dramatic effect on long-term interest rates? Here the conclusion is different from the traditional one. There is no evidence that there was a dramatic fall in the consol yield brought about by the conversion. Until now Nevin (1955) has been alone in arguing that the conversion did not dramatically usher in an era of cheap money. The present results support his view.

APPENDIX

The following summarizes the technique used in the chapter. A detailed discussion can be found in the references given in the text.

Let us assume that, in the absence of any intervention, an interest rate, x_t, can be modelled by a mixed autoregressive moving average process:

$$\gamma(B)x_t = \theta(B)a_t, \tag{A1}$$

where B is the backshift operation such that $B^k x_t = x_{t-k}$; a_t is a sequence of independently distributed normal variables having mean zero variance σ_a^2 (i.e. white noise); $\gamma(B) = 1 - \gamma_1 B - \gamma_2 B^2 \ldots \gamma_P B^{P1}$; and $\theta(B) = 1 - \theta_1 B - \theta_2 B^2 \ldots \theta_q B^q$ are 'autoregressive' and 'moving average' polynomials in B of degrees p_1 and q respectively, the roots of $\theta(B)$ lying outside and those of $\gamma(B)$ lying on or outside the unit circle.

To represent a homogeneous nonstationary series, the operator $\gamma(B)$ may be factored as

$$\gamma(B) = (1 - B)^d \phi(B), \tag{A2}$$

where the roots of $\varphi(B)$ all lie outside the unit circle. Thus the process (Equation A1) with the factorization (Equation A2) represents an autoregressive—integrated—moving average model of orders ($p = p_1 - d$, d, q), i.e. an ARIMA (p, d, q) model.

An intervention may be regarded as an exogeneous event occurring at time T which has an effect (either permanent or transitory) on the level of x_t. If a single intervention is considered, this may be modelled by extending Equation A1 to

$$x_t = \Big(w(B)/\delta(B)\Big)\mathrm{I}_t + \Big(\theta(B)/\gamma(B)\Big)a_t, \tag{A3}$$

where $w(B) = w_0 + w_1 B + w_2 B^2 + \ldots + w_r B^r$ and $\delta(B) = 1 - \delta_1 (B) - \delta_2 B^2 \ldots -\delta_q B^q$, the roots of $w(B)$ lying outside and those of $\delta(B)$ outside or on, the unit circle.

The intervention I_t can usefully take three forms. A 'step' intervention is defined as

$$\mathrm{I}_t = \eta_t^{(T)} = \begin{cases} o & t < T \\ 1 & t \geq T \end{cases} \tag{A4}$$

Similarly, a 'pulse' intervention is defined as

$$\mathrm{I}_t = \xi_t^{(T)} = \begin{cases} o & t \neq T \\ 1 & t = T \end{cases}$$

These forms can be combined to define an 'extended pulse' intervention as

$$\mathrm{I}_t = \xi_t^{(T_1,T_2)} = \sum_{T-T1}^{T1} \xi_t^{(T)} = \begin{cases} o & t < T_1, t < T_2 \\ 1 T_1 \leq t \leq T_2 \end{cases} \tag{A5}$$

Box and Tiao (1975) and Jenkins (1979) discuss examples of the dynamic effects (or response functions that result from assuming specific orders for the polynominals w (B) and $\delta(B)$). In the results to be presented we shall be interested in the response functions depicted in Figure 8.3.

Other useful functions are examined in the above references. As can be seen from Figure 8.3, a pulse intervention will produce a transitory response from x_1, whereas a

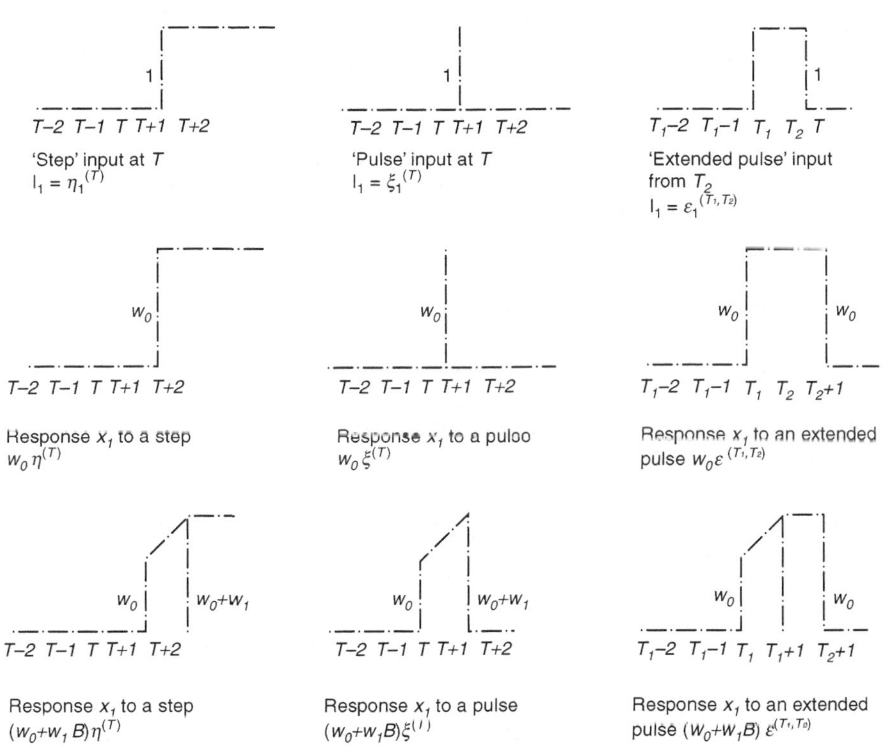

Figure 8.3. Response functions associated with particular interventions

step intervention will produce a permanent response, the forms of the polynominals *w (B)* and *δ(B)* determining the speed and strength of the response.

In general, Equation A3 can be extended to incorporate *n* interventions, yielding the model,

$$\chi_t = \sum_{i=1}^{A} \Big(w_1(B)/\delta_1(B)\Big)\mathrm{I}_t + \Big(\theta(B)/\gamma(B)\Big)a_t \tag{A6}$$

and the identification and estimation of such models is discussed by Box and Tiao (1975) and Jenkins (1979), being an extension of the iterative modelling procedure developed by Box and Jenkins (1970).

REFERENCES

Barro, R. J. (1974) 'Are Government Bonds Net Wealth?' *Journal of Political Economy,* 82, 1095–111.

——(1978) 'Public Debt and Taxes', in M. J. Boskin (ed.), *Federal Tax Reform*, San Francisco: Institute of for Contemporary Studies.

Box, G. E. P. and Jenkins, G. M. (1970) *Time-Series Analysis, Forecasting and Control*, San Francisco: Holden-Day.

——and Tiao, G. C. (1975) 'Intervention Analysis with Applications to Economic and Econometric Problems', *Journal of the American Statistical Association,* 70, 78–9.

Cagan, P. (1972) *The Channels of Monetary Influences on Interest Rates*, New York: National Bureau of Economic Research, Columbia University Press.

Capie, F. H. (1978) 'The British Tariff and Industrial Protection in 1930s', *Economic History Review,* 31, 399–409.

——and Webber, A. (1984) *Monetary Statistics of the Untied Kingdom, 1870–1982,* London: Allen & Unwin.

Clay, H. (1957) *Lord Norman*, London: Macmillan.

Economist, The (1932) 20 August.

Feinstein, C. H. (1972) *National Income, Expenditure and Output of the United Kingdom*, Cambridge University Press.

Friedman, M. and Schwartz, A. J. (1983) *Monetary Trends in the US and UK*, Chicago: National Bureau of Economic Research, Chicago University Press.

Hansard (1932) Volume 267 (30 June).

Harley, C. K. (1976) 'Goschen's Conversion of the National Debt and the Yield on Consols', *Economic History Review* (February), 101–6.

Howson, S. (1975) *Domestic Monetary Management in Britain 1919–38*, Cambridge University Press.

Jenkins, G. M. (1979) *Practical Experiments with Modelling and Forecasting Time Series*, Jersey: Gwillam Jenkins Press.

Kaldor, N. (1982) *The Scourge of Monetarism*, Oxford: Blackwell.

Morning Post (1932) 'City Facts and Figures,' 12 July.

Nevin, E. T. (1955) *The Mechanism of Cheap Money: A Study of British Monetary Policy 1931–1939*, Cardiff: University of Wales Press.

Sayers, R. S. (1976) *The Bank of England 1891–1944,* 3 Vols, Cambridge University Press.

Tobin, J. (1961) 'Money, Capital and Other Stores of Value,' *AER Papers and Proceedings*, 51, 26–37.

9

Policy-Makers in Crisis: A Study of Two Devaluations*

Studies of economic policy-making generally examine the policy-maker in the normal business of life; going about whatever is his day-to-day business. Indeed, if the studies are statistical (using reaction functions, for example) they have no choice, for they must use data series which have sufficient observations to permit meaningful statistical manipulation. In this chapter we take an entirely different course, and consider the policy-maker out of his day-to-day routine, in circumstances when, at any rate from his point of view, things seem to be going badly wrong. We consider the policy-maker in crisis.

To widen our range of observations and to see whether comparisons are revealing we consider two episodes. After both the First and Second World Wars, the United Kingdom returned to an exchange rate close to that of before the wars. In each case, it held to that rate for only a few years. After returning to gold (at $4.86 to the £) in 1925, sterling was floated in 1931; in 1946 the £ was pegged at $4.04, the rate which had been adopted at the outbreak of war, and it was devalued in 1949 to $2.80, a rate which then held for almost twenty years. In this chapter we study and compare these two episodes. Throughout we have two questions particularly in mind. The first is, were there common factors in the way policy-makers reacted to these exchange crises, or were they both unique events treated uniquely in the world of policy-maker? Whatever the detailed answer to that, it is clear that to policy-makers the events had at least one feature in common: they were both major crises. As will emerge

* We are indebted to Dr Alan Webber for his assistance in providing data for this chapter, to Professor Leslie Pressnell for detailed guidance at certain points, and to Professors Donald Hodgman, Roland Vaubel, and John Woolley for their comments on a draft version. For the sake of clarity, it should be noted that throughout this chapter exchange rates are quoted in units of foreign currency per £1. Thus, for example, an 'overvaluation' is when sterling buys 'too many' (by some criterion) units of foreign currency.

Originally published as Forrest Capie and Geoffrey Wood (1987) 'Policy Makers in Crisis: A Study of Two Devaluations', pp. 166–92, in Donald R. Hodgman and Geoffrey E. Wood (eds), *Monetary and Exchange Rate Policy* (Palgrave Macmillan), reproduced with the permission of Palgrave Macmillan.

below, the approach to 1931 was characterized by increasingly frantic discussion of measures to defend the £. And of 1949, Sir Alec Cairncross, who was at that time in the Economic Section of the Cabinet Office, wrote (1983): 'To those who took part in it, the devaluation of Sterling in September 1949, from $4.03 to $2.80 to the pound was one of the most dramatic episodes in the post-war history of the United Kingdom.'

Were the events as important to the economy as they were to 'those who took part' in the decisions; and if not, why not? That is second issue on which we focus.

The structure of the chapter is as follows. We initially examine each episode separately, starting in each case with the decision to fix the parity, so as to understand the context in which the 'crisis' exchange rate decisions were taken. Then we examine the pressures on that parity and the response to them, culminating with the parity's being abandoned. The consequences for the economy of the depreciation are then considered. Last, we compare the two episodes.

THE END OF THE GOLDEN AGE

Britain suspended gold convertibility in 1914, and resumed it in 1925 at the 1914 parity. About the resumption two questions arise. Why did Britain return to gold? And why did it do so at the 1914 parity? The case for the return to gold was stated very clearly by the Treasury.

> Whatever its imperfections gold had for centuries commanded the confidence of the civilised world and has continued to command it. If the Gold Standard fails to give complete stability, its adoption is nevertheless the most simple and direct method of obtaining a high degree of stability. It is not proved that any other standard would give even as good results. All countries which have successfully restored stability and confidence in their currencies after the disturbances of the last ten years have done so on a gold basis. (Treasury Memorandum, Gold Standard Bill, 28 April 1925)

This confidence was based on two types of evidence. One was the experience of countries without the restraints of gold—there had been wide swings in prices and output after the adoption of 'managed money' in 1914, and particularly during 1918–24 when wartime controls were forsaken and Germany, Austria, and others had undergone alarming inflationary experiences. That was part of the evidence that gold was the best available option. Second were perceptions of how the gold standard had worked before 1914.

THE WORKING OF THE GOLD STANDARD

Britain had been on the gold standard (and at an unchanged parity) since 1717 (with the exception of the years of the Napoleonic Wars) until the outbreak of the First World War. Therefore 1870–1914 was the continuation of long experience, and a most satisfactory continuation. UK prices were steady, first drifting downwards and then upwards. Output too fluctuated moderately, while long bond yields (as expected given the performance of prices) moved scarcely at all, and an adequate reserve of gold was maintained by small movements in short rates. The UK was at the heart of the gold standard system, chronically exporting capital, and accommodating balance of payments fluctuations by modest changes in its rate of export of capital produced by small interest rate changes.

According to a survey in *The Economist*, November 1907, interest rate changes had very little effect on economic activity, affecting only inventory holding. It seems plain, from both the data and the comments of contemporary observers, that these interest rate changes were regarded as transitory fluctuations about a stable expected mean, and therefore did not affect long-term decisions. As Hawtrey (1938) observed, the relationship between changes in Bank rate and Consol yield 'seems to have been both very slight and capricious'. This is clear in the data, and is as one would expect in a period of price stability. It reflects the fact that interest rate changes were designed only to offset transitory, random fluctuations in the balance of payments. The world was a stable one. It is no wonder that there was a strong desire to return to gold.[1]

THE DECISION TO RETURN

The decision to return seemed well-founded in experience. Sayers (1960) describes it as a policy aimed at increasing employment by providing a stable international financial setting for world trade. The next issue policy-makers addressed was: when, and at what parity, should it be done? There are now many narrative of this—Moggridge (1969), Howson (1975), and, most recently, Cairncross and Eichengreen (1983). Discussion here can be brief.

[1] Williams (1963) argues that the system was in fact in many ways a sterling system, working as smoothly as it did because sterling was regarded by foreign central banks as being 'as good as gold'. Further discussion of the working of the gold standard, and the UK's experience from 1870 to 1914 can be found in Bordo (1984) 'The Gold Standard: The Traditional Approach', in Bordo and Schwartz (1984).

Sterling had been pegged throughout most of the First World War, and thus kept close to its pre-war rate despite the suspension of the gold standard. After the War, the rate was allowed to move, and slid to a low point of \$3.20 in 1920. But from 1919 it had been government policy to return to gold, and this probably underpinned the rate. At any event it rose to \$4.70 by March 1923, fell to \$4.26 by January 1924, and thereafter rose towards the pre-war parity. This timing was convenient, for the wartime measures modifying the gold standard had in 1920 been replaced by the Gold and Silver Export Embargo Act, an act with a fixed five-year term. Sayers (1960) remarks that there was no particular element of choice in that term: five years was a normal period for temporary legislation. That term did, however, mean that by 1925 a decision to do something had to be taken—the option of deciding to do nothing was not available.

The announcement of the decision to return to gold, at the pre-war parity, was made by Mr Churchill in his budget speech of April 1925. Partly because it ended a period of uncertainty, the decision was initially welcomed widely, with few reservations about the exchange rate.[2] Criticism did not develop extensively until the summer of 1925, when Keynes published his polemic, *The Economic Consequences of Mr Churchill*, and Stamp criticized the decision in an Addendum to a report on the Coal Industry Dispute. Churchill himself became increasingly concerned by his decision, and came to believe that the return to gold was 'the greatest mistake of his life' (Grigg, 1948). But was it? The decision was certainly not precipitate. The case had been argued in 1919 by the Cunliffe Committee. In 1922 British delegates to the Genoa Conference had argued for a worldwide return to gold, wherever possible at pre-war parities. The Association of Clearing Banks had supported the return, as had the Federation of British Industry. At the time of return, unemployment was still high, but was concentrated in industries which were experiencing the continuation of a pre-First-World-War decline, resulting largely from competition from overseas producers whose comparative advantage was such that a modest sterling devaluation would not have helped. Further, unemployment was also due to a depression of world markets, itself partly a product of currency disorganization.

How big a devaluation was considered desirable? Those few who opposed the return gathered around Keynes, who, on the basis of Purchasing Power Parity (PPP) calculations, claimed sterling was overvalued by around 10 per cent. The case for return was not really disputed—attention focused on the rate. Not all accepted Keynes's calculation, however. Gregory (1957) showed that the overvaluation appeared much less when a more appropriate price index was used,[3] and there was a substantial body of opinion which held it to

[2] See the advice of the Federation of British Industry to the Chancellor, in a letter of 18 March 1925.

[3] Keynes used one for the State of Massachusetts, not for the US; Sayers (1960) remarks of this, in a footnote, that 'Keynes used the wrong index numbers, and Gregory the right, yet Keynes

be a matter of principle that sterling should return to gold at the old parity—for to do otherwise would be a partial repudiation of debt. This attitude was clearly expressed by Sir Henry Strakosch, in the course of a controversy with Keynes carried on in the correspondence columns of *The Times*. Strackosch wrote of 'devaluation—more appropriately called repudiation' (*The Times*, 3 July 1925). This attitude persisted certainly until after the Second World War. Choice of parity was then influenced by the consideration that, whatever Britain's economic difficulties with the parity, a devaluation would make still poorer the poor countries of the Empire, who had trusted Britain by holding their foreign exchange reserves in sterling (see pp. 196–9). Even more recently, in 1967, it was conjectured in the press that similar views on the morality of a devaluation by an economy with substantial liabilities owed to foreigners and denominated in its own currency prompted the resignation of James Callaghan as Chancellor of the Exchequer after the devaluation of 1967.

Despite the existence of this 'moral' view, there was considerable discussion of the plan to return to gold before the event, and the discussion was conducted in economic terms. Whether there should be a return, at some time, was discussed and some discussion concentrated on the parity.

The reasons advanced for a return to gold were various. Undoubtedly part of the attraction lay in the prosperity which had been associated with the gold standard—whether it had been caused by it was little discussed, and has, indeed, seldom been properly examined to date.[4] The issues were discussed in the 'Report to the Committee on the Currency and Bank of England Note Issues' (1925). That report largely took the case for return as self-evident, and ruled out devaluation as wholly unworthy. It focused on when the return should take place. The authors (and their later critics) recognized PPP as the appropriate guide (an approach which persisted after 1945), and observed that at the then present exchange rate, 'The adjustment of price levels required to restore and maintain pre-war parity needs to be only some 1½ per cent larger than that required to hold the exchange at its present rate.'[5]

Prices were required to adjust to parity—as opposed to the view of Keynes, who wanted the parity adjusted to prices. (Both parties accepted PPP as a guide to policy, and wished both price and exchange stability after the one-off adjustment.)[6]

got the right result and Gregory the wrong. So much for PPP as a guide to policy!'. What that means is obscure—in what sense was Keynes's answer 'right'? And indeed, the view is inconsistent with Sayers's own paper, where the subsequent problems of the UK economy were expressly ascribed to factors *other* than the parity.

[4] See Easton (1984), 'Real Output and the Gold Standard Years'; and Wood (1984), 'Comments on Easton', in Bordo and Schwartz (eds) (1984).

[5] Section 20 of the report. It should be observed that the years previous to this calculation had seen periods of tight money, connected with the aim of returning to gold at the pre-war parity.

[6] See Keynes, letter to the City Editor of *The Morning Post*, 1 August 1925.

The views of industry, at least as expressed by the Federation of British Industry, were clearly expressed but far from unambiguous. Stable exchanges would be welcome—they would benefit trade and capital movements. This was in contrast to flexible exchanges, which were thought to be primarily of benefit to speculators in the City. The rise of the pound was 'viewed with satisfaction as an indication of returning economic power' (Aden Brown, 1929). But, at the same time, industry almost certainly did not wish a further credit and monetary squeeze to bring UK prices into line with PPP. Rather they wished to wait for prices overseas to rise. None the less, objection to sterling strengthening was very muted—for it was only one problem among many, and by most businessmen not separately identified. When pressure from the exchange rate was identified, blame was placed, not on the rise in sterling, or on the force causing it, but on the forces inhibiting price level and cost adjustment. What were called the 'sheltered' industries—those not engaged in foreign trade and, particularly, municipal undertakings—were blamed for keeping up their prices in the absence of direct foreign competition and thus slowing the adjustment of costs in the rest of the economy.[7] Some indeed thought that whatever the temporary difficulties for industry, the promise of stability that a return to gold gave would, when delivered, benefit industry. This view does not seem to recognize fully the arguments of Keynes that there could be stability at another parity. But it could also reflect the belief that if the parity had been changed other than at times of war, it could be changed again, and the guarantee of stability was therefore gone. This was certainly argued by Kiddy (editor of the *Bankers Magazine*) in the course of a speaking trip to provincial industrialists.

Nor was there much objection from politicians to the choice of parity. Cole was violently against it:

> Are we not artificially manufacturing a good half of our present unemployment? . . . There are people who think it more important to maintain British Commercial Credit represented by the worship of par than to make British industry prosper. The Treasury and the Bank appear to take this view. I do not. I want moderate bank inflation because I believe it will reduce it (i.e. the unemployment problem) to manageable proportions. (*Morning Post*, 13 July 1924)[8]

But the majority Labour view was that expressed by Philip Snowden, in the House of Commons: 'We do not by this amendment oppose a return to the gold standard—we register our protest against haste' (*Hansard*, 83, col. 62, 4 May).

[7] See the 'Survey of Industrial Relations' of the 'Committee on Industry and Trade' (Balfour Committee, 1932).

[8] It is not clear from the context, or his other writings, whether by inflation he meant a continuous process—and thus can claim early discovery of the Phillips Eurve—or the acceptance of the once-for-all rise in prices that returning to gold at a lower parity would have entailed.

It is clear, then, that the decision to return was not a precipitately taken one; and it is also clear that the choice of parity was thought about, albeit with the distinction between a fixed parity and fixing at *the old* parity somewhat confused; the parity chosen was not wildly wrong in the light of information available at the time; and opposition to the move, although vigorous, was not widespread.[9]

In some degree it could be said the policy worked. The UK did experience difficulties after the return. But by 1929 world trade had grown and many industries were exporting more than at the 1913 peak. Some of those that did not were in secular decline and others were affected by the competitive devaluations of France and Belgium.

Summarizing so far, it can be said that the problems of 1931, and the crisis of that year among policy-makers, were not simply the product of a hasty and obviously wrong decision six years earlier and subsequent panic about undoing it.[10] What then did go wrong between 1925 and 1931?

THE COLLAPSE

Two aspects of UK domestic policy have been considered candidates for the role of having pushed the UK off gold. These are budgetary policy and the choice of the exchange rate in 1925.

(a) Budgetary policy

The government of the day was concerned by the size of its deficit. Efforts, including cuts in unemployment benefit, were made to reduce it. Despite this concern among contemporaries, it is hard to argue that the budget deficit was the cause of the collapse of sterling.

The budget deficit was not growing at a rate so rapid that monetization with eventual inflation was inevitable.[11] Indeed, a good part of the deficit was cyclical, and therefore transitory. Unemployment stood in 1931 at over 3m, being 21 per cent of the insured work force—equivalent on the present definition to an unemployment rate of around 16 per cent.[12] This manifestly contributed a substantial transitory component to the deficit.

[9] Redmond (1982) maintains that, on an effective exchange rate basis, sterling was overvalued by as much as 25 per cent but the data for that calculation were not available at the time, and indeed the effective rate concept was not clearly articulated.

[10] Sayers (1976) argues that nothing went wrong, but that the system was bound to fail because London's financial situation changed. It was not able to 'push the main burden of adjustment on to other countries'.

[11] For a detailed description of this process, see, for example, Sargent and Wallace (1983).

[12] Ideally, to ascertain whether the budgetary position was transitory or permanent—permanent in the sense that it required policy action rather than economic recovery to correct—one

It is fairly clear that the *underlying* budgetary position was not at fault in pushing the UK off gold.

What of the actual budgetary position? Could that be responsible? This is in principle a possibility—bond sales could raise interest rates, and thus reduce the demand for money. The *excess* supply of money could then produce once-for-all depreciation. But bond yields were not rising throughout the years 1925–31, and short rates only started to rise after the exchange rate came under pressure. This route, too, can be ruled out.

(b) A sterling overvaluation

Two versions of the argument that it was sterling overvaluation which produced the crisis of 1931 can be found. Some of the traditional export industries remained depressed throughout the second half of the 1920s. This led Montague Norman (in October 1929) to express the fear that sterling would be forced off gold. To this problem were added a scramble for liquidity throughout Europe following the collapse of the Credit Anstalt in May 1931 and, in Germany, the temporary closure of the Danat Bank in June. At the same time (1931) the Macmillan Report was published, and revealed that Britain's short-term liabilities were much greater than had been thought. Balances started to be withdrawn from London, and American and French credits replaced only a small part of the loss. The Bank was left with few reserves and, in the wake of the Invergordon Mutiny[13] (15 September), Britain left gold on 21 September.

Moggridge (1972) focuses not on the merchandise trade account, but on the deteriorating invisible balance, itself in part a product of the contraction of world trade. Falling interest rates reduced receipts from overseas investments and the contraction of trade reduced income from shipping and financial services. In this account the scramble for liquidity only brought matters to a head.

should calculate the constant employment budgetary position. Only that can reveal whether a surge in the deficit in any one year is an economy-induced fluctuation or a shift of policy to a new, and conceivably unsustainable, course. Budgetary calculations of that nature are not straightforward and the results can differ widely. There are in existence, however, two independent calculations of the constant employment budgetary position of the UK in the 1920s and 1930s—the work of Thomas (1979) and Middleton (1981). Fortunately, these studies produce similar results. The main focus of these studies was to consider whether fiscal policy was operated in what is generally viewed as a stabilizing way—deficits varying counter-cyclically. As a preliminary to that, both authors calculated constant employment deficits. Both found that on a constant employment basis the deficits was low—indeed, in 1931, the Budget on that definition was in small surplus.

[13] The refusal of some seamen to accept wage cuts and to stay on their ship in September 1931, when their ship was berthed at Invergordon, constitutes the mutiny. According to some, when foreigners saw the British navy defying the government, the end of the road had been reached.

Table 9.1 Growth in the United Kingdom

	Growth of base	Growth of M3	Growth of prices (% pa)
1920–21	−5.80	−0.35	−9.00
1921–22	−5.80	−7.50	−19.20
1922–23	−4.80	−7.17	−5.00
1923–24	0.29	−0.95	0.81
1924–25	1.00	−0.69	0.40
1925–26	−1.20	−0.46	−2.00
1926–27	0.22	1.50	−2.80
1927–28	1.60	1.66	−0.80
1928–29	−1.70	1.80	−1.30
1929–30	1.25	0.28	−3.80
1930–31	−1.80	−1.02	−6.20
1931–32	0.92	1.92	−2.80

Source: Capie and Webber (1984) Vol. 1 (Data Sources and Methods).
Column 1: table I (1)
Column 2: table I (3)
Column 3: table III (II)

(c) Monetary policy

The claim that the events of 1931 were the consequence of over-expansionary monetary policy has seldom been advanced. Table 9.1 makes the reason plain. There is no hint there of excessive monetary expansion.

1931 IN PERSPECTIVE

The evidence discussed above, evidence from both the time of the decision to return to gold and from the years between then and 1931, all suggests that Britain's problem was neither a grossly overvalued exchange rate in 1925 nor inappropriate fiscal and monetary policy thereafter. What happened in 1931?

Devaluation was not a carefully considered policy—indeed, it was explicitly rejected only a few months earlier (a familiar story!). In his arguments to the Macmillan Committee, Keynes opposed devaluation—stability should be the goal, as it was when gold was restored. For the sake of stability, the decision once taken should be stuck to. This was the view also of Norman. Only Bradbury and Bevin supported devaluation—viewing it as preferable to protection. (A difference resulting perhaps from perspective, the others putting great weight on the stability of the international *system*.)

Nevertheless, stability of the parity became a cause for concern in May 1930, when gold losses resumed after abating in 1928. Both France and the US bought sterling on the foreign exchanges for the remainder of that year. Snowden

(Labour Chancellor of the Exchequer) drew the attention of the Cabinet to the continual pressure on sterling in a meeting in January 1931. In February 1931 discussion started in the press, and on 11 February the Chancellor observed that there were foreign reservations about the UK budgetary position. This may have been to lend support to the desire to establish the 'Committee on National Expenditure' (the May Committee), but it should be observed that in France, for example, the UK's unbalanced budget was thought to be the cause of the UK's difficulties; the example of Poincaré was commended to the UK.[14]

Little was done before July—apart from some tentative steps to budgetary balance. Some (notably Keynes in his evidence to the Macmillan Committee) argued that the problem was deflation overseas. Gold outflows resumed in July. From 13 July to 1 August the Bank lost some £33m in gold and £21m in foreign exchange (⅓ of the Bank of England's gold reserves). Bank rate had been raised on 23 July, and again on 30 July, but the gold drain continued. The Bank continued to intervene but that was the extent of policy. Some gave curious advice. Hopkins, the Controller of Finance and Supply Services at the Treasury, sent a memorandum to the Chancellor in which he blamed foreign events for the difficulties and then recommended UK policy changes (Cairncross and Eichengreen (1983, p. 64).

Reserve losses continued. Keynes (1931: in Moggridge, 1981) now recommended devaluation; Henderson, in contrast, argued for budgetary economies. Budget cuts were prepared. The government resigned on 23 August, and was replaced by a 'National Government' on 24 August. It announced its new budgetary policies on 10 September—but the run continued. The Bank intervened massively—losses went on. On Sunday, 20 September, gold was abandoned. Is that story one of panic or of reasoned action? There certainly was panic; but nothing would have defended the system, because the system's rules were flouted. Policy makers in the UK were helpless spectators—but because of others. The return to gold had been a considered act. Policy after the return was consistent with making the parity stick. The cause of the abandoning of gold primarily lay elsewhere; the central banks of the US and France no longer played by 'the rules of the game'.

Britain's position was precarious. She had fewer reserves and more short-term liabilities than before; and was no longer a dominant force in world capital markets, able to draw funds from abroad by a twitch of bank rate. Under these conditions, assistance from other central banks was often likely to be necessary—and it was seldom forthcoming. After the death of Benjamin

[14] This does lead to two issues. There was clearly a scramble for liquidity on the Continent. Under a fixed rate system this would tend to push up interest rates in the UK. The deficit would have the same tendency. But the authorities were keen to see rates come down (see Capie, Mills, and Wood, 1983). This may have increased willingness to break financial links with the rest of the world, and thereby alleviate domestic interest rate pressures. Second, markets may simply have taken fright (irrationally on the above arguments) because of the deficit.

Strong, President of the Federal Reserve Bank of New York, in 1928, the US was no longer willing to lend gold freely. Meanwhile, France, the other major gold holder, had been reluctant to lose gold to the UK throughout the period. This had been due partly to a desire to replenish her own gold holdings, and partly due to the hostility to the UK created by Montague Norman's encouraging the development of Central Banks in regions not friendly to France. Central bankers no longer played the rules of the game; they no longer lent gold freely among themselves to meet liquidity pressures (see Clarke, 1967, for a discussion of the collapse of the system which sets out the above position in detail).

What of the impact of abandoning gold on the economy? Because the link with gold was broken, monetary policy was freed from external constraints. The UK, therefore, did not import the deflationary policies of the Federal Reserve and experienced a much less severe recession than the US (as did those countries which followed the UK in leaving gold, either because they too used the £ or as deliberate policy act). Figure 9.1 shows just how different

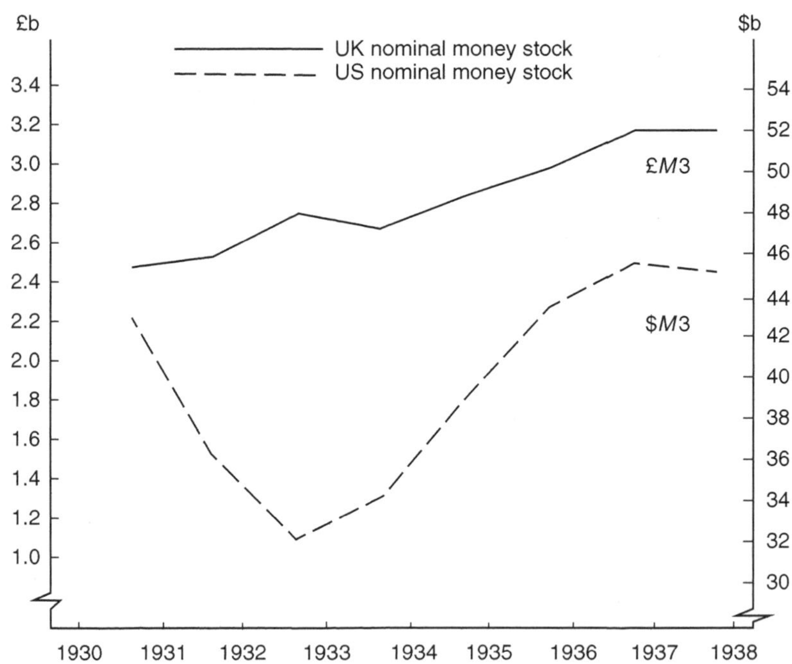

Figure 9.1. The growth of the UK and US money stock 1931–38

Sources:
UK: Capie and Webber (1984), (Data Sources and Methods) table 1 (3).
US: Friedman and Schwartz (1982), table 4.8.

money growth was in the UK from in the US between 1931 and 1938. This would not have been possible on the gold standard. After the abandoning of gold, interest rates—short and long—fell, economic recovery started and there was little rise in prices. The turmoil that preceded the event in the world of policy-makers certainly did not carry on in the world outside after the decision was taken.

It is now time to turn to 1949. Before doing so, though, it is worth giving provisional consideration to the main questions posed at the outset of this paper: 1931 was unique moment, not handled by any prearranged scheme; this is not surprising, given that it appears largely to have been brought about by the refusal of others to obey a set of rules that had governed international monetary arrangements for at least fifty years, and among some countries longer. It was traumatic for policymakers—it even required a new government—but it had little effect, except by accident, on the economy.

DEVALUATION IN 1949

We start examination of this episode by setting out the particular circumstances of the immediate post-war years—the changed trading accounts of the sterling area; the changed nature of Britain's indebtedness; some conventional assessments of exchange rate pressure. We then conclude on the nature of the event and reflect on the appropriateness of Atlee's remark to Dalton: '1931 all over again'. But first we set out the simple sequence of events.

At the end of the Second World War a supposedly radical Labour Government was elected, one that was committed to, and pursued, a policy of 'cheap money'. Along with that there was the great switch from wartime to peacetime production at a time when, just as following the First World War, there was a considerable degree of liquidity in the economy and a pent-up demand for consumer and capital goods; though of course there was also a great panoply of controls that seemed likely to persist for some time.

There was American pressure for the abolition of sterling area—that is, for the full convertibility of sterling—and that, together with a budget which was still in deficit in 1946 and the fuel crisis in the bitter winter of 1947, led to a severe crisis for sterling in the middle of 1947. Aid was forthcoming from the Americans, but a jitteriness surrounded sterling in the following eighteen months and, of course, rumours of devaluation, and denials of them, both abounded. In September 1949 sterling was devalued by 30 per cent against the dollar—though this has been reckoned to be about 10 per cent on a trade-weighted basis.

CHANGED POSITION OF BRITISH ECONOMY

The war proved exceedingly costly to the British economy and left it in no position to provide a key currency in international trade. From having been the greatest of creditor nations Britain had become the greatest of debtors. By one estimate of time there had been external disinvestment of over £4000m. There was realization of capital assets of £1118m. Overseas loans totalled £303m and in the sterling balances held abroad there was a floating indebtedness of £2756m. To this has to be added the US and Canadian loans negotiated immediately after the war and totalling £1400m (Hawtrey, 1954).

The need at the time was seen as being a massive export programme. Using 1939 as a base of 100, exports stood at 31 in 1944 and the post-war aim was to raise that to 175 while trying to keep imports down.

THE STERLING AREA

Something that might loosely be called the sterling area had been in existence since the early part of the nineteenth century. In this area there was a tradition that embraced most Empire countries (and several others) of keeping their currencies stable in terms of sterling and of these countries holding some, or even all, their international reserves in claims on London (Pressnell, 1978). However, on a stricter definition, a currency area suggests inconvertibility, and so long as sterling was a fully convertible currency there was no sterling area (Sargent, 1952). After 1931, when sterling was no longer convertible into gold, a period of confusion followed, and after 1933 the countries of the loosely-defined sterling area more formally became the sterling bloc and in the period of floating rates they kept constant the rate of exchange of their own currencies into sterling.

The sterling area of the 1940s was a much different affair. In 1939 countries not involved in the war severed their connection with the sterling bloc, and then the introduction of exchange control (September 1939) provided the condition for the development of the sterling area. This was a complicated system, but Table 9.2 captures the essence of the arrangements. Several qualifications have to be added to the simple picture presented. In the first place there were import restrictions which often meant that while there was freedom to make a payment there was not necessarily freedom to make a purchase. Second, there were various provisions governing control of capital movements between some areas. And third, not all sterling owned by members was freely available. At the end of 1949 sterling balances are estimated to have been £2352m. About £930m, belonging to India, Pakistan, Ceylon, and Iraq, was blocked.

Table 9.2. The sterling exchange control system

	Freely transferable within area shown		Freely transferable to outside area shown	
Sterling held by residents of:	*for current transactions*	*for capital transactions*	*for current transactions*	*for capital transactions*
American Account Area	Yes	*	Yes	*
Sterling Area	Yes	Yes	Yes	No
Transferable Account Area x	Yes	No	No*	No
Bilateral Area and Group	No	No	No**	No

* Sterling balances only; sterling held as form of securities can be transferred outside sterling area only in the event of repayment.
x Sterling on transferable account only.
Except for payments to residual group and sterling area.
** Except for payments to sterling area.
Source: Sargent (1952).

This then was a complicated set of arrangements which has a bearing on any discussion of the problems of sterling. It was during the Second World War that closer cooperation between member countries developed, and it was at this time that a central reserve of foreign exchange was built up. The arrangement was that the UK undertook to make dollars available to member countries to cover unfavourable balances on dollar transactions. And on the other side, member countries were obliged to make available to the UK any surplus gold or dollars they acquired in international transactions. That system persisted after the War and is the reason sometimes given for viewing sterling's problems in terms of the area as a whole.

Table 9.3 brings out some of the problems suffered by sterling area countries in the Second World War. Whereas in 1938 the overall sterling area current account had a deficit of £100m, in 1947 this was a frightening £950m. Improvements were seen in 1948 and 1949 but the deficits were seen as still intolerably high. As a percentage of Gross Domestic Product (GDP) the deficits were 2.9 and 3.2 per cent of UK GDP respectively. These do not seem notably large now, but it is important to note that comparisons were then made with the years before 1939, when the UK was more often than not in surplus on current account. Although all the major countries of the area had deficits, it was the UK that dominated the deficits between the war and 1947; but then it improved and it was South Africa that dominated in 1948 and 1949. Bearing in mind that South Africa was on the point of leaving the area, the problems for the area as a whole seemed to be easing and in the British case to have disappeared altogether.

Table 9.3. Sterling area current balance (£m)

Member country	1938	1947	1948	1949	1950
United Kingdom	−70	−545	29	21	221
Ireland	−3	−38	−29	−17	−36
Australia	−15	8	37	−4	−2
New Zealand	−5	−9	−4	−5	17
South Africa	−9	−180	−175	−114	−7
Southern Rhodesia	-	−11	−13	−24	−21
India	−12	−91	−75	−136	46
Pakistan			−2	37	−11
Ceylon	−2	−14	2	−2	11
Colonies	−20	−50	−20	−50	140
Other	10	−37	−13	-	-
Total Rest of sterling area	−56	−422	−292	−389	137
All sterling area	−100	−950	−300	−350	350

Source: Conan (1952, p. 65).

Table 9.4. Dollar trade of the sterling area ($m)

	Exports			Imports			Balance		
Member country	1934–8 (av.)	1947	1948	1934–8 (av.)	1947	1948	1934–8 (av.)	1947	1948
United Kingdom	280	386	580	805	1862	1331	−525	−1476	−751
Australia	28	131	161	86	297	153	−58	−166	8
New Zealand	16	39	44	31	114	52	−15	−75	−8
South Africa	13	113	141	80	481	575	−67	−368	−434
India and Pakistan	76	289	327	37	444	357	39	−155	−30
Ceylon	19	41	64	2	51	21	17	−10	43
Colonies	226	475	538	72	446	405	154	29	133
Others	9	18	27	21	173	84	−11	−155	−57
Total rest of sterling area	387	1106	1302	329	2006	1647	58	−900	−345
Sterling area	667	1492	1882	1134	3868	2978	−466	−2376	−1096

Source: Conan (1952, p. 70).

The trade of sterling area countries with the dollar area is shown in Table 9.4. The striking feature of this table is the soaring imports from the dollar area, almost all attributable to the demands of war and the immediate aftermath. Where British imports from the dollar area averaged £805m between 1934 and 1938, in 1947 they were £1862m; they had dropped to £1331m by the following year. The trade balance for the whole of the sterling area had averaged £466m before the War, deteriorated to £2376m in 1947 and dramatically improved the following year to £1096m. Again, the evidence on the balance of payments suggests that whatever the problems created by war, these were not going to be long lasting—all the signs were that a reduction in 'dollar' imports, and improvement in 'dollar' exports, were both working quickly to erode that deficit. This was being supported by an improvement in the sterling trade of the OEEC countries. This was favourable immediately after the War and the surplus increased in 1948. It faltered a little in 1949 but for the whole sterling area it was still favourable.

For those, then, who looked to the balance of payments for information on the exchange rate, there is no suggestion in the annual figures of anything other than diminishing pressure. It is true, though, that the quarterly figures in 1949 gave cause for some alarm—there was clear deterioration in the second quarter. This is reflected in the dollar reserves of the sterling area. Where these had been $2200m just before the War, and a little more right at the end of the War, by 1948 they were slipping and in the course of 1949 fell dangerously low. In the first quarter they were $1912m, in the second $1651m and in the third $1425m.

CONVERTIBILITY

An ultimate ambition after the War was the restoration of the full convertibility of sterling. The Americans were very keen that it should come about as quickly as possible and, given that they were providing fairly substantial loans to Britain, they were in a position to force the pace. Indeed, it was part of the loan agreement that sterling would become convertible into hard currencies—that is, dollars. A further condition of American aid (Marshall Aid replaced the loans—the first payment coming in June 1948) was that recipients should maintain 'valid rates of exchange'.

When convertibility came into operation in July 1947, more than half the US loan was used up. Clearly, the conditions for convertibility (at the existing parity) did not hold and it became necessary (because of the loan conditions) to get US consent to suspend convertibility. (It was eventually restored in 1958.) Essentially conditions were not right, since the UK economy could not produce the goods being asked of it, whereas the US economy could. There was, therefore, an excess demand for dollars and a deficient demand for sterling at the rate of exchange at which it was being held. British industry was in a state of over-full employment, but instead of there being a restrictive monetary policy there was in fact an easy one ('cheap money').

SOME ECONOMIC CALCULATIONS

The economic section of the Cabinet office was involved in discussion of the choice of exchange rate at the end of the War. (There may also have been discussions in the course of reaching the Bretton Woods agreement; but we have not had access to the Bretton Woods archives.) Among its members James Meade was notable in arguing that sterling should be allowed to float. The general view opposed this, discussing the parity to be chosen with (so far as we can find) no discussion via memoranda of whether or not the rate should actually be fixed at all. It is clear that morality was important in this view. Several countries, notably India, had maintained extensive sterling balances, and there was concern to ensure they did not suffer for this. Indeed, in 1944 Keynes had given a pledge to that effect to representatives of the Indian government.[15]

Keynes's memorandum on the choice of the rate has been published in a revised form.[16] That memorandum elicited a response from 'Otto' Clarke. Clarke's memorandum is noteworthy in two respects. It makes clear that PPP calculations played a part in the decision, intermingling with questions of morality just as they had in 1925, and it anticipates (perhaps as a result of discussion with James Meade) later work on policy assignment.

The correspondence opens by Clarke saying he was slightly more pessimistic than Keynes about the likely extent of the UK's post-war indebtedness. He then continues as follows:

> I cannot help feeling it would be very premature for us, with internal wage rates pretty well fixed, to agree to fix: —
>
> a) the exchange rate; and
> b) our powers of import limitation; and
> c) our powers of export stimulation (by taking the pledge against export subsidies) until we can see the position more clearly ahead.
>
> We must have something left we can manipulate.
> (Clarke, Memoranda, 1948–49)

The next section draws attention to PPP:

> I feel that Keynes is a little over optimistic about our competitive position. The U.S. Administration has been quite unexpectedly successful in maintaining wage and price control, and I do not think that even on the \$4 exchange rate the position is more favourable to us than it was before the war with a \$4.86⅔ exchange rate.
> (Clarke, Memoranda, 1948–49; see Appendix for further discussion of the price controls)

[15] We are indebted to Professor Leslie Pressnell for this information. This pledge did not, of course, rule out devaluation. Compensation could have been paid to offset the devaluation. This option does not appear in any of the documents.

[16] Keynes (1979), pp. 256–95.

Clarke then went on to compare labour costs in various industries, and to discuss how overhead costs might be allocated in determining the selling price for exports.

1949 IN PERSPECTIVE

As with the return to gold in 1925, at the end of the Second World War the exchange rate seems to have been arrived at on the basis of a mixture of moral considerations and PPP calculations, albeit calculations carried out with highly misleading price indices, so that sterling was overvalued quite substantially against the US dollar. How did the problems of 1949 emerge against that background, and how were they dealt with?

Balance of payments problems of the immediate post-war years were handled by loans, the quick abandoning of convertibility, and the developing of trade within the sterling area. There *was* discussion of devaluation in 1948. It was initiated by 'Otto' Clarke (1948–49), who saw it as a way of 'mobilizing ordinary commercial incentives for the task of righting our dollar balance of payments', in other words, as a device to allow the removal of controls. But the scheme for discussion was quickly sat on. As Cairncross (1983) points out, many of the ministers of the time were actively in favour of government by controls—controls were not even a necessary evil.

Outside opinion continued to expect devaluation—because of the gap between the control-sustained official rate and the rate in the free market (which was located primarily in Portugal).Within official circles, the debate renewed as the current balance seemed to be headed towards surplus; although it was roughly in balance in 1948, dollars remained scarce. The idea, again, was to stimulate dollar trade. Again the plan foundered, a result of Board of Trade and Bank of England resistance to plan floated by a divided Treasury.

None the less speculation continued, and it was believed that the US administration favoured a sterling devaluation—on the grounds that it would allow freer multilateral trade and end, or at least reduce, discrimination against the dollar.

Meanwhile, there was a deterioration in the trade account (June 1949) and reserves fell rapidly. As a result, Cripps proposed spending cuts and tightening controls on $ trade so as to avoid devaluation. He carried the day, no doubt with the support of those ministers who had their eye on the prospect of an election in the autumn, and were concerned to delay devaluation till after that date.

Some officials argued for a less expansionary monetary policy, but ministers would have none of it. As discussion continued it became clear that devaluation, or further controls and spending cuts, were the choices. Three ministers,

Gaitskill, Jay and Wilson, put a paper proposing devaluation to the Prime Minister. Devaluation was eventually agreed without any difficulty and discussion focused on the accompanying measures. The new rate was soon agreed—a devaluation so big as not to leave the prospect of another was sought. Floating was rejected. In the House of Commons, Dalton said of floating that if it implied that 'all our exchange and import controls should be taken off and the pound allowed to find its own level, we could not possibly think of such a course' (*Hansard*, 27 September 1949, House of Commons, column 12). (This conclusion seems to have been reached without any discussion; the position may simply reflect acceptance of the IMF Articles of Agreement.)

COMPARISON

All this is very different from 1931. The resemblance spotted by Atlee could scarcely have been slighter. Pressures were again partly external—but they were to change UK policy, rather than simply a run on the UK's reserves. Devaluation was a replacement for controls. (Just as quotas have a tariff equivalent, so do controls have a tax equivalent—see Phylaktis and Wood, 1984.) Rather than a last ditch float, the decision was founded on a considered decision to free up at least a part of the economy.

Both changes were undertaken under stress—but the first was the consequence of external pressures upsetting broadly sound policy, while the second was brought about by pressure to change a policy thought by many, both inside and outside the UK, to be misguided. (It seems highly likely that the pressure could be exerted in good part because when the rate was set in 1945 insufficient allowance was made for the effect of price controls.)

The first change in exchange rate policy was beneficial to the UK, but by accident. The second, too, was beneficial, albeit moderately. The war in Korea broke out only nine months after the devaluation, but enough time had already passed for it to be seen that the policy had 'worked'. Gold and dollar reserves rose by 70 per cent in those nine months. British prices rose more than American ones, but only slightly, over the next five years, and British exports rose very rapidly—perhaps too rapidly to be ascribed wholly to the devaluation. Most important, controls on foreign trade were not tightened. Neither event produced turmoil outside the circle of policy-makers, although there was turmoil in plenty within that circle.

Trying to arrive at any precise timing of decisions to devalue does not seem to us to be profitable. The nature of the exercise means that although at some stage the authorities may have accepted that a new rate was inevitable there was secrecy, rumour, and counter-rumour surrounding the event that make identification of the time of the decision to act difficult. It would require tracing and interpreting statements by the principal persons, which would change from day to day as pressure eased or intensified. (The statements could influence the event at that critical stage.) We have written as if the decision was taken immediately prior to the event and implicitly assumed that the authorities acted when there was no other way to go. That, however, may not always be the case, and the probable lack of general application is another good reason for not pursing the issue.

CONCLUSIONS

As can be seen, 1931 and 1949 were very different events. The first was scarcely discussed in advance—because devaluation was almost inconceivable. Indeed, it required a national government—a coalition—before the policy could be carried through. Consent had to be widespread, for it was a step into unknown territory. However, 1949 was a step back towards conventional policies, and away from the use of controls—so it was agreed with much less difficulty. Both were none the less crises for policy-makers: they involved the abandoning of previous commitments. To answer the first of the two questions posed at the outset of this paper, they were both unique events treated uniquely. As to the second question, both episodes were important to the economy—but beneficial, not, as the behaviour of policy-makers before the event would have led one to believe, damaging. Policy-makers were in turmoil because of the difficulty of changing course, rather than because of the prospective effect of the change on the economy. That leads finally to a common lesson of those episodes. Once a course; a policy rule, has been adopted, it requires great pressure before that course is abandoned. Change is not easy. It is therefore not surprising that politicians are often unwilling to commit themselves to a policy which has implications for a number of years. Economic policy, as well as the economy, has considerable inertia.

APPENDIX

Some recent work highlights just how right Clarke was to be concerned about the different degrees of effectiveness of UK and US price totals. Friedman and Schwartz (1983, p. 101) write of these wartime controls as follows:

> The behaviour of reported prices in the United States during World War II . . . is distorted by the effects of price control, since control meant that price increases took

indirect and concealed forms not recorded in the indexes. The large rise in price indexes when price control was repealed in 1946 consisted largely of an unveiling of the earlier concealed increases. Hence the recorded price indexes understate the price rise during the war.

Their estimated price index and that reported by Kuznets are as follows:

Price Index (1929 = 100)

	F&S	K
1943	111.7	107.6
1944	120.0	110.8
1945	125.3	114.1
1946	126.4	122.2

They also correct the UK price indices for the effect of controls. The corrected and uncorrected series are shown below:

Price index (1929 = 100)

	Reported	Corrected
1939	99.9	–
1940	109.0	114.7
1941	118.4	127.4
1942	126.6	134.8
1943	131.4	142.0
1944	139.0	145.7
1945	143.3	146.2
1946	145.6	150.0
1947	158.5	–

Carrying out a PPP calculation with the corrected indices suggests an appropriate exchange rate for £ against the $ would have been $2.816 to £1. That figure is, of course, close to what £ moved to in 1949, and $0.30 above what sterling was trading at in the free market in Portugal just after the end of the War. Before devaluation, the rate was $4.04 to the pound; it moved to $2.80 to the pound.

PRICE CONTROLS

In connecting the indices, Friedman and Schwartz made use of a method they had developed for another purpose, and described in 'The Interpolation of Time Series by Related Series' Milton Friedman, NBER Technical Paper 16, 1962. They estimated the price indices by interpolating between previous and succeeding values primarily on the basis of movements in nominal income (Friedman and Schwartz, 1982, p.102).

For the UK, only the years 1940–46 were corrected, although price controls covered a longer period, because only these years seemed to be outliers from the pattern of price and nominal income deviations from trend.

REFERENCES

Aden Brown, W. (1929) *England and the New Gold Standard, 1919–1926*, New Haven: Yale University Press.

Bank of England Statistical Summary.

Bordo, M. D. and Schwartz, A. J. (eds) (1984) *The Classical Gold Standard Reappraised*, University of Chicago Press.

Cairncross, A. and Eichengreen, B. (1983) *Sterling in Decline*, Oxford: Basil Blackwell.

Capie, F. and Webber, A. (1984) *A Monetary History of the United Kingdom, 1870–1982*, Vol. 1, London: Allen & Unwin.

——Mills, T. and Wood, G. E. (1983) 'What Happened in 1931', Paper presented to the City University Conference on Financial Crises.

Carse, S., Williamson, J., and Wood, G. E. (1980) *The Financing Practices of British Foreign Trade*, Cambridge University Press.

Clarke, R. W. B. ('OTTO') (1948–49) Public Record Office Treasury Records, OF 145/146/09.

Clarke, S. V. O. (1967) *Central Bank Co-operation: 1924–1931*, New York: Federal Reserve Bank.

Conan, A. R. (1952) *The Sterling Area*, London: Macmillan.

Dimsdale, N. H. (1981) 'British Monetary Policy and the Exchange Rate, 1920–38', *Oxford Economic Papers*, 33 (supplement).

Easton, S. (1984) 'Real Output and the Gold Standard Years', in M. D. Bordo and A. I. Schwartz (eds), *The Classical Gold Standard Reappraised*, Chicago University Press.

The Economist (1907) November.

Eichengreen, B. J. (1981) 'Bank Failure, Balance of Payments and the 1931 Sterling Crisis', Harvard Institute of Economic Research, Discussion Paper no. 869, December.

Friedman, M. (1962) 'The Interpolation of Time Series by Related Series', NBER Technical Paper 16, New York.

——and Schwartz, A. J. (1982) *Monetary Trends in the United States and the United Kingdom*, Chicago University Press for the NBER.

Grassman, Sven (1973) *Exchange Reserves and the Financial Structure of Foreign Trade*, Farnborough: Saxon House.

Gregory, T. E. (1957) 'The "Norman Conquest" Reconsidered', *Lloyds Bank Review*, October.

Grigg, P. J. (1948) *Prejudice and Judgement*, London: Hutchinson.

Hawtrey, R. G. (1938) *A Century of Bank Rate*, London: Longman, Green, & Co.

Hawtrey, R. G. (1954) *Towards the Rescue of Sterling*, London: Longman, Green & Co.

Howson, S. (1975) *Domestic Monetary Management in Britain*, 1919–38, Cambridge University Press.

Keynes, J. M. (1925) *The Economic Consequences of Mr Churchill*, London: Hogarth Press.

——(1979) *Collected Writings of John Maynard Keynes*, vol. XXIV: *Activities 1944–46: The Transition to Peace*, London: Macmillan, 256–95.

McKinnon, R. I. (1979) *Money in International Exchange: The Convertible Currency System*, Oxford University Press.

Middleton, Roger (1981) 'The Constant Employment Budget Balance and British Budgetary Policy, 1929–39', *Economic History Review*, 34(2), 266–86.

Moggridge, D. E. (1969) *The Return to Gold 1925: The Formulation of Economic Policy and Its Critics*, Cambridge University Press.

——(1972) *British Monetary Policy, 1924–1931: The Norman Conquest of $4.86*, Cambridge University Press.

——(1981) (ed.) *Collected Writings of John Maynard Keynes 1929–1931: Rethinking Employment and Unemployment Policies*, vol. 20, London: Macmillan Press.

Phylaktis, K. and Wood, G. E. (1984) 'An Analtyical and Taxonomic Framework for the Study of Exchange Controls', in J. Black and G. S. Dorrance (eds), *Problems in International Finance*, London: Macmillan Press.

Pollard, S. (ed.) (1970) *The Gold Standard and Employment Policies Between the Wars*, London: Methuen.

Pressnell, L. (1978) '1925: The Burden of Sterling', *Economic History Review*, 31(1), 67–88.

Redmond, J. (1982) 'The Norman Conquest of $4.86, was the Pound Overvalued?', University of Birmingham Faculty of Commerce and Social Sciences, Discussion Paper no. 9.

Report of the Committee on Currency and Foreign Exchanges after the War (Cunliffe Committee) (1919), Cmd 464, B. P. P. 1919, vol. XIII, p. 493.

Report of the Committee on Currency and Bank of England Note Issues (1925), Cmd 2392, B. P. P. 1924–25, vol. IX, p. 435.

Report of the Committee on Industry and Trade (Balfour Committee) (1932), Cmd 3282, B. P. P. 1928–29, vol. VII, p. 413.

Report of the Committee on Finance and Industry (Macmillan Committee) (1931), Cmd 3897, B. P. P. 1930–1, vol. XIII, p. 219.

Report of the Committee on National Expenditure (May Committee) (1931), Cmd 3920, B. P. P. 1930–1, vol. XVI, p. l.

Sargent, J. R. (1952) 'Britain and the Sterling Area', in G. D. N. Worswick and P. H. Ady (eds), *The British Economy 1945–50*, Oxford University Press.

Sargent, T. J. and Wallace, N. (1983) 'Some Unpleasant Monetarist Arithmetic', in B. Griffiths and G. E. Wood (eds), *Monetarism in the U.K.*, London: Macmillan Press.

Sayers, R. S. (1976) *The Bank of England 1891–1944*, Cambridge University Press.

——(1960) 'The Return to Gold, 1925', in L. S. Pressnell (ed.), *Studies in the Industrial Revolution*, London: Athlone.

Thomas, T. (1979) 'Aggregate Demand in the UK 1918–1945', in R. Floud and D. McLoskey (eds), *The Economic History of Britain since 1700,* vol. 2, Cambridge University Press.

The Times (1925) 3 July.

Williams, D. R. (1963) 'London and the 1931 Financial Crisis', *Economic History Review,* 15 (April), 513–28.

Wood, G. E. (1984) 'Comments on Easton', in Bordo and Schwartz 1984.

10

Price Controls in War and Peace: A Marshallian Conclusion*

INTRODUCTION

In the twentieth century in Britain price controls were used both in war and in peace; they were used in the Second World War, and again in the 1960s. The methods used did, however, differ quite substantially as between the two periods. Our aim in this chapter is to indicate, and contrast the effectiveness of, the different methods of price control. Comparison of a period of war with one of peace does of course raise a problem. Patriotism, an influence which we do not attempt to measure, is likely to play a larger part in war than in peace. But even after recognizing this difficulty we would argue that the comparison is useful, for the methods of control used in the war were in an important respect radically differently from those in the 1960s. As the contrast between methods of control is very sharp, the comparison is a useful addition to the counterfactual normally used to assess the impact of price controls, that of no control. Our confidence in this is reinforced by the relevance to the comparison of a neglected policy recommendation of Alfred Marshall's, to which we turn at the end of this paper.

In the current climate where deregulation is popular, all kinds of controls are being removed. In many of the 'transition' economies price controls have been in use as part of the transition process. But even these have been disappearing. What contribution if any they made in the pursuit of price stability is difficult to say, because distance from the event is required, together with good data, before a proper assessment can be made. That is one reason why an analysis such as ours may provide some illumination: it can help reach some perhaps generalizable conclusions.

* The authors are indebted to two particularly perceptive referees for their comments on an earlier version of this chapter. Originally published as Forrest Capie and Geoffrey Wood (2002), 'Price Controls in War and Peace: A Marshallian Conclusion', *Scottish Journal of Political Economy*, Vol. 49 (February), no. 1, pp. 39–60, reproduced with the permission of the Scottish Economic Society.

The structure of the chapter is as follows. We first set out what we mean by saying price controls had 'worked'. That done, we turn to our two episodes, taking them in chronological order and for each episode describing the methods of control, the actual path of prices, and various counterfactuals derived within each episode. The methods used to derive the counterfactuals are not identical between the two periods; the reason for this difference is set out below. Next we compare the two episodes, and advance an explanation for the contrast, which we discover, between them. The chapter then concludes with a brief review of the main points of our argument, and a summary statement of our main conclusions.

THE MEANING OF 'WORKED'

If we said that price controls had worked, we would mean that they had made the rate of inflation lower than it would otherwise have been. That does assume 'other things unchanged'—which might well not have been the case in the absence of price controls. For example, if price controls had not been used, monetary policy might have been more restrictive. Nevertheless, we consider our definition appropriate, for we are simply trying to see whether a particular policy instrument had a particular kind of impact. We are not engaged in the exercise of trying to judge how policy-makers would have behaved in the absence of a particular policy instrument.

This definition of 'worked' is admittedly narrower than that used by some contemporary observers in the 1960s, one of the periods we study. Some then argued that controls reduced wage disputes. (Others held that they only displaced them to matters other than wages.) But their core purpose was the control of prices; any other effects were in addition to that core purpose. Accordingly, we confine ourselves to the narrow definition. The problems of testing are substantial enough without going further.

WARTIME

We start by examining Britain's inflation and price control experience during the Second World War. The economic objective in wartime is to obtain command of resources so as to win the war. This simplification of objectives was pointed out by Lionel Robbins (*The Economic Problem in Peace and War*) who also drew attention to what is particularly important in the present context, the great increase in the scale of the task. Resources are used by the government on a scale much greater than in peacetime, and, quite often, the increase to this scale is very rapid. Even when preparation was made in advance the outbreak of war brings a sudden quickening of the pace of resource mobilization.

In principle, resources can be found through taxation and borrowing, the normal means of government financing. If these means are used appropriately there would be no need for controls. But in practice governments have generally relied on controls as well as making use of the traditional tools of government finance. This was certainly the case in Britain in the Second World War. In those years the British government also imposed a second task on itself. This was to win the war with as little inflation as possible. Keeping the lid on prices was seen as necessary to preserve social stability and to secure the full cooperation of the labour force. The government took this decision without reference to the objectives of allies and trading partners. Consciously or unconsciously, then, external influences on inflation were ignored; it was declared in the budget of 1941 that prices would be held at their then current level for the duration of the war.

How did prices behave in the war? What measures were taken to control the general level of prices?

What were the contributions of each of these measures? And was policy-makers' neglect of external influences on prices justified by events? We consider these questions in turn and then attempt to assess the effectiveness of the anti-inflation policy. To anticipate, we find that measures taken were in total fairly effective, and that the key element was probably rationing. But first, we examine briefly why inflation was a concern.

It is plain both from discussions within government and civil service and from outside commentators that there was great concern lest the war be accompanied by inflation. In the light of both economic theory and previous experience it is worth asking why there should have been this concern. Theory can suggest it is rational for there to be a positive inflationary surprise—a jump in the inflation rate—in wartime. There are three reasons for this. First, there may be a temporary stimulus to output. Second, the government will get increased revenue from the inflation tax. Third, there will be a capital levy on all nominally denominated government bonds.[1] A government might produce inflation for these reasons even though it had avoided inflation before the war on the grounds that the costs of inflation—transaction costs and economizing on cash balances, for example, outweighed the only permanent benefit from inflation, the use of inflation as a tax.

[1] Was this theory which has recently become fashionable available in 1939? In our view significant parts of it were. Consider first David Hume's advocacy of modest inflation as a stimulus to output—and his explicit assumption that the inflation was never fully anticipated. Second, recollect that there had already been published a simplified version of the *General Theory*, in which an increase in the stock of money increased output (Hicks, 1937).

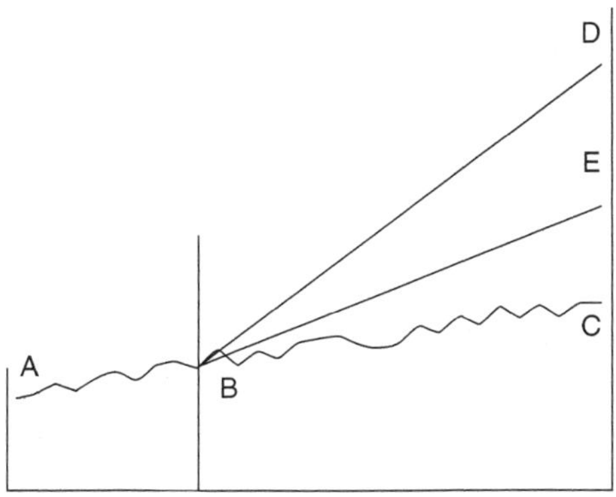

Figure 10.1. Price level

The argument for inflating can thus be put quite strongly but it neglects the social disruption that could follow—a lesson learnt early in the First World War. Accordingly, then, the desire to avoid inflation can be regarded as rational—for although wartime inflation appears sensible and useful from a purely resource-raising view point, there is the risk of social unrest, or at minimum of lack of cooperation.

It is useful now to set out a simple framework that separates out the effects of specific anti-inflationary measures in a peace-time period, and then, to refine it for wartime. The period is captured in a highly simplified way in Figure 10.1. We start by plotting the actual course of retail prices prior to the implementation of any controls(A-B). We then model the time series (by a means it is unnecessary to specify at the moment) and forecast the course that prices would take from B on. When we do this, in the figure we would reach a point such as, for example, C. For wartime it is helpful to view the problem in a slightly different way. First, if we posed the admittedly grand counterfactual that there was no war, we can then model prices as before and produce the point that the price level would have reached under those conditions (C in Figure 10.1). But at the outbreak of war substantial resources are demanded by the government. If we therefore pose a different counterfactual, that there is war but that it is financed entirely by monetary means (no taxes raised, etc.) we could predict considerable inflation, which would take us to some point such as D. That point represents where prices would finish up if the authorities effectively ignored the inflation problem. However, measures were immediately taken to combat inflation and the actual price index moves through time to a point such as E. This is below D if the measures taken are at least better than doing nothing. But given the enormous pressures of war it is unlikely that the price level could be reduced to a point at or below this, which would have been realized in the absence of war. So E lies between D and C. Finally, there could be a point F: where prices would have reached if price controls had not been used but all the other anti-inflation measures the authorities took were in place.[2] We do not yet know where F would lie relative to the other points.

Modelling prices

Now to the actual calculation of these points. Point C is obtained by statistical modelling of the time series for prices, and assumes that in the absence of war the world carried on as it had been, and the exchange rate regime did not impart any new shocks. Point E is straightforward—the point at which the published price level actually finished. Point D is more problematical. Our approach is to employ a simple quantity theory framework: $MV = PY$.[3] We then use estimates of M, and make assumptions on V. Real output figures have been published, and we can in addition obtain a real output estimate by simply extrapolating from the past on the grounds that the course of real income is unexciting and we can expect to be wrong by no more than a few per centage points.[4] With these three obtained we can then produce 'P' in our quantity identity and hence provide an indication of where point D lies. The difference between points D and E is then one indication of how successful the whole package of anti-inflation measures has been.

Point E is an indication of what actually happened to prices. There are three price indices available for the general course of prices. During the war the indicator used was the Ministry of Labour's cost of living index (devised soon after the outbreak of the First World War when there was concern over what was happening to the standard of living of the working class). It was heavily biased to working-class expenditure, and by the end of the 1930s some items in the index were no longer in production. For what it is worth the index moved, from a base in 1936–38 of 100, to 131 in 1945. That is a fairly modest inflation of 28 per cent in the course of the war. According to this index the great bulk of that came in the first eighteen months; indeed, between 1941 and 1944 there was almost no change in prices.

With the publication of Feinsteins's (1972) data we were able to get a slightly different view of the behaviour of prices. Feinstein's retail price index shows a greater rise in prices—an inflation of 48 per cent over the war

[2] One could also think another point, which represents where a 'true' price index taking account of quality change ended up.

[3] The result of this simple procedure is problematical because of the answer it gives. The inflation is so striking that it is hard to credit it, even as a counterfactual. But we would argue that it is of interest, simply because governments (not, fortunately in the UK) have on some occasions tolerated higher inflations than we discover here.

[4] We do not mean to imply by the above that changes in money induced by changes in income have no effect on prices.

years. The implicit GNP deflator derived from Feinstein's data provides an almost identical picture. The course of all the indices is however, very similar. Feinstein's two show that the worst year was 1940—retail prices rose 13.3 per cent and the deflator 9.2 per cent, but thereafter the rate of inflation fell each year until the end of the war.

These three indices all contain the effects of subsidies and price controls, and of course they do not reflect quality change. Friedman and Schwartz (1982) attempted to correct for price controls; the index they produced is the implicit deflator with the effect of price controls removed. Their method was a complicated one. It involved interpolating on the basis of movements in nominal income and adjusting with real income. However, as they pointed out, nominal income contains the price movements that they were seeking to correct for. They remarked that their result was 'at best a crude approximation'. The Friedman and Schwartz index in fact differs little from the GNP deflator. Both show an inflation of about 50 per cent between 1939 and 1946. One would have to conclude from this similarity that price controls had little effect. However, we leave the conclusions until later.

We now go on to construct the other points. We have noted that the recorded price index moved to a level of 145. Where was C, where prices would have moved to in the absence of the war? We are conscious of the magnitude of such a counterfactual, but there is justification of it as we regard the number as only an estimate of orders of magnitude, not a precise 'forecast'. To assess the course of retail prices in the absence of war, we estimated a time series model for retail prices for the period February 1927 to December 1938 using data from December 1926 onwards. We used the estimated equation to forecast prices over the subsequent period.

We began with the data from the retail price index (RPI) which covered the period January 1926 to December 1945 and we estimated a price equation for the period 1927–38 on monthly data. This equation is then used to forecast prices for the period 1939–45. The results of this statistical exercise are a price index figure of 118. That is, in the absence of war the price level would have reached 118 in 1945 from a base of 100 in 1939.

A question that must hang over this estimate is posed by Britain's leaving the gold standard in 1931. A straightforward solution might appear to be simply to estimate the model for, say, 1932 to 1938. That would, however be hazardous as the forecast period would be as long as the estimated. And we would argue that truncating the estimated period so drastically is unnecessary. Had Britain *and every other* gold standard member stayed on gold after 1931, then the price level might have drifted on down, due to economic growth interacting with a gold stock, additions to which were modest. But such generalized deflation did not set in; the sharp decline in Britain's prices after the end of the First World War had come to an end by 1926; and finally, a detailed study of prices and price expectations around the leaving of gold found no substantial effect on either. In summary, the evidence is that while the rule, which constrained monetary policy from 1925, was abandoned in 1931, this had no measurable effect on the outcome of monetary policy.

Our point D is derived from estimating a purely money-financed war. This result, therefore, is in a sense the opposite of the preceding one. We more from the 'no war' conterfactual to the 'war with entirely inflationary finance' conterfactual.

It is essential first to set out the extent of the finance required. We calculate pre-war tax revenue, and increase this by the effect of nominal income growth on this revenue. No estimates of tax elasticities are available so we have carried out two calculations, assuming first a tax elasticity of unity and then one of 0.5. The final result is little affected.

With regard to bonds, we assume that bond finance continued at its 1939 level. As we are going to have higher inflation than actually occurred, we do have to choose whether bond finance continues unchanged in nominal terms or in real terms. We decided to hold it unchanged in real terms; otherwise efforts at bond financing would be easing, not remaining unchanged as the war proceeded.

We consider two models for price expectations. The first is to assume stationary expectations, so that each year's rise in prices is treated as a once and for all event. The second is to let expectations change, so that the government ends up collecting the inflation tax. In fact we ended up following only the first course; for it emerged when calculating the inflation that would result under the second assumption that even the revenue maximizing inflation rate did not yield enough revenue.[5] Accordingly, then, we treat each year's inflation as a one-off event. By this route, we find prices would have risen by 5098 per cent by the end of the war. This is our point D. This point may seem remarkably high, but compared to some inflations it would have been modest. (See e.g. Friedman, 1956; and Capie, 1986.)

War finance

According to the conventional account by the historians of this episode, the Keynesian approach adopted to pay for the war was highly successful (Pollard,

[5] This is a result of the low interest elasticity of the money demand function. It is of interest to reflect briefly on what would have happened had inflation been tried. In his study of inflation in revolutionary France. Eugene White (1990) observed that the actual inflation rate was far above the revenue maximizing rate. He could offer no rational explanation for this. It could well, though, have been the result of politicians learning from experience. Higher inflation had previously brought in higher revenue, so why not keep on raising inflation? Would the same have happened in the UK?

1962). Keynes was installed at the Treasury from the beginning of the war and his ideas (outlined in *How to Pay for the War*) were, after a little resistance, accepted and acted on. (Kingsley Wood's budget of 1941 was conceived in national income terms and was accompanied by the first ever official estimates of national income and expenditure.) The essence of this budgetary analysis was that there was an inflationary gap of around £500m, of which approximately one half was to be found in increased personal savings and the remainder from additional taxation. The former was to be achieved by making attractive financial instruments readily available to the personal sector. Pollard (1962) says that borrowing was carried out as if by a discriminating monopolist—the offer of separate terms to each sector of the market, each at the lowest rates necessary to bring forth the loans. For the small saver National Savings Certificates and Defence bonds were available. Treasury Bills and Treasury Deposit Receipts were used to tap any idle balances in the banking system. (Ways and Means Advances, which had been resorted to in World War I, were regarded as inflationary and to be avoided if possible.) Increased tax receipts were to be achieved from raising the standard rate of tax to 10 shillings in the pound (i.e. 50 per cent) and by raising purchase tax. PAYE was introduced in 1943 to ease and speed the flow of tax receipts.

Tax receipts fell short of total expenditure each year and the balance was substantially gathered in by borrowing. However, this does not mean that all monetary pressure was removed. Monetary growth was considerable. M1 and M3 were growing at very rapid rates, and when, we bear in mind the limited output that could be bought we can see there was still a potentially powerful inflationary force. The monetary base also grew rapidly, showing the extent to which the authorities 'printed money' the monetary base grew by 128 per cent. The money multiplier fell a little, not as a result of anything the banks did but rather because, as one would expect in the uncertainty of wartime, the currency ratio rose.

Starting from the point that money growth causes inflation, money growth can be used to predict inflation, and these predictions compared with the actual course of prices. The difference in a period of controls could be ascribed to these controls. (In a time of war the direct controls on capital and trade mean that we can regard the economy as near to closed and money growth as under the control of the government, and can therefore use the simple closed economy notion of changes in money being independent of changes in income.)

We can indicate the effect monetary pressure had on the price level by finding some idea of the 'excess', growth of money relative to purchasable output. We calculated how much the amount of money demanded would have grown over the war years, and treated the excess of money growth over this as excess which would produce a rise in prices. This led to a predicted price rise of about 95 per cent.[6] This suggests that controls were dramatically effective. This calculation of the effect of controls must, of course, be qualified. First, there are lags in the money–price relationship. One would not expect the money growth of 1945 to affect prices in 1945. In fact, on the basis of the established relationship, 1938 money affects 1940 prices and so forth. Accordingly, cumulative money growth from 1937 to 1943 should be compared with growth in money demand from 1939–45. This yields excess money of 65 per cent and therefore a price rise of 65 per cent. Our point F would, then be 165, suggesting a still important benefit from controls.

Two further comments are in order, however. We should examine the money-to-income ratio, and then consider the role of ration coupons. It is usually suggested that the money-to-income ratio will rise in wars, as there is a 'precautionary' flight to highly liquid assets. This is not prima facie obvious for inconvertible paper currencies, but there does appear to be a rise in the ratio in the Second World War, by which time sterling was such a currency. The rise is, perhaps surprisingly, much larger than in the First World War.

The explanation may lie in the system of rationing that was adopted in the Second World War. With goods rationed 'excess' money could not be spent on rationed goods, and these comprised some 75 per cent of the index. Rationing by coupons can quite plainly have played a crucial role in the working of the anti-inflation policy. We discuss the role of coupons again below.

Certain other problems can only be noted—not even rough adjustments can be made to take account of them. First, interest rates were pegged; hence if inflationary expectations did rise (thus reducing the amount of money demanded) this would not be reflected in the interest rate we use. (In view of the generally accepted low interest elasticity of money demand this is unlikely to be important.) Second, is the behaviour of the output series. This grew and then fell away finishing about where it started. (Real output *fell* in the last two years of the war. Indeed, the fall from 1944–45, 7.1 per cent, would be regarded as a major recession.) Third, the *concept* of GNP, used in our money demand function, is somewhat unclear at a time of war, even aside from any problems of measurement. Accordingly, then, the above estimates of monetary pressure should be regarded as no more than a well-informed guess—an indication, no more.

[6] As part of our work on UK monetary history we estimated a money demand function for the UK. This function is for a broad aggregate, which includes interest-bearing accounts at commercial banks—this was a result simply of data limitations. See Capie and Webber (1985, ch. 2–4) for discussion of the data, and Forrest Capie and Ghila Rodrik-Bali (1985) for details on the estimation of the function. The function has the following properties—a unitary income elasticity and an interest elasticity of—0.05. On the basis of that, we can readily obtain an estimate of 'excess money'—the amount by which money supply growth exceeded money demand growth. Over the war years (1939–45) real income grew by 9.95% and M3 by 104.7%, while interest rates were kept steady. Hence as shown in the text excess money was 94.8%, leading one to expect the price rise over the war years of 94.8%.

The price controls

There were two principal means of controlling prices, direct price controls and subsidies. Both means were adopted in the very early months of the war and both were greatly refined or extended in early 1941. There were other measures too, such as rent control and rationing, that either extended control over the cost-of-living index or backed up other measures. The cost of living index was made up of five groups, as follows: food, rent, clothing, fuel and light, and other.

The first price control legislation came in the middle of November 1939. This froze prices on a range of clothing and household goods and allowed for certain specified increases on others. Enforcement was left to price-regulation committees, with possible penalties of three months' imprisonment for the first offence. A number of increases in price were allowed in the course of 1940. In 1941 there was a second piece of legislation. This amended the 1939 Act and contained further provisions for preventing 'excessive' price rises. Powers were extended to cover second-hand goods. These two price control acts focused primarily on clothing and household goods.

The other main weapon for directly influencing the price index was the subsidy. As early as August 1939 the Cabinet resolved that the prices of essential foodstuffs would be kept down. A decision was taken in December 1939 to subsidize food. Price increases on bread, flour, meat, butter, cheese, milk, and bacon were to be deferred by exchequer subsidy. In the 1941 Budget the Chancellor promised to stabilize, if necessary by subsidy, prices of all essential services such as coal, gas, and electricity. Subsidies grew steadily from £47m in 1939 and £102m in 1940 to £258m in 1944 and £302m in 1945. Food was also the subject of a price control order in January 1941. The Rent and Mortgage Interest Restrictions Act 1939 amended related legislation of the previous twenty years. Its principal effect was to freeze rents at their 1939 level on all properties below a specified rateable value. It should be noted that there was an upward pressure on the prices of some goods which were the subject of increase in customs and excise duties. These were duty increases on beer, spirits, wines, sweets, tobacco, and sugar. Of these, though, only tobacco and sugar were in the index.

The problem of subsidies

We noted above that the price index may give a misleading indication of inflation because price controls produced a deterioration in the quality of goods, so that the quality adjusted index was really higher. Here we turn to a second problem, one raised by the Treasury at the time. Did subsidies in fact keep the prices down? Or did they just affect the index, with offsetting rises occurring in the prices of goods not in the cost-of-living index?

In *How to Pay for the War*, Keynes (1940, pp. 51–57) discussed subsidies in some detail. He argued that they would not keep down inflation—for as wages were pulled up by increased demand for labour, subsidizing some items of spending would simply leave income to be spent elsewhere so that the price of unsubsidized goods would rise by more than the others would. That is plausible. There is also another way of looking at the question which leads to a similar conclusion. What does *financing* the subsidy do to prices? Consider the quantity identity, $MV=PT$. Can raising resources to subsidize some good (or goods) affect V or T so that, given M (a crucial point, as subsidies are supposed to make prices lower than they would otherwise be), P turns out to be lower? V has to be lowered or T increased. Subsidies will not increase T—although they might affect its composition. (Recollect, too, that T was initially increased by the war; what could subsidies do additionally in an economy that may actually have been close to physical capacity?) We have to fall back on V. But there are two possibilities. Either V is a passive random variable—in which case we do not know how subsidies will affect it. Or it is determined by utility maximizing money holding behaviour. In that second case, why should subsidies affect the amount of money demanded?

In other words, there are good reasons for thinking that subsidies, to the extent that they depressed the published price index, did so by pushing other prices up. Point E, in other words, is because of subsidies, a downwards biased measure of the course of prices in general.[7]

Conclusion on war

The published index shows that Britain had lower inflation in the Second World War than in the First. The containing of inflation was an objective of policy, and it appears to have been a success. It was also a well-chosen policy objective—for if inflation had been used to raise revenue, its contribution could only have been modest, and the post-war problems from the resulting inflation rate could have been enormous. Taxes contributed substantially to this success, as did bond finance.[8] Both these traditional instruments of policy reduced very considerably the need to print money. Some discussions at the

[7] Another way of looking at this question is to ask how subsidies could be financed. Indirect taxes would raise other prices. Printing money would push up uncontrolled prices. Bond sales would affect present prices indirectly, by pushing up V, and also the price of future goods by raising the interest rate. Income taxes would create cost pressures.

[8] Mention of bond sales raises the issue of Ricardian equivalence. Savings may have risen (on 'Ricardian' grounds) as a result of the vast growth in the stock of bonds. But although 'Ricardian' arguments may well have assisted patriotism in encouraging bond sales, they do not affect the amount of money demanded unless money is held to meet future tax liabilities. As bonds were so

time gave much credit to subsidies, but we would support those (Keynes and the Treasury generally) who argued that subsidies affected only relative prices, and not the general price level.

Price controls, however, do seem to have played a significant part in containing inflation. They held the end of war index to 150, as compared to a counterfactual (by our calculations above) of either 165 or 195. But it should be emphasized that these controls were bolstered by an extensive system of rationing. Indeed, rationing alone may well have accomplished all that we found.

The Economic Section set out clearly what the failings of price controls would be in the absence of other measures:[9]

> To attempt to remedy such an 'inflationary' process by the mere imposition of maximum price orders raises as many problems as it solves. Even if the prices of every commodity bought and sold were rigidly fixed, the operation of 'inflationary' forces already described would not be suspended. They would merely manifest themselves in other ways.
>
> (a) There would be disorderly and inequitable distribution. The fixing of maximum prices cannot, in itself, balance demand and supply; and, if demand is not allowed to push prices upwards, all that will happen will be queues and shop shortages and the general exhaustion of stocks.
>
> (b) The effect of general price fixing, unaccompanied by other measures, would be no less serious on production. To fix prices regardless of costs might easily bring it about that many commodities will cease to be produced. If costs rise above money prices so that the producer is making losses, then he will discontinue production.

We would argue, on exactly these grounds, that rationing was crucial to the effectiveness of controls, but we turn to this again after we have considered price controls in a time of peace.

THE 1960s[10]

A survey of controls

There were several attempts to control the growth of wages in the early 1960s. These attempts were based on the belief that rising wages caused inflation.

abundantly available to be held in anticipation of the obligations, it is unlikely money demand increased; so our monetary calculations are unlikely to have been affected.

[9] PRO CAB 71/3 26 March 1941. Quoted by Alan Both 'Economists and Points Rationing in the Second World War', *Journal of European History* (1985).

[10] A detailed economic history of these can be found in Blackaby (1978).

Only when a Labour government took office in 1964 were prices as well as wages brought within the controls. Responsibility for prices and incomes policies was given to a new ministry, the Department of Economic Affairs, and the policy was to be carried out by the National Board for Prices and Incomes, set up in early 1965. Initially restraint was voluntary. The Board was intended to 'educate public opinion' (Blackaby, 1978, p. 368)

Formal controls were introduced in July 1966 (Cmnd 3073). The policy was intended to run from July 1966 to July 1967, and to be in two phases—first 'standstill' (July 1966 to December 1966) and second 'severe restraint' (January 1967 to July 1967).

Under the first phase, the only price increases allowed were those deriving from increases in the cost of imports, changes in supply of seasonal goods, and tax changes. Controls applied to all enterprises, public and private. Plans for the second period were outlined in Cmnd 3150, published in November 1966. Price increases were allowed only when higher costs could not be absorbed. That lasted until July 1967, when a policy under which increases could be delayed but not forbidden was introduced. Then, in April 1968, a productivity, prices, and incomes policy was announced (Cmnd 3590). There was a 3.5 per cent ceiling on wage and salary increases. The NBPI's delaying power over price increases was lengthened to twelve months, reductions in prices could be required where this was recommended by the NBPI, and housing rent increases which had been planned were reduced. There was also a list of goods and services subject to 'Early Warning Arrangements'.

In summary, price controls of one sort or another were in place from mid 1966 to a little beyond June 1970. There was, however, a change of government in June 1970. The end of controls was in sight from then, so we regard that date as the end of the controlled period.

MEASURING EFFECTIVENESS IN PEACE

We use a variety of methods to construct a hypothetical 'control-free' index. One of these is basically the same as that used for wartime. The other, in many ways preferable, is completely different, and as will emerge below could not be used for the wartime period because of the above-discussed rationing system.

A monetary approach

Although there is a robust long run relationship between money and prices, this approach is not very well suited to the present problem, for two reasons.

First, simple equations relating past money to current prices can be very misleading in a fixed exchange rate regime.[11] Second, the method we use produces a much smoother series than we would wish, because we exploit the availability of higher frequency data than are available for our earlier period to forecast the course of prices not just their end point. Be that as it may, the method does give an indication. The approach is a basic and standard one. Our variables are the RPI (monthly) and the M3 measure of money. These were both transformed into logs and then into growth rates. We expect money to affect prices with a lag, but we have no theoretically determined views on lag length. Accordingly, we used fairly long polynominally distributed lags (Almon) so that the data were free to determine the lag length. This common procedure is far from ideal for the present purpose, for the effect of lagged money on prices is smoothed out by application of the mean lag—a problem, as we wish to compare the month by month movements of the actual RPI with the hypothetical controlled RPI.

These are all substantial problems, and we report our best equation (shown below) only for completeness.

Dependent variable = p (rate of inflation)
Independent variable = M (rate of money growth)

Independent variable	*coefficient*	*standard error*	t-*statistic*
Constant	−0.015	0.0097	−1.51
M3 GR1	0.011	0.051	0.22
M3 GR2	0.03	0.016	1.79
M3 GR3	0.04	0.013	3.13
M3 GR4	0.034	0.016	2.05
M3 GR5	0.09	0.06	1.45

$R^2 = 0.31$
DW = 0.29
Mean Lag = 21.3 (months)
(3.48)
Sum of lag coefficients = 1.29
(0.27)
Standard errors are in parenthesis.

As this is the best equation, our low expectations of the usefulness of the simple monetary approach for this purpose are plainly confirmed.

[11] See Mills and Wood (1978); and Friedman and Schwartz (1982).

A 'microeconomic' price index

This approach exploits information on how the weights in the RPI are chosen, and the fact that identical controls were not imposed on every good. Data on the RPI, including its composition, are available in some detail. It is possible to use this information to construct an index free of some (but not all) of the distortions caused by price controls. If this index differs substantially from the published one, we would argue the controls were effective; and conversely, if the two series are similar, then the controls were ineffective. We defer for the moment the question of how similar is similar.

The relevant control period begins in 1967, since the weights used for 1966 would have been decided in January 1966 on the basis of consumers' expenditure in the preceding three years when there were few controls.

The weights in the index could change from the demand side, because tastes changed or because spending patterns changed with rising incomes; or they could change from the supply side because of changes in supply conditions. Alternatively, they could change because of the constraints imposed by price controls. A two commodity example makes the distinction clear.

Assume there are two goods, X and Y. (They are imperfect substitutes in consumption.) Without controls, equilibrium in each market is at (PX_0X_0) and (PY_0Y_0) respectively, in Figure 10.2a. Now the price of X is controlled at PXc.

The effect on Y will be increased demand to D_1 and this would raise the price of Y to PY_1 and quantity to Y_1. In other words, controls on X affect both price and quantity of Y. This highlights why we could not use this method for wartime. Rationing inhibited substitution.

Suppose now that aggregate demand is increasing (as a result of monetary expansion) and that this is temporarily increases aggregate supply. This is the

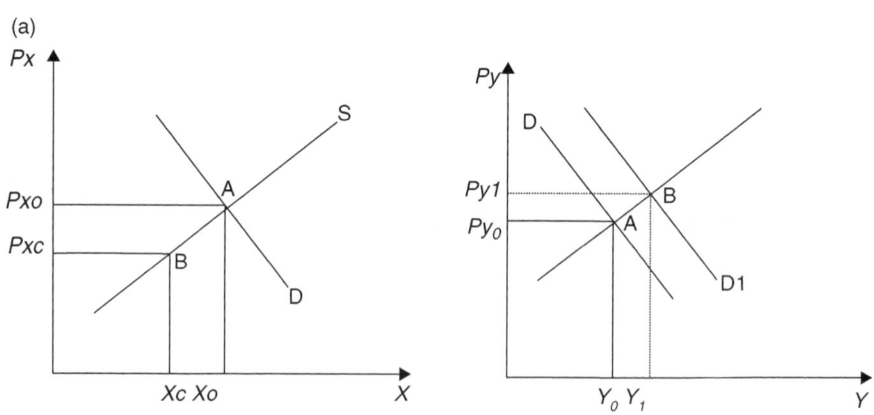

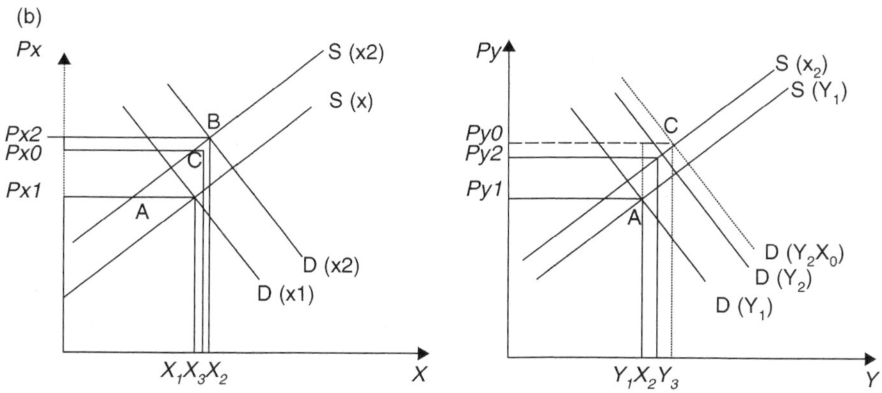

Figure 10.2 Substitution with and without rationing

case depicted in Figure 10.2b, where point A is the situation in Year 1 and point B the situation in Year 2. We have assumed that higher costs (e.g. wages) also shift supply curves upwards, but not enough to make the aggregate supply curve vertical. So in Year 2 prices of both goods will be higher at PX_2 and PY_2 respectively.

Now suppose that *the price of good X is controlled and is not allowed to rise beyond PXc*. This will imply (under 'no black market' assumption) that the constrained equilibrium will be at point C, and in market *Y* the demand curve will move to D (Y_2Xc), and equilibrium to point C. So the new equilibrium is:

$$X = (PXc, X_3)$$
$$Y - (Pyc, Y_3).$$

Observe that again prices and quantities in *both* markets, controlled and uncontrolled, are affected by controls in one market. Thus controls affect nominal expenditure on both goods, and thus in turn the weights assigned to them in the index.

In contrast, if the controls had been totally *ineffective* and there had been no change except inflation, the weights would not have changed. By constructing an index using the unchanged (i.e. base) weights and the new (current) prices (to allow for inflation) one can get an idea whether controls had a significant effect on the pattern of spending. If controls are effective, this 'hypothetical' index should lie below the actual index, as it will be giving a higher weight than did the published index to the price controlled good. And the more effective are controls, the farther apart will the two indices lie.

This procedure does involve certain assumptions. These should be made explicit. It is assumed that all changes in weights can be ascribed to controls, and none to changes in tastes or in supply conditions. This has two dangers. On the one hand, it may overstate the effect of controls if part of the change in weights has some other cause. Alternatively, if the other factors would have changed the weights in the *opposite direction* from that resulting from controls, the effect of controls would be understated. Which of the dangers appears to be present here?

The 'reformed' and the alternative series move closely together. This difference between the two can be put in context by noting that the official RPI started the period at 118.5 and ended it at 145.0, while the alternative index started at 118.7 and ended at 144.8. It thus appears on the basis of this method that controls were for all practical purposes ineffective.

There is of course the possibility, noted above, that tastes or supply changed in such a way as *exactly* to offset the distorting effects of controls. The offset required seems to be so exact as to be implausible. But implausible is not impossible, so we turn next to consider a third method of constructing a counterfactual index. This method requires the assumption of *no change* in structure, If it yields results consistent with the 'microeconomic' method, it lets us eliminate the possibility of offsetting structural change.

An atheoretical approach

We construct a time series model of the RPI, estimated during the period free of price controls, and then use it to 'forecast' the RPI during the period of controls. The model is estimated over the period February 1957 to June 1966, and then used to forecast prices over the subsequent period July 1966 to June 1970.

We estimated a moving average model of the order (1) (i.e. the lags on the error term were of the order 1). Beginning with the initial variable RPI, the monthly index of retail prices in level form, we estimate a model whereby past prices enable us to predict current prices. The data were deseasonalized and detrended. (Otherwise a spurious fit could be obtained.) Essentially, this enables us to obtain a stationary time series and model the process which has generated that stationary series. Full details are in the Appendix.

The results are, as with the 'alternative index' method, fairly striking (see Table 10A). The forecast index tracks the controlled index very closely. It is therefore essential to consider some assumptions and qualifications.

Qualifications

(i) Structural change

As emphasized at several points above, our methods involved assumptions about the structure of the economy. In particular, the way in which prices are generated should remain unchanged. This raises a major question. Does the

Table 10.1. Price index composition weights

Year	All items	A	B	C	D	E	F	G	H	I	J	K
1961	1000	350	71	80	87	55	66	106	68	59	58	
1962	1000	319	64	79	102	62	64	98	92	64	56	
1963	1000	319	63	77	104	63	64	98	93	63	56	
1964	1000	314	63	74	107	66	62	95	100	63	56	
1965	1000	311	65	76	109	65	59	92	105	63	55	
1966	1000	298	67	77	113	64	57	91	116	61	56	
1967	1000	293	67	72	118	62	59	92	118	61	58	
1968	1000	289	65	68	123	64	60	91	122	61	57	
1968	1000	263	63	66	121	62	59	89	120	60	56	41
1969	1000	254	64	68	118	61	60	86	124	66	57	42
1970	1000	255	66	64	119	61	60	86	126	65	55	43

Note on categories:
A: Food
B: Alcoholic drink
C: Tobacco
D: Housing
E: Fuel and light
F: Durable household goods
G: Clothing and footwear
H: Transport and vehicles
I: Miscellaneous goods
J: Services
K: Meals bought and consumed outside the home.

imposition of price controls count as a change in policy regime? If so, then as Lucas has argued we would have no way of interpreting econometric forecasts based on pre-regime change estimates. In the present context, this would mean that our finding that the constructed index traced the published one was just accidental, with no significance for the interpretation of controls. Actual index weights are shown in Table 10.1. But every writer who has argued for controls has written as if they are 'controls'—as if they contain pressures, not as if they remove them by somehow changing the economy's structure. No case has been advanced that controls change underlying behaviour.

Second, even if the imposition of controls were regarded as a regime change, it is not clear how important the implication would be in the present case. The reason is that although the controls eventually lasted for some years, they were continually presented as short-term measures. Would people incur the costs of changing price-setting behaviour for a purely transitory regime change?[12]

[12] Also requiring remark is that the 1967 devaluation of sterling seems to have had no effect on the performance of the estimated as compared to the actual price series. The actual price series did not show a jump; the post-devaluation attempts to contain price rises were by and large successful. Nor did the process generating price level increases alter. This is likely to be due to the fact that it was the exchange rate, not the exchange rate regime, the changed. Britain was still importing monetary policy from the US, the dominant country in the Bretton Woods system.

(ii) Testable qualifications

Here we turn to two qualifications to our results less sweeping than that discussed above, and, by virtue of that, capable of being tested. We constructed an index partially corrected for any distorting effects controls might have, and found that this index tracked closely the official RPI. Had controls restrained the official RPI, there would be excess demand for the controlled goods. Our partially corrected index should under those circumstances differ significantly from the published RPI. There is no evidence of this. It is however possible that the excess demand simply led to temporary accumulation of assets; this possibility can and should be examined.

We also constructed a moving average model of prices for the control price period, and used this model to forecast prices in the controlled period. The 'forecast' index was scarcely distinguishable from the reported index for the controlled period. This implies one of two things. Either the process generating the RPI did not change—so controls had no effect; or controls did have an effect, but some exactly offsetting effect impinged on the process from some other source.

Both approaches therefore yielded the conclusion that subject to some qualification, different in each case, price controls did not affect the behaviour of the RPI. That the qualifications were different in each case in itself suggests that price controls had little impact. It is however possible to carry out certain straightforward checks on the above-noted qualifications.

If there had been accumulation of financial assets in anticipation of the ending of controls, this would have impinged on bank deposits, or possibly deposits at building societies. We therefore checked to see whether the growth of either of those assets accelerated to a higher rate at the start of the period of controls, and, if they did so, if they sustained that rate. No acceleration is apparent.

What of the qualification to the second approach? What offsetting change could have occurred to the process generating prices so that price controls were exactly offset? Three possibilities seem worth exploring. Money growth could have accelerated, thus pushing up the trend of prices; unemployment could have been persistently lower; or we could have been in a different phase of the business cycle.

In fact, none of these indicates the likelihood of offsetting changes in the price-generating process. Money growth did not accelerate. Unemployment was not lower in this period than before; in fact it was higher. The British economy was not in a different phase of the cycle from the preceding years. It was first in a downswing; then there was a whole upswing; and finally the start of another downswing.

Accordingly, we conclude that the 1960s' controls were ineffective. This of course contrasts with our results for wartime. Confidence in both findings would be reinforced if the difference can be explained. We now turn to providing an explanation.

RATIONING—A SYMETALLIC ANALYSIS

The notable feature of the system of rationing in place in the wartime period is that many goods had to be paid for by a combination of two 'moneys'—sterling and coupons. Without both the goods could not legally be purchased. The system was thus exactly parallel to the symetallic monetary system proposed by Alfred Marshall, under which money would be linked to a fixed weight of gold *and* silver, the metals being in combination (1897, pp. 355–75). For example, the standard unit of currency might comprise 0.02 oz of gold *plus* 0.3 oz of silver, and the monetary authorities would buy and sell such units at the price of one pound sterling.

The purpose of Marshall's scheme can most easily be seen by extending it to imagining a situation when the 'standard bundle' comprises a large number of commodities, in relative magnitude proportionate to their weights in the wholesale price index. Then keeping fixed the £ price of such a bundle would be conducting monetary policy so as to stabilize the wholesale price index. Marshall's scheme, then, extended through more channels the stabilizing mechanisms of the gold standard. Looked at the other way round, it also prevented the price level from being disturbed by a change in supply conditions of one metal alone. For example, sudden technical progress in gold extraction would, without parallel change in silver production, leave the prices of goods in general unaffected, for the increase in gold alone would have no effect on the supply of money.

That was how the money/coupon combination worked. In principle, increasing the supply of money could have no effect on the demand for goods unless there were a matching increase in the supply of coupons. Of course the money/price relationship is flexible. Nevertheless, the difference between the effectiveness of the price controls in the two periods is striking and is paralleled by an additional mechanism of enforcement in the period when controls 'worked'. The rationing system seems to have been crucial to the effectiveness of Second World War price controls.

CONCLUSION

In comparing price controls in different time periods and in war and peace, it has to be borne in mind that many factors differed between the two periods. Nevertheless, it is notable that as between the two periods, by any method we tried we found controls to be effective in one period and not in the other. The period when controls did work, wartime, was a period when they were supplemented by requiring coupons as well as money to be tendered for goods. That brought into play an additional method of restraining prices, one described by Alfred Marshall in the course of setting out his proposal for a symetallic monetary standard. It is to that tardily adopted Marshallian proposal that we ascribe the effectiveness of Second World War price controls in Britain.

Appendix

Modelling the Retail Price Index

Let $\ln P_t$ be the log of the monthly retail price index.

Seasonal Adjustment:

$$\Delta \ln P_t = \ln P_t - \ln P_{t-12} \tag{1}$$

where $\Delta \ln P_t$ is the twelfth difference of the series. Since we are using logs, this gives us the rate of the inflation (i.e. the twelve monthly rate of inflation).

De-trending

In order to de-trend the above series we take first differences again, such that:

$$\Delta_1\Delta_1 \ln P_2 = \Delta_{12} \ln P_t - \Delta_{12} \ln P_{t-1}. \tag{2}$$

Equation (2) is then the rate of change of the twelve monthly rate of inflation. Substituting (1) into (2) we can rewrite the detrended series in the following form:

$$\Delta_1\Delta_{12} \ln P_t = (\ln P_t - \ln P_{t-12}IP) - (\ln P_{t-1} - \ln P_{t-13}) \tag{2.1}$$

Before estimating the relevant models, we examined the properties of both series as represented by (1) and (2). Essentially, we want to find a stationary series. The results suggested that $\Delta_{12} \ln \mathrm{P}_t$ was not stationary and in addition also displayed significant autocorrelation coefficients up to the tenth lag. The de-trended series $\Delta_1\ \Delta_1 \ln P_t$ was however found to be stationary. It did not have any significant autocorrelation coefficients.

Given the above there are two options for the form of the final equation. For equation (1) the appropriate model would be an ARIMA (1), which would take the following form:

$$\Delta_{12} \ln P_t = \beta\Delta_1 2 \ln P_{t-1} + \varepsilon t + \theta\varepsilon_{t-12} \qquad \text{[MODEL A]}$$

Where (ε_{t-12}) is the first order moving average term, and for equation (2) the appropriate model would be an MA(1), of the form:

$$\Delta_1\Delta_{12} \ln P_t = \rho\varepsilon_{t-12} \qquad \text{[MODEL B]}$$

This last model is a simple first order moving average process. If β takes the value one, then models A and B would be equivalent. We opted for model B, and estimated this using the Box-Jenkins (maximum likelihood) method.

The estimation of the above model will yield values of the parameters ρ and θ. These can then be used to forecast future prices. The forecasting equation will then take the following form:

$$(\ln P_t - \ln P_{t-12}) - (\ln P_{t-1} \ln P_{t-13}) = \rho\varepsilon_t + \theta\varepsilon_{t-12}$$

which by rearranging one can write:

$$\ln P_t = \ln P_{t-1} + \ln P_{t-12} - \ln P_{t-13} + \rho\varepsilon_t + \theta\varepsilon_{t-12}.$$

Equation (3) is then used for forecasting. It is important to observe that the results of our forecasts do depend crucially on whether we use actual past prices on the right-hand side of equation (3) or predicted prices. The latter exercise would imply dynamic simulation of equation (3); it has the advantage of not utilizing any of the actual prices during the forecasting period. We have used both methods, but report only the more demanding, dynamic method.

*Estimation results**

$$\Delta_1\Delta_{12} \ln P_t = \rho\varepsilon_t + \theta\varepsilon_{t-12} \qquad (3)$$

Dependent Variable	Independent Variable Coefficient on:	R2	S.E.	F.STAT (2.11)
ϵ_t	ϵ_{t-12}			
0.00	-0.89484	0.47	0.000546	99.31147
	(0.00016)	(0.0314)		

*Standard errors in parenthesis.

We know the forecasting equation is:

$$\ln P_t = \ln P_{t-1} + \ln P_{t-12} - \ln P_{t-13} - 0.89484\varepsilon_{t-12}.$$

Estimation period was 1957:2 to 1966:6. So from 1966:7 to 1970:6 we want to forecast in P_t using only predicted values and not actual values. So for example:

$$\text{In } P_{t(\text{July 1966})} = \ln P_{t(\text{June 1966})} + \ln P_{t(\text{July 1965})} - \ln P_{t(\text{June 1965})} - 0.89484\, \varepsilon_{t-12}.$$

Clearly our forecast for the first month (July 1966) will contain actual values but as we move on, we will be using predicted values, that is,

$$\ln P_{t(\text{Aug 1966})} = \ln P_{t(\text{July 1966})} + \ln P_{t(\text{Aug 1965})} \\ -\ln P_{t(\text{July 1965})} - 0.89484\ \varepsilon_{t-12}.$$

So here In P_t (July 1966) is a predicted value not an actual value

$$\ln P_{t(\text{Sept 1966})} = \ln P_{t(\text{Aug 1966})} + \ln P_{t(\text{Sept 1965})} \\ -\ln P_{t(\text{Aug 1965})} - 0.89484\ \varepsilon_{t-12}.$$

and so on, until we get to:

$$\ln P_{t(\text{July 1967})} = \ln P_{t(\text{June 1967})} + \ln P_{t(\text{July 1966})} \\ -\ln P_{t(\text{June 1966})} - 0.89484\ \varepsilon_{t-12}.$$

Note however that for the forecast of July 1967, $\epsilon_{t\ -12}$ is the error in July 1966, which by definition is equal to zero. Therefore from July 1967 onwards the last term ($\epsilon_{t\ -12}$) will disappear. Hence, for example, the forecast for August 1967 will be:

$$\ln P_{t(\text{July 1967})} = \ln P_{t(\text{July 1967})} + \ln P_{t(\text{Aug 1966})} \\ -\ln P_{t(\text{July 1966})}.$$

Finally, note that the forecast for July 1967 contains only one actual value, that is June 1966, and the forecast for August 1967, contains no actual values. Thus, it is

Table 10A.1. Actual and forecast prices

Year (month)	LPR	LFPR	Year (month)	LPR	LFPR
1966:7	4.75875	4.76302	1968:7	4.83231	4.82565
1966:8	4.76473	4.76478	1968:8	4.83390	4.82979
1966:9	4.76303	4.76657	1968:9	4.83469	4.83306
1966:10	4.76559	4.76701	1968:10	4.83945	4.84224
1966:11	4.77153	4.77208	1968:11	4.84182	4.84528
1966:12	4.77322	4.77358	1968:12	4.85515	4.84844
1967:1	4.77491	4.77606	1969:1	4.86059	4.85845
1967:2	4.77576	4.77596	1969:2	4.86599	4.86551
1967:3	4.77576	4.77866	1969:3	4.86984	
1967:4	4.78332	4.78580	1969:4	4.88053	4.88762
1967:5	4.78248	4.78571	1969:5	4.87901	4.88133
1967:6	4.78666	4.78615	1969:6	4.88356	4.88301
1967:7	4.78080	4.78238	1969:7	4.88356	4.88436
1967:8	4.77828	4.78678	1969:8	4.88129	4.88515
1967:9	4.77744	4.77658	1969:9	4.88432	4.88208
1967:10	4.78499	4.7800	1969:10	4.89185	4.88908
1967:11	4.79082	4.79093	1969:11	4.89410	4.89422
1967:12	4.79744	4.79251	1969:12	4.90082	4.90743
1968:1	4.80074	4.79913	1970:1	4.90897	4.90626
1968:2	4.80566	4.80159	1970:2	4.91412	4.91437
1968:3	4.80893	4.80566	1970:3	4.91998	491797
1968:4	4.82671	4.81649	1970:4	4.93519	4.93067
1968:5	4.82751	4.82587	1970:5	4.93806	4.93367
1968:6	4.83151	4.83169	1970:6	4.94093	4.94261

Notes:
LPR = log of actual prices.
LFPR = log of forecast prices.

worthwhile pointing out at this stage, that we are not using any actual values from the whole of the forecasting period. The last actual value used is June 1966, which is part of the estimation period. The results are reported, and compared with the actual index, in Table 10A.

REFERENCES

Blackaby, F. T. (ed) (1978) *British Economic Policy 1960–74*, Cambridge University Press for the N.I.E.S.R Economic Studies, 31.

Booth, A. (1985) 'Economists and Points Rationing in the Second World War', *Journal of European History*, 14(2), 297–317.

Capie, F. H. (1986) Conditions under which Very Rapid Inflation has Appeared', *Journal of Monetary Economics, Carnegie Rochester Proceedings*, 24, 115–68.

——and Rodrik-bali, G. (1985) 'The Money Adjustment Process in the United Kingdom, 1870–1914', *Economica*, 52(25), 117–22.

——and Webber, A. (1985) *A Monetary History of the Untied Kingdom 1870–1982 1 Data, Sources, Methods*, London: George Allen and Unwin.

Feinstein, C. H. (1972) *National Income, Expenditure and Output of the United Kingdom, 1855–1965*, Cambridge University Press.

Friedman, M. and Schwartz, A. J. (1982) *Monetary Trends in the United Kingdom; Their Relation to Income, Prices and Interest Rates 1867–1975*, University of Chicago Press for the NBER.

Friedman, M. (1956) *Studies in the Quantity Theory of Money*, Chicago University Press.

Hicks, J. R. (1937) 'Mr Keynes and the 'Classics'; A Suggested Interpretation', *Econometrical* 5 (April) 147–59

Keynes, J. M. (1936) *General Theory of Employment, Interest and Money*, London. Macmillan. Also in J. M. Keynes (1973), *The Collected Writings of J. M. Keynes*, Vol. VII, *The General Theory*, London: Macmillian St. Martins Press for the Royal Economic Society.

—— (1940) *How to Pay for the War*, London: Macmillan and Co.

Marshall, A. (1897) 'Remedies for Fluctuations of General Prices', *Contemporary Review*, 51.

Mills, T. C. and Wood, G. E. (1978) 'Money Income Relationships and the Exchange Rate Regime', *Federal Reserve Bank of St Louis Review*, August.

Pollard, S. (1962) *The Development of the British Economy 1914–1950*, London: Edward Arnold Publishers.

Robbins, L. (1947) *The Economic Problem in Peace and War; Some Reflections on Objectives and Mechanisms*, London: Macmillan.

White, E. N. (1990) 'Deficits, Inflation, and the Bankruptcy of the French Revolution', Rutgers University, Mimeo.

Part Three

11

Modelling Institutional Change in the Payments System, and its Implications for Monetary Policy*

Many institutional changes have taken place to payments systems. Indeed, they have been in continual change ever since money first emerged as the dominant technology for conducting transactions. Means of settlement between banks have changed: cheques replaced cash in many transactions, and they have in their turn been replaced partially (much more in some countries than others) by cards. Technology is even developing whereby mobile telephones can be used to effect instantaneous settlement of transactions. These have all affected the relationship between the quantity of money demanded and income. But none of the innovations has threatened to move us from a money-using society to one which transacts by some other means.

The implications for monetary policy have therefore been, in theory at least, trivial. And this has also been true in practice. Central banks have remained able to use monetary policy to influence, and to contral within surprisingly narrow limits, the course of the price level. Indeed, as the short-to-medium relationship between money and income has become looser (as evidenced by increasing difficulty in fitting well-behaved money demand functions), central bank control of inflation has improved. The changed constitutional relationship between central bank and government that has occurred in many

* The authors are grateful to Peter Andrews, Willem Buiter, Charles Goodhart, Mervyn King, Andrew Liliko, Stefan W. Schmitz, Martin Shubik, seminar participants at the Austrian Academy of Sciences, the Bank of England, the European Central Bank, and the 2003 International Conference of Game Theory, Mumbai, India. All remaining errors are ours.

Originally published as Forrest H. Capie, Dimitrios P. Tsomocos, and Geoffery E. Wood (2006), 'Modelling Institutional Change in the Payment System, and its Implications for Monetary policy, pp. 62–80, in Stefan W. Schmitz and Geoffery Wood (eds), *Institutional change in the Payment System and Monetary Policy* (Routledge), reproduced with the permission of Taylor & Francis Books.

countries appears to have produced benefits which have more than offset the increasing difficulty of using monetary policy to control inflation.

But how long can that benign outcome last? It would be too much to expect still further improvements to inflation control; that would be an excessive demand on monetary policy and central banks. Our concern is whether the *present* benign situation can persist. Will developments which appear to be on the horizon loosen the money-income relationship still further, or even end it by eliminating money as a transactions technology?

The aim of this chapter is to appraise one such possible technological development, and to model both it and money as transactions technologies. By comparing the models, we shall be able to appraise the future of fiat money.

The structure of the chapter is as follows. We first set out an outline of the technology that may replace money. Then we provide an informal description of the model we use to appraise both this technology and fiat money as means of conducting exchanges. This is followed by the development of our formal model. We then develop the implications of our analysis for the survival (or otherwise) of fiat money. This leads to a discussion of economic policy, and then to a concluding overview of our findings and policy conclusions.

One preliminary remains: definition. McCallum (1985; 2003) distinguishes very clearly between a monetary system of exchange, a barter system of exchange, and an accounting system of exchange. The first is one which uses a 'tangible mechanism of exchange'; a 'monetary system of exchange', he goes on, is '. . . one in which the vast majority of transactions involve money on one side'. This he contrasts with barter, 'in which commodities are directly exchanged without any intermediate conversion into money'. The third type of system is one in which 'there is no money [by which McCallum means at this point a medium of exchange] but exchanges are conducted by means of signals to an accounting network, with debits and credits to the wealth accounts of buyers and sellers being effected with each exchange'. McCallum goes on to say that he regards that system as non-monetary, as a 'highly efficient form of barter'.

In the present chapter we follow him in that. It must be noted, though, that whether such a system would dominate barter conducted electronically but *without* an agreed medium and unit of account should be demonstrated rather than assumed. We do, however, leave for another paper whether electronic barter with a mechanism and a unit of account would dominate electronic barter without these two features. The question is interesting, for only if the former does dominate is the concept and controllability of a price level a logically possible subject for discussion in an electronic barter world. But making the comparison would require detailed modelling of transactions costs in the two systems, and the results would not be relevant to the present chapter's conclusions.

TECHNOLOGY AND EXCHANGE

The development of electronic, and in particular of computer, technology has led to speculation that electronic technology will replace fiat money in facilitating exchange. Just as barter was supplanted first by commodity money and then by fiat money because these were superior transactions technologies, so, it is argued, information storage and transmission will be so facilitated by computer technology that in its turn fiat money will be displaced.

Central to analysis of this proposition is the medium-of-exchange function of money. The crucial distinction is between a money-using economy and a barter economy; whether it is one of primitive or of electronic barter, is that in the former a medium of exchange is used. Our aim in this chapter is to establish a simple formal framework which will let us examine the crucial determinants of whether or not a medium of exchange will be used. To do this, we construct a model of exchange with costs of transacting an intrinsic part of it; for if there are no costs of transacting then there are no transactions costs on which a medium of exchange can economize.

As was observed some years ago by George Stigler (1972), a world without transactions costs would seem a very strange place. There would be no firms—and therefore no banks, insurance companies, or other financial institutions. And further, there would be no money. The essence of our argument is that so long as there are transactions costs there will be money, and that even electronic barter will not, except under very special circumstances which we set out later in this chapter, be able to replace 'fiat' money because it will not be as effective in reducing transactions costs. To develop the economic intuition underlying our model, we first argue informally why some form of money to mediate trade in mass anonymous markets evolved as a device to reduce the costs of transacting. Then, we go on to show that once the *concept* of using money had developed, still further cost reductions were achieved by a further development—convergence to a very small number of commodities which were used as money. Indeed, a single money is, subject to certain constraints on its issuance, the optimal outcome. We would remark at this point that, while all the subsequent arguments are set implicitly or explicitly in an exchange economy, the conclusions would be expected to hold a fortiori in an economy with production, for if there is production then the *number* of exchanges will exceed these in an exchange economy with the endowment that our production economy produces.

Barter, whether with or without electronic accounting, involves the double coincidence of wants. The buyer must want what the seller is selling—and vice versa. That could be eliminated by what Meltzer (1998) calls 'barter credit'—supplying goods now in exchange for a promise of goods later. But such transactions are rare even in economies with developed and reliable legal systems. Why? The reason is that there is a cheaper way of transacting. Credit, whether barter credit or not, requires the seller to know about the buyer—about his or her creditworthiness, and the features (such as income) which contribute to that. If a money which is widely accepted and recognized is available, then the personal attributes of the buyer become irrelevant. All that matters is what he is offering. *Less information has to be gathered, so trade becomes cheaper*. This expands the possibilities for trade, so both buyer and seller gain. (The analogy with a tariff reduction is clear.)

For something to *evolve* as the *sole* medium of exchange of a society, rather than be imposed as such, two conditions have to be satisfied. These are as follows. First, not all goods are equally suitable for use as money; the costs of acquiring information must depend on the good selected. Second, the marginal cost of acquiring information about whatever is used in exchange falls the more frequently it is used. These two features let us explain the once widespread use of precious metals as a means of payment. Such metals can be assayed for fineness, are divisible, can be readily quantified by weighing, and are homogeneous—an ounce of gold of a certain fineness is identical to another ounce of that fineness. Alternative monies—cattle, stones, and tablets of salt—did not possess these attributes to anything like the same extent. These are the attributes that guide us towards the monetary commodity. But, it should be emphasized, the information-economizing attribute is crucial. Precious metals are not always available. If they are not, something else is used. Cigarettes were used as money in German prisoner-of-war camps in the Second World War.[1] They were used because everyone could recognize them, and knew that everyone would accept them in any exchange.

We can thus see that a society will tend to evolve towards the use of a very few commodities as money, given the assumption that not all commodities are equally good at satisfying the medium of exchange function; and that one good will come to dominate if the marginal cost of acquiring information about that good falls the more it is used.

Not only does the use of money eliminate the need to know about the buyer in a transaction; when it has evolved into use as a unit of account, another saving is achieved. Without a medium of account and unit of account, any transactor must know the bilateral exchange value of each commodity for every other commodity.[2]

[1] Radford (1945).

[2] McCallum (2003) emphasizes that the choice of a *medium* of account is of great importance and that, once that choice has been made, the subsequent choice of a *unit* of account is of little significance. The example he gives is that the choice of gold or silver as a medium of account can be vital, but once that choice is made, the quantity of it which is the unit of account is unimportant. The debate over bimetallism in the US in the run-up to the Presidential Election of 1896 makes the point.

> If there are n commodities, there are at least $(n(n-1))/2$ separate values. The number of bilateral exchange ratios (prices) rises quickly. With $n = 100$ commodities, there are at least 4950 prices to know. At $n = 500$, the number is 124,750, and with 1000 commodities there are at least 499,500 prices. Without a unit of account, trade would be very limited by costs of information. Use of a unit of account to express value reduces the number of prices from $(n(n-1))/2$ to n. (Meltzer 1998, p. 12)

So far we have argued that evolution to the use of a few commodities and subsequently to one commodity as money, is beneficial. Subject to certain constraints going beyond that brings still further benefits. Paper money, so long as there is not overissue that leads to inflation, brings a resource saving if it substitutes in whole or in part for the commodities which heretofore had served as money.

To summarize, we have argued that the concept and use of money emerged through a process of search and discovery. Its advantage over barter credit, which has some advantages over simple barter, is that it reduces transaction costs still further by shifting attention from the qualities of the prospective purchaser of a good to the qualities of what he is offering to pay for it. From (in Allan Meltzer's (1998) words) 'a unique and possibly obscure set of attributes to a common and widely known set of attributes'. A money-using society requires less information than a bartering society.

Before going on to develop a formal demonstration of these conclusions, and then to show their relevance to the future of electronic barter and paper money, it is useful to place the arguments in their historical context, for the view of the development and role of money set out earlier is not new. A thorough exposition of it was provided over 100 years ago by Carl Menger (1892).[3] He maintained that money was a 'social' creation, a product of the invisible hand. His was an example of an invisible hand explanation—in contrast to a government-based explanation—of a social institution.[4] The basic point was not original to Menger, either. (It is a bold writer who asserts that he has found the original inventor of any economic concept!) Adam Smith had made the point in the *Wealth of Nations*:

> In order to avoid the inconvenience of such situations [where the would-be seller of a good does not want what the would-be buyer offers] every prudent man in every period of society, after the first establishment of the division of labour, must naturally have endeavoured to manage his affairs in such a manner, as to have at all times by him, besides the peculiar product of his own industry, a certain quantity of some one commodity or other, such as he imagined few people would be likely to refuse in exchange for the product of their industry. (Smith 1776/1981 edition, pp. 37–38)

[3] The complete text of this chapter has been translated into English and is available in Latzer and Schmitz (2002).

[4] See Latzer and Schmitz (2002).

And that money was originally a social institution, although it had subsequently become a government one, was also noted by Keynes (1935, pp. 4–5):

> Thus the Age of Money had succeeded to the Age of Barter as soon as men had adopted a money-of-account. And the Age of State money was reached when the state claimed the right to declare what thing should answer as money to the current money of account—when it claimed the right not only to enforce the dictionary but also to write the dictionary.[5]

Now, it is not logically necessary for the medium of exchange to save also as the medium of account. But as several authors have emphasized, if they do not coincide, the 'computational benefits' of having a medium of account are incomplete unless the simple step of having it coincide with the medium of exchange is taken.[6] Severe inflation can disrupt this, but it does need to be severe; the two seem to continue to coincide even at inflation rates well into three figures per annum.

STRATEGIC MARKET GAMES: A BIRD'S EYE VIEW

Strategic market games provide a framework rigorously to introduce money, other financial instruments as well as financial intermediaries to closed models. The need for accounting clarity, institutional detail, and the criterion of 'playability' is such that minimal institutions (e.g. clearing houses, central banks and other financial intermediaries, credit, default, etc.) and well-defined price formation mechanisms (sell-all, bid-offer, double auction) naturally emerge as logical necessities in the rules of the game and the equilibrium concept used. Ultimately, this class of games contributes to the development of formal micro foundations to money, financial economics, and macroeconomics.

Strategic market games are related to the design of resource allocation methods introduced by Hurwicz (1960; 1973). They were introduced formally by Shubik (1973), Shapley (1976), Shapley and Shubik (1977), Dubey and Shubik

[5] The most fully developed modern statement of the 'transactions cost' theory of money can be found in the work of Karl Brunner and Allan Meltzer. The most detailed statement of their view is given in Brunner and Meltzer (1971). Alchian (1977) also develops the argument and Yeager (1968) draws out the implications of it for the behaviour of the macroeconomy. The argument that money evolved as a result of private initiative of course leaves unexplained why all money is now state money. Some scholars (e.g. Goodhart (2000)) argue that state money is an inherently superior 'institutional symbol of trust' (to use Shubik's definition of money), while others (e.g. Glasner (1989)) point to the successful existence of private mints until they were extinguished by law and maintain the opposite. A formal model of an explanation for the dominance of state money can be found in Monnet (2002). An additional factor which may predispose a society to state rather than private fiat money is the comparative irrelevance of the solvency of the state. See also footnote 13.

[6] Wicksell (1935), Niehans (1978) and McCallum (1985).

(1978; 1980) and Shubik and Wilson (1977). Three main price formation mechanisms were introduced: a one-sided Cournot type of model, a two-sided Cournot type and a double auction (or two-sided Bertrand-Edgeworth model). Fiat or commodity money is used and other market structures are also modelled. For example, foreign exchange markets whereby no natural *numéraire* or fiat money is a medium of exchange, then one can employ a modified price formation where trading posts between any two instruments or commodities are set and consistent prices that clear all markets are determined via a giant clearinghouse.

Endogenous default, credit, financial intermediaries, and incomplete asset markets are introduced and, therefore, one can formally model and analyse payment systems, monetary, fiscal, and regulatory policies. For an excellent presentation of these models one can consult Shubik (1990; 1999); and for a more technical analysis Giraud (2003). In principle, inefficiency in this class of models arises due to insufficient liquidity, or oligopolistic effects, or institutional restrictions. Hence, active policy has non-neutral effects and possibly, but not always, ameliorates welfare losses because of the transactions technology present in the models. Last but not least, abstracting from the oligopolistic effects, there exists a large literature on monetary general equilibrium models which is akin to the strategic market games one, since money and institutions are introduced into the standard Arrow-Debreu model.[7]

In sum, since the institutions of society in general, and the financial institutions in particular, are the carriers of economic process, a *mathematical institutional economics* is needed as it has been argued by Martin Shubik. This is what strategic market games attempt so as to achieve a better understanding of production, distribution, policy and, more generally, of political economy.

FORMAL MODEL

We use the strategic market game developed in Shubik and Tsomocos (2002). Money depreciates (i.e. it wears out through deterioration of notes' and coins' quality) when used in exchange, and its replacement is costly.[8] The stipulated means of exchange is fiat money and all transactions need cash in advance (see footnote 14 for the motivation of this constraint). Thus, agents borrow fiat money to make their transactions. The government extracts seigniorage costs

[7] See e.g. Lucas (1980); Grandmont (1983); Dubey and Geanakoplos (1992, 2003); and Drèze and Polemarchakis (2000).

[8] Calculations of the rate of depreciation of various types of money can be found in Shubik and Tsomocos (2002).

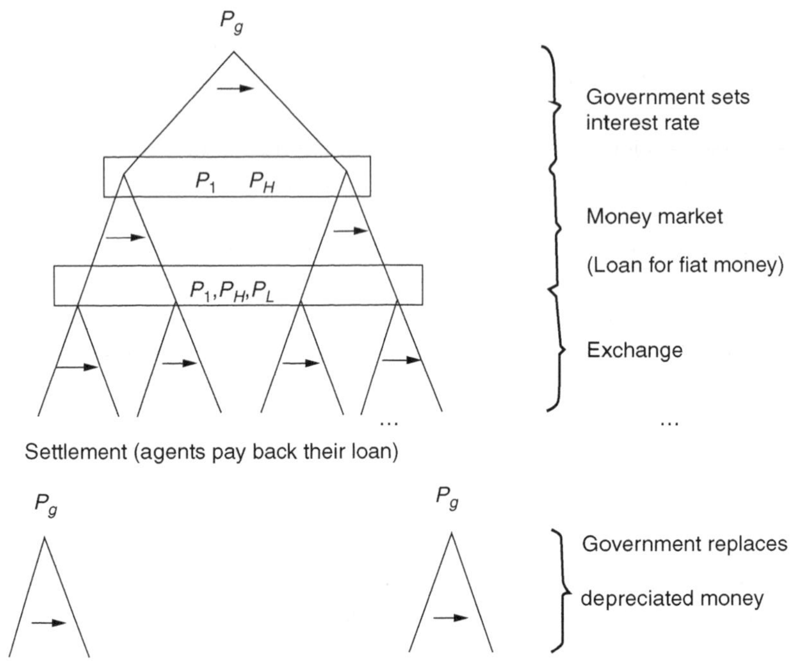

Figure 11.1. Trade with seigniorage cost of fiat money

from the players in the form of interest rate payments. In order to do so, it participates in exchange and bids to provide for its inputs of production. The objective function of the government for the purposes of our argument, without loss of generality, is to minimize the interest rate subject to the requirement to replace worn out fiat money used in exchange, and the interest rate which is a choice variable of the government determines its revenues. We assume that the initial money supply enters exogenously. Figure 11.1 shows the extensive form of the game. The exchange game is a one-period game with four subperiods. At each subperiod, as we explain below, an agent or a group of agents move. We first modify the game to admit both fiat money and electronic barter. We conceptualize electronic barter mediated as through a giant clearing house run by an institution, perhaps the government. We then analyse the condition under which fiat money dominates electronic barter.

At the first move the government, P_g, determines the interest rate. At the second move, individuals, $P_1, \ldots, P_H$, obtain fiat money in the money market at the predetermined interest rate. At the third move, individuals exchange commodities and the government buys inputs of production to be used in the replacement of depreciated fiat money. We maintain simplicity of strategy sets by assuming a continuum of traders, simultaneous moves, and a minimum of information at the second and the third stage. Then traders pay back their loans, and finally the government replaces depreciated money.

The government levies seigniorage costs to replenish depreciated money and also participates in exchange.[9]

Let $h \in H = \{1, \ldots, H\}$ be the set of agents and $l \in L = \{1, \ldots, L\}$ be the set of tradable commodities. Each agent is endowed with a vector of commodities $e^h \in \mathfrak{R}^L_+$. The utility functions of agents are of the form $u^h : \mathfrak{R}^L \to \mathfrak{R}$.

The following assumptions hold:

(i) $\sum_{h \in H} e^h \gg 0$
(i.e. every commodity is present in the economy)

(ii) $e^h \neq 0, \forall\, h \in H$
(i.e. no agent has the null endowment of commodities)

(iii) u^k is continuous, concave and strictly monotonic $\forall\, h \in H$
(i.e. the more consumption the better)

Agents maximize their utility of consumption subject to the following constraints:

$$\sum_{i \in L} b_l^h \leq v^h \tag{1}$$

(i.e. expenditures in commodities $\leq$ borrowed money)

$$q_l^h \leq e_l^h, \forall l \in L \tag{2}$$

(i.e. sales of commodities $\leq$ endowment of commodities)

$$(1 + r)_{\imath'}{}^h \sum_{l \in L} p_l q_l^h + \Delta(1) \tag{3}$$

(i.e. loan repayment $\leq$ receipts from sales of commodities + money at hand) where, $b_l^h \equiv$ money bid of h for the purchase of commodity $l \in L$,

$q_l^h \equiv$ quantity of commodity $l \in L$ offered by h,
$v^h \equiv$ loans *contracted* by h,
$r \equiv$ loan *interest* rate,
$p_l \equiv$ commodity *price* of $l \in L$ and
$\Delta(1)$ is the difference between the right- and left-hand sides of equation (1).

As can be seen from the budget constraints (1) and (3), receipts from sales of commodities cannot be used contemporaneously for financing purchases of other commodities. This is the essence of the cash-in-advance constraint which can also be thought of as a liquidity constraint.

[9] A more extensive presentation and discussion can be found in Shubik and Tsomocos (2002).

The exogenously fixed money supply M depreciates at a rate η. Thus, if the total amount of fiat money borrowed by the agents from the government (or central bank) is $\sum_{h \in H} \upsilon^h = \bar{\mu}$ and the expenditure of the government for the purchase of inputs of production is $\bar{g}$ then $\eta[\mu + \bar{g}]$ is the depreciated amount of money, since $[\bar{\mu} + \bar{g}]$ is the total amount of money in circulation.

The government's production function for money exhibits decreasing returns to scale in order to generate a unique optimum.[10]

$$z_{L+1} = F(x_1^g, \ldots, x_L^g) \tag{4}$$

with

$z_{L+1} \equiv$ amount of fiat money produced,
x_l^g inputs of production.

We impose the standard technical assumptions on the government's production set, $y^g \in \mathfrak{R}_+^L$, that guarantee feasibility and the existence of a solution to the government's maximization problem.

(iv) $0 \in y^g$,
(v) y^g is convex and closed
(vi) $\exists B > 0 \ni if(x_1^g, \ldots, x_L^g; Z_{L+1}) \in y^g$ then $x_l^g \in B, \forall l \in L$ and $Z_{L+1} \leq B$

The government seeks to minimize interest rates because it simply aims to levy the necessary seigniorage to replace depreciated fiat money. Thus the government's optimization problem becomes,[11]

$$\max_{r, b_l^g, l \in L} {}^{12} - r$$

$$\text{s.t. } Z_{L+1} = \eta \left[\sum_{h \in H} \upsilon^h + \sum_{l \in L} b_l^g \right] \tag{5}$$

$$\sum_{l \in L} b_l^g = r \sum_{h \in H} \upsilon^h \tag{6}$$

Where (5) is the amount of depreciated money that needs to be replaced, and (6) is the budget constraint of the government (i.e. its expenditures to finance the cost of production come from seigniorage).

[10] For example, a Leontief production technology with coefficients $\gamma_l, \forall l \in L, Z_{L+1} = \min[\gamma_l x_l^g, \ldots, \gamma_L x_L^g]$. If another technology were chosen, a unique equilibrium could be guaranteed by an exogenous institutional constraint, such as a price level target.

[11] Government purchases are all used in the production process, i.e. government does not obtain utility from consumption.

[12] Mathematically, minimization of r is equivalent to maximize $-r$.

The final allocations for the agents and the government are:

$$x_l^h = e_l^h - q_l^h + \frac{b_l^h}{p_l}, \forall l \in L \tag{7}$$

(i.e. consumption = initial endowment – sales + purchases) and

$$x_l^g = \frac{b_l^g}{p_l} \tag{8}$$

(government's inputs of production = money offered/prices).

Note that the relation between η and r is a complicated one and depends on gains from trade that in turn determine the volume of transactions. The interest rate r is set by the government to raise seigniorage revenue for the financing of fiat money production so as to replace depreciated money.

Finally, a Nash equilibrium (NE) or $\Gamma(H, u^h, e^h, \eta, M, x^h, x^g)$ is a set of strategy choices, $s = (s^h, s^g) = (b_l^h, q_l^h, x_l^h, b_l^g, p); \forall h \in H$ and the government, and $\alpha = (\alpha^h, \alpha^g) \in \sum = \mathrm{X}_{h \in H} B^h \times B^g, \ni$

$$\pi(s/\alpha) \leq \pi(s) \tag{9}$$

where B^h, B^g are the choice sets of the agents and the government (i.e. $B^h = ((b_l^h, q_l^h, v^k)_{l \in L} : (1){-}(2)\text{hold})$ and $B^g = ((r, b_l^g)_{l \in L} : (5){-}(6)\text{hold}))$ and (s/α) is s with either s^t or s^8 replaced by any other strategy choice α^t or α^g.[13] Also, $\Pi(\cdot)$ represents the payoff functions of agents ($\Pi^h(\cdot) = u^h$) and of the government ($\Pi^8(\cdot) = -r$).

Prices are formed using the Dubey and Shubik (1978) price formation mechanism. Prices are by that mechanism formed as the ratio of the aggregate cash bid in a particular market to the aggregate quantity of commodities offered for sale. This is equivalent to an equilibrium condition; its accounting clarity allows for cash flows in the economy to be traced precisely.

$$\text{Thus}, p_l = \left\{ \begin{array}{ll} \dfrac{\sum\limits_{h \in H} b_l^h + b_l^g}{\sum\limits_{h \in H} q_l^h}, & \mathit{if} \sum\limits_{h \in H} b_l^h + b_l^g; \sum\limits_{h \in H} q_l^h > 0 \\ 0, & \mathit{otherwise} \end{array} \right\} \tag{10}$$

The existence and inefficiency theorems for these outcomes are stated and proved in Shubik and Tsomocos (2002). Here we will focus our attention on

[13] Without loss of generality, we consider the case of perfect competition (i.e. a continuum of agents). Thus, agents regard prices as fixed in the optimization problems.

the relative efficiency of using alternative means of payments (on fiat money versus electronic barter).

TRADE WITH FIAT MONEY VERSUS ELECTRONIC BARTER

We conceptualize exchange using fiat money as follows. Consider a simple case in which $L = 4$. Fiat money can be exchanged against every commodity but commodities cannot be exchanged with each other. Figure 11.2 describes the situation. The arcs connecting m with commodities 1, 2, 3, and 4 indicate that money can be exchanged against all commodities. On the other hand, commodities cannot be exchanged with each other (i.e. there are no arcs connecting them).[14]

Thus, there exist four markets. If on the other hand we want to conceptualize 'electronic barter' we assume that commodities can be exchange with each other, perhaps via an accounting device of e-barter, which now becomes the stipulated means of exchange, through a clearing house that matches demand and supply. In this case there will be $\frac{L(L-1)}{2}$ markets, that is, six markets altogether.[15] Thus, in Figure 11.3 arcs connect all commodities with each other indicating that exchange occurs via electronic barter.

Let us assume that the combined cost of gathering and then processing information on each transaction is c. On the other hand trade with fiat money, by virtue of its anonymity, divisibility, fungibility, and its other properties does

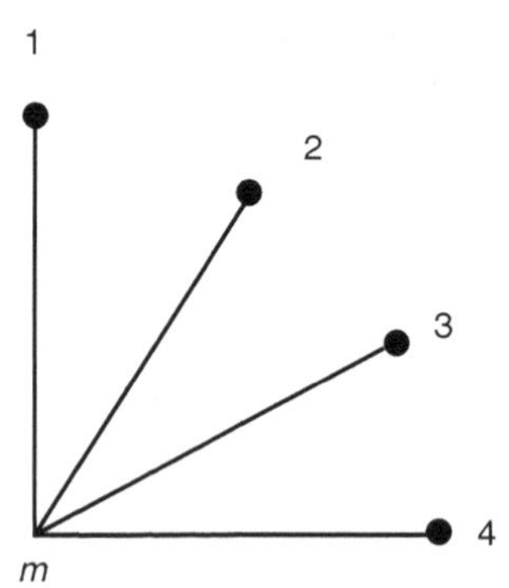

Figure 11.2. Trade with fiat money

[14] Note that the constraint that goods cannot be directly exchanged for goods is not imposed but naturally emerges as a consequence of our prior argument that trade with money dominates primitive barter.

[15] Extensive discussion on various market structures and how these affect exchange is contained in Shubik (1999).

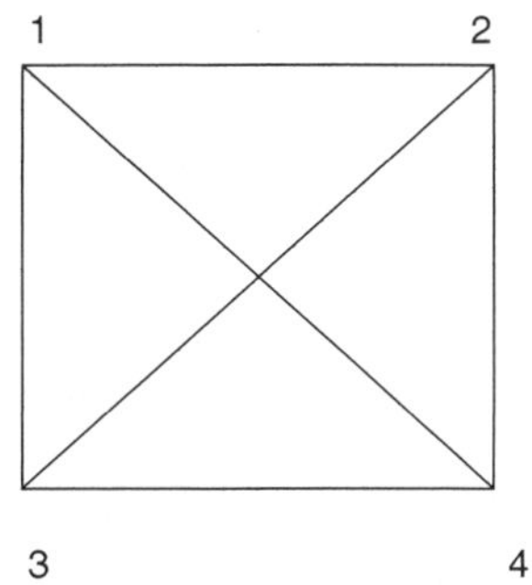

Figure 11.3. Trade via electronic barter

not require any additional costs except its production and replacement costs. These are covered in its production process as described in equation (4). Also, information costs concerning the creditworthiness of borrowers in a fiat money economy are dealt with by commercial banks and not by the original issuers of money (i.e. central banks) or by those who accept money in exchange for goods or services. These costs cannot be avoided by the operators of the central clearing house (or a similar transactions institution) that implements electronic barter. Then the total cost of exchange with e-barter is:

$$\overline{C} = \frac{cL(L-1)}{2}(H+1)^{16} \tag{11}$$

We note that each agent participates in only one side of the market since wash sales (i.e. the same individual participating in both sides of a particular market) are not profitable in a strategic market game without oligopolistic effects. If we assume that set-up costs for establishing either of the two market structures are negligible we have proposition 1. We also note that the total cost of fiat money and of electronic barter is endogenously determined; both depend on the volume of transactions; see equations (6) and (11).

Proposition 1

The cost of exchange with fiat money is lower than exchange with e-barter provided that,

$$\frac{L(L-1)}{2}c(H+1) - rM > 0, \text{where } M = \sum\nolimits_{h \in H} \upsilon^h$$

[16] We implicitly assume that we are in equilibrium such that agents participate in all markets.

Proof

The cost of exchange with fiat money is $r\sum_{h\in H} \upsilon^h(*)$, since replacement of depreciated money is financed by seigniorage which is levied by interest rates. Hence, $(11)-(*) = \frac{L(L-1)}{2}c(H+1) - r\sum_{h\in H} \upsilon^h$ represents the cost difference of exchange with electronic barter versus fiat money.

One point can usefully be made here about this relationship. If we imagine technical progress lowering c, the very same process is likely to increase the number of commodities, L. Indeed, over time we have seen a proliferation of traded commodities most of them being associated with technical progress. Note also that while the lower bound of r is zero, that of c is inevitably above zero.[17]

Proposition 1 underlines the fact that fiat money is a decoupling device that economizes on transaction costs regardless from where they emanate (i.e. processing, information acquisition, etc.). On the other hand, electronic barter is a centralized accounting mechanism that requires detailed knowledge of every transaction. Thus, it inevitably entails higher aggregate costs in complicated market systems with multiple markets and commodities. It is not a coincidence that the advent of money (or equivalently the decline of barter) occurred contemporaneously with the development of the market system.

Proposition 2

The equilibria of $\Gamma(H, u^h, e^h, \eta, x^h, x^g)$ with trade with fiat money coincide with those of the corresponding game with e-barter only if $r = 0$ and $c = 0$.

Proof

If $r = 0$ and $c = 0$ the two alternative methods of financing trade produce the same commodity allocations. To get the same prices and allocations set

$$\frac{\sum_{h\in H} b_l^h}{\sum_{h\in H} q_l^h} = p_l \text{ and } x_l^h = e_l^h - q_l^h + \frac{b_l^h}{p_l} \forall l \in L, h \in H.$$

[17] Why money is replaced by barter as a result of hyperinflation is summarized in the relationship given above. In hyperinflation, the nominal interest rate rises enormously. See Capie (1986) for a review of some such episodes.

Then, regardless whether trade is conducted with fiat or through electronic barter, the same equilibrium obtains.

Proposition 2 underlines the fact that alternative methods of financing become distinct only when transactions costs are present in the economy. Unless one introduces process and the organizational details of market transactions, it is difficult to delineate the differences between alternative media of exchange. Both of them, without transactions costs, are identical units of account. Money is both neutral and super-neutral. Trade, no matter how organized, generates the same allocations. Whenever $r = 0$ and $c = 0$ then money is a 'veil'.[18] Even in the case of bimetallism or multiple means of exchange, as long as there are determinate conversion rates among the media of exchange, the analysis can be conducted in terms of a 'primary' means of payment. However, the allocations generated by the two methods of financing trade are not unambiguously Pareto ranked whenever $r, c \neq 0$. It remains an open question to determine the conditions on r and c that allow one method to generate Pareto superior allocations over the other.

A natural question that emerges from this analysis is whether it is possible for fiat money and electronic barter to coexist in equilibrium; in particular, whether fiat money can be used for a subset of commodities and electronic barter for the rest. This issue is complicated and beyond the scope of our present analysis, since the volume of transactions with each medium of exchange is endogenously determined and in turn determines the subset of commodities whose trade might occur with each medium of exchange. Also, the gains from trade of each commodity influence the marginal benefit and cost using different methods of financing trade. For example, if there exist big gains from trade in a specific commodity, the government may reduce the marginal cost of trading in that market by introducing electronic barter and thus avoiding depreciation of fiat money used in this particular very liquid market.

THE PRICE LEVEL—MEANINGFUL AND DETERMINATE

The intrinsic informational superiority of central bank issued base money will ensure that demand for it is not extinguished by the growth of e-barter. Demand will remain from the non-bank public, and, because of that, derived

[18] For more on this, see and Tsomocos (1996, 2003a, 2003b), Shubik and Tsomocos (2002).

demand will remain from the banking sector. The central bank will thus retain control of short-term interest rates.[19] This might seem at first glance sufficient for it to retain control of the price level; for in many models a short rate is the sole transmitter of monetary policy actions. For example, much recent work on monetary policy uses small macroeconomic models which include an IS function analogous to that in a basic IS-LM model. These can be backward looking, and thus very close to the traditional specification,[20] or forward looking, embodying rational expectations.[21] But whatever the specification, a common feature is that demand for current output is a function of the real rate of interest, and that rate in turn is typically assumed to be a short-term nominal rate. There is a crucial assumption of slow price level adjustment; monetary policy in such models affects output and inflation only through its effects on the real rate of interest. This is surely a somewhat hazardous assumption in the present context. Sluggish price adjustment is a result of price adjustment being costly. In a world where transaction costs have been drastically reduced by technical progress, it would be strange to assume that the costs of price adjustment remained unaffected. Accordingly, it also seems strange to continue to argue that monetary policy depends crucially for its effectiveness on prices being sticky.

It is all the stranger since no such dependence is necessary. Viewing the short rate as the sole transmitter of monetary policy is unnecessarily restrictive both theoretically and empirically. Allan Meltzer (1999a) has recently summarized the body of theory and evidence which considers that specification to be inadequate. He argued that, while so long as prices are sticky the real interest rate is indeed affected by central bank operations, so too is the real monetary base, and changes in the latter affect aggregate demand in ways additional to the effect of changes in the real interest rate. Meltzer (1999b) reports empirical results for the United States which support this argument, as does Nelson (2000) for the United Kingdom,[22] who provides a clear summary of his results as follows:

> The common feature of the regressions is that for the United States and the United Kingdom, real money growth enters output regressions sizeably, positively, and significantly. The real interest rate generally enters with a negative sign, though both the sign and the significance of the real interest rate term appear to be less consistent across sub-samples than those of the money growth terms. (Nelson 2000, 13)

[19] We do not imply that without such demand it would lose control of short rates. The argument in Goodhart (2000) that the central bank can control rates through its being able to sustain losses seems to us to be correct, despite objections by Selgin and White (2002).

[20] See e.g. Fuhrer and Moore (1995).

[21] See e.g. McCallum and Nelson (1999a).

[22] The result is not novel; earlier work (e.g. Mills and Wood (1977)) found a relationship between the base and the price level over long runs of data in the United Kingdom.

These empirical results are consistent with two quite distinct bodies of analysis. One is on an approach which assumes utility is non-separable in consumption and real money holdings. This justifies a real money balance term in the IS function as a result of optimizing behaviour. Koenig (1990) reports results which support this; but others suggest that the coefficient on real balances is likely to be small.[23]

A *direct* role for money is perhaps better defended and explained by an approach with much earlier origins. David Hume (1752) thought that money affected the economy through a wide variety of channels, and expressed this thought in a metaphor—water flowing from one place to another—that frequently recurs in the discussions of the money transmission process.[24]

> Money always finds its way back again by a hundred canals, of which we have not notion or suspicion.... For above a thousand years, the money of Europe has been flowing to Rome, by one open and sensible current; but it has been emptied by many secret and insensible canals. (Hume 1752/1955 reprint, p. 48)

The many channels view is also articulated by Friedman and Schwartz (1962, pp. 486–87).

> The attempt to correct portfolio imbalances (resulting from an increase in the money stock) raises the prices of the sources of service flows relative to the flows themselves which leads to an increase in spending both on the service flows and then produce a new source of service flows.... Sooner or later the acceleration in nominal income will have to take the form of rising prices, since the initial position was assumed to be one of equilibrium and we have introduced nothing to change the long-run trend of nominal income.

This argument is also expressed in Brunner and Meltzer (1993) and was stated very succinctly in Meltzer (1999b, p. 10), as follows:

> Monetary policy works by changing relative prices. There are many, many, such prices. Some economists erroneously believe.... monetary policy works only by changing a single short-term interest rate.

He also argues (1999a, pp. 10 11) that money balances are crucial in the transmission mechanism. He sees 'the gap between desired and actual real balances as a measure of the relative price adjustment required to restore full equilibrium'.

Our formal model, which compared fiat money with e-barter, also yields the result that control of the issue of fiat money controls the price level without any intermediation through an interest rate channel. Our model manifests *real* as well as *nominal* determinacy as has been shown in Tsomocos (1996; 2003a;

[23] See e.g. McCallum (1999).

[24] See Wood (1995) for a discussion of the development of the quantity theory and the history of the 'water' metaphor.

2003b). This is unlike the classical competitive model which possesses a 'finite' number of equilibria with respect to real allocations; only relative prices can be determined. Our model resolves nominal indeterminacy through the presence of *private liquid wealth*.[25] By liquid wealth we mean a commodity or a monetary instrument which can be used interchangeably with money in real, financial, or bank transactions, and its conversion rate is institutionally predetermined. The essence of the determinacy argument and consequently of the non-neutrality result is that monetary policy affects nominal variables, yet if private liquid wealth is non-zero then monetary changes directly affect the endowments of agents, resulting in different optimization choices and consequently different real consumption. The issues of determinacy and money non-neutrality are intimately connected and are analytically equivalent.

Finally, if a model does not possess equilibria that are nominally determinate then any discussion of exchange with a particular means of payment (either fiat or e-barter) is not legitimate. If multiple price levels support the same equilibrium real allocations then it is impossible to compare the relative virtues of exchange with different means of payment.[26]

CONCLUSION

In this paper we first set out the argument (a very traditional one) that money evolved to reduce transaction costs by economizing on information.

A formal model in which money existed by virtue of that property was then developed and the costs of operating a fiat money system were compared with the costs of operating a system of e-barter. The key cost parameters were identified. It was shown that within this framework fiat money dominates—is cheaper than—e-barter, unless inflation drives up the nominal interest rate. Second, increases in the number of commodities increase the costs of e-barter faster than they do the costs of using fiat money; and finally that the lower bound to the cost of using fiat money is always below that of e-barter. Thus fiat money is a superior transaction technology to e-barter; transaction chains that use it have intrinsically lower information requirements. The resulting demand for fiat money by the non-bank public will in turn give rise to demand by the banking sector. Their joint demands will ensure both that central banks survive and that they will retain control of a price level measured in the money

[25] Tsomocos (1996).

[26] McCallum (2003) reaches this same conclusion by a different route. It is, however, clearly related to the above argument in that it focuses on a voluntary demand for base money on the part of banks—that is, of demand for it in the absence of reserve requirements. He, as an alternative, suggests that payment of interest in reserves could also achieve such a demand.

they issue. Institutional change in the payments system will no doubt have quantitative implications for central bank operations, but it will not have qualitative implications for them.

REFERENCES

Alchian, A. A. (1977) 'Why Money?' *Journal of Money, Credit and Banking*, 9, 133–40.

Brunner, K. and Meltzer, M. (1971) 'The Uses of Money: Money in the Theory of an Exchange Economy', *American Economic Review*, 61, 784–805.

——(1993) *Money and the Economy: Issues in Monetary Analysis*, Cambridge University Press.

Capie, F. H. (1986) 'Conditions in which Very Rapid Inflation Appears', *Carnegie-Rochester Conferences on Public Policy*, 24, 115–65.

——and Gomez, Y. (2002) 'Electronic Money: A Survey of "Potential Users"', Bank of Finland Economic Trends, Helsinki.

Clower, R. W. (1969) 'Introduction', in R. W. Clower (ed.), *Readings in Monetary Theory*, London: Penguin.

Drèze, J. and Polemarchakis, H. M. (2000) 'Monetary Equilibria', in G. Debren, Neuefeind, W., and Trockel, W. (eds), *Economic Essays: A Festschrift for Werner Hildenbrand*, Heidelberg: Springer, pp. 83–104.

Dubey, P. and Geanakoplos, J. (1992) 'The Value of Money in a Finite-Horizon Economy: A Role for Banks', in Dasgupta, P. and Gale, D. et al. (eds), *Economic Analysis of Markets and Games*, Cambridge, MA: MIT Press.

————(2003) 'Monetary Equilibrium with Missing Markets', *Journal of Mathematical Economics*, 39, 585–618.

——and Shubik, M. (1978) 'The Non Cooperative Equilibria of a Closed Trading Economy with Market Supply and Bidding Strategies', *Journal of Economic Theory*, 17, 1–20.

————(1980) 'A Strategic Market Game with Price and Quantity Strategies', *Zeitschrift für Nationalokonomie*, 40, 25–34.

Friedman, M. (1956) 'The Quantity Theory of Money: A Restatement', in M. Friedman (ed.), *Studies in the Quantity Theory of Money*, University of Chicago Press.

——and Schwartz, A. J. (1962) *A Monetary History of the United States*, Princeton University Press.

Fubrer, J. C. and Moore, G. R. (1995) 'Monetary Policy Trade-Offs and the Correlation Between Nominal Interest Rates and Output', *American Economic Review*, 85, 219–39.

Giraud, G. (2003) 'Strategic Market Games: An Introduction', *Journal of Mathematical Economics*, 39, 355–75.

Glasner, D. (1989) *Free Banking and Monetary Reform*, Cambridge University Press.

Gomez, Y. (2001) 'Electronic Money and the Monetary System', unpublished PhD thesis, City University, London.

Goodhart, C. A. E. (2000) 'Can Central Banking Survive the IT Revolution?' *International Finance*, 3, 189–202.
Grandmont, J.-M. (1983) *Money and Value*, Cambridge University Press.
Hume, D. (1752) 'Of Money'. Reprinted in E. Rotwein (ed.) (1955), *Writings on Economics*, London: Nelson.
Hurwicz, L. (1960) 'Optimality and Informational Efficiency in Resource Allocation Processes', in K. J. Arrow, S. Karlin, and P. Puppes (eds), *Mathematical Methods in the Social Sciences*, Stanford University Press.
——(1973) 'The Design of Mechanisms for Resource Allocation', *American Economic Review*, 63, 1–30.
Keynes, J. M. (1935) *A Treatise on Money*, Vol. 1, London: Macmillan.
King, M. (1999) 'Challenges for Monetary Policy: Old and New', paper prepared for the Symposium on New Challenges for Monetary Policy, 27 August, sponsored by the Federal Reserve Bank of Kansas City at Jackson Hole, Wyoming.
——(2002) 'No Money, no Inflation—The Role of Money in the Economy', *Bank of England Quarterly Bulletin*, Summer, 162–74.
Koenig, E. F. (1990) 'Real Money Balances and the Timing of Consumption: An Empirical Investigation', *Quarterly Journal of Economics*, 105, 399–425.
Latzer, M. and Schmitz, S. W. (2002) *Carl Menger and the Evolution of Payment Systems: From Barter to Electronic Money*, Cheltenham: Edward Elgar.
Lucas, R. E. (1980) 'Equilibrium in a Pure Currency Economy', in J. H. Kareken and N. Wallace (eds), *Models of Monetary Economies*, Minneapolis: Federal Reserve Bank of Minneapolis.
McCallum, B. (1985) 'Bank Regulation, Accounting Systems of Exchange, and the Unit of Account: A Critical Review', *Carnegie-Rochester Conference Series on Public Series*, 23, 13–45.
——(1989) *Monetary Economics: Theory and Policy*, New York: Macmillan.
——(1999) 'Theoretical Analysis Regarding a Zero Nominal Bound for Interest Rates', *Journal of Monetary Economics*, 32, 163–72.
——(2003) 'Monetary Policy in Economics with Little or No Money', National Burean of Economic Research Working Paper, Cambridge, December.
——and Nelson, E. (1999a) 'An Optimising IS-LM Specification for Monetary Policy and Business Cycle Analysis', *Journal of Money, Credit and Banking*, 31, 296–316.
Meltzer, A. H. (1998) 'What is Money?', in G. E. Wood (ed.), *Money, Prices and the Real Economy*, Cheltenham: Edward Elgar, pp. 8–18.
——(1999a) 'The Transmission Process', Working Paper, Carnegle-Mellon University.
——(1999b) 'A Liquidity Trap', Working Paper, Carnegle-Mellon University.
Menger, C. (1892) 'On the Origin of Money', *Economic Journal*, 2, 239–55.
Mills, T. C. and Wood, G. E. (1977) 'Money-Substitutes and Monetary Policy in the UK 1922–1971', *European Economic Review*, 10, 19–36.
——(1982) 'Econometric Evaluation of Alternative UK Money Stock Series, 1870–1913', *Journal of Money, Credit and Banking*, 14, 245–67.
Monnet, C. (2002) 'Optimal Public Money', Typescript, Frankfurt/Main: ECB.
Nelson, E. (2000) 'Direct Effects of Base Money on Aggregate Demand: Theory and Evidence', Bank of England Working Paper no. 122, London.
Niebans, J. (1978) *The Theory of Money*, Baltimore: John Hopkins University Press.

Radford, R. A. (1945) 'The Economic Organisation of POW Camp', *Economica*, 12, 189–201.

Selgin, G. A. and White, L. H. (2002) 'Mengerian Perspectives on the Future of Money', in M. Latzer, S. W Schmitz (eds), *Carl Menger and the Evolution of Payments Systems: From Barter to Electronic Money*, Cheltenham: Edward Elgar, pp. 133–58.

Shapley, L. (1976) 'Noncooperative General Exchange', in S. Lin, (ed.), *Theory of Measurement of Economic Externalities*, New York: Academic Press, pp. 155–75.

——and Shubik, M. (1977), 'Trade Using one Commodity as a Means of Payment', *Journal of Political Economy*, 85, 937–68.

Shubik, M. (1973) 'Commodity Money, Oligopoly, Credit and Bankruptcy in a General Equilibrium Model', *Western Economic Journal*, 10, 24–38.

——(1990) 'A Game Theoretic Approach to the Theory of Money and Financial Institutions', in B. M. Friedman and F. H. Hahn (eds), *Handbook of Monetary Economics*, Amsterdam: North Holland, pp. 171–219.

——(1999) *The Theory of Money and Financial Institutions*, Cambridge, MA: MIT Press.

——and Tsomocos, D. P. (2002) 'A Strategic Market Game with Seigniorage Costs of Fiat Money', *Economic Theory*, 19, 187–201.

——and Wilson, C. (1977) 'The Optimal Bankruptcy Rule in a Trading Economy Using Fiat Money', *Zeitschrift für Nationalokonomie*, 37, 337–54.

Smith, A. (1776) *The Wealth of Nations*, University of Chicago Press, 1981 edn.

Stigler, G. J. (1972) 'The Law and Economics of Public Policy: A Plea to Scholars', *Journal of Legal Studies*, 1, 1–12.

Tsomocos, D. P. (1996) 'Essays on Money, Banking and General Economic Equilibrium', unpublished PhD thesis, Yale University.

Tsomocos, D. P. (2003a) 'Equilibrium Analysis, Banking, Contagion, and Financial Fragility', Bank of England Working Paper No. 175, London.

——(2003b) 'Equilibrium Analysis, Banking and Financial Instability', *Journal of Mathematical Economics*, 39, 619–55.

Wicksell, J. (1935) *Lectures in Political Economy*, Vol. 2, London: Routledge and Kegan Paul.

Wood, G. E. (1995) 'The Quantity Theory in the 1980s', in W. Eltis (ed.), *The Quantity Theory of Money: From Locke and Hume to Friedman*, Cheltenham: Edward Elgar.

Yeager, L. B. (1968) 'Essential Properties of the Medium of Exchange', *Kyldos*, 21. 45–69.

12

Can EMU Survive Unchanged?*

INTRODUCTION

Although EMU, the economic and monetary union of (some parts of) Europe, has now proceeded to a stage where for many observers it is irrevocable, there is nevertheless still discussion of whether it might break up and of how it has to evolve, politically and economically, to ensure it does *not*. It has not, therefore, yet reached the status of that monetary union which comprises the United States of America; discussion of whether that will survive as a monetary union, or of what has to be done to keep it together, is essentially unknown. The US monetary union has become like the Rocky Mountains: its existence is for all practical purposes taken as given. EMU has not reached that state.

In this chapter we seek first to consider why the future of EMU is still seen as so unsettled as to be a subject worthy of frequent and intense analysis and discussion. Having set out why we consider that to be the case we then proceed to consider various aspects of monetary unions that existed in the past, some of which have survlved and some of which have not. What factors contributed to survival? And what factors—if any, in addition to absence of those necessary for survival—contributed to break-up? That leads to a study of a monetary union already mentioned: how did the US develop into a single currency area and how long was it before it functioned well as one? Further, how did it survive in the turmoils of the inter-war years, when so many similar monetary arrangements did not? Next, in the chapter's penultimate section, we turn to the role of fiscal policy in monetary unions. This has been discussed analytically and econometrically; but it has not been discussed in the light of the experience of an earlier monetary union in which explicit attention was paid to the public finances of the constituent parts. We then conclude by drawing out the common lessons from the episodes we have studied, and

* Originally published as Forrest Capie and Geoffrey Wood (2002) 'Can EMU Survive Unchanged?', pp. 93–117, in A.M.EL-Agraa (ed.), *The EU and Britain: Implications of Moving into the EMU* (*Financial Times*–Prentice Hall), reproduced with the permission of Pearson Education Limited.

reflecting on what they suggest for both the future of EMU and for debate over whether Britain should join. In particular with regard to the latter, we consider whether the institutional structure of EMU is stable and whether history supports claims that political unity close to subordination of nationhood is necessary for EMU to survive.

The methods used in this chapter are both analytical and historical. We do not attempt to build an econometric model to assess the likely future of EMU. We eschew that partly because it has been done several times in the fairly recent past. But we avoid it also for two other reasons. The first is that there is surely a strong case for thinking that the formation of EMU is a 'regime change'. Europe has moved from the ERM, in which a collection of national central banks followed the policy of the Bundesbank, a central bank with a clear reputation such that expectations about its future policies at any time, although of course uncertain in detail, were absolutely clear in outline. (See Capie and Wood, 2002, for discussion of the evolution of the Bundesbank.) Monetary policy in Europe is now run by a completely new central bank, with a low inflation mandate but with a completely untested constitution and no incentives to keep to its mandate.[1] Expectations are no longer anchored as they were under the Bundesbank; so, as argued in Lucas (1976), reactions to shocks such as policy changes are likely to be quite different from what they were in the past. Our second reason for pursuing the methods of this chapter is that discussion of EMU, while sometimes drawing on the history of monetary unions, has done so to only a modest extent. There is much more to be learned from that history. After all, history is the only laboratory economists have. We wish to use it.

WHY IS EMU STILL DEBATED?

EMU is still debated, it will be argued here, because the body of analysis used to appraise EMU is based on Robert Mundell's (1961) paper, 'A theory of optimum currency areas'. Max Corden (1972) observed some years ago that that body of literature seems to relate not to the optimality of a currency area, but rather to its feasibility. In this section of the present chapter we review briefly the main contributions to the optimum currency area literature and set out why in our view it is indeed the case, as Corden (1972) conjectured, that it guides not on the optimality of an area, but rather, and that fairly imprecisely, on its feasibility. We conclude this section by explaining why we think this lies behind the continuing debate on EMU.

[1] See Wood (2002) on the ECB's constitution.

The best known early papers in the area are Mundell (1961), McKinnon (1963), and Kenen (1969). We consider them in that order, as well as looking at Mundell's important (but much less frequently discussed) 1973 contribution. The problems these reveal are then compared to the rather similar problems which beset another and quite different area of economic analysis, and some implications of this similarity are drawn out.

The optimum currency area concept (and the term) was invented by Mundell (1961). The crucial trade-off he identified for determining optimality is, to quote McCallum (1996), that 'an extension of the area over which a single currency prevails enhances [microeconomic] efficiency but reduces the possibility of monetary policy responses to shocks [or conditions] that affect various subareas differently' (p. 258). The wider the area, that is to say, the greater are the efficiency benefits of possessing a single medium of exchange and unit of account, but the smaller the area, the greater are the possibilities of tailoring monetary policy to (temporary) local conditions. Somewhere between one currency for the entire world and one for each city lies the optimum.

A textbook by Obstfeld and Rogoff (1996, pp. 632–34) develops this point by listing four main benefits and four main costs which accrue to a pair of countries as a result of having a common currency. These (in the words of Obstfeld and Rogoff) are as follows, with benefits listed first (B for benefits, C for costs):

- **B1** Reduced transaction costs from currency conversion
- **B2** Reduced accounting costs and greater predictability of relative prices for firms doing business in both countries
- **B3** Insulation from monetary disturbances and speculative bubbles that might otherwise lead to unnecessary fluctuations in real exchange rates
- **B4** Less political pressure for trade protection because of sharp shifts in real exchange rates
- **C1** Individual regions in a currency union cannot use monetary policy to respond to region-specific macroeconomic disturbances
- **C2** Regions in a currency union give up the option to use inflation to reduce the real burden of public debt
- **C3** Political problems arise in determining how member countries split seignorage revenues
- **C4** Avoiding speculative attacks in the transition from individual currencies to a common currency can be a major problem

A list of the Obstfeld-Rogoff type can be extended by noting that the existence of a common currency tends to bring a greater degree of integration to financial and non-financial markets in the two countries. (See last part of this section and Mundell, 1973a.)

Merely stating that this optimization problem exists does nothing to solve it in any particular case. The relevant issue for the present section of this chapter is how the optimization problem should be handled in practice. In his original paper, Mundell (1961) emphasized factor mobility, especially labour mobility, as a crucial consideration. Subsequent contributions by McKinnon (1963), Kenen (1969), and others have proposed other criteria. McKinnon emphasized openness, measured by the share of tradeable goods in a country's output and Kenen focused on the extent of product diversification in production. McKinnon was concerned that an area could be 'too small' to sustain its own currency as a result of being so open to trade that any exchange rate change impacted directly and completely on domestic prices. Kenen, meanwhile, saw diversification as important for reducing susceptibility to shocks.

All the criteria are very sensible. None, therefore, can by itself define an 'optimum currency area'. Further, each of the criteria is extremely difficult to implement quantitatively. It seems impossible to avoid the conclusion that the optimal currency area (OCA) concept is in practice non-operational. The concept reflects an important and interesting trade-off, but in practice it seems that one cannot go beyond the conclusion that currency unions 'will be relatively more attractive for small, open economies that engage in a large volume of international trade (relative to their size)' whereas 'floating rates . . . are more suitable for large and relatively self-contained economies' (McCallum, 1996, p. 225).

Bayoumi and Eichengreen (1996; 1997) have, however, been able to go a little further. In their 1997 paper they develop quantitative measures (or proxies for them) for size, trade linkages, and dissimilarity of aggregate shocks for different European countries, each relative to Germany. An index of suitability for membership in the contemplated currency area is constructed (for each country except Germany) by using coefficients obtained in a cross-section regression whose dependent variable is the variability of bilateral exchange rates with Germany. This index indicates that Austria, Belgium, Ireland, the Netherlands, and Switzerland would be relatively suitable for inclusion in the union, whereas Denmark, Finland, Norway, Portugal, Spain, Sweden, and the UK would be relatively unsuitable. These groupings seem unexceptionable.

Bayoumi and Eichengreen have made significant progress towards operationalization of OCA theory. Nevertheless, their approach yields only rankings of suitability, not actual cost-benefit measures that would indicate where the line separating included from excluded countries should be. Accordingly, one could still maintain that true operationality of the OCA concept has not been achieved: To emphasize this point, it should be observed that if there were ever a situation that required application of the OCA calculus, it was the January 1999 creation of the European Monetary Union. But Bayoumi's and Eichengreen's (1996) review of numerous studies indicates that none actually provides estimates indicating which countries should, and which should not, be members of the euro area.

That the concept is operational only in this very limited sense is important for the arguments and approach of this chapter, so it is worth setting out and developing the conclusion a little further. Krugman and Obstfeld (1994, pp. 611–17) provide a diagram which lets the point be made with particular clarity. The construction of the diagram is in three stages (see Figures 12.1–12.3).

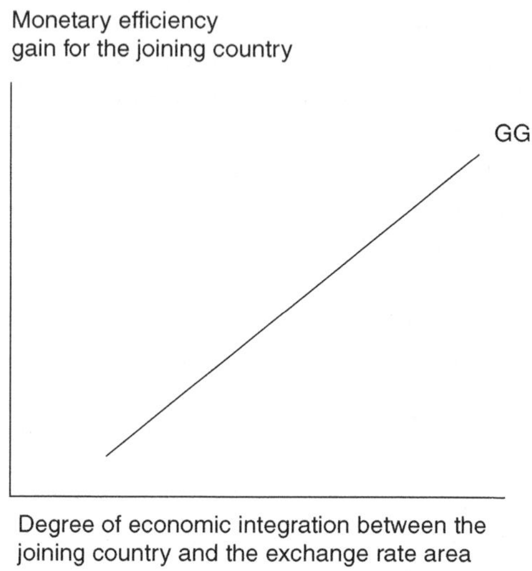

Figure 12.1. Monetary efficiency gain

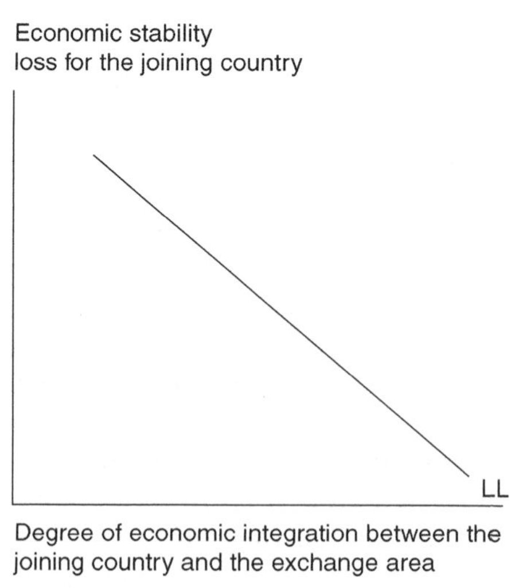

Figure 12.2. Economic stability loss

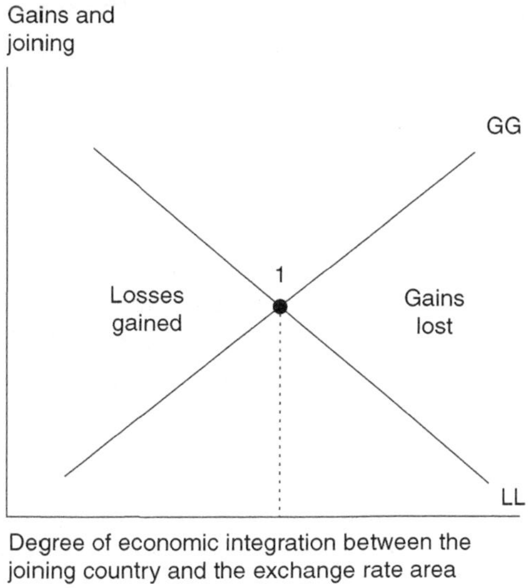

Figure 12.3. Gains and joining

In Figure 12.1, the upward sloping GG schedule shows that a country's monetary efficiency gain from joining a fixed exchange rate area rises as the country's economic integration with the area rises. In Figure 12.2, the downward sloping LL schedule shows that a country's economic stability loss from joining a fixed exchange rate area falls as the country's economic integration with the area rises. And, finally, in Figure 12.3, the intersection of GG and LL at point 1 determines a critical level of economic integration between a fixed exchange rate area and a country considering whether to join. At any greater level of integration, the decision to join yields positive net economic benefits to the joining country.

The analysis shows the relevant issues: but reading the labelling of the axes shows how far the theory is from being operational.

It may therefore be useful to approach the concept of an optimum currency area in a different way.

Rather than starting by listing the conditions which make a currency area optimal and seeing which areas satisfy these conditions, one could start with the following definition: the basic definition of a currency area of optimum size is that it can maintain itself indefinitely in competition with currency areas of other sizes.

That definition may seem familiar. Familiarity would not be surprising. The definition is taken, with one modification, from the 4th (1987) edition of George Stigler's *The Theory of Price*. The change is that 'currency area' has been substituted for 'firm'. Stigler produced that definition on the basis of concluding that 'the theory of the economies of scale has never achieved scientific prosperity' (1958, p. 4). He went on: 'A large cause of its poverty is that the central concept of the theory—the firm of optimum size—has eluded confident measurement' (1958, p. 14). He then argued that we should judge the optimum size by whether firms survive or not. Trying that led him to find a wide range of optimum sizes. We see the same when we look at currency areas which have survived without the protection of exchange controls.[2] What can we do with this concept? We can borrow from Stigler again and look at various factors popularly said to contribute to currency area size, as he did for firm size. (For example he looked at and rejected advertising expenditure.) We could look at labour mobility; at price stability; at commodity composition of output. Given the reluctance of governments to abandon national currencies, we could focus on how competition led them to adopt policies necessary for their currencies' survival.[3]

The theory thus restated has an immediate application in considering EMU. We can consider any proposed currency area and ask if it falls within the range of existing areas. If, as the euro area does, the answer is 'not quite', we can then compare it with a successful currency area of almost the same size (considering both economic and geographical dimensions) and ask if it has the same attributes. The obvious comparison is with the USA. The answer from that comparison would appear to be that some factors are lacking and, if optimality develops over time (as Hugh Rockoff, 2002, suggests that it does) the road to it could be bumpy. These points are developed in the following sections.

Our conclusion so far would therefore be that EMU remains debated because there is no body of analysis which can be used to consider whether or not EMU is an optimal currency area. Rather the literature suggests that there is a wide range of such optimal—or perhaps feasible (to use Corden's term)—areas. EMU is an outlier in that range (if it is in the range at all) and so discussion of it is particularly vigorous. Why, one might ask, is the US not similarly discussed? The answer may be that its having survived for a long time has promoted almost unthinking acceptance of it. (Martin Feldstein, 1997, has observed that if the US were now separate currency areas—two to four, perhaps—no one would suggest forming it into one.) Further, it is one country.

All in all, then, our approach of drawing on a wide varlety of precedents to see what lessons they teach for various aspects of EMU, rather than approaching EMU with a single model, seems unavoidable and fully justified. There is no single model appropriate to the task.

[2] It also prompts questions such as 'What is an area?' Is it an economic concept (measured, say, by GNP) or a political or geographic area? How big a currency area is Australia?

[3] When this approach is taken it becomes much harder to defend the claim that the clear association between the abolition of exchange controls and the downward trend in inflation as seen over the past two decades is just a coincidence.

A NEGLECTED ARGUMENT FOR UNIONS

Mundell elaborated a further argument for the fixing of exchange rates between countries. To quote from Mundell (1973a): 'A fixed exchange rate system is a device for automatic cushioning of shocks without destroying the image of the international moneyness of the national money in the public mind' (p. 115).

He summarizes the argument behind this by a very simple example:

> If we consider two different countries, one with internationally acceptable gold as money, and the other with inconvertible paper money, the state with the gold is better off since, other things equal, the gold can be spent abroad—used as an emergency reserve—if the rest of the world is on a gold standard and the state in question does not make up too large a share of the world (as measured by reserves). Inconvertible paper money is not a reserve for the state as a whole, except insofar as it can be marketed abroad. (1973a, p. 114)

Fixed exchange rates thus, Mundell argues, facilitate international borrowing and lending and help smooth out asymmetric shocks.

Now, that is indeed an argument for countries having fixed exchange rates, or even a common currency, between them. It does not, of course, guide us in deciding the 'optimal' domain of a currency, except insofar as it suggests a presumption in favour of large rather than small, domains (other things equal).

His view on how smoothly the system would work are summed up in the following quotation:

> The adjustment mechanism if it is run correctly, works just like the interregional mechanism of adjustment between the twelve districts of the United States, which runs so smoothly that most people are not even aware that there are twelve Federal Reserve district currencies. (1973b, p. 146)[4]

But in a penetrating and wide-ranging paper, Balassa (1973) set out how important 'others things equal' qualifications are in this case. In considering the regional adjustment mechanism within the US, he observed as follows:

> For one thing, the literature on interregional payment mechanisms leads to the conclusions that reserve flows are not solely responsible for the equilibrium of regional balances of payments and that short-term as well as long-term capital movements, income changes, government transfers as well as labour migration all contribute to it. (p. 174)[5]

[4] The paper from which this quotation comes, which appears in the same volume as 1973a, is surely the reason Mundell is sometimes called the 'Father of European Monetary Union'. His earlier and better known (1961) paper would surely, if placing him in any group, place him in one opposed to European Monetary Union.

[5] A pioneering and unjustly neglected paper by Hartland (1949) makes some of these points. See further discussion of this paper in the next section.

So we are still left with 'optimality' not being a clear-cut phenomenon and Corden's 'feasibility' being perhaps the more accurate term for the issue examined in the literature on the appropriate domain of a currency.

PREVIOUS MONETARY UNIONS

There is no strict historical precedent for the European Monetary Union, but there are some similarities with previous experience which can be instructive. Two important points need to be made at the outset, however, and should be held in view throughout. The first is that previous unions of any size or significance are found in the nineteenth century at a time when metallic monetary standards were almost universally used. This makes for considerable differences from any union that might take place now in a world of fiat money. The second point is that the nineteenth century was the century of the nation state, when there was widespread desire among small states for political union.

This section considers the principal attempts at political and monetary unions. In the first category are Switzerland, Germany, and Italy. In the second are the Latin Monetary Union and the Scandinavian Currency Union.

Political union through common money

Switzerland

Although a territory recognized as Switzerland has been around for many hundreds of years, serious political union did not take place until 1848. There were twenty-two cantons in the union and many different currencies. There was discussion about how to rationalize such a system and the preference was for the French franc-based system which came into being in 1850. The Swiss silver franc happened to coincide with the French franc and by the early 1850s 80 per cent of Swiss coins originated in France. An act of 1860 allowed for the reduction of the metal content in coins and that led to some problems with Switzerland's monetary partners in the Latin Monetary Union (to which we will return). In the 1880s and 1890s the Swiss franc depreciated against the French franc and Swiss banks began losing silver.

Paper money was in use in Switzerland. But bank notes were not legal tender and their regulation was left to individual cantons. In 1876 a Konkordat was made agreeing to a rationalization of the bank notes and in 1907 the Swiss National Bank was founded following discussion and legislation of 1904. The Bank was given a monopoly on the issue of bank notes.

The main point to make about the Swiss experience is that the organization of the currency was simply a rationalization of a system that had come after political union had been achieved.

Germany

Germany is more interesting in the present context and at least at some levels would appear to have some striking parallels with the EMU—principally that substantial moves toward *economic* union clearly preceded political union; although it should be stressed that political union was the objective. There were hundreds of German states in the early nineteenth century. Some attempts were made at removing obstacles to trade: first of all in the formation of the Zollverein in 1834. The real starting point for the process of German unification, however, can be found at the Congress of Vienna in 1814. After that, thirty-five principalities and four free cities had full sovereignty and, particularly, the authority to regulate their own money systems. They had independent fiscal systems too, but in most cases the power of princes to tax had been heavily circumscribed and customs duties remained an important source of revenue. In most of the territories a silver standard was in use. There was some government paper but it was not a significant proportion of the total stock of money. Fiscal needs were invariably the source of such paper.

In 1837 the Munich Coinage Treaty was signed. It was a step taken toward monetary union. Some states renounced their rights of monetary sovereignty. In 1838, following the Dresden Coinage Convention, each state was obliged to adopt either the Thaler or the Gulden. Additionally, to promote the idea of a unified system a common coin was minted (the Vereinsmünze, meaning 'union coin'). It was equal in value to 2 Thaler and 3.5 Gulden. What was tending to happen, however, was that the Prussian Thaler was beginning to penetrate all over Germany.

An important aspect of the Dresden Convention was that it established permanently fixed exchange rates between the two currency areas of the Zollverein. However, some states within the Zollverein had opt-out clauses and did not participate in these arrangements (e.g. Luxembourg) and other important German states were outside the Zollverein.

The political turmoil of 1848 brought some changes in Europe but the political movement for German unification failed. The Vienna Coinage Treaty of 1857 must be regarded as the next important further step towards German monetary union. It standardized the silver coinage system, laid down strict rules on the circulation and minting of gold coins and prohibited the conversion of gold to silver at a fixed exchange rate, so preventing a bimetallic system from emerging. It also touched on the issue of paper money. This was aimed at Austria, whose paper money was inconvertible. The treaty insisted on convertibility. Thus coinage was on a common standard after 1857.

In 1871 the German Reich was founded. At that point there were still different coinage systems in place and paper money was highly diverse. But coinage acts of 1871 and 1873 unified the coinage across the Reich. The set of rules meant that in fact something dose to a common currency existed; paper money remained a small proportion of the total.

There is some disagreement in the case of Germany over whether monetary union led or followed political union. There can be no doubt that political union was a desired objective, as it was for some other states. And it does seem that steps taken in that direction were frequently of an economic kind so that it could be argued that the path to monetary union was well advanced by 1871.

As to how this union performed over the next thirty years, it has recently been argued that because the central authority had limited taxing powers and limited income from the individual states, strains emerged and problems developed which led directly to World War I and on to the hyperinflation that followed. Ill-designed fiscal federalism (which happens to look surprisingly like that of the EU) proved fatal (Hefeker, 2001).

Italy

The story of Italy can be treated at less length. The drive for political union was a romantic vision of the nation state that drove the separate kingdoms and territories along in the course of the nineteenth century, so that by 1861 unification under the King of Sardinia was achieved. When that union was completed it became necessary to remove many of the obstacles to trade, some of which came in the form of the many different currencies that were in existence. Steps therefore followed to convert the country to a monetary union as well. In 1862 a unified system based on the Sardinian lira was introduced. Sardinia was French oriented which accounts in part for the adoption of a system closely related to the French. A bimetallic standard was adopted in common with Italy's main trading partners and also to allow for the fact that silver coin predominated in the south of Italy. The main reason for not saying more here is that we turn next (and briefly again) to the Latin Monetary Union of which, of course, Italy was a founder member.

Common money pure and simple

Latin Monetary Union

In 1865 France, Switzerland, Italy, and Belgium made an agreement to co-ordinate their monetary systems. It was this that became known as the Latin Monetary Union. Some have seen it as an attempt at establishing bimetallism but Redish has argued convincingly that it was not (Redish, 1994). These countries all had strong monetary links and were on a de facto gold standard. It is not without significance that the union was formed soon after the rapid fall in the gold price that was consequent upon the Californian and Australian gold discoveries. This drove silver out of circulation. The four countries of the Latin Monetary Union had close connections but had different token coins and the union established a common token currency. The agreement between them also stated the type of token and the quantity that would be issued and the conditions of convertibility.

When the price of gold started to rise in the 1870s it might have been imagined that the *de jure* bimetallic standard would have restored a de facto silver standard. In fact union members abandoned bimetallism. Again the important fact was the nineteenth-century climate of economic integration.

Some background may be helpful. In 1798 the French had invaded the Netherlands and imposed the new French monetary system. When the Belgian provinces revolted and went their own way they kept the French monetary system. In 1798 the French had also invaded Switzerland and instituted a system there, based on the franc. By 1852 the silver coins of France, Belgium, and some Italian states were made legal tender. (Napoleon had already introduced the French system to Italy in 1793.) We noted earlier that when Italy was unified in 1861 it led to the adoption of the French system with which large parts of the country were already familiar. It was thus the case that the coins of Belgium, Switzerland, and France all had legal-tender status. So by 1852 these countries all used the same unit of account and gave legal-tender status to each other's coins. It must be regarded as no great leap forward to form what they called a union—a currency union was in effect already in place.

Interestingly, Duisinberg recently drew the following lesson from this experience: 'Monetary unification of countries with different monetary systems is not easily attained; a treaty aimed at unification is ultimately doomed to failure if it is more or less imposed on the other signatories to the treaty' (quoted in van Thoor, 1996).

Scandinavia

Much the same might be said for the Scandinavian countries Norway, Denmark, and Sweden as for the Latin countries. These countries had a long history of close connection and had similar units of account—principally the riksdaler—and exchange of coins. They were on a silver standard. After long discussion and with a view to joining the increasingly prosperous club, these countries joined the gold standard—Norway and Denmark in 1874, and Sweden in 1874. In 1873 they formed a currency union and at that point the krona replaced the riksdaler. Gold and other coins circulated freely.

In the 1870s these countries had considered various proposals—of joining the LMU; of joining the German Union; of joining the sterling area. They opted for the less adventurous course of forming their own union. It must be said it was not so much imposed as the natural evolution of these similar countries' gradually using each other's coins. The main step taken to enlarge the union was in 1885 when the 'central banks' established inter-country drawing rights. This clearing arrangement cleared notes at par.

By 1901 bank notes circulated freely and the most complete form of the union came about. However, no sooner had that happened than political problems between Norway and Sweden in 1905 brought strains and the system was doomed in 1914 with the beginning of the end of the gold standard.

The principal points that can be made about these unions which are of interest from our point of view are as follows. First, some were principally driven by a desire for political union. Those that resulted in political union were successful and those that did not failed. Second, they were essentially currency unions among countries using the same metallic standard. As such it can hardly be regarded as a great advance to make the formal announcement that all their notes and coins were acceptable to one another. Third, they did not have fully developed central banks; but insofar as they did, they did not have an explicitly unified monetary policy.

The fact that it was the unions that were political unions that succeeded leads to the question, is it necessary for a monetary union to be supported by a fiscal union? Study of the US bears on this issue.

The United States

A major part of the economic analysis of monetary unions is concerned with whether or not the territories covered make, in the jargon, an optimum currency area. As noted earlier this is not an easy concept to make operational. It is straightforward to list the basic requirements such as price flexibility, labour mobility, capital mobility, and so on, but much more difficult to say at what stage the combined factors have defined an optimum currency area. The originator of the concept, Robert Mundell, has in fact come out in support of the idea that the different European states would certainly become an optimum currency area even if they are not one at present. There can perhaps be no denying that; but the questions would then be, how long would that take and might there be unacceptable costs to some parts of the territory along the way. This is a question that has been addressed in relation to the US (Rockoff, 2002). The US was a political union from an early date and that may no doubt have smoothed the monetary experience. Nevertheless, the question can still be put—might some parts of the US have been better off with their own currencies floating against the US dollar?

Rockoff traces US experience from the origins of the monetary union, which date from the ratification of the Constitution in 1788. Prior to that, currency differed among the different colonies. The central question that he puts is, might the US have been better off if some of the regions had had their own currency? He shows that there were bitter disputes during the 150 years after ratification. Typically what happened was that one region would experience a shock—commonly a fall in demand for an agricultural product—and the local banking system would suffer, perhaps even collapse, leading in turn to falling money supply and a further fall in real income.

In the Civil War there were effectively three monetary regions: the East and the Mid West used greenbacks; the South had a Confederate dollar; and the Pacific coast stayed on gold. After the war there was a long struggle towards acceptance of monetary reunification. Rockoff shows too that in terms of optimum currency area criteria some regions differed highly from others and that in many ways they were separable currency areas.

The most extreme experience was the Great Depression of 1929–32. While the whole country suffered there were big differences. It was at that point, argues Rockoff, that important institutional changes were made, such as the development of federally funded transfer programmes which 'redistributed reserves lost through interregional payments deficits' (p. 35). These and the increasing integration of the labour market helped to bring the US closer to an optimum currency area. But the answer he gives to the question 'How long did it take the United States to become an optimum currency area?' is roughly 150 years.

The experience of the US in the 1930s is of considerable interest. An early contribution to this literature, albeit made for a different purpose, came from Hartland (1949). There was, of course, a fiscal union in place in the USA in the 1930s. But there was a danger of monetary break-up as a consequence of the loss of gold reserves by individual states following on from the collapse of a state's banking system. In fact no state's system collapsed entirely since there were transfers from federal resources to alleviate poverty. Hartland concludes that these transfers were essential to the system's survivial.

She does not ask if fiscal transfers can offset asymmetric shocks, but her study does bear directly on the problem. By the inter-war years the US had a common currency, a central fiscal authority, a central bank and, crucial for the study, no nationwide banking system other than the Federal Reserve itself. All other banks could do business across one state (at most); and some states, such as illinois, prohibited even intrastate branch banking. Hartland used this combination of facts to consider how the US, effectively on a gold standard, held together as a monetary system when the international gold standard broke apart. It may be said that there was complete confidence that it would. But there was nevertheless a good analogy to monetary break-up as a consequence of the loss of gold reserves. This was collapse of a state's banking system consequent upon a loss of gold reserves. Although many problems were experienced, no state's system collapsed entirely. Why not? Hartland examined the flows of reserves through the Fed's accounts (the only means of monetary movement apart from shipments of cash). When a state was experiencing a net loss of reserves on private sector accounts, this was offset by inflows from the central government's account, arising not as a financial stabilization measure but as a result of transfers from federal resources made to alleviate poverty and depression.

The conclusion was that these transfers were essential to the system's survival. It must be admitted that the counterfactual was not explicitly posed—what would have happened had there not been such transfers? Would confidence in the continued integrity of the US as a currency area have been such that private sector funds would have responded? In response to that question, it has to be said that given the degree of economic difficulties of the time it seems unlikely. The risk would have been too great.

This all points strongly to the conclusion that while monetary union may not lead automatically to political and fiscal union, without such union a monetary union may well not last. This conclusion would appear to be particularly robust in that it does not depend on asymmetric shocks to cause problems before it becomes relevant, for in the 1930s the problem was quite plainly an asymmetric response to a common shock.

It seems, then, that as a matter of fact there has been a close connection between monetary union and fiscal union. Sometimes that has been a consequence of the assertion of political power. Whether they need to go together when the desire to assert political will is absent is another question. But the historical evidence looks highly suggestive. In some cases there seem to have been agreements over the sharing of seigniorage—paralleled in EMU. And the US experience suggests that a monetary union might only be viable if it is associated with a fiscal union.

FISCAL CONSTRAINTS IN EMU

As well as agreeing to adopt a common money, the countries which participated in EMU agreed limits in public sector debt to income and public sector borrowing to income ratios (60 per cent and 3 per cent respectively). These have been criticized. Some query whether there will be enough 'room' to stimulate the economy should there be a recession. Some criticize them as non-optimal. But surely a basic question is why there need be any fiscal constraints on individual members in a monetary union. We start by considering two possible theoretical justifications.

The first was formalized in Sargent and Wallace's 'Unpleasant Monetarist Arithmetic' (1984). Their point is simple. Governments, like everyone else, face a budget constraint. Spending must equal revenue. They have three sources of revenue: taxes, borrowing, and money creation.

Thus,

$$\mathrm{GS} = \mathrm{T} + \Delta B + \Delta \mathrm{MB}$$

Spending is identically equal to taxes plus net bond sales plus net creation of base money. If bonds cannot be sold—because there may be doubts about redemption, or even just because the stock is so high that the terms are unacceptable—and no further tax can be raised, then only one source of revenue remains, money creation. This can lead to inflation.

In the instances of very high inflation studied by Capie (1986) this was exactly the problem. Governments desperate for revenue fell back on money creation, and inflation—in some cases, hyperinflation—resulted. As one of the countries to experience this was Germany, it is easy to understand why Germany should wish fiscal constraints to prevent money creation resulting from excess borrowing. But that is to neglect an important point. The ECB is supposedly independent: it has an inflation target and no EU government, or any EU agency, supposedly can give it instructions. Accordingly, then, the ECB's constitution should render 'unpleasant monetarist arithmetic' irrelevant.

There is, however, a body of theory, quite recent in origin, which suggests that fiscal policy can be sufficient—that is, without consequent monetary expansion—to cause inflation. The main papers in this literature are Sims (1994), Woodford (1994), Cochrane (1998), and Begrin (2000). The feature which differentiates these models from all those which suggest that inflation is a monetary phenomenon is that the price level follows a path very similar to that of the stock of government bonds and not at all like, or even connected to, the path of the monetary base. Further, and a particularly striking feature of the literature, the models used are generally of a type in which Ricardian equivalence usually holds. Usually when that holds, bond-financed tax changes have effects on no important macroeconomic variable. The results of the 'fiscalist' models are thus, to use McCallum's (2002) words, 'truly startling'.

It is hard to confront the fiscalist position empirically, for usually bonds and money both increase in a period of inflation and it then can be disputed how to disentangle the effects empirically.[6] But, using history as this chapter does, it is surely appropriate to remark on episodes from quite far back in time which seem relevant. British economic history contains two notable and useful

6 The position is certainly not free of problems at the theoretical level (see Buiter, 1998, and McCallum, 1998).

examples of such episodes. Under Henry VIII, there was a major currency debasement, but no increase in the stock of government debt. Yet prices rose, broadly in line with the nominal quantity of money. Then, somewhat later, between 1688 and 1790, the debt-to-income ratio rose from zero to something over 100 per cent. There was insignificant movement in the price level.

Accordingly, the 'fiscalist' theory of inflation cannot provide a robust justification for the fiscal constraint in EMU. And even if it could in principle, we would be cautious in claiming that such a novel and complex theory as the explanation.

What can history suggest? There is an interesting, and actually quite close, precedent—the monetary union between Austria and Hungary, a well-known nineteenth-century union, discussion of which we have deferred until this point as it is particularly illuminating on the role of fiscal constraints.

The Hapsburg economic union lasted from 1867 to 1914, without significant disruption. It had much in common with today's EMU: the two independent countries had a common central bank (inherited from Austria) yet retained national sovereignty over fiscal matters. There was, however, no 'stability pact'. The only restraint on government borrowing—and both governments wished to borrow substantially—came from the markets. How did matters work out?

The Austro-Hungarian currency, an inconvertible paper one, was established in 1867. In September of that year, an agreement was reached between Hungary and Austria whereby the Hungarians promised not to allow any bank of issue in their part of the Empire. There was thus one money, one exchange rate and one bank of issue, and monetary matters were all run (from Vienna) by that bank of issue. Following a stock market crash and economic stagnation in 1873, there was agitation by Hungary for greater control over monetary matters. This was gained in 1878, when the bank became the Austro-Hungarian Bank. Then in the 1890s the currency, which had previously floated, was put on gold. This ended the (rather limited) ability the two separate governments had previously possessed to coin silver and thereby hardened up the governments' budget constraints. The main restraint on government borrowing was now the capital market. Hungary was a new borrower, with no reputation. (All previous borrowing had been by the Austro-Hungarian empire (managed from Vienna) or by Austria.)

It was recognized by both countries that the terms on which one borrowed influenced those available to the other. This led to the common central bank's acquiring considerable power. For the capital markets required higher rates on currencies without gold clauses than on those with such clauses. Managing a gold debt was harder when the currency floated than when it was on gold. Hence market discipline led via gold clauses to a gold standard and to a central bank which could impose a hard fiscal constraint on governments.

The question this poses in the present context is why the founders of the euro have explicit constraints on fiscal profligacy, rather than relying on the market discipline which worked in a previous situation with close structural parallels to EMU. Market discipline led to an accretion of power to the central bank. Was that feared by the founders of the euro? Or was it feared that market discipline would not trouble some traditionally high-inflation members, and that they, unconcerned by reputation, would drag the reputation of others down with them? Either way, it would appear that behind the fiscal constraints may well be a lack of trust: lack of trust in the constitution of the euro area, with fear of accretion of power to the ECB; lack of trust of member states; or both. Among these three the evidence is insufficient to suggest a choice.

LESSONS THAT EMERGE

It is clear from the point of view of economic analysis just why there is still debate over EMU and its future. Economic analysis cannot say whether EMU is an 'optimal' or even a sensible currency area. That is why the prospects for EMU are still discussed among economists. But that said, both certain aspects of theory and an overview of the performance of past monetary unions suggest that if EMU is to survive, further institutional development of it is necessary.

Fiscal constraints are hard to rationalize unless one sees them as a way of constraining irresponsible EMU member states so as to prevent power accuring, via a 'hard' fiscal constraint, to the ECB. It is difficult to believe in the durability of a monetary union whose members trust each other so little and fear their central bank so much. Evolution to promote greater political trust is manifestly desirable from that point of view. Such evolution could, too, lead to the creation of a European political body of sufficient importance that the ECB could sensibly be made accountable to it.

Second, examination of the history of monetary unions shows that only those which become political ones survive. Focusing on the history of the US as a monetary union reinforces that conclusion, showing that even as recently as the 1930s, over a century and half after the US became a monetary union, it required the political cohesion of a long-established community to hold it together as a monetary union in the face of a large common shock.

It is thus clear that further political developments are necessary in the EMU zone; and it is equally clear that those who claim that there are profound political and constitutional implications for Britain should that country choose to join are abundantly supported by history in making that claim.

ANNEXE

A Brief History of the Austro-Hungarian Union

There is a fascinating study of this union by Marc Flandreau (2001). Flandreau is perhaps best known for his work on bimetallism and the working of the French monetary system in the middle of the nineteenth century; and that of course included the relationship with the Latin Monetary Union. He raises here the question as to how useful the study of historical experience can be for guidance on the sustainability of modern monetary unions. He points out, correctly in our view as we noted earlier, that most of the arrangements that went under the name of 'monetary unions' can be found in the nineteenth century when most countries adhered to some form of metallic monetary standard. So as we have seen, unions such as the Latin Monetary Union or the Scandinavian Monetary Union turn out on closer examination not to be monetary unions of the kind we currently have in mind but rather simply currency unions. The countries involved simply agreed to accept each other's currency. Given that these were coins with specified metal content there was little to get excited about and much of the activity was already taking place without any formal agreement. These unions had no common monetary policy and no common central bank. Where the driving force was political union things were different—different currencies had to be rationalized in order to facilitate political union or as a sensible practice after political union was achieved, or some combination of both of these. Insofar as the European monetary union is supposed to be about separate states and not political union these latter examples should be of little interest to us. And yet, as has been stressed by many contributors to this debate, European monetary union is a political agenda and has been carried along with 'devilish cleverness by a politically astute clique intent on achieving their own ends' (Goodhart, 2001).

Be that as it may, Flandreau tried instead to find an experience which might fit our purposes more closely—a monetary union between two independent states; this is found in the alliance between Austria and Hungary. This was an arrangement whereby both countries surrendered monetary sovereignty to a common central bank but retained fiscal sovereignty. The Hapsburg monarchy operated without the kind of agreement that exists in Europe today to keep public expenditure within certain limits. There were great pressures to raise public spending in the nineteenth century to promote economic development, and it was left to the capital market to discipline the fiscal authorities. The 'compromise of 1867' was the agreement struck between the two countries for a period of ten years and reviewed regularly until 1917. Flandreau traces the monetary and fiscal experience of this union. He shows how the two states were continuously concerned about their reputation in the market. There was some competition over reputation and as they standardized their debt instruments the market could better read the price signals.

REFERENCES

Balassa, B. (1973) 'Comment', in H. G. Johnson and A. K. Swoboda (eds), *The Economics of Common Currencies*, Cambridge, MA: Harvard University Press, 173–79.

Bayoumi, T. and Eichengreen, B. (1996) 'Operationalising the Theory of Optimum Currency Areas', CEPR Discussion Paper 1484.

——(1997) 'Exchange Market Pressure and Exchange Rate Management: Perspectives from the Theory of Optimum Currency Areas', in M. I. Blejer et al., (eds.), *Optimum Currency Areas: New Analytical and Policy Developments*, Washington, DC: IMF.

Bergin, P. R. (2000) 'Fiscal Solvency and Price Level Determination in a Monetary Union', *Journal of Monetary Economics*, 45, 1, 37–53.

Buiter, W. H. (1998) 'The Young Person's Guide to Neutrality, Price Level Indeterminacy, Interest Rate Begs, and Fiscal Theories of the Price Level', NBER Working Paper 6396.

Capie F. H. (1986) 'Conditions in which Very Rapid Inflation has Appeared', *Carnegie-Rochester Conference Series on Public Policy*, 24(d), 115–68.

——and Wood, G. (2001) 'The Birth, life and Death of a Currency', *Economic Journal*, 472, 449–61.

————(eds) (2002) *Monetary Unions: Theory, History, Public Choice*, London: Palgrave.

Cochrane, J. H. (1998) 'A Frictionless View of U.S. Inflation', NBER Working Paper 6646.

Corden, W. Max (1972) 'Monetary Integration,' *Essays in International Finance*, 93. Princeton, NJ: Princeton University.

Feldstein, M. (1997) 'EMU and International Conflict', *Foreign Affairs*, 76(6), 60–73.

Flandreau, M. (2001) 'The Economics of Cacania, 1867–1914: Austro-Hungarian Monetary Lessons for Euroland', in Capie and Wood (eds) (2001b).

Goodhart, C. A. E. G. (2002) The Future of EMU: Comments on Borodo and Jonung', in Capie and Wood (eds) (2001b).

Hartland, P. (1949) 'Interregional Payments Compared with International Payments', *Quarterly Journal of Economics*, 63, 392–404.

Hefeker, C. (2001) The Agony of Central Power: Fiscal Federalism in the German Reich', *European Review of Economic History*, 5(1), 119–42.

Kenen, Peter B. (1969) 'The Theory of Optimum Currency Areas: An Eclectic View', in R. A. Mundell and A. K. Swoboda (eds), Monetary Problems of the International Economy, Proceedings of the Conference on International Monetary Problems, September 1966, University of Chicago Press, pp. 41-60.

Krugman, P. and Obstfeld, M. (1994) *International Economics*, New York: HarperCollins.

Lucas, R. E. (1976) 'Econometric Policy Evaluation—A Critique', *The Phillips Curve and Labor Markets Carnegie-Rochester Conference Series on Public Policy*, 1, 19–46.

McCallum, B. T. (1996) *International Monetary Economics*, New York: Oxford University Press.

——(1998) 'Indeterminacy, Bubbles, and the Fiscal Theory of Price Level Determination', NBER Working Paper 6456.

McCallum, B. T. (2002) 'Theoretical Issues Pertaining to Monetary Unions' in Capie and Wood (eds) (2001b).

McKinnon, R. I. (1963) 'Optimum Currency Areas', *American Economic Review*, 53, 717–25.

Mundell, R. (1961) 'A Theory of Optimum Currency Areas', *American Economic Review*, 51, 657–64.

—— (1973a) 'A Plan for a European Currency', in H. G. Johnson and A. K. Swoboda (eds), *The Economics of Common Currencies*, London: Allen & Unwin.

—— (1973b) 'Uncommon Arguments for Common Currencies', in H. G. Johnson and A. K. Swoboda (eds), *The Economics of Common Currencies*, London: Allen & Unwin.

Obstfeld, M. (1996) 'Models of Currency Crises with Self-Fulfilling Features', *European Economic Review*, 40, 1037–48.

——and Rogoff, K. (1996) *Foundations of International Macroeconomics*, Cambridge, MA: MIT Press.

Redish, A. (1994) 'The Latin American Union', in M. Bordo and F. H. Capie (eds.), *Monetary Regimes in Transition*, Cambridge University Press.

Rockoff, H. (2002) 'How Long Did it Take the USA to Become an Optimum Area?' in F. H. Capie and G. E. Wood (eds) (2002b).

Sargent, T. and Wallace, N. (1984) 'Some Unpleasant Monetarist Arithmetic', in B. Griffiths and G. E. Wood (eds), *Monetarism in the United Kingdom*, London: Macmillan.

Sims, C. A. (1994) 'A Simple Model for the Study of the Determination of the Price Level and the Interaction of Monetary and Fiscal Policy', *Economic Theory*, 4(3), 381–99.

—— (1997) 'Fiscal Foundations of Price Stability in Open Economics', Working Paper presented to Hong Kong Meeting of the Far Eastern Region of the Econometric Society, 24 July.

Stigler, G. J. (1958) 'The Economies of Scale', *Journal of Law and Economics*, 54–71.

—— (1987) *The Theory of Price*, New York: Macmillan; London: Collier Macmillan.

Van Thoor, Wim. F. V. (1996) *European Monetary Union Since 1848*, Chettenham: Edward Elgar.

Wood, G. (2002) 'Is the European Central Bank too Independent?' in P. Schacht (ed.), *Studies in Money, Banking and Finance: Essays in Honour of Stephen Frowen*, London: Palgrave.

Woodford, M. (1994) 'Monetary Policy and Price-Level Determinacy in a Cash-in-Advance Economy', *Economic Theory*, 4(3), 345–80.

——(1995) 'Price-Level Determinacy without Control of a Monetary Aggregate', *Carnegie-Rochester Conference Series on Public Policy*, 43, 1–46.

——(1998) 'Public Debt and the Price Level', Working Paper prepared for Bank of England Conference: Government Debt Structure and Monetary Conditions, 18–19 June.

13

Central Banks and Inflation: An Historical Perspective*

After several decades (and in some countries much longer) when the relationship between central banks and governments was taken for granted and seldom discussed, it has now become a subject of debate. In particular, whether the conduct of monetary policy would be improved if the central bank were 'independent' is a question attracting considerable attention. Several factors have led to this. At the academic level, the analytical impetus was provided by two papers (1983a and b) by Robert Barro and David Gordon. These papers show that a politically determined monetary policy will produce high inflation; hence the recommendation to remove political influence, by giving the central bank independence.

In this chapter we aim to test the conclusions of this model against some historical evidence. The evidence is drawn from two distinct *types* of experience. First, we consider extreme inflations. Would the central bank's freedom from political influence have prevented these episodes? Second, we look at the connection between central bank/government relationship and the inflation rate in more normal times, to see if any systematic pattern emerges.

The structure of the chapter is as follows. First we set out the Barro and Gordon model, to show how it relates to the debate on central bank independence. We briefly consider a criticism of the model, and a way of amending it to take account of that criticism. Then we discuss what is meant by 'independence'.

The next section examines some dramatic episodes of very rapid inflations to see what, if any, common cause led to these extraordinary monetary expansions, and whether an 'independent' central bank could have prevented

* Originally published as Forrest Capie and Geoffrey E. Wood (1991), 'Central Banks and Inflation: An Historical Perspective—Part I', pp. 27–46, Central Banking, Vol. 2 (Autumn 1991), No. 2, and Forrest Capie and Geoffrey Wood (1991), 'Central Banks and Inflation: An Historical Perspective–Part II', pp. 38–57, Central Banking, Vol. 2 (Winter, 1990) No. 3 reproduced with the permission of Central Banking Publications Inclusive Media. Additional research by Ashraf A. Mahate.

them. We then move on to less dramatic events. The next section contrasts the inflation performance of several economies among which the relationship between central bank and government displays (by measures which we develop in this section) different degrees of independence. The chapter concludes with a summary of the main points that can be drawn from the preceding discussion.[1]

Governments have more than one incentive to inflate. By inflating they gain tax revenue if the tax system is non-indexed (as almost all are). Even were the tax system perfectly indexed, they get revenue from money creation; this incentive is discussed further below.[2] Here we focus on a third type of incentive, that most frequently discussed: the desire to win elections. The formal model which draws out the monetary policy implications of this objective was developed in Barro and Gordon (1983a). Monetary policy ultimately affects only the general price level. That proposition is generally accepted. Also widely, though not universally, accepted is the assumption that unexpected monetary fluctuations have temporary effects on output—in the jargon, there is an expectational Phillips Curve.[3] To these propositions Barro and Gordon add two more. Increases in output are attractive to voters, and hence to politicians. And finally, inflation itself is undesired—it is valued only because of the output effects of unexpected inflation. What will be the equilibrium output/inflation combination in such a setting?

THE ANALYTICS OF INDEPENDENCE

a. Formal Models

Barro and Gordon assume that the expectations of voters are rational—so that actual inflation is not *systematically* different from expected inflation. Another way of putting this is that errors in inflation expectations are random, or alternatively, that expectations are on average correct. This is a conventional

[1] A large number of scholars have argued that price stability can best be attained by abolishing central banks, and having competing privately issued currencies. An excellent recent review of this literature can be found in Glasner (1989). The conclusions to date of this discussion are manifestly related to the present chapter; but we set them aside simply on the grounds that to do otherwise would divert attention from the point we wish to address. Our doing so does not imply that we reject the arguments of the authors.

[2] Phelps (1973) points out that a positive inflation rate is on welfare-cost-minimizing grounds part of an optimal tax structure. We do not consider how a central bank might be designed to produce this optimal inflation rate for two reasons. First, the Phelps recommendation is not operational. Second, even if it were it is highly likely to imply an inflation rate so low that it would approximate to a working definition of price stability. See Garfinkel (1989).

[3] It does not matter for our purpose whether this is produced by Lucas (1972) type confusion; Taylor (1975) type contracts; or by any other means.

assumption in modern monetary economics. We emphasize it because it is crucial to the Barro and Gordon result. In this framework, politicians have a double incentive. They are motivated to promise zero inflation—for inflation is disliked. But they are also motivated to deliver inflation at a rate higher than that—an inflation surprise. Why? If voters believe the promise, they set all prices, including in particular wages, in the expectation of zero inflation. Once that has happened, there is an incentive to deliver non-zero inflation—an inflation surprise—so as to boost output.

However, as expectations are rational the government cannot systematically deliver surprises. But it has an incentive to try to do so. What stops it? In the presence of discretion, only an appropriate incentive—the loss of votes from higher inflation must be as great as the gain in votes from higher output. Barro and Gordon conclude that if a policymaker can bind himself not to inflate, then a lower inflation and no worse employment equilibrium, hence a preferred equilibrium, will emerge. In this light, having a bank independent of government is viewed as a way of binding government's hands.[4]

In a subsequent paper Barro and Gordon (1983b) went on to consider the possibility of a low inflation being reached through reputation. In this model people's expectations of inflation depend on the past performance of the authorities. The monetary authorities' choice of inflation rate assigns weight to the effect of the current inflation rate on future inflationary expectations. This holds down rates of money growth—how far below the pure discretion result of the earlier model depends on the authorities' discount rate. The model approximates to a monetary rule—the lower the discount rate and hence the greater concern about future votes, the closer the approximation.

This latter model shows reputation to be an *imperfect* substitute for abandoning discretion, for tying the policy-makers' hands. However, the basic case for an independent central bank which the model makes remains infact.

b. Formal models modified

It is striking that, although as Barro and Gordon (1983a) point out, some of the model's predictions are manifestly consistent with the data, one is troubling. The model predicts a high and steady inflation rate. And yet in the world around us we observe inflation fluctuating. This can be resolved in several ways, of which Cagan's (1986) is particularly appealing, not requiring for example a fluctuating natural rate of unemployment. He writes:

[4] They also claim that the model predicts cyclical monetary policy, as unemployment reductions are valued more greatly in slumps. But this would seem to beg the question of why we have business cycles.

> It is not deception that keeps the desired goal of price stability out of reach. It is the public's insistence, shared and accepted by the authorities, not to subordinate low unemployment to other objectives. (p. 32)

How can allowing for this lead to the kind of inflation fluctuations we see? Cagan lets prices be sticky, responding with a lag to changes in the rate of growth of money. Hence monetary expansion at first lowers unemployment. But it has subsequent inflationary consequences, and a rise in unemployment to reverse this is tolerated only when inflation exceeds some threshold rate. Hence there is an upward bias to the price level, as in the Barro and Gordon model, without the implausible prediction that it be produced by a steady rate of inflation. Prices rise continually because the electorate will tolerate a rise in unemployment to slow inflation, but not enough (or long-lasting enough) to produce a fall in prices to their pre-inflation level. Again, the de-politicizing of monetary policy would seem to be required. The implication of this analysis, then, is that to avoid an inflationary bias to policy, we require an independent central bank.[5]

These seem to be the grounds on which both proponents and opponents of central bank independence debate. As noted above, proponents see independence from politically motivated concern with unemployment as necessary for price stability; and opponents fear independence *because* it will allow that concern to be ignored. It therefore seems useful to see whether such concern, produced by political pressure, is in fact the only or likely cause of monetary over-expansion. But before doing so, a discussion of 'independence' is useful. For its meaning is far from clear-cut.

c. *The concept of independence*

Independence can have several meanings. One is trivial, but worth eliminating from the discussion for the sake of clarity. In any bureaucracy some functions are delegated to particular agencies. If within the administrative hierarchy there were a separate organization, charged with monetary policy, which was subordinate to the executive but independent in routine decisions, this would not be independence in the sense usually meant in this discussion. What is usually meant is that the central bank be an independent branch of government—like the judicial branch. It would operate subject to a set of laws; but, once these laws had been enacted, it could not be further instructed by the government. Such instruction would require a change in the law.

[5] There is also the possibility, as is common with a regime based on reputation, of multiple equilibria. For if people base future beliefs on policymakers' past actions, policymakers may have an incentive to validate the beliefs on some occasion.

The law would of course embody an objective. The proponents of independent central banks, who appear to have this notion of independence in mind although we can so far find no explicit statement of it, wish the objective to be price stability. The concept of independence is thus very clearly analogous to that enjoyed by the Bank of England under the gold standard. The Bank was privately owned. It was not a branch of government. But it was constrained by a public objective—maintenance of gold convertibility. Nowadays the public objective would be price level stability.

We will now examine, first, episodes of extreme inflation and, second, the relationship between central bank–government relations and inflation at rather lower levels of inflation. This will provide evidence on two crucial questions raised by the above discussion. Is the lack of independence really, as the model suggests, the source of the trouble? And can independence, even if it is useful, be maintained in the face of extreme economic difficulties? The study of hyperinflation bears on the latter question; of normal inflations, on the former.

The historical record: extreme circumstances

If central banks were independent, would that mean that the worst excesses of government would be avoided? The answer is, unfortunately not. In this section we look briefly at some of the worst experiences of inflation in history before the middle of the twentieth century. Whether a central bank was dependent or not, or indeed whether one existed, appears to have made no difference.

A survey of the period from the Roman Empire until the middle of the present century reveals very few cases (perhaps a dozen or so) of inflation over 100 per cent p.a. What stands out as the critical element in almost all of these cases was severe civil disorder (at worst civil war), or perhaps weak government. Serious social unrest or actual disorder provokes large-scale spending by the established authority in an attempt either to suppress or placate the rebellious element. At the same time there is a sharp fall in revenue. The need is therefore for the printing press to be brought into action and the government to reap the inflation tax. As Keynes wrote in 1923, inflation is the form of taxation which the public find hardest to evade and even the weakest government can enforce it.

Remarkably, there were no examples of rapid inflation before the advent of central banks, although central banks were not always involved in inflationary episodes. The first major inflation was in the American War of Independence. Paper money financed the rebellion and inflation reached more than 200 per cent p.a. The second was the well-known experience of France in the 1790s when the assignat was issued in abundance during the Revolution. Inflation raced to more than several hundred per cent per annum. In America during the Civil War in the 1860s inflation in the Confederacy was running at over

100 per cent p.a. The next group of inflations were clustered at the end of the First World War. At some point between 1919 and 1925 five countries experienced severe inflation. In Austria, Hungary, Poland, Russia, and Germany from the beginning to the end of their hyperinflations (defined by Cagan and usually lasting around a year) prices increased by the following multiples: 14,000 per cent, 23,000 per cent, 2.5m per cent, 4m per cent, and 1000m per cent. In the second half of the 1940s there were similar powerful pressures for inflation around the world and many serious outbursts, but the worst three, where inflation indisputably soared to hyperinflationary heights, were Hungary, Greece, and China.

What generalizations—of the kind that would be suggested by economic theory—can be made about these episodes? What were the conditions in which inflation appeared and accelerated rapidly? In most of the qualitative accounts of these episodes there are some obvious 'proximate' factors. A huge growth in money supply and accompanying budget deficits stand out. The first and most striking feature common to all episodes is that of an unbacked paper currency. The fact that paper currency was rare prior to the twentieth century undoubtedly explains why rapid inflation was also rare. Without a paper currency, the metals used and the technology available for increased production would not allow a sufficient expansion of the money supply, or a rise in velocity, sufficient to produce the rapid rise in prices. All pre-twentieth century experiences with unbacked paper money resulted in inflation though they did not always degenerate into very rapid inflation.

Monetising budget deficits

Most of the qualitative accounts also draw attention to the fact that the inflationary monetary growth derived from fiscal deficits. The view that deficits ultimately require monetising is quite widespread. It is implicit in much of the literature and explicit in some. When government was unable to cover the gap by borrowing it resorted to the printing press. Where there was little prospect of revenue covering expenditure, the whole debt had to be monetized.

In the examples of very rapid inflation before the twentieth century, there is little doubt that when deficits and debt soared, monetary growth followed quickly. Again, the data do not allow rigorous testing even of the precise timing of the relationship, but the accounts of these cases all suggest that this was the sequence of the variables, and that this sequence preceded the price explosion. Fiscal demands led to monetary growth and so to inflation. The American Revolution, the French Revolution, and the Confederacy in the American Civil War are all examples. Austria, Germany, Hungary, and Poland all had substantial and growing deficits built up prior to or coincidental with their inflations. This was also the case with Russia. Of the fewer examples in the 1940s a notable one is China, and Greece provides further support. All these cases confirm the story of government budget deficits leading to very rapid money growth and then inflation.

Causes of large budget deficits

Given that very rapid inflation has always appeared in a period of monetary expansion following or contemporaneous with growing budget deficits, the question arises: what circumstances produced the latter? And there is second question: did deficits and monetary growth lead inexorably to high inflation? Sometimes 'war' has been put forward as an explanation. But that is clearly unsatisfactory. The history of the world is essentially a chronicle of conflict, frequently on a huge and prolonged scale; and in two world wars in the twentieth century, when scores of countries were involved, there were still only a few cases of very rapid inflation. In the seventeenth and eighteenth centuries there were many wars and they often lasted longer than in the nineteenth and twentieth centuries, yet the cases of rapid inflation were fewer. War of itself is certainly not an explanation of the phenomenon of rapid inflation. It is perhaps worth recalling here that Germany's deficits in the First World War grew rapidly from 1914 onwards and were accompanied by a substantial growth in the money supply, but the very rapid inflation did not develop until 1923, and the First World War cannot really be seen as its prime source.

A closer look reveals that it was not war between nations, but rather civil war or revolution or, at a minimum, serious social unrest that was present in almost all cases: eighteenth century America and France, America in the 1860s, Russia after 1917 (and in 1991?), Hungary in 1919, and Poland in the early 1920s. In Germany too in the early 1920s there were attempted communist coups, widespread unrest (and a Bolshevik government in Bavaria). Austria was similar. China and Greece were plunged deep into civil war after the Second World War, and Hungary was a particular victim of Soviet influence.

Governments have always been keen to get hold of resources, and in times of great difficulty the temptation has been simply to confiscate them. The easiest method is to generate inflation and benefit from the tax. The authorities maximize their revenue when inflation is in excess of 100 per cent p.a. (Cagan, 1956), but at these rates the government must be in serious danger of losing power. In other words while the inflation tax may have the appearance of an attractive short-term policy, it is clearly potentially calamitous in anything but the shortest term. The tax may be useful, however, the political consequences are potentially dire. In what circumstances would it be worth taking such risks? The answer must be when the state is seriously threatened from within. The reason the external threat is not critical is that it usually stimulates patriotism. Tax revenue is then easier to raise and so is borrowing. It could be argued that there were occasions when such risks were rational.

The number of cases of rapid inflation in world history rises sharply after 1950, because of the available technology for the production of paper money and the absence of any commodity standard. All over the world, and especially in Latin American countries, there have been many examples of the kind of inflation rates discussed above. Interestingly, a casual inspection again suggests that civil unrest and revolution were root causes. But the main point is that all of the cases noted above, together with the more recent examples, were illustrations of political difficulties superseding economic considerations.

Central banks irrelevant?

In all the cases of extreme inflation rates that we have examined, the status, or even the existence of the central bank was or would have been irrelevant. From the earliest times until the middle of the twentieth century there have been very few examples of rapid inflation as we have defined it. In all cases (with the exception of Hungary in 1946 where exceptional circumstances obtained) there was serious social unrest, with breakdown threatened, imminent, or actual. Our argument is that the niceties of distinction between dependence and independence are irrelevant. Governments clinging to power in the face of rebellion will ultimately resort to confiscating resources. No independent central bank could in such conditions maintain a hold on to its independence.

It is, for example, inconceivable that an independent central bank in Russia in 1917 could have been allowed to follow a strict monetary policy and deprive the revolutionaries of the resources necessary for the achievement of their goals. And that is surely true of all such circumstances. On a much more modest scale we have seen recently in Germany how the world's most independent central bank was overridden when an important political objective arose.

NORMAL TIMES

The importance of bank/government relations in what we regard as normal times—all circumstances bar inflations of the type discussed in the previous section—is our next subject. There have been several other studies of monetary performance and the effect of bank/government relations over recent years. These are summarized below. Our work differs from them in three main respects.

First, we examine a long run of data. If institutional factors are important, we would expect the effect of them to be long lasting, and to show up in long runs of data. If a stable relationship emerges over a long period, it rules out, for example, the occasional but at times major importance of individuals. (A vivid description of two such occasions can be found in Friedman, 1962). Second, taking a long run also ensures that the full effect of money on prices is apparent—since, although the average lag before money affects prices may be two to three years, the lags can on occasions be much greater. Third, by taking a long run of data, we can in several cases examine the same country with more than one bank/government relationship. This certainly does not give us a perfect 'other things equal' controlled experiment, but it is a step towards one.

There is also a disadvantage. All the economies we examine are to some degree open. It is widely, and correctly, believed that open economies under fixed exchange rates cannot control their own monetary conditions. Slower money growth (after adjusting for demand) than the rest of the world, means that money is drawn across the exchanges. Faster money growth, and it flows out. The classic description of this situation is Hume (1752); there have been many since. There are two qualifications to the above conclusion. The reserve centre—the country which sets the pace of money growth, either by agreement, tacit or explicit, or by chance—has monetary freedom. But more important for our purposes is the word 'fixed' in the preceding description of monetary dependence. The result holds if the exchange rate is fixed—as it was for Hume, who described a system with metallic coinage usable, perhaps after melting and recoining, in any country.

There is a crucial difference between a *fixed* rate and a *pegged* rate. Under the latter, with the ever-present possibility of exchange rate changes, there is the friction of uncertainty to impede monetary integration. And there is also the possibility for a country with a pegged rate to pursue its own monetary policy, validating its independence by occasional discrete exchange rate changes. This was the practice of the UK in the years from the inception of Bretton Woods to floating. Excess monetary expansion produced reserve losses, 'runs on the pound', packages of emergency measures and then a devaluation which reimported the inflation that the previous policy had exported. It reimported it in the form of a sharp boost to the price level. (It is worth emphasizing that this is not to imply that devaluations cause price level increases. In the British case they were a channel of transmission for such an increase, as the trigger for the devaluations was a current account deficit. The devaluation was allowed to produce a surplus, which led to an increase in reserves, and growth in money.) This process is described in detail, and several examples of it examined, in Williamson and Wood (1976). And of course, in the Bretton Woods era, Britain was far from alone in changing its exchange rate.

Looking further back in history, we find that few countries regarded the gold standard parity as being as immutable as it was regarded in Britain. Latin American countries were not alone in abandoning parity from time to time. Italy too, did so, for example. This means that the relationship between money and prices could be lagged to a much greater extent than would be expected under floating rates; this further justifies the use of long runs of data.

Comparison with previous studies

Two further differences between this study and previous studies which have examined non-hyperinflationary times should be outlined at this point. Several of these studies (such as Alesina, 1989) have looked at the effects of central bank/government relationship on inflation *and unemployment.* We focus on inflation; and we would regard any other focus as inappropriate. It would of course be out of keeping with the spirit of the motivating Barro and Gordon (1983a, 1983b) model—for in that model monetary policy has no persistent effect on the level of unemployment. Simply looking at the average level of unemployment is therefore not useful in this context. Indeed, in view of the abundant evidence of long run monetary neutrality (see for example Friedman and Schwartz (1982); Schwartz (1987); Capie, Mills, and Wood (1991); and Mills and Wood (1992)) we cannot see why anyone should expect to find central bank/government relations affecting unemployment over a long period.

A case could be constructed for saying that, if the lags in the economy are appropriate, an activist, politically inspired, monetary policy would deliver a more variable unemployment rate. We do not, however, pursue that hypothesis because so many factors can produce changes in the rate of unemployment (including among these factors those which change the natural rate) that we regard variability in unemployment as telling nothing about monetary policy; it is an indicator which gives too much information to be useful for our purpose.

Finally, in this description of differences from previous studies, we carry out a rudimentary 'sensitivity analysis'. As will emerge below, it is possible in several of the cases we examine to argue that the central bank should not be in the dependent category but in that of independent banks. We have perforce drawn sharp boundaries where there is in fact a continuum. Because of this when we examine the effect of bank/government relations on long-run inflation performance, we carry out our examinations with these marginal candidates first in one category (our preferred classification of them) and then in the other (that which we regard as less appropriate but nevertheless defensible). This will help to reveal whether a classificationary scheme which inevitably has some degree of arbitrariness about it has biased our results.

A number of previous studies have considered the relationship between central bank dependency and inflation. Among the first was Bade and Parkin (1987—although this paper dates back to 1978). They consider central banks from twelve countries, and their average inflation rates over the floating exchange rate period of 1973–86. The central banks are classified into four groups depending on the level of government influence. The classifications are based on two aspects namely, 'financial type' and 'policy type'. The financial type refers to the level of government influence in selecting board members, their salaries, budgets and the distribution of profits. Policy type refers to the level of government influence in board meetings and whether it decides the final policy. The statistical procedure employed to determine the relationship between central bank type and inflation was to estimate a first order autoregression for each country.

Central bank classification

Further attempts to classify central banks have been carried out by Masciandaro and Tabellini (1988). Central banks from five 'Pacific basin' countries (Australia, Canada, Japan, New Zealand, and the US) are classified according to their dependency. These are based on government influence in the appointment of the board and the conduct of monetary policy. Although the study is primarily concerned with the relationship between central bank dependency and the fiscal deficit, it nevertheless considers the relationship with inflation. Average inflation rates for the period 1970–74, 1975–79, and 1980–85 are calculated for each of the five countries, and compared against the respective degree of dependency of the central bank. Other studies considering the relationship between central bank dependency and inflation have employed the classifications carried out by earlier authors. Alesina (1988 and 1989) ranks the central banks according to their dependency, based on classifications carried out by Bade and Parkin, and by Fair (1980). Again average inflation rates are calculated, over the period 1973 to 1986, for each of the countries and compared against the respective central bank.

Our study differs from previous research in this area in a number of respects. First, we attempt to carry out our own classification of central bank dependency for fifteen countries. Our classifications are based on factors considered by both Bade and Parkin (1987) and Masciandaro and Tabellini (1988). In addition to these we consider the ownership of the bank and whether it has the sole right to issue notes and coins. The latter is important because some central banks have only relatively recently received this privilege.

Second, this research, unlike any previous work in this area, considers the relationship between central bank dependency and inflation for the period 1871 to 1989. Previous studies have tended mainly to focus on the floating exchange rate period. By using long-run data, we illustrate how central bank dependency can change from time to time. Finally, studies carried out by Bade and Parkin (1987), Masciandaro and Tabellini (1988), and Alesina (1988, 1989) take the average inflation rate for each country over the whole period under consideration. Our research takes average annual inflation rates for groups of countries.

RESULTS

Figure 13.1 shows our basic classification of central bank dependence/independence. Any such classification requires a considerable element of judgement, or as some might say, arbitrariness. It turns out, however, not to matter greatly, as we will demonstrate shortly. Figure 13.2 shows the average inflation rates for all the countries with independent central banks over the period 1870 to 1990. The only qualification for inclusion here is that the country's central bank be independent in any given year. If a bank were independent for a period of, say, only five years then that country's inflation rate would be included for those five years. Figure 13.3 then does the same for countries with dependent central banks. And finally, Figure 13.4 shows them combined for the period 1930 to 1989.

The general pattern that is thrown up is one that must be familiar to most monetary economists/historians. There was considerable price stability before 1900 with some deflation in the 1880s; then the well-known inflationary bursts of wartime show up in the two world war periods and there is the hyperinflation of the 1920s. In the 1970s, when the entire world resorted to a 'fiat' money regime for the first time in history, we can see another burst of inflation. The figures in Table 13.1 show that it was worse in the case of dependent banks.

What is striking is the remarkable similarity over such a long period between the performance of dependent and independent central banks. Table 13.1 provides the five-yearly averages of the inflation rates and from these it can be seen that the actual differences in inflation rates were seldom different to any interesting degree. The differences were rarely large, and various dependent central banks from time to time produced inflation rates lower than the average of independent central banks.

As we mentioned at the outset, there is a considerable degree of freedom of movement in saying what is and what is not independent. For that reason we adjusted the classification in several places where our doubts over the initial

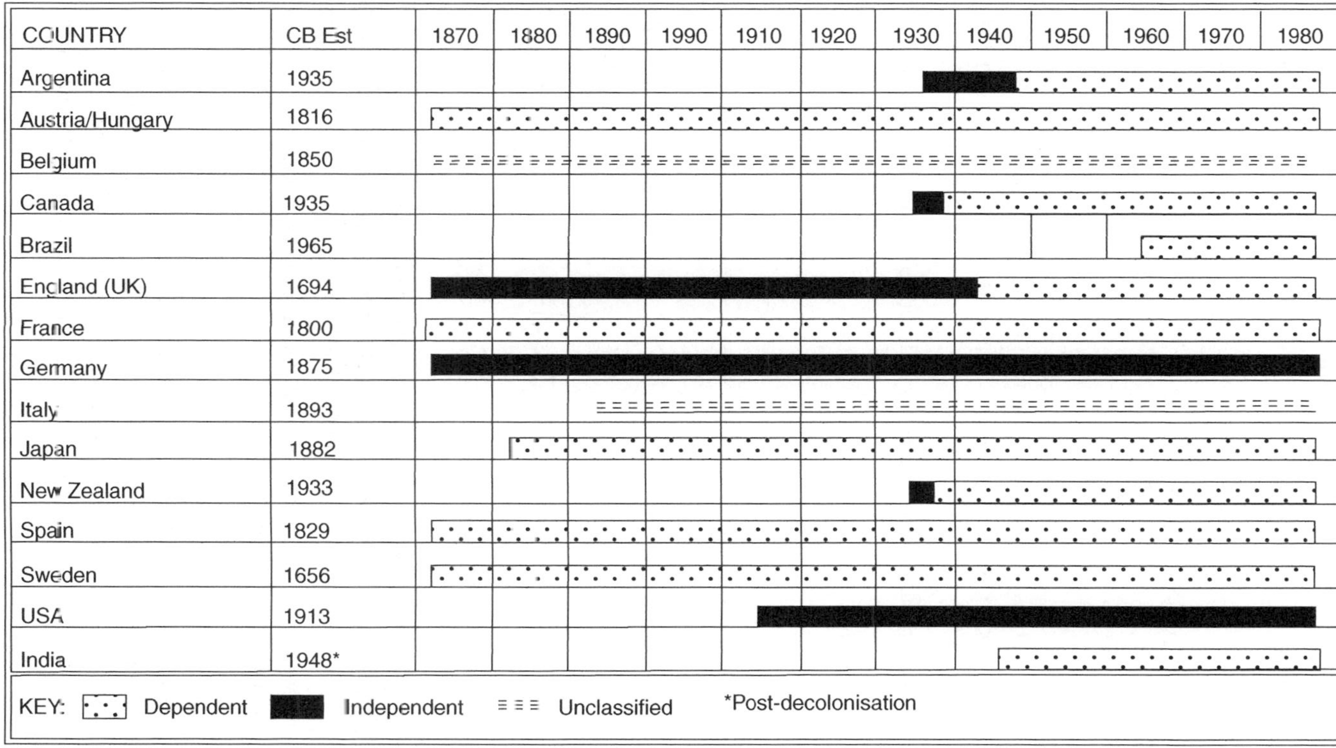

Figure 13.1. Classification of central banks, 1870 to 1989

Sources: These classifications are based on readings and evidence from Conant C. A. (1927), Kisch C. A. and Elkin W. A. (1932), Creighton J. H. (1933), Stokes M. C. (1939), Plumptre A. F. W. (1940), Neufeld E. P. (1955), Sayers R. S. (1952 and 1962), Quintero Ramos A. M. (1965), Auburn H. W. (1966), Pressnell L. S. (1974), Weston R. (1980), Goodhart C. A. E. (1986), Lees, F. A., Botts J. M., and Cysne R. P. (1990), Smith V. (reprint 1990).

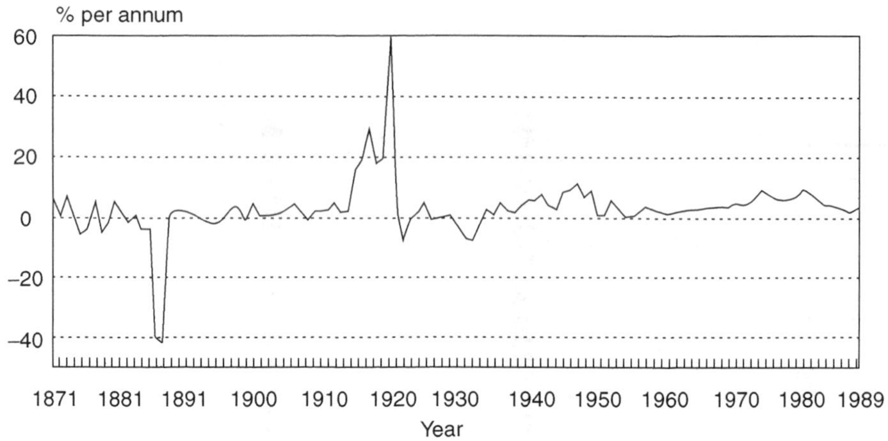

Figure 13.2. Average annual inflation rates for independent central banks, 1871 to 1989

Sources: Mitchell, B.R. (1981, 1982, 1983), IFS, Datastream.

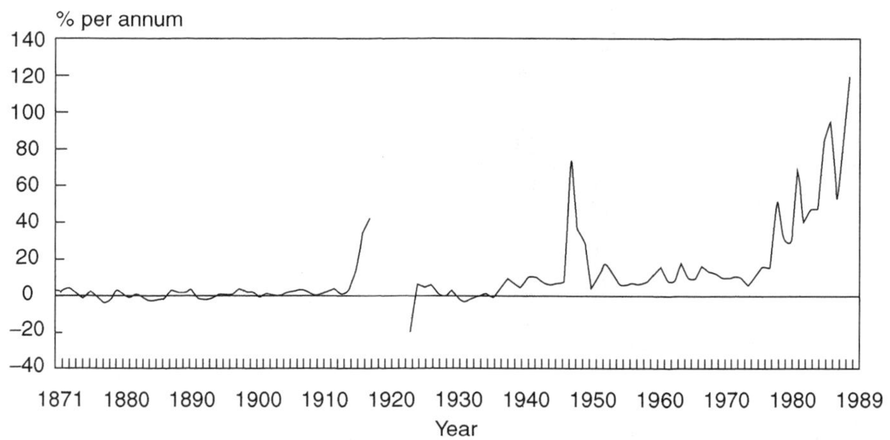

Figure 13.3. Average annual inflation rates for dependent central banks, 1871 to 1989

Sources: Mitchell, B.R. (1981, 1982, 1983), IFS, Datastream.

classification were strongest. We then repeated the exercise above and the results are shown in Figure 13.5 and Table 13.2. From these it can be seen that nothing of significance has changed. However, there are differences between our results and others that reflect how sensitive the results can be to classification changes.

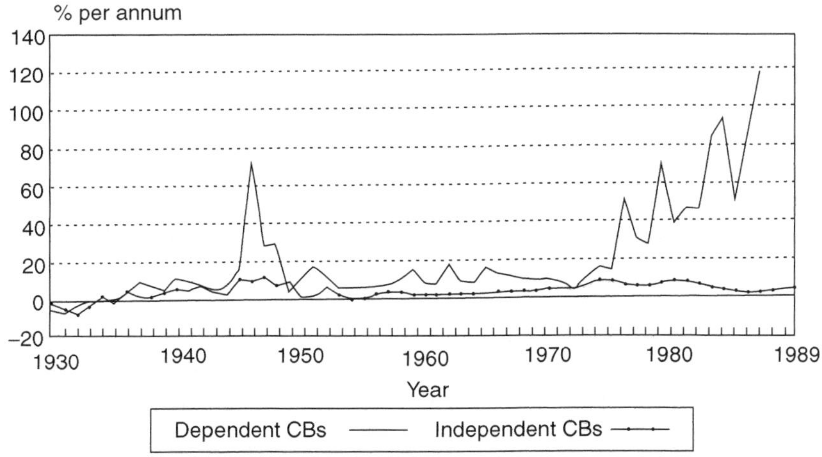

Figure 13.4. Central bank dependency and average annual inflation rates, 1930 to 1989

Sources: Mitchell, B.R. (1981, 1982, 1983), IFS, Datastream.

Table 13.1. Five-year average inflation rates and standard deviations for dependent and independent central banks

	Dependent central banks*		Independent central banks*		Dependent central bank (excluding Latin America)	
Years	Average	Std. Dev.	Average	Std. Dev.	Average	Std. Dev.
1871/4	2.62	2.82	2.89	5.66	2.62	2.82
1875/9	−1.41	2.76	−2.58	4.98	−1.41	2.76
1880/4	0.24	2.31	−0.36	3.16	0.24	2.31
1885/9	−0.89	3.13	−8.49	24.29	0.89	3.13
1890/4	−0.49	2.62	−0.31	2.08	−0.49	2.62
1895/9	1.08	2.13	0.41	2.19	1.08	2.13
1900/4	0.01	1.17	1.10	1.80	0.01	1.17
1905/9	1.37	1.50	1.57	2.16	1.37	1.50
1910/4	1.49	2.22	2.20	1.34	1.49	2.22
1915/9	36.29	38.32	20.06	11.72	36.29	38.32
1920/4	121.29	530.06	13.46	42.02	121.29	530.06
1925/9	2.02	7.32	0.72	2.84	2.02	7.32
1930/4	−1.93	4.70	−3.76	4.26	−1.93	4.70
1935/9	79.43	374.55	2.23	4.12	79.43	374.55
1940/4	7.58	7.90	4.56	3.35	7.58	7.90
1945/9	29.91	82.15	8.39	7.02	30.09	85.87
1950/4	9.85	14.69	1.31	3.98	5.67	6.99
1955/9	8.06	18.32	1.67	1.14	3.32	3.46
1960/4	9.73	22.03	1.70	0.75	3.59	2.40
1965/9	13.12	22.67	2.89	1.18	4.72	2.69
1970/4	9.85	8.36	5.32	2.39	7.92	7.06
1975/9	38.86	101.62	6.37	2.47	10.47	4.19
1980/4	61.81	151.72	6.14	3.15	9.51	4.19
1985/9	159.56	498.59	2.64	1.39	5.77	3.29

Notes and data source: *For a list of dependent and independent central banks please see Figure 13.1 Datastream (mainly for data from 1975 onwards). Int. Financial Statistics (for Argentina and Brazil in the mid 1970s). Mitchell (1981, 1982, 1983) for all other data.

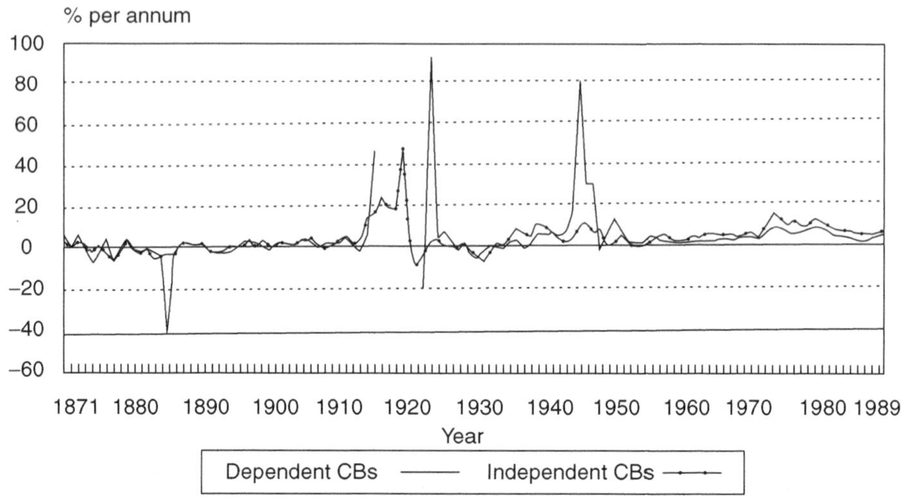

Figure 13.5. Central bank dependency and average annual inflation rates, 1871 to 1989 (excluding Latin American countries)

Sources: Mitchell, B.R. (1981, 1982, 1983), IFS, Datastream.

When we calculate a rank correlation coefficient for Alesina's dependency and inflation performance it is very high at 0.9657. But we disagree with his classification, in particular the placing of Japan in the most independent group, and our reclassification yields a result of 0.6679. Our own classification is a slightly different version of the above and gives a moderately good relationship between the degree of dependence and inflation performance (0.6099). When we remove the Latin American countries from the sample (being extreme observations, at any rate for this period) the rank correlation falls to 0.3636—a weak relationship. Further indication of a weak relationship is found in Masciandaro and Tabellini, a rank correlation coefficient of 0.4 (see Table 13.3).

One difference that continues to show up is the more pronounced inflation in the last two decades in countries with dependent central banks. Much of this, though, is attributable to the Latin American countries and indeed when they are removed from the set the difference between the two classifications is much less pronounced. (See Tables 13.1 and 13.2 above for five-year averages of inflation rates.) One final point that is worthy of note is that the independent series is more variable than the dependent series. At first sight this may

Table 13.2. Five-year average inflation rates and standard deviations for dependent and independent central banks with a reclassification of Japan

	Dependent central banks*		Independent central banks*		Dependent central banks (excluding Latin America)	
Years	Average	Std. Dev.	Average	Std. Dev.	Average	Std. Dev.
1871/4	2.62	2.82	2.89	5.66	2.62	2.82
1875/9	−1.41	2.76	−2.58	4.98	−1.41	2.76
1880/4	0.24	2.31	−0.36	3.16	0.24	2.31
1885/9	−0.89	3.13	−8.49	24.29	−0.89	3.13
1890/4	−0.49	2.62	−0.31	2.08	−0.49	2.62
1895/9	1.08	2.13	0.41	2.19	1.08	2.13
1900/4	0.01	1.17	1.10	1.80	0.01	1.17
1905/9	1.37	1.50	1.57	2.16	1.37	1.50
1910/4	1.49	2.22	2.20	1.34	1.49	2.22
1915/9	36.29	38.32	20.06	11.72	36.29	38.32
1920/4	133.71	554.40	10.37	38.11	133.71	554.40
1925/9	3.49	7.36	−0.42	3.46	3.49	7.36
1930/4	−1.56	3.05	−3.68	5.54	−1.56	3.05
1935/9	2.85	6.85	2.32	5.89	87.65	394.31
1940/4	7.90	8.70	5.18	4.07	7.57	8.25
1945/9	14.85	26.81	45.75	118.14	13.58	29.06
1950/4	9.72	14.62	3.35	5.36	5.69	6.93
1955/9	9.26	19.08	1.82	1.66	3.54	3.50
1960/4	9.69	22.05	2.91	1.87	3.36	2.39
1965/9	11.77	16.01	3.80	1.53	4.67	2.80
1970/4	9.84	8.24	7.55	4.37	7.66	7.16
1975/9	39.79	101.37	10.37	5.28	10.78	5.75
1980/4	62.69	151.41	6.44	4.05	10.21	3.84
1985/9	148.54	481.73	2.93	1.98	5.86	3.28

Notes and data source: *For a list of dependent and independent central banks please see Figure 13.1. Datastream (mainly for data from 1975 onwards). Int. Financial Statistics (for Argentina and Brazil in the mid 1970s). Mitchell (1981, 1982, 1983) for all other data.

appear surprising but we believe it can be explained in the following terms. Independent central banks do not engage in interest rate smoothing, while dependent central banks, on the others hand, a price series do. The result is that the latter produce a less variable price series, albeit with a slightly firmer upward trend.

Table 13.3. Classification of central bank dependency, 1973 to 1986

Central Bank Ranking*	Alesina's Classification[2]	Reclassification of Alesina[2]	Masciandaro and Tabellini's Classification[3]	Our Classification[1]
1	Spain (2)	Spain (2)	New Zealand (1)	Brazil (2)
2	New Zealand (3)	Japan (14)	Japan (5)	Argentina (1)
3	Australia (6)	New Zealand (2)	Australia (2)	India (8)
4	Italy (1)	Canada (11)	Canada (3)	Spain (3)
5	UK (4)	Australia (6)	USA (4)	Japan (11)
6	Finland (5)	Italy (1)		New Zealand (4)
7	France (7)	France (7)		Canada(9)
8	Denmark (8)	UK (4)		Austria (12)
9	Sweden (9)	Finland (5)		France (6)
10	Norway (10)	Denmark (8)		UK (5)
11	Canada (11)	Sweden (9)		Sweden (7)
12	Belgium (12)	Norway (10)		USA (10)
13	Holland (15)	Belgium (12)		W. Germany (13)
14	USA (13)	Holland (15)		
15	Japan (14)	USA (13)		
16	Switzerland (16)	Switzerland (16)		
17	W. Germany (17)	W. Germany (17)		

* 1 refers to the most dependent central bank and 17 to the least dependent.
[1] In our study Belgium and Italy are unclassified.
[2] Central bank dependency ranking and inflation rates from Alesina (1989).
[3] Central bank dependency ranking and inflation rates from Masciandaro and Tabellini (1988).
Figures in brackets relate to the ranking of inflation rates.

Appendix and Reference List

Key to tables and background notes:

Ownership: J–Joint; G–Government; P–Private; MB–Member banks of the system
Management: J–Joint; G–Government
Money issue: J–Joint issuer; S–Sole issuer; M–one of many issuers; X–did not issue
Monetary policy: I–Independent; D–Dependent; U–Unclassified

In each country table, notes are given explaining classification under the four properties of central banks and the final overall classification given in note 4 (monetary policy)

Argentina

Banco Central de la Republica Argentina Established 1935

One of the main reasons for setting up the bank was to 'minimize the ups and downs which so frequently affected the Argentine economy'. In order to set up an institution to deal with this problem, the government in 1933 asked the Bank of England for help. Under the leadership of Sir Otto Niemeyer, a director of the Bank of England at the time, a report was published and shortly afterwards the bank established.

		1935	1946	1988
1	Ownership	J	G	G
2	Management	J	G	G
3	Money issue	J	S	S
4	Monetary policy	J	D	D

1 When the bank was established in 1935 the government subscribed half the capital, of Peso mn (moneda nacional) 30m, private shareholders the rest. The private shareholders consisted of 49 banks, including 12 foreign banks, and no bank was allowed to own more than 10% of the capital. However the ownership structure was changed in March 1946 when the newly elected socialist government nationalized the bank. All shareholders prior to nationalization were expropriated through a 2.5% treasury bond.

2 Prior to 1946 the president and vice-president were appointed on the advice of the senate for a period of seven years. The senate obtained three nominations from each member bank. The rest of the twelve directors were selected for a period of three years by member banks, including two directors by foreign banks.

Since 1946 the president and vice-president have been selected as before. The ordinary directors, now thirteen, are all selected by the president of the country for three years. The directors can be reappointed without limitation. As from 1946 all directors have to be Argentinian by birth.

3 Initially the bank issued notes and coins above peso mn 5 only, while the government issued notes and coins below this sum. However, the government could not issue above peso mn 20 per inhabitant. After nationalization the bank became the sole issuer of all notes and coins.

4 Between 1935 and 1946 the bank acted as an agent for the government. After 1946 the bank acted solely as a department of the government.

Source: Quintero Ramos (1965).

Austria (Austria-Hungary)

Chartered Austrian National Bank (until 1878)

Austria Hungarian Bank (until 1922)

Austrian National Bank

Established 1816 (refers to Chartered Austrian National Bank)

The bank was formed primarily to regulate the circulation of notes and coins. The bank has always been privately owned; however it has gone through a number of changes. The main change occurred at the time of the union with Hungary, which resulted in the bank having to merge with the Austro-Hungarian Bank. When the union between the two countries was dissolved, after the First World War, the bank returned to being a purely Austrian Central Bank.

		1816	1878	1922	1988
1	Ownership	P	P	P	P
2	Management	J	G	J	J
3	Money issue	S	S	S	S
4	Monetary policy	D	D	D	D

1 The bank is wholly owned by private shareholders.
2 Until 1878 the governor and his deputy were selected by the government and the rest of the directors by the shareholders. After 1878, the governor was appointed on the advice of Ministers of Finance from Austria and Hungary. The ministers also appointed a deputy each, although Goodhart (1986) notes that Austria had the majority on the council.

In 1922 a new charter was passed creating the Austrian National Bank. The bank continued to be a private concern with the chairman appointed by the president of the country for five years. The vice-chairmen (of which there were two) were selected by the board on the approval of the government. Ordinary directors were selected at general meetings by shareholders. However, there existed guidelines which made sure that certain sectors in the economy were represented. The charter allowed for foreigners to be directors but limited their number to four.
3 The bank was set up as a sole issuer of notes and coins and this was its primary function. After the union with Hungary in 1867 Austrian notes and coins were legal tender in Hungary. This formed part of the agreement with Hungary, as did the opening of bank branches in Hungary.
4 Although a privately owned bank it has never been outside the influence of the government. By 1841 the bank behaved more like a department of the government than an independent organization. In 1899 the government was given greater power in the management of the bank. Goodhart (1986) claims that during the period 1890 to 1910 it was the bank 'most under the thumb of the government'.

Sources: Conant (1929), Kisch and Elkin (1932), Goodhart (1986).

Belgium

National Bank of Belgium Established 1850

The historic relationship between the bank and the government is not well documented. However, the government is part shareholder in the bank with half of the representation on the council.

		1850	1945	1988
1	Ownership	J	J	J
2	Management	J	J	J
3	Money issue	S	S	S
4	Monetary policy	U	U	U

1 The bank is partly owned by the state (via the government) and partly by private shareholders.
2 The governor is nominated by and can be dismissed or suspended by the government. The appointment is for a fixed period but can be renewed. The rest of the board of directors appointed by the government represent various economic groups. There is also a permanent government representative who has the power to veto any decision. All members of the board of directors have to be Belgian.
3 The bank is the sole issuer of notes and coins.
4 Unclassified throughout. Conant (1929) claims that 'the history of banking in Belgium is a history of greater freedom from state interference and entanglement with the finances of the government than that of most other European countries'. However, the government does have the right to oppose any measures which it considers contrary to the laws, statues or interests of the state.

Sources: Contant (1929), Kirsch and Elkin (1932), Weston (1980), Goodhart (1986).

Brazil

Central Bank of Brazil Established 1965

Before the establishment of the central bank, monetary regulation was the responsibility of the superitendencia da Moeda e do Credito (SUMOC). The currency was issued by the Federal Treasury.

		1965	1988
1	Ownership	G	G
2	Management	G	G
3	Money issue	S	S
4	Monetary policy	D	D

1 Since the establishment of the bank it has been wholly owned by the government.
2 All the directors of the bank are appointed by the president of the country. They are not appointed for fixed time periods but instead can be dismissed at any time.
3 Lees et al. note that 'the executive branch of the government retained most of its former authority (i.e., before the establishment of the central bank) in matters relating to money and credit creation. The printing of money remained under the control of the Minister of Finance'.
4 The government has a strong influence on the central bank and since 1965 has made the most important monetary and foreign exchange decisions via the National Monetary Council.

Source: Lees, Botts, and Cysne (1990).

Canada

Bank of Canada Established 1935

The prime objective for setting up the bank was to regulate the credit and currency in the best interests of the state. The bank initially had private shareholders but in 1938 it was nationalized after a number of capital injections by the newly elected Liberal government.

		1935	1936/7	1938	1967	1988
1	Ownership	P	J	G	G	G
2	Management	J	J	G	G	G
3	Money issue	S	S	S	S	S
4	Monetary policy	I	I	D	D	D

1 Although initially a private bank it soon received a number of capital injections from the government. By 1937 the government owned a substantial part of the bank. The process was completed in 1938 when it was nationalized and all private shareholders forced to sell.
2 The Bank of Canada Act 1934 (i.e. the Act which led to the establishment of the bank), states that after the first governor and his deputy all future governors and deputies should be selected by the directors with the approval of the Governor-in-Council. The term of office of the governor and his deputy was to be seven years with eligibility for reappointment. Between 1936 and 1938 (i.e. during the periods of capital injections) the government had an average of ten voting rights while private shareholders had seven. The governor had a veto.
3 The bank is sole issuer of notes and coins.
4 From 1935 to 1938 the bank was largely independent from government. From 1938 onwards the bank became more of a government department than a separate organization. This relationship between bank and government was formalized by the Bank of Canada Act 1967. Under this Act the bank had to consult the finance minister and set out a formal procedure, and in case of disagreement the government could after further consultation issue a directive.

Source: Creighton (1933), Stokes (1939), Neufeld (1955), Weston (1980).

France

Banque de France Established 1800

The original idea for the bank came from an influential French banking institution, Le Couteulx de Canteleu et Perrgaux, and it was immediately welcomed by Napoleon. Before the establishment of the bank, the Paris bankers used the Caisse des Comptes Courants, which provided some central bank facilities.

		1800	1801	1806	1848	1945	1988
1	Ownership	J	P	P	P	G	G
2	Management	J	J	G	G	G	G
3	Money issue	M	M	M	S	S	S
4	Monetary policy	D	D	D	D	D	D

1 Napoleon persuaded the shareholders of Caisse des Comtes Courants to dissolve the company and merge it with the Banque de France. This provided for some of the initial capital of FF36 million while the rest was obtained from the government and private shareholders. In 1801 Napoleon sold the government holding in the bank. Later in 1945 the bank was nationalized by the newly elected Socialist government.
2 Prior to 1806 the directors of the bank were selected largely by the shareholders. Because of Napoleon's dislike and distrust of the bankers and also because he assumed they were furthering their own interest he felt that the government should select the directors. Even after Napoleon the government continued to select the directors of the bank.
3 The bank achieved complete note issuing monopoly in 1848 although the process had started in 1802. This monopoly was challenged for a very brief period in the 1860s by the Bank of Savoy.
4 The bank has always been dependent on the government.
Sources: Kisch and Elkin (1932), Goodhart (1986), Smith (reprint 1990).

Germany

Reichsbank (until 1945)
Bundesbank (from 1945)
Established 1875 (Reichsbank)

The bank was set up in order to unify and organize the note issue. The post WW2 central bank has been modelled on that of the US. The Bundesbank is not subject to direct instruction on monetary policy by the German government.

		1875	1891	1945	1988
1	Ownership	P	P	G	G
2	Management	J	J	G	G
3	Money issue	M	E	S	S
4	Monetary policy	I	I	I	I

1 The bank was originally a private concern but was nationalized in 1945.
2 Prior to 1945 the directors consisted of both private shareholder appointees and governmental appointees. Since 1945 the governor and the directors of the bank, of which there are no more than ten, have been appointed by the president. They are appointed for a fixed period of eight years, on the advice of the Council of the Bank. The Council consists of eleven presidents of the 'Land' Central Banks nominated by parliament, the governor and the directors of the bank.
3 The main purpose of the bank was to unify and organize the note issue. This was a somewhat difficult task as there were many note issuers at the time. In view of the large number of local banks issuing notes, the Federal Council decided to review the situation every ten years starting from 1891. The banks who did not agree to this law found that their notes were not be accepted outside their state. As recently as 1922 there existed more than one issuer of notes and coins. In fact the Bank Law of 1924 gave the bank exclusive rights to issue notes above a certain denomination in addition to giving rights of issue of lower denominations to four other banks. Also notes of a value less than RM10 could be issued with the consent of the government.
4 The bank has always been independent of the government. This situation was formalized in the postwar structure whereby the government is responsible for fiscal and exchange rate policy and the bank for monetary policy.

Source: Conant (1929), Kirsch and Elkin (1932), Goodhart (1986), Smith (reprint 1990).

India

Reserve Bank of India Established 1935

The bank was established while India was under British rule and therefore there is a similarity between the structure of the two banks. With decolonization and separation in 1948, India decided under Nehru to follow the socialist path. One result of this was an end to the private central bank in which the shareholders elected half the board of directors. Instead came government ownership, government appointed directors, and government direction.

		1935	1948	1988
1	Ownership	P	G	G
2	Management	J	G	G
3	Money issue	S	S	S
4	Monetary policy	D	D	D

1 The bank was established as a private bank with a capital of Rs5 million, of which Rs220,000 was reserved for the government of India. The government holding was held by directors nominated by it. The 1948 Reserve Bank Act nationalized the bank, and all shareholders were paid Rs118.10 per share in the form of a government promissory note bearing 3% interest p.a.
2 Prior to 1948 the government selected the governor, two deputies and four directors. The government also appointed an official who was present at all board meetings. The remaining eight directors were selected by the shareholders. After nationalization all directors were appointed by government.
3 The bank took over the sole control of the note issue from the government. The new socialist government continued to keep note issue under the sole control of the bank.
4 A dependent bank. In the early years the government was the only major customer of the bank and had a large representation on the board. The result of this was that monetary policy was largely dependent on the government. Nationalization formalized this relationship between the bank and government, where the former was subservient to the latter. The 1948 Act allowed the central government to give directions to the bank which it considered to be in the interest of the public.

Sources: Sayers (1952).

Italy

Banca D'Italia Established 1893

The bank is a private concern formed as a result of a merger between four of the six banks of issue at the time. It gained the sole right to issue notes in 1926. Any monetary policy measures by the bank have to be approved by the 'Inter-ministerial Committee for Credit and Savings'.

		1893	1926	1988
1	Ownership	P	P	P
2	Management	P	P	P
3	Money issue	M	S	S
4	Monetary policy	U	U	U

1 The bank was a result of a merger between four banks of issue and all previous shareholders continued to own shares in the new bank. The Banking Law of 1936 limited ownership of the bank to public law banks savings banks, banks of national interest, social security institutions, and insurance companies.
2 The governor of the bank is appointed for an indefinite period by the board, on the approval of the president. The remaining thirteen directors are elected by the shareholders for a three-year period with reappointment allowed.
3 The bank gained the sole right to issue notes and coins in 1926, prior to which there existed many issuing banks.
4 Unclassified. The bank has to seek approval from the Inter-ministerial Committee for Credit and Savings for any monetary policy measure.
Sources: Sayers (1952).

Japan

Bank of Japan Established 1882

After the Meiji restoration, the Japanese looked to the West for a central bank model, and found one in the National Bank of Belgium. However, in practice the bank is significantly different from its original model.

		1882	1885	1942	1988
1	Ownership	J	J	J	J
2	Management	G	G	G	G
3	Money issue	X	S	S	S
4	Monetary policy	D	D	D	D

1 The government is a partner but is allowed to own only half the capital.
2 Prior to the Second World War the governor and his deputy were selected by the Crown on the advice of the government. The period of governorship was fixed at five years with reappointment allowed. The government also appointed two-thirds of the ordinary directors, while the shareholders selected the remaining third. Ordinary directors were selected for a fixed period of four years. After the war the governor and his deputy were appointed by the cabinet. The ordinary directors are selected by the Minister of Finance from recommendations of the governor. All positions are for a fixed period of four years for the governor and his deputy and three for the ordinary directors.
3 Monopoly authority to issue notes and coins was given to the bank in May 1884, although these did not reach circulation till 1885. Prior to 1884/85 the bank did not issue any notes or coins.
4 The Bank of Japan Act 1884 states that 'The Government shall control all the operations of the Bank of Japan, and shall prevent not only any operation which is contrary to the Act or By-laws, but also any measure that the Government may deem disadvantageous for the state'. This tight grip on the Bank continued after the war, when the bank was subject to extensive supervision. Pressnell (1974) notes 'The Minister of Finance is empowered to issue general directives and may give supervisory orders to the bank. The Minister also appoints the Comptroller of the Bank of Japan, who superintends its business. The Minister can also dismiss the officers of the Bank. In addition to this general supervision, the government has the power to permit, approve and decide various individual matters of the Bank's business, so that almost all aspects of its activities including policies, organisation, note-issue and accounting, are under the government's control.'

Source: Conant (1929), Kirsch and Elkin (1932), Pressnell (1974), Goodhart (1986).

New Zealand

Reserve Bank of New Zealand Established 1933

The bank was initially jointly owned by private shareholders and government. However, the Labour government of 1936 nationalized the bank and formalized the relationship between the two.

		1933	1936	1988
1	Ownership	J	G	G
2	Management	J	G	G
3	Money issue	S	S	S
4	Monetary policy	D	D	D

1 The bank began life jointly owned by the government and private shareholders. Private shareholders were allowed to invest in one-third of the bank's capital of £NZ1.5 million and the government the remainder. No single shareholder was permitted to own more than £NZ2,500 of the bank's capital. However, the newly elected Labour government of 1936 nationalized the bank.
2 Prior to 1936 the directors were selected on the basis of three by the state and four by the shareholders. After 1936 all directors are selected by the government. The changes in 1936 gave the Secretary of the Treasury voting rights which were previously denied to him.
3 The bank is sole issuer of notes and coins.
4 Before nationalization the bank had some degree of independence from the government. In 1936, this independence was lost and the bank behaved more as a department of the government than as a separate institution.

Source: Plumptre (1940).

Spain

Bank of San Fernando (until 1856) Bank of Spain (from 1856) Established 1829 (Bank of San Fernando)

The bank's privileges and activities were initially restricted to Madrid and to places where it had branches. The Act of 1856 extended the bank's privileges to all parts of Spain.

		1829	1874	1931	1988
1	Ownership	J	J	J	J
2	Management	J	J	J	J
3	Money issue	M	S	S	S
4	Monetary policy	D	D	D	D

1 The Bank Law of 1921 increased the capital of the bank to P177 million with a facility to increase it on the approval of the shareholders and government. Shareholders receive a guaranteed 10% p.a. from net profits and any excess is shared with the government.
2 The governor is appointed by the government and the two assistant governors by the council of the bank. The council of the bank consists of twenty-one members of which fifteen are elected by shareholders. Of the remainder three are selected by various official organizations and three by the state. Apart from the three state appointed directors all directors have to deposit a given number of shares as guarantee. Only Spanish citizens are eligible to be directors.
3 The Bank Law of 1874 gave the bank the exclusive privilege to issue notes and coins. The existing banks were forced to liquidate their circulation and transfer it to the Bank of Spain.
4 A Dependent bank. The bank has to seek the approval of the Minister of Finance on matters of monetary policy.
Source: Conant (1929), Kisch and Elkin (1932).

Sweden

State Bank of Sweden Established 1656

This is the world's oldest central bank. From its establishment until the 1830s it was the only bank in Sweden.

		1656	1668	1809	1988
1	Ownership	P	G	G	G
2	Management	P	G	G	G
3	Money issue	M	M	S	S
4	Monetary policy	D	D	D	D

1 The bank was originally established as a private concern, which became a state institution in 1668.
2 The Constitution of 1809 stated that the president of the bank and his deputy should be selected by the Crown. It also stated that five ordinary directors be appointed for three years by the Riksdag (i.e. the Parliament) All directors including the president and his deputy are answerable to the Riksdag. Only Swedish citizenship directors of other banks can be directors of the bank.
3 Article 72 of the 1809 constitution gave the bank the sole right to issue notes. However, this did not become fully effective until 1904.
4 The 1809 constitution put the bank under the guarantee of the Riksdag. It also increased the political pressures placed on the directors. All matters regarding monetary policy have to be approved by the Minister of Budget and Economics.
Source: Conant (1929), Kisch and Elkin (1932), Goodhart (1986).

United Kingdom

Bank of England Established 1694

The Bank was founded as a private institution which carried out some functions as an agent for government. The newly elected Labour government of 1945 nationalized the Bank.

		1694	1844	1946	1988
1	Ownership	P	P	G	G
2	Management	P	P	G	G
3	Money issue	M	S	S	S
4	Monetary policy	I	I	D	D

1 The bank was a private concern until 1946 when it was nationalized by the recently elected Labour government of 1945.
2 The directors of the bank consisted of 13 ordinary directors, a governor and his deputy. The directors were selected by shareholders owning shares to the value of £500 or more. All directors have to be natural born or naturalized British subjects. After nationalization directors were appointed by the government.
3 When the bank was established there existed a number of banks which issued notes and coins. However the Bank of England Act of 1844 gave it a monopoly of note issue. Banks which had previously issued notes were allowed to continue at a fixed rate of their average level prior to 1844. However, this did not extend to Scottish banks who still issue their own notes.
4 Prior to nationalization the bank was largely independent from the government. However, at times it obeyed the government in return for certain favours and privileges. After nationalization it was largely a dependent central bank.
Source: Kisch and Elkin (1932), Goodhart (1986), Smith (reprint 1990).

USA

Federal Reserve System Established 1913

Before the Fed was established, one of the most extensive studies regarding central banks was carried out. The study began in 1908 and ended in 1912. The following year the

		1913	1988
1	Ownership	MB	MB
2	Management	J	J
3	Money issue	S	S
4	Monetary policy	I	I

1 The bank is owned by all the member banks of the Federal System.
2 The seven members of the Federal Reserve Board are selected by the president of the country, on the approval of the senate, for a fixed period of fourteen years. Two members from the board are selected by the president of the country to be chairman and vice-chairman for a four-year period with reappointment allowed.
3 Article 16 of the 1913 Constitution gives the bank the sole right to issue notes and coins.
4 Decisions relating to matters of monetary policy are made by the Open Market Committee consisting of the members of the Federal Reserve Board, the president of the Federal Reserve Bank of New York, and four presidents from the Federal Reserve Banks. The four presidents from the Federal Reserve Banks are selected for a fixed one-year period on a rotating basis. Decisions made by the committee are reached by a simple majority.
Source: Conant (1929), Kisch and Elkin (1932), Goodhart (1986), Smith (reprint 1990).

Federal System of banks was established in order to furnish an elastic currency, to afford a means of redistributing commercial paper and to establish a more effective supervision of banking.

The basic case for an independent central bank—a formal model

The model draws out the monetary policy implications of one of the principal incentives to inflation—a government's desire to win elections. The algebra follows Neumann (1990) rather than Barro and Gordon, whose model is more complex. The simpler model makes the valid point—that policy-makers have to have their hands tied if they are to deliver zero inflation once they have promised it.

The government has realized that inflation is costly, so announces as an inflation target $\pi^* = 0$. But it also wants unemployment below the natural rate. (Presumably the natural rate is too high because of distortions, such as non-lump sum taxes, which the government chooses not to eliminate.) Employment above the natural rate is achieved by surprise inflation $\pi_t > \pi_t^e$. (It is assumed that the choice of π_t has no effect on the future output/inflation trade-off. This lets an infinite horizon maximization problem be collapsed to a single period one.)

$$\text{The government maximizes} \quad \alpha(\pi - \pi^e) - \frac{\beta(\pi - \pi*)^2}{2} \quad \text{with } \pi* = 0.$$

The first, linear, term describes the profit deriving from the employment goal; the second, quadratic, term the cost associated with deviating from price stability. The 'profit' function is linear, the loss function quadratic; α and $\beta/2$ are by assumption fixed weights.

There are two possibilities to consider. First, the government announces its objective as $\pi^*=0$, and the public believes them and acts accordingly, i.e. $\pi^e = \pi^* = 0$. It now pays the government to inflate. It chooses the inflation rate which maximizes its profit function given π^*. The policy is 'time inconsistent', in the sense that policymakers have an incentive to deviate from the announcement once private agents are committed to acting as if the announcement were to be followed (see Kydland and Prescott, 1977). Maximizing the 'profit equation' with respect to π produces $\pi = \alpha/\beta$, i.e. π does not turn out to be zero. Alternatively, let private agents assume $\pi = \alpha/\beta$ in their wage contracts; they are rational, and act in anticipation of what the government will do. There is no output gain from delivering $\pi = \alpha/\beta$. The first term in the government's profit function is equal to zero, and total negative—it loses popularity. To summarize, because the government has an incentive to disregard its announced zero inflation objective the moment wage bargains are concluded, the announcement is not credible.

The problem arises because there is no mechanism to bind the government; there can only be incentive. The incentive has to be inflation sufficiently high for the loss from further inflation to equal the gain from higher output. In this simple model, the rate is positive—and thus too high, as the desired rate is zero. Barro and Gordon (1983a) develop a Nash equilibrium solution where, regardless of the desired rate, the actual rate is too high. The above is of course a special case of this.

REFERENCES

Alesina, A. (1988) 'Macroeconomics and Politics', *NBER Macroeconomic Annual 1988*, Cambridge, MA: MIT.

——(1989), 'Politics and Business Cycles in Industrial Democracies', *Economic Policy*, April, 55–98.

Auburn, H. W. (1966) *Comparative Banking*, London: Waterlow & Sons.

Bade, R. and Parkin, M. (1987) 'Central Bank Laws and Monetary Policy', *University of Western Ontario Department of Economics Discussion Paper.*

Banaian, K., Laney, L. O., and Willett (1983) 'Central Bank Independent: An International Comparison', *Federal Reserve Bank of Dallas Economic Review*, March, 1–13.

Barro, R. J. and Gordon, D. B. (1983a) 'A Positive Theory of Monetary Policy in a Natural Rate Model', *Journal of Political Economy*, 91(4), 589–610.

——(1983b) 'Rules, Discretion and Reputation in a Model of Monetary Policy', *Journal of Monetary Economics*, 12(1), 101–22.

Cagan, P. (1956) 'The Monetary Dynamics of Hyperinflation', in Friedman (ed.), *Studies in the Quantity Theory of Money*, University of Chicago Press for NBER.

——(1986) 'Conflict between Short and Long Run Objectives', in Campbell and Dougan (eds), *Alternative Monetary Regimes*, Baltimore: John Hopkins University Press.

Capie, F. H., Mill, T. C., and Wood, G. E. (1991) 'Money and Prices in the Great Depression', in Foreman-Peck (ed.), *Reinterpreting the later Victorian Economy*, Cambridge University Press.

Conant, C. A. (1927 reprint 1969) *A History of Modern Banks of Issue*, London: Augustus M. Kelly.

Creighton, J. H. (1933), *Central Banking in Canada*, Vancouver: Clarke & Stuart.

Fair, D. E. (1980) 'Relations Between Government and Central Bank: A Survey of Twenty Countries', *Committee to Review the Functioning of Financial Institutions*, Cmnd 7937 Appendix 8 pp. 557–72. Summarized in *The Banker*, October, 31–41.

Friedman, M. (1962) 'Should There be an Independent Monetary Authority?' in Leland B. Yeager (ed.), *In Search of a Monetary Constitution*, Boston, MA: Harvard University Press.

——and Schwartz, A. J. (1982) *Monetary Trends in the United States and in the United Kingdom 1870–1970*, University of Chicago Press for NBER.

Garfinkel, M. (1989) 'What is an Acceptable Rate of Inflation?,' *Federal Reserve Bank of St Louis Review*, 71, 3–15.

Glasner, D. (1989) *Free Banking and Monetary Reform*, Cambridge University Press.

Goodhart, C. A. E. (1985) *The Evolution of Central Banking: A Natural Development*, London: School of Economics and Political Science.

——(1986) 'Financial Innovation and Monetary Control, *Oxford Review of Economic Policy*, Winter 2(4), 79–102.

Hume, D. (1752, reprint 1906) *Political Discourses*, Walter Scott.

Kisch, C. A. and Elkin, W. A. (1932) *Central Banks: A Study of the Constitutions of Banks of Issue, with an Analysis of Representative Charters*, London: Macmillan.

Kydland, F. E. and Prescott, E. C. (1977) 'Rules Rather than Discretion: The Inconsistency of Optimal Plans, *Journal of Political Economy*, 85, 473–91.

Lees, F. A., Botts, J. M., and Cysne, R. P. (1990) *Banking and Financial Deepening in Brazil*, London: Macmillan.

Lucas, R. E. (1972) 'Expectations and the Neutrality of Money', *Journal of Economic Theory*, April, 103–24.

Masciandaro, D. and Tabellini, G. (1988) 'Monetary Regimes and Fiscal Deficits: A Comparative Analysis,' in Cheng (ed.), *Monetary Policy in the Pacific Basin Countries*, Norwell, MA: Kluwer Academic.

Mills, T. C., and Wood, G. E. (1992) 'The Gibson Paradox Reexamined', in Broadberry and Crafts (eds), *Money Trade and Business Cycles: Essays in Honour of A. G. Ford*, Cambridge University Press.

Mitchell, B. R. (1981) *European Historical Statistics 1750–1975*, London: Macmillan.

——(1982) *International Historical Statistics: Africa and Asia*, London: Macmillan.

——(1983) *International Historical Statistics: The Americas and Australasia*, London: Macmillan.

Neufeld, E. P. (1955) *Bank of Canada Operations 1935–1954*, University of Toronto Press.

Neumann, M. J. M. (1990) 'Precommitment to Stability and Central Bank Independence', Sonderforschungsbereich 303, Discussion Paper B 152.

Phelps, E. A. (1973) 'Inflation in the Theory of Public Finance', *Swedish Journal of Economics*, 75, 67–82.

Plumptre, A. F. W. (1940) *Central Banking in the British Dominions*, University of Toronto Press.

Presnell, L. S. (1974) *Money and Banking in Japan*, London: Macmillan.

Quintero Ramos, A. M. (1965) *A History of Money and Banking in Argentina*, University of Puerto Rico Press.

Sayers, R. S. (1952) *Banking in the British Commonwealth*, Oxford: Clarendon Press.

——(1962) *Banking in Western Europe*, Oxford: Clarendon Press.

Schwartz, A. J. (1987) *Money in Historical Perspective*, Chicago University Press for NBER.

Smith, V. (reprint 1990) *The Rationale of Central Banking*, London: Liberty Press.

Stokes, M. L. (1939) *Central Banking in Canada*, Toronto: Hunter Rose.

Taylor, J. E. (1975) 'Monetary Policy during a Transition to Rational Expectation,' *Journal of Political Economy*, 83(5), 1009–22.

Weston, R. (1980) *Domestic and Multinational Banking*, London: Croom Helm.

Williamson, J. and Wood, G. E. (1976) 'The British Inflation—Indigenous or Imported?', *American Economic Review*.

14

The IMF as an International Lender of Last Resort*

INTRODUCTION

The international monetary system has been in some turmoil and is currently under review. There is widespread and recurrent discussion on the need for a new international financial architecture. The last great debate was in the 1930s and early 1940s when there was disenchantment with the floating exchange rates which had come to replace the defective restored gold standard of the 1920s. Out of that previous discussion a new international monetary system was designed—one that came to be called the Bretton Woods system, and which had the International Monetary Fund at its centre. The 'system' came to be described as working (or being in place) from 1946 to 1971/73, although some commentators preferred to date it from 1958 (when currency convertibility was restored) until the late 1960s. But as more questions have been asked the whole notion of a system has been called into question.

This article considers the origins of these previous discussions and the design they produced. It questions the extent to which the design really came into being, and the role that the IMF then played, for perhaps the Fund played a role other than the one planned. But be that as it may, when floating rates returned the Fund seemed to have lost its role altogether, and yet it has survived and even flourished. How it has done this is then considered before we raise some questions about its possible future role: can it be a lender of last resort; or a crisis manager; a policeman or a fireman; or would it be better if it were wound up? We conclude that the case for the last has been gaining force.

* Originally published as Forrest Capie and Geoffrey E. Wood, 'The IMF as an International Lender of Last Resort', *The Journal of International Banking Regulation*, Vol. 1 (1986), No. 3, reproduced with the permission of Palgrave Macmillan.

BACKGROUND

The proximate origins of the IMF can be found in the period between the two world wars. The story has several strands that need to be identified. After World War I the nationalism that played its part in bringing the war about continued and even intensified. This was manifest in various ways, finding its economic expression in increased barriers to trade, wrangling over war debts, and reparation payments. It generally soured international relations. While there were some attempts at putting the world economy together again in its nineteenth century form, the noble sentiments expressed on the world stage seldom found support at the national level.

It was this climate, together with the failure of the faulty restored gold standard, compounded by the ineptitude of the Federal Reserve in the years 1928–32, that initiated and exacerbated the Great Depression in the US, which in turn had worldwide ramifications. The resulting mixture of dirty/managed exchange rates in the 1930s provoked a series of competitive devaluations—something future designers of the international monetary system would want to avoid.

What has to be remembered throughout this discussion is that the principal participants were the US and the UK—the two major economies in the free world and the key currency countries; though there was to be an attempt to destroy the latter concept. This is important because the final outcome—the IMF and other associated institutions—had perhaps more to do with British and American monetary and trade matters than with a wider concern with, and analysis of, the world economy, though some of that was obviously involved.

An important element in the story was capital movements. World War I and its unsatisfactory outcome in terms of the resolution of many issues had created a great deal of political uncertainty in Europe and stimulated a corresponding amount of capital flight. Some flight was prompted by fear that the capital would not be able to be moved. From World War I through the 1920s there was flight from all parts of Europe. There was too a 'normal' change in the direction of capital flows when, for example, American investment in Germany began to be returned in the late 1920s as the New York stock exchange boomed. But the really large movements of capital were provoked by the increasing uncertainty generated at the turn of the decade by the spreading world depression and further political developments. When the Nazis emerged as the second-largest party in the Reichstag in 1930 things got worse. In the summer of 1931 the Bruning government introduced exchange controls, and a standstill on short-term debt owed abroad was negotiated. Not surprisingly, capital flight increased. There were fears that Britain would do something similar and in September 1931 it did. Many other countries followed suit soon after, and it was at that point that exchange controls proliferated.

Although Britain did not suffer greatly in the Great Depression (output fell less than 6 per cent against the US fall of around 35 per cent) it did nevertheless behave as if it were affected. For example, it reversed its free trade policies of almost a century and introduced a general tariff. At the same time Britain saw in its Empire a possible solution to trade and output concerns, for it contemplated turning the Empire into a customs union. At the Ottawa conference of 1932 it did something less than that but nevertheless did sign a large number of trade agreements with Empire partners, and more significantly extended preferential treatment to Empire countries—imperial preference. This is of significance because of the extent to which it upset Britain's biggest trading partner, the US (we return briefly to this issue below). Tension between the US and UK had also blown up earlier over Britain's share of reparation payments from Germany after World War I.

Ever-spreading trade barriers, arising in part out of the depression and some in part from retaliatory strikes against the US for the introduction of the Smoot-Hawley tariff in 1930, provoked further impediments to international discourse. All manner of obstacles appeared: quotas, bilateral settlements, clearing arrangements, exchange controls, and invisible barriers to trade. Some would go so far as to say that all this led inexorably to World War II. Whether or not that is too strong, it is clear that great damage was done to the international economy: international trade collapsed between 1930 and 1935 and had barely made any recovery by 1939. International economic relations had deteriorated, to an actual or potentially disastrous extent depending on one's view of the origins of World War II.

Lying as an irritant within this, as noted above, was the British favourable treatment of its Empire partners. The US was bitterly opposed to this discriminatory system. Thus it was that soon after the US granted lend-lease to the UK early in 1941 the Americans presented the bill for their services: '. . . a commitment was required from Britain to work with the US towards elimination of trade restrictions . . . and in particular Britain's system of imperial preference . . . ' (Pressnell, 1997).

It is here that we begin to see the direct link with the 1930s. Given that what was widely accepted would be Britain's balance of payments position after the war (little to export with still strong demand for imports) it was felt that some safeguards would be needed if Britain were to abandon the imperial preferential apparatus. In order to allow Britain to do this Keynes drafted in 1941 his proposal for an International Clearing Union—which was the basis of the 'Keynes Plan' for the new international monetary system. Keynes himself described it as utopian. It seemed to cover all international finance from post-war reconstruction through development finance, an investment board, and so on. And of course the British were keen to restore the position of sterling after the war in part to demonstrate Britain's ability to maintain its status as a leading power. It was not at all clear that the US was supportive of Britain's stance. The scheme would attend primarily to short-run balance of payments adjustments. The institution would issue a new international currency (the 'bancor') which would be held and used by central banks for settling the external account. The union would be there to provide liquidity with a view to keeping exchange rates stable. The plan was put forward in the midst of continuing Anglo-American talks on monetary and trade matters that ran through the war. Through Harry Dexter White, the US proposed a more limited stabilization fund. It is important to remember at this stage that the US had established their own exchange stabilization fund in 1934 to operate under the control of the Secretary of the Treasury. The White plan was more conservative than Keynes's in that it saw the new institution's reserves being made up of national currencies and gold rather than the institution having the power to create a new money.

By the spring of 1944 the two proposals had been combined into 'The Joint statement of Experts on the Establishment of an International Monetary Fund'. As is well-known, the plan adopted was closer to the White plan than to the Keynes plan, but it inclined in some respects to the international clearing union in that it sought to avoid interference with domestic policies. The concentration was on developed industrial countries and although the stabilization fund had initially envisaged the new institution being a policeman with discretionary powers, it was to rely on the member countries behaving responsibly. Later that year it had developed into the Bretton Woods Agreements to establish the IMF and the World Bank. The White plan reflected the interests of a creditor nation, the Keynes plan those of a debtor.

Following the upheavals of the inter-war years the aims for the new international financial architecture of the time were to have stable and 'realistic' exchange rates, with countries in difficulty having access to adequate international reserves to smooth out short-term problems. Good behaviour would be expected and some codes of behaviour put in place. This ambition in a manner aimed to incorporate the good aspects of the past (the international pre-1914 gold standard) with the removal of problems of the 1930s (restrictions and emphasis on domestic survival).

THE BRETTON WOODS AGREEMENT

Following several years of Anglo-American discussions, more than 300 representatives of 44 countries met in the US in the small New Hampshire town of Bretton Woods in the summer of 1944. These meetings were to reach agreement on the details of the drafts submitted. The essence of the agreements was that the IMF would provide assistance to member countries to manage balance of payments in a way consistent with stable exchange rates, and would supply credit where needed. The principal obligation of members was to allow free convertibility for current account transactions—capital account controls were permitted. The Fund was established in 1945 and began operations in 1947. But it had become apparent immediately that there was going to be a longer transition period than anticipated—the British were unsuccessful in their attempt (made under strong US pressure) to restore convertibility in 1947. Countries were therefore allowed a longer period in which to do this. The major industrial countries achieved some limited current account convertibility in 1958. However, most countries did not and persisted with exchange controls, at least on the capital account, to the 1990s.

It was increasingly being recognized that the world never, or at best for a very short time, followed the Bretton Woods rules. As McKinnon (1993) has recently summarized it, the post-war monetary order envisaged by its designers had six main elements:

- fixing a foreign par value for domestic currency by using gold, or a currency linked to gold;
- keeping the exchange rate within 1 per cent of its par value in the short run;
- free currency convertibility for current account but use of capital controls;
- use national monies symmetrically in foreign transactions;
- draw on official reserves and IMF credits for shortrun payments imbalances and sterilize domestic monetary impact of exchange market intervention; and
- each country to pursue its own price level and employment policies.

The rules were intended to apply to all nations equally, but each country was to be free to pursue its own macroeconomic policies and this could result in differential inflation rates; hence the requirement for long-run flexibility in the exchange rate. This feature was in fact the opposite of the pre-1914 gold standard.

However, although this had been the intention, in fact the US emerged as the only country that could really behave autonomously, while 'other countries were caught in a straight jacket—that is a new and apparently unplanned international monetary standard—where the elbow room for exercising national macro autonomy was limited' (McKinnon, 1993).

So, in fact, a fixed rate dollar standard emerged for the period 1950–70. For industrial countries other than the US this meant a par value for the currency with the US dollar as numeraire, and keeping the exchange-rate within 1 per cent of this value indefinitely; free currency convertibility for the current account but using capital controls, though the latter should be gradually freed; using the US dollar as the intervention currency; subordinate long-run growth in domestic money supply to the exchange rate and US inflation rate; and limiting current account imbalances by using fiscal policy to offset imbalances between private saving and investment. The US had to remain passive in the foreign exchanges, keep capital markets open, pursue independent monetary policy; and maintain its position as net creditor by limiting fiscal deficits. All this was clearly very different from the original intention (McKinnon, 1993).

How did this change from the original intention come about? It might be thought in some ways obvious that it would be very difficult to draw up a set of rules in wartime that would be able to be applied in a post-war world that was bound to be in some turmoil and more uncertain than usual. Feldstein says that instead of accepting 'an arrangement in which exchange rates were determined in the market and national governments had responsibility for some domestic policies, the architects of the system created rules that appeared to be logically attractive but that were inapplicable in practice' (Feldstein, 1993). But following the spread of controls in the 1930s and the collapse of world trade it was not surprising that stable exchange rates should be uppermost in designers' minds.

McKinnon (with others) argues that the Bretton Woods articles never came into effect, for something that was not anticipated was the impact of the Marshall Plan. One of the unknowns that was to materialize quite quickly at the end of the war was the extent of the threat of communism: the Soviet Union had attended the Bretton Woods conference though it was always unlikely it would be a participant. The urgency of containing communism was what prompted the US to support recovery programmes in many countries. Recovery in Europe, and particularly in Germany, was essential and the US made extensive loans to European countries. When the worst harvest of the century and the most severe winter followed one another in 1946 and 1947, problems were exacerbated. In Europe reserves had been nearly exhausted and a desperate shortage of dollars and gold developed. It was here that the Marshall Plan came in. Without it there would have been a huge reduction in the extensive investment programmes which were designed to speed recovery—and so contain the communist threat. The argument in theory was that if a country balanced its budget and let its currency find its level in the market there would be no balance-of-payments 'problem'; though while there can be little argument with that as a proposition, the real question centred on the policy's cost in terms of its effect on output and employment. In normal times these might be pains that had to be borne, but in the context of the 1940s they had to be avoided 'at all costs'. What the plan provided was several billion US dollars for a speedy first-year recovery programme in the form of a mixture of grants, loans, and conditional aid. But its importance for the purposes of this article lies in how it changed the basis of the international monetary system.

Part of the recovery project was the establishment of the European Payments Union in 1950. This helped to restore current account convertibility in Europe using the dollar as the unit of account for calculating credit balances. For the system to work, each country had to declare an exact dollar parity and then follow policies to keep this parity. This began in 1948 and was a means of trying to restore trade and financial stability in Europe which of course were in a mess following the war. Mundell supports some of this story. He says there never was a 'Bretton Woods system'. Instead the Bretton Woods Agreement 'accommodated the rest of the world to an international system that already existed' (Mundell, 1993). He argues that, following the Tripartite Agreement of 1936, 'the essential structure of the gold-dollar standard was already determined' (Mundell, 1993). When World War II came, European currencies became inconvertible, which strengthened the position of the dollar as the international means of settlement and standard of value.

All the immediate and more or less predictable difficulties consequent on the end of the war, together with some exogenous and other unanticipated problems, meant it was impossible for the Fund to behave as planned. Pressnell maintains that the IMF was 'effectively sidelined until the Suez crisis of 1956' (Pressnell, 1997). The failure of sterling convertibility in 1947, the big French devaluation of 1948 (with multiple rates for hard currencies) and Italy's use of multiple rates, followed by Britain's devaluation of 1949, all damaged any prospect of the system working as intended. And of course the US granting of loans and then the Marshall Plan changed the nature of the system.

We have traced the origins of the IMF in the arrangements and discussions of the 1930s and 1940s and noted how in fact a different system came into being than the one intended. Nevertheless, it was a system of pegged exchange rates and the Fund made some contribution to its working by providing short-term resources to countries with balance of payments difficulties. But when President Nixon closed the gold window and the dollar's link with gold was severed at the start of the 1970s, in the event that function appeared to have been made redundant. Yet it was only a few years later in 1976 that a team from the Fund appeared in Britain laying out the kind of monetary policies that should be implemented and followed. The Fund seemed to be carrying on much as before, channelling resources here and there and setting out conditions for the recipients.

The oil price rises and OPEC surpluses of the 1970s presented problems as countries faced the challenge of re-cycling these balances. The resulting problems in turn produced the debt crisis of the 1980s—commercial banks had lent indiscriminately and countries had borrowed too readily. It was then hoped that the crisis could be handled by an external agency—the IMF. While the Federal Reserve and the Bank for International Settlements (BIS) acted quickly they wanted to be assured that others too would help and it was this organizational task that fell to the IMF. Here was the beginning of another possible role—crisis management.

THE IMF AS CRISIS MANAGER

For some years the IMF has seen itself as a 'manager' of international financial crises. It has played this role in Mexico (1994), in Russia, and in East Asia. But what is that role? And, indeed, what is an international financial crisis? In considering these questions we do not touch on the case of Russia; for that seems to the authors to raise interesting and complex issues rather different from the problems in Mexico and the Far East, and which may point to a useful future role for the IMF unlike that which it has recently been trying to achieve.

First it is necessary to be clear about the distinction between fixed and floating exchange rates. The gold standard is the best example of a fixed rate regime. Under that standard, financial problems, including crises, were readily transmitted from one country to another.

Gold flows, capital flows, and trade flows, all held movements in prices together across national borders. To break or weaken these links, the standard had to be abandoned. Without doing so, it was inevitable that (for example) a monetary contraction in one country would affect others: independent national monetary policies were impossible. Under floating exchange rates that is not true. Exchange rates adjust and transmit some shocks; but by adjusting they restrict monetary shocks to the country in which they originated. How, then, under present-day circumstances can a national financial crisis become international, and require the IMF to manage it?

Two arguments have been advanced, both having in common the importance of 'contagion'. Suppose a country experiences some sort of financial panic or crisis in its banking system. Lenders in other countries are then, quite reasonably, unwilling to lend to it. One argument for this causing international problems is that third countries, untarnished by these domestic difficulties, nevertheless lose their creditworthiness. This is sometimes called the 'tequila effect', after what supposedly happened in the aftermath of Mexico's 1994 difficulties. It is argued on the same basis that a ballout of the original country is required, lest contagion produce a wave of crises across the world, with quite likely disastrous effects.

What evidence is there for this 'contagion' actually occurring? Models can undoubtedly be constructed to show it is likely. But has it happened in recent years? Two cases are often cited—Argentina in 1995 as a result of Mexico in 1994, and the problems in the rest of Asia after the collapse of Thailand's currency (the baht) on 2 July, 1997. We consider these in turn.

Argentina had adopted an arrangement in all essential features comprising a currency board in March 1998. The peso was convertible one to one with the US dollar. Inflation fell and fiscal discipline was restored. Then private capital started to flow in. Unfortunately, while monetary and fiscal arrangements had been reformed, no such changes had affected the banking system. It was undercapitalized and, although the central bank had regulatory powers, no improvement in the banking system was effected. Nor, in the event that problems hit this frail system, was the central bank in a position to act as lender of last resort: a currency board arrangement prevents this.[1]

The Argentinian banking system was thus not only fragile: it had no possibility of central bank liquidity support. A cliché is sometimes apt and that is the case here: the Argentinian banking system was an accident waiting to happen. Thus the conventional view of Argentina's problems, in which Argentina is an innocent victim of Mexico's circumstances, misses an important part of the story. The timing is correct: after Mexico's problems, depositors at Argentinian banks did withdraw their pesos and convert them into US dollars, producing, as was inevitable in the absence of a lender of last resort, a sharp monetary contraction. Gross domestic product fell by over 5 per cent in 1995, and unemployment rose from 10 per cent to 17 per cent. This led in turn to a sharp move into deficit by the public sector. No fewer than 205 banks failed in 1995.

It may be the case that observing Mexico led Argentinians to a careful evaluation of their own country's economic situation, and thus to the Argentinian crises. But was that contagion? Rather it was the reverse: it was rational action prompted by a warning from elsewhere, not irrational panic in response to an irrelevant signal.

And what of South East Asia? There can be no claim that Thailand was an innocent victim of bad luck. The baht collapsed not for that reason, but because of surging short-term foreign borrowing, a banking system whose main activity was speculative property lending, and a corrupt government.

What about the other countries which suffered in the fallout? Indonesia, Malaysia, and the Philippines all had to give up their exchange rate pegs. Was this 'contagion'? The case for that is not persuasive. Every one of these countries had adopted an exchange rate peg as a way of reducing inflation. That policy worked: low inflation and manifest investment opportunities led to large capital inflows. These inflows were allowed to affect the domestic money supply.[2] In consequence, prices rose, first of non-tradeables and then, via the pressure of these on costs generally, of tradeables. The real exchange

[1] See Schwartz (1992) for a full discussion of this, and also the section of this article that discusses the meaning of the term 'lender of last resort', though there could be an arrangement as under the gold standard.

[2] What could have been done about this is considered when we discuss the feasible range of exchange rate regimes in a world of mobile capital later in this article.

rates started to appreciate despite the nominal rates being pegged. This led to a rapidly widening current account deficit—far from always bad, but invariably a signal that the cause should be investigated.

It started to be noticed that the banking systems of these countries were not lending prudently what they had borrowed. Non-performing loans were high and rising, especially in the state-owned banks. Local lenders were quite well informed and there was, in consequence, a risk premium on domestic securities. This led banks (and firms) to borrow in foreign currency; while lending substantially in domestic currency. Again like Argentina, the situation was an accident waiting to happen. Thailand may have been the catalyst, but these countries were not innocent bystanders affected by the resulting explosion. Thailand, after all, was followed only by those countries who were themselves in dangerous situations.

Whether these countries might have got by had Thailand not triggered their collapse is an interesting question; but only superficially so, for it is unanswerable. It is plain, though, that they could not go on as they were.

In summary, it is hard to make the case that contagion was a source of problems in these often-cited episodes. The 'tequila effect' on the basis of these episodes—including the one which gave it its name—is an effect without consequences.

Despite the lack of evidence for contagion, it is worth thinking briefly about whether IMF bailouts can be justified. 'Bailouts' were planned at the June 1995 Halifax Summit. The IMF was to establish an 'emergency financing mechanism' the objective of which was to '. . . provide faster access to Fund arrangements with strong conditionality and larger upfront disbursements in crisis situations'. It is worth asking why the IMF is doing this in the absence of spillover effects in episodes where it did not. Such a facility did not exist for Mexico in 1995; its absence led to it being many weeks before a US-organized US$50 on rescue package was assembled. Note that even so, evidence of contagion is lacking. Second, what was that US-organized package used for? It paid off foreign institutions which had invested in Mexico, an action that may be described not only as unnecessary but also as perverse: it protected high-risk–high-reward investments at the expense of the general body of taxpayers. Some IMF spokesmen have defended such bailouts by saying that their absence penalizes the populace in general, and not those who made the policy errors. This raises a remarkable number of points. Who got the bailout money? In the Mexican case, foreign investors. The population then had to struggle to pay back the loan. In Thailand, it ended up bailing out the politically well connected. And of course, too, it raises a more general point. All governments, democratic or not (with the exception of extreme kleptocracies with a very short time horizon), wish for successful economic policies and prosperous economies. They do not deliberately try to impoverish their countries. The availability of these loans does, however, encourage them to take risks, and the risks do not always pay off. They take the loan, not in the expectation that it will be dramatically more expensive to repay than they think, but in the hope that things will work out well. The loans are a permanent temptation to regard 'something will turn up' as a prudent policy.

In short, the case for IMF crisis management as currently practised is fragile.

AN INTERNATIONAL LENDER OF LAST RESORT

It has been argued in several quarters recently that the world would benefit from the creation of an international lender of last resort (LOLR), and that the IMF not only could evolve into this role, but that it is the natural body to take it on and therefore should do so. To clarify discussion of this it is essential first to say what is meant by LOLR in the domestic context, and why it came into being.

THE ORIGINS OF LOLR

The concept has its origins in a problem which can occur in a domestic banking system in a scramble for liquidity as follows. Suppose a bank fails. This gives rise to fears on the part of other depositors about the soundness of their own banks and they go to get their cash accordingly (in the nineteenth century in the form of gold or in Britain as Bank of England notes). But banks do not hold all funds deposited with them as cash, so all banks together cannot cope with a mass withdrawal. One bank could, by getting cash from other banks: but the only and ultimate source of cash in a system with a central bank for the whole system is the central bank.

The problem and the solution were both described well by two eminent nineteenth-century writers on monetary economics. First, the problem:

> If any bank fails, a general run upon the neighbouring banks is apt to take place, which if not checked in the beginning by a pouring into the circulation of a very large quantity of gold, leads to very extensive mischief. (Thornton, 1802)

and then the solution:

> What is wanted and what is necessary to stop a panic is to diffuse the impression that though money may be dear, still money is to be had. If people could really be convinced that they would have money . . . most likely they would cease to run in such a mad way for money. (Bagehot, 1873)

Acting in the way Bagehot prescribed could, it was asserted, prevent the problems associated with a banking system collapse. These problems are many, but most basic is the unanticipated collapse in the stock of money which it would produce. Such collapses cause severe recession, of which the Great Depression in the US is the archetype. But they can be prevented by the following action.

The central bank that experiences such a shock should lend freely on collateral. It should not restrict lending to the classes of security (usually quite narrow) that it would accept for discount at normal times. Advances should be made without limit, on demand, but at a rate of interest above the pre-crisis rate. These loans should be made to the market—that is, to anyone who brings in acceptable security. In addition (and argued in particular by Bagehot) it should be made clear that the central bank will act in that way should there ever be a crisis: this reduces the likelihood of runs because knowledge that the central bank will supply liquidity makes it seem less urgent to scramble for it.

That is the theory. Does it work in practice? There can be no doubt that it does. One often cited item of evidence is that there has been no such banking crisis in Britain since 1866—by 1875 the Bank had accepted Bagehot's advice. The Governor of the Bank of England from 1875 to 1877. H. H. Gibb,[3] described the 1866 crisis as 'the Bank's only real blunder in his experience': but he did not criticize the then Governor, for '. . . the matter was not as well understood then as it is now. . . .'

The other example is the Great Depression in the US. There were several contributing factors, but the major one was undoubtedly the failure of the recently established Federal Reserve System to act adequately as lender of last resort in the waves of bank failures from 1930 to 1933. The Federal Reserve's failure led in 1934 to the establishment of deposit insurance—a perhaps unhappy precedent to which we return.

Less well-known examples are France and Italy. In both countries LOLR action prevented bank runs, and its absence allowed them.

That, then, is the essence of domestic LOLR action. It is rapid, involves the abundant supply of domestic money on the basis of provision of collateral, and does not involve bailing out individual institutions.[4]

We turn now to proposals for an international LOLR before first comparing that proposal with a domestic (i.e. a classic or traditional) LOLR, and then appraising it more generally.

[3] It is worth noting that until the tenure of Montagu Norman (Governor of the Bank of England 1920–44), the Governor usually served only a two-year term.

[4] Even so, there is some degree of moral hazard. This was pointed out by Thomson Hankey, Deputy Governor of the Bank of England, at the time Bagehot wrote. Hankey maintained that without LOLR banks would hold larger reserves. This is undoubtedly true; but subsequent writers have judged this modest increase in moral hazard a price worth paying to insure against crises.

AN INTERNATIONAL LOLR

The most clearly and thoroughly articulated proposal for such an institution was set out by Stanley Fischer in a talk entitled. 'On the Need for an International Lender of Last Resort' given to a joint luncheon of the American Economic Association and the American Finance Association on 3 January, 1999. His talk was in two parts: the first on LOLR, the second on possible activities for the IMF. The key distinction he makes in the first section of his paper is between central banks lending to the market in a crisis, and banks, sometimes central, acting as 'crisis managers'. He calls both 'LOLR' even though in the second activity no lending is involved.

The concept of domestic LOLR has already been discussed. What of crisis management? The UK's 1890 Baring crisis is an excellent example of the Bank of England acting in that role. When that crisis broke there was consternation both in the Bank of England and in government. The reason was that, although Barings was not one of the country's biggest banks, it was one of very high reputation: when the British government introduced its first Treasury bills in 1877 Walter Bagehot praised them as being 'as good as Barings'. There was a fear that if Barings failed, there would be such a run on London that Britain might be forced off the gold standard or, at the least, have to suspend it.

A hurried inspection of Barings suggested that the situation could be saved, but that £10m was needed to finance current and imminent obligations. A consortium was organized, initially with £17m of capital. By 15 November, the news had leaked, and there was some switching of bills of exchange into cash. But there was no major panic and no run on London or on sterling. The impact on financial markets was small. Barings was liquidated, and refloated as a limited company with additional capital and new (but still family) management.

That was an episode of the central bank acting as 'crisis manager'. It ensured that a collective interest was preserved—the stability of London money markets and, indeed, the stability of London as a financial centre. This it achieved by coordinating the various private participants in the rescue of Barings. Coordination might well have been possible without Bank of England action; but even by 1890 the bank had the authority and reputation in the City to make it a natural 'crisis manager'.

Now, it cannot be overemphasized that the role of crisis manager is completely distinct from that of lender of last resort. The former manages events, assures coordination, perhaps coordinates the provision of capital (either long or short term) from a variety of sources. It can be done by any institution with the necessary reputation. LOLR, by contrast, involves the provision of liquidity, not of capital; possibly in almost limitless amounts; and on security.

The aim of this section of the article is not to argue that the IMF has no role as crisis manager. Rather that, as has been the case so far, the crisis manager role is not, and should not be, confused with the role of lender of last resort; we now go on to argue that there can be no international lender of last resort in any useful sense.

One point remains before turning to the ILOLR concept. This is the claim that illiquidity and insolvency can be hard to distinguish in a crisis. Fischer states this well:

> ... the line between solvency and liquidity is not determinate in a crisis—it depends on how well the crisis is managed—[therefore] the task of distinguishing insolvent from illiquid becomes more difficult and an official lender of last resort is likely to be needed to restore normalcy. (Fischer, 1993)

Whether that is relevant internationally is considered below. But international relevance cannot be inferred from domestic, for there is none. As Hawtrey pointed out in 1932, one of the purposes of last-resort lending being on collateral is to avoid having to look at the solvency of the institution which offers the collateral (Hawtrey, 1932). As to valuing the collateral, Bagehot argued (as observed above) that it should be valued at a rate above the precrisis one, but below that (should there be one) would have cleared the market in the crisis.

Nor can domestic LOLR action justify bailout internationally. Here too, Fischer is in error.

> ... Given the externalities that can follow from the failure of a large institution ... the precept (i.e. lend only to the market) cannot be accepted as a general rule of conduct for the lender of last resort. (Fischer, 1993)

Now, what are these 'externalities'? Fischer does not itemize any. Presumably what he has in mind is that one firm's failure imposes losses on others. That is of course true whatever the type or size of firm. Unpaid debts always cause problems. It is hard to see, though, how that can justify the injection of taxpayers' funds. Failure can have its consequences mitigated by orderly liquidation—a matter for the law and, perhaps, for a crisis manager. But the consequences of failure cannot fall on taxpayers: once might be supportable, but even once would be a precedent.

Now we come to dealing directly with the international LOLR concept. Unless the IMF or some other body can issue any currency it wishes on demand and without limit, it cannot act as international LOLR. Many of the advocates of this scheme come close to recognizing this, and urge that the IMF should be given more reserves to enable it to lend more freely. The trouble with that, apart from its ignoring the fundamental point that an international LOLR has not yet been justified, is that the more resources it has, the more it will need. Only when it has enough to be able to replace on demand the entire money stock of an economy with US dollars (assuming that to be the money demanded) will it have enough.

But why should there be such a body in any event? A domestic one is needed because banks cannot suddenly declare that, for example, US dollar deposits at it are no longer redeemable in dollars, but only in a currency of the bank's own issuing which floats against the US dollar. That option is always available to a country; a country can always float its exchange rate.

Of course it may be claimed that countries may wish to avoid that option. Then they can if they wish either adopt another currency ('dollarize') or adopt a currency board and hold reserves equal in value to the domestic money stock. It is always possible to be pushed off an 'adjustable peg'.

In the presence of capital mobility, only truly fixed or freely floating rates are sustainable in the long term. The choice of 'fixed but adjustable' rates is not available: recent experience—Europe in 1992 and 1993, Mexico in 1994–95, East Asia in 1997–98—has gone to confirm Milton Friedman's extraordinarily perceptive 1953 statement:

> Because the exchange rate is changed infrequently and only to meet substantial difficulties, a change tends to come well after the onset of difficulty, to be postponed as long as possible, and to be made only after substantial pressure on the exchange rate has been accumulated. In consequence, there is seldom any doubt about the direction in which an exchange rate will be changed, if it is changed. In the interim between the suspicion of a possible change in the rate and its actual change, there is every incentive to sell the country's currency if a devaluation is expected—or to buy it if an appreciation is expected. (Friedman, 1958)

This conclusion is supported by both the above-cited examples and by the recently burgeoning analytical and empirical literature on currency crises. The conclusion of this now substantial body of literature is that 'fixed but adjustable' exchange rates are not a viable option, as they require a central bank to defend an exchange rate regardless of what is happening to the economy—even though there is freedom not to defend the exchange rate; central banks and governments will not do that, and it is known they will not.

It must also be remembered that when the IMF was set up most countries still had exchange controls. Thus a country, no matter how creditworthy, could not borrow on international capital markets, but only through official agencies. Countries can now borrow on the markets. The claim that sometimes even countries with sound domestic policies cannot do this seems to the authors not well founded. The fall-outs from neither Mexico nor South East Asia affected countries with unblemished domestic financial systems. It is of course true that when the South East Asia crisis broke, many analysts claimed it was unprecedented. Countries with sound government finance and low inflation were experiencing crises. That reaction simply showed that these commentators had little knowledge of financial crises. Such events were common in the nineteenth and early twentieth centuries, when governments were very small, inflation lower than now, and budgets in or close to balance. For a further discussion of this, see Wood (1999).

Accordingly, then, the authors conclude that not only is an ILOLR not feasible but that happily, given that conclusion, it is not necessary either. Note, though, that the authors do not accept Fischer's conflation of LOLR and crisis management. These are separable functions.

CONCLUSION

The IMF was born out of the turmoil that afflicted the international monetary arrangements in the 1930s—competitive devaluations, managed/dirty/floating exchange rates, exchange controls, and so on. But the new arrangements designed at Bretton Woods never got off the ground. Instead post-war conditions resulted in a pegged system based on a US dollar standard being established, something that lasted until the beginning of the 1970s. As James has put it:

> The institutions created at Bretton Woods were fundamentally unsuited to the combination of the international political climate of the early Cold War and the prevalence and persistence of the managed exchange and trade regimes inherited from the 1930s and the experience of war. The Marshall plan and the initiatives associated with it, especially the European Payments Union, produced a much more effective mechanism for promoting recovery and creating incentives for the earliest steps toward trade liberalization. Running what became more and more a key currencies system with the legal obligations and institutions created at Bretton Woods (which had been intended for the management of a quite different international financial order) was like trying to drive along a road with a machine constructed for flying. It can be done, but it is rather cumbersome and might appear to many observers as counterproductive. (James, 1996)

This judgement then is that the IMF was unsuited to the job to which it was assigned. After 1971 it was searching for a different role altogether. A variety of suggestions has been put forward but none has been convincing. The roles of either fireman or policeman have their problems. And we have shown how it cannot be a lender of last resort, while crisis management was something that was done entirely satisfactorily by interested parties in the nineteenth century. But perhaps there is a role in the twentieth century for an external agency with good knowledge of, and relations with, all the central banks. Yet all these problems and doubts together with disaffection over the Fund's behaviour as a surreptitious agency for US foreign aid have led Schwartz to conclude:

> ... two institutions (the ESF and the IMF) that are administered by unelected officials who are not accountable for their actions.... In a democratic society these two institutions should have no right to exist. (Schwartz, 1998)

REFERENCES

Bagehot, W. (1873) *Lombard Street: A Description of the Money Market*, Homewood, IL: Irwin, reprinted 1962.

Feldstein, M. (1993) 'Lessons of the Bretton Woods Experience', in M. Bordo and B. Eichengreen (eds), *A Retrospective on the Bretton Woods System*, University of Chicago Press.

Fischer, S. (1993) in M. Bordo and B. Eichengreen (eds), *A Retrospective on the Bretton Woods System*, University of Chicago Press.

Friedman, M. (1958) 'The Case for Flexible Exchange Rates', in M. Friedman (ed.), *Essays in Positive Economics*, University of Chicago Press.

Hawtrey, R. (1932) *The Art of Central Banking*, London: Longmans Green & Company.

James, H. (1996) *International Monetary Cooperation since Bretton Woods*, Oxford University Press.

Magee, S. and Brock, W. (1986) 'Third World Debt and International Capital Market Failure as a Consequence of Redistributive Political Risk Sharing', in X. Chandon (ed.), *World Debt Crisis*, Cambridge, MA: MIT Press.

McKinnon, R. (1993) 'The Origins of the Fixed Rate Dollar Standard: Bretton Woods or the Marshall Plan?' in M. Bordo and B. Eichengreen (eds), *A Retrospective on the Bretton Woods System*, University of Chicago Press.

Mundell, R. (1993) 'An Agreement not a System', in M. Bordo and B. Eichengreen (eds), *A Retrospective on the Bretton Woods System*, University of Chicago Press.

Neihans, J. (1985) 'International Debt with Unenforceable Claims', *Economic Review*, 65–79, Federal Reserve, San Francisco.

Pressnell, L. S. (1997) 'What Went Wrong? The Evolution of the IMF 1941–1961', *Banca Nazionale del Lavoro Quarterly Review*, 201, 1997.

Schwartz, A. J. (1992) *Do Currency Boards Have a Future*, Occasional Paper No. 88, Institute of Economic Affairs, London.

——(1998) 'Time to Terminate the ESF and the IMF', CMRE Monograph No. 54, December.

Thornton, H. (1802) *An Enquiry into the Effects of the Paper Credit of Great Britain*, Fairfield, NJ, Augustus Kelly (reprinted 1978 with an introduction by F. A. Hayek).

Vaubel, R. (1996) 'The Political Economy of International Money and Finance', in F. Capie and G. Wood (eds), *Monetary Economics in the 1990s*, Basingstoke: Macmillan.

Wood, G. E. (1999) 'Great Crashes in History: Have they Lessons for Today?' *Oxford Review of Economic Policy*, Autumn.

15

Financial Crises from 1803 to 2009: The Crescendo of Moral Hazard*

INTRODUCTION

Since late 2007 the banking systems of the world have been in turmoil. Despite this, there has been little discussion of the classic lender of last resort (LoLR), essentially no consideration of whether the use of that technique could have prevented these banking difficulties leading to the recent sharp economic slowdown and severe recession in many countries, both developed and developing. Our aim in this chapter is to consider why this was; to discuss whether LoLR operations could have prevented or at least mitigated the consequences of what has been often called a worldwide financial crisis; and, if the answer is negative, what this implies for both the LoLR and the range of policy tools which are currently available for the preservation of financial stability.

WHAT IS A FINANCIAL CRISIS?

An implicit definition of a financial crisis was developed in parallel with the policy for how to deal with such episodes. The policy was what has become known as a lender of last resort operation, and, very soon after Francis Baring's 1797 use of the term (in French) Henry Thornton (1802) provided a statement of what the LoLR was, why it was necessary, and how it should operate. This statement was an essentially complete description of the LoLR role as it worked up to the beginning of this century. His statement was made

* Written for the conference and volume in honour of David Lewellyn on the occasion of his retirement. Orginally published as Forrest Capie and Geoffrey Wood (2011), 'Financial Crises from 1803 to 2009: The Crescendo of Moral Hazard', pp. 134–51, in Christopher J. Green, Eric J. Pentecost, and Tom Weyman-Jones (eds), *The Financial Crisis and the Regulation of Finance* (Edward Elgar Publishing Ltd), reproduced with permission.

in a particular institutional context, and it is as well for the sake of subsequent clarity to set out what this context was.

There were many banks in England, all (except the Bank of England) constrained to being partnerships of six or fewer. The joint stock form was not generally allowed until 1826, and limited liability not until 1858. Even with the care that unlimited liability surely brought, failures were common. It is here that the Bank of England comes in:

> If any bank fails, a general run upon the neighbouring banks is apt to take place, which if not checked in the beginning by a pouring into the circulation of a very large quantity of gold, leads to very extensive mischief. (Thornton, 1802, p. 182)

And who was to 'pour in' this gold? The Bank of England:

> if the Bank of England, in future seasons of alarm, should be disposed to extend its discounts in a greater degree than heretofore, then the threatened calamity may be averted. (p. 188)

This was not incompatible with allowing some individual institutions to fail:

> It is by no means intended to imply that it would become the Bank of England to relieve every distress which the rashness of country banks may bring upon them: the Bank by doing this, might encourage their improvidence. . . . The relief should neither be so prompt and liberal as to exempt those who misconduct their business from all the natural consequences of their fault, nor so scanty and slow as deeply to involve the general interests. (p. 188)

Concern should be with the system as a whole. And the reason a 'pouring into the circulation' (to use Thornton's phrase) would stop a panic and thus protect the system was described with great clarity by Bagehot in 1873:

> What is wanted and what is necessary to stop a panic is to diffuse the impression that though money may be dear, still money is to be had. If people could really be convinced that they would have money . . . Most likely they would cease to run in such a herd-like way for money. (1873, pp. 64–5)

In the kind of banking system which Britain had by the mid to late nineteenth century, a system based on gold but with the central bank the monopoly supplier of notes, the responsibility for diffusing 'the impression that . . . money is to be had' clearly rested with the central bank.

That summarizes nineteenth-century theory on the subject. Because the central bank was the main note issuer it was the ultimate source of cash.[1] If it does not by acting as LoLR supply cash in a panic, the panic will continue, get worse, and a widespread banking collapse ensue, bringing along with it a sharp monetary contraction.

[1] After 1844 it gradually became the only note issuer, as other banks which before that date had been banks of issue lost that right as they amalgamated or were taken over.

The practice of that theory developed with remarkable rapidity. Sterling returned to its pre-war gold parity in 1821. The first subsequent occasion for emergency assistance from the Bank was in 1825. A stock market boom developed, particularly in Latin American stocks. There had been a substantial external drain of gold, and there was a shortage of currency. A panic developed, and there were runs on banks. The type of bills the Bank would normally discount soon ran out and the panic continued. If a wave of bank failures was to be prevented, the banks would have had to borrow on the security of other types of assets. On 14 December 1825 the Bank of England suddenly deviated from its normal practice, and made advances on government securities offered to it by the banks instead of limiting itself to discounting commercial bills. Of that change of policy Jeremiah Harman, a director of the Bank, spoke as follows when giving evidence before a Parliamentary Committee in 1832. The Bank had lent money 'by every possible means and in modes we had never adopted before; we took in stock on security, we purchased Exchequer bills, we made advances on Exchequer bills, we not only discounted outright but we made advances on the deposit of bills of exchange to an immense amount, in short by every means consistent with the safety of the Bank, and we were not on some occasions over nice'.

As Hawtrey (1932) wrote of these now famous remarks, 'In reality the advances he describes were of a highly conservative character' (p. 122). But to continue that quotation from Hawtrey:

> The importance of the change in practice was that it admitted a class of borrowers on irreproachable security, who had nevertheless been barred by the previous limitations. The concession was a real one, and it stayed the panic.

Several steps followed in the next few decades. In the 1830s the usury laws were relaxed at least for the Bank. In the 1840s, following the tighter definition of the gold standard in 1844, there was the Chancellor's letter that relieved the Bank of the need to hold to the 1844 Act. That became understood in the 1850s to be a precedent. Interestingly, across these decades the general philosophy was laissez-faire and in banking we do indeed see a steady deregulation. The next step was taken in 1866, with the Overend, Gurney Crisis.

Overend, Gurney, and Co. originated with two eighteenth-century firms, the Gurney Bank (of Norwich) and the London firm of Richardson, Overend and Company. By the 1850s the combined firm was very large; its annual turnover of bills of exchange was equal in value to about half the national debt, and its balance sheet was ten times the size of the next largest bank. It was floated during the stock market boom of 1865. By early 1866 the boom had ended. A good number of firms were failing. Bank rate had been raised from 3 per cent in July 1865 to 7 per cent in January 1866. After February, bank rate started to ease, but on 11 May Gurney's was declared insolvent.

To quote the *Bankers' Magazine* for June 1866, 'a terror and anxiety took possession of men's minds for the remainder of that and the whole following day'. The Bank of England for a brief time made matters worse by hesitating to lend even on government debt. The Bank Charter Act (which, among other things, restricted the note issue to the extent of the gold reserve plus a small fiduciary issue) was then suspended, and the panic gradually subsided.

The failure in 1878 of the City of Glasgow Bank was much less dramatic. The bank had started respectably, was managed fraudulently, and failed. There was fear that the Bank Charter Act would have to be suspended again (see Pressnell, 1968), but no major problems appeared.

Then in 1890 came the (first) Baring Crisis, Barings was a large bank of great reputation; in 1877, when Treasury bills were introduced, Bagehot praised them as being 'as good as Barings'. It nevertheless became involved in a financial crisis in Argentina. The Argentinean government found difficulty in paying the interest on its debt in April 1890; then the national bank suspended interest payments on *its* debt. This precipitated a run on the Argentinean banking system. There was a revolution on 26 July. Barings had lent heavily to Argentina and on 8 November it revealed the resulting difficulties to the Bank of England. The Bank (and the government) were horrified, fearing a run on London should Barings default. A hurried inspection of Barings suggested that the situation could be saved, but that £10m was needed to finance current and imminent obligations. A consortium was organized, initially with £17m of capital. By 15 November the news had leaked, and there was some switching of bills of exchange into cash. But there was no major panic and no run on London or on sterling.

Why the great difference between the first, second, and third of these episodes? The Bank of England had both learned to act as lender of last resort and it had become clear that it stood ready so to act. What the Bank had done wrong in 1866 was to lend 'hesitatingly, reluctantly, and with misgiving... (But) to make large advances in this faltering way is to incur the evil of making them without obtaining the advantage' (Bagehot, 1873). The Bank learned the appropriate action quickly; H. H. Gibb, governor of the Bank from 1875 to 1877 described the 1866 crisis as 'the Bank's only real blunder in his experience'; but he did not criticize the then governor, for 'the matter was not as well-understood then as it is now'.

So by 1866 the lesson that was learned in Britain was that a banking crisis could be stopped by prompt LoLR action. One concern does however arise from drawing that conclusion solely on the basis of British nineteenth-century experience, and it is a concern that, it will emerge, is of particular relevance to current difficulties. It is not quite so clear as Bagehot maintained that the Bank of England's taking on the LoLR role was what brought stability to Britain after 1866, for branch banking was starting to spread rapidly. By the fourth quarter of the nineteenth century, mergers among banks, leading to banks with wide geographical diversification and diversification by type of customer, were well advanced. Branched banks are more robust, at any rate to localized shocks, than unit banks; note that of the 9036 banks which failed in the US in the Great Depression, only ten were branched (Benston, 1990). (This may of course reflect not just the effect of branching, but also of other factors such as scale.) The British experience thus provides somewhat contaminated evidence of the success of LoLR action. A brief glance at some developments in France and in Italy, however, provides evidence free of such contamination.

The Banque de France can trace its origins to a bank founded in 1800 by a group of Parisian banks. Early in its history it was willing to discount commercial paper very freely in the face of liquidity crises. It did so in 1810, 1818, and 1826. But on other occasions it did not, and here the demonstration of the importance of LoLR is clear. In 1848 it allowed the failure of all provincial banks of issue. There is dispute over why it allowed these failures, but whatever the explanation the French experience supports the view that LoLR action contains a crisis, while absence of such action allows a localized panic to turn into a widespread banking crisis.

Italy confirms that lesson. The Kingdom of Italy was established in 1861. After the new state was founded the currency was unified, but there remained several banks of issue. In the 1880s there was a series of crises. Banks had rapidly expanded their loans to industry, and to real estate speculation. Following a rapid expansion in construction, prices collapsed and numerous real estate companies and banks failed. The banks of issue, themselves involved in this, were pressed by government to rescue other banks and in consequence got into severe problems. In 1893 the Banca d'Italia was founded and the number of banks of issue reduced from six to three. By 1907 the Banca d'Italia had adopted the Bagehot principle of lending freely in a crisis (it referred to Bagehot in its 1907 report and accounts), and in 1910 acted in accordance with his principles. In its report of that year, the Bank of Italy wrote:

> At that particular time, what was important to the Italian business community was not so much to obtain funds at reasonable conditions, but to know that credit was still available for good risk transactions. And the Bank did not fail to provide this type of credit.

In contrast to the 1880s, despite there still being a system of many banks each with at most a few branches, there was no crisis in the sense of a run on the banking system. Problems were contained by LoLR action. It thus seems reasonable to conclude that such action is sufficient to prevent localized panic leading to general crisis. This conclusion, based on nineteenth-century and early twentieth-century episodes, was re-emphasized recently, first in Argentina and more recently still in South East Asia. Argentina had adopted what was in all essential features a currency board, fixing the peso against the

US dollar in April 1991. Inflation fell, fiscal discipline was restored, and private capital started to flow in. But there had been no reforms to the banking system. It was undercapitalized, and while the central bank had regulatory powers, because of the currency board arrangement it could act as LoLR to only a very modest extent. The banking system was thus both fragile and without access to abundant central bank liquidity provision in a panic.

Seeing the fall of the Mexican peso (in 1995) depositors at Argentinian banks had the similarities between Mexico's and Argentina's circumstances thrust before them. They withdrew pesos and converted them to US dollars. Inevitably in the absence of a LoLR, there was a sharp monetary contraction. GDP fell by over 5 per cent in 1995, and unemployment rose from 10 per cent to 17 per cent. The still more recent South East Asian experience is similar. In the wake of the collapse of the Thai baht, attention turned to Indonesia, Malaysia, and the Philippines. Banks had been lending extensively in domestic currency while borrowing in foreign currency. When depositors started to withdraw their funds, no liquidity could be provided by the central bank. Again consequent upon lack—indeed impossibility—of LoLR action, severe problems followed.

A brief summary of the evidence, up to the early twentieth century, on the effectiveness of LoLR action in the traditional sense would be that whenever it was used in a banking crisis the crisis ended, and wherever in such times of crisis it was not used, the crisis continued and got worse, usually with serious consequences for the economy affected. This conclusion was reinforced by a very brief glance at the experience of some developing countries late in the twentieth century.

How did the LoLR perform—indeed, was it called on—in Britain, the country of its birth, in the twentieth century?

BRITISH BANKING IN THE TWENTIETH CENTURY

The first problem to hit British banking (and much else besides) in the twentieth century was the outbreak of the First World War. Just like the outbreak of the Napoleonic Wars in 1793, the first economic impact was felt through failure, and the expectation of failure, of remittance from abroad.

The Balkan Wars had left a legacy of political tension in Europe, and there was a widespread belief that problems were not over. Nevertheless the tension was chronic rather than acute until the assassination of the heir to the throne of Austria on 29 June 1914. Even then there was a temporary calm until 24 July, when Austria sent its ultimatum to Serbia. This ultimatum, together with the fear that hostilities would encompass all Europe, created a financial panic.

On the London Stock Exchange in the last two weeks of July there was a rush to sell, and it started to be feared that foreign borrowers would not be able to remit payment to the accepting houses.[2] When war broke out between Austria and Serbia on 28 July there was an immediate scramble for liquidity. The banks called in loans from the stock exchange and the discount market, leading to further falls on the former and forcing the latter to borrow from the Bank of England. Bank rate was raised from 3 per cent to 4 per cent on 30 July. On 31 July the stock exchange closed to trading and bank rate was raised to 8 per cent. The next day bank rate was raised again to 10 per cent. The panic had by this time spread to the general public, and the banks, fearing a drain of gold, refused to pay out gold coin to their customers.

On 2 August there came the formal declaration of war between Russia and Germany. The next day, a Monday, was a bank holiday in Britain, and to provide thinking time the closure of the banks was extended for three days. In addition, to protect the accepting houses from their immediate difficulties a moratorium on bills of exchange was declared. By 6 August the main measures to deal with the crisis had been decided. (Meanwhile Britain had declared war on Germany on 5 August; in those days the British government could walk and chew gum at the same time).

A general moratorium was then declared, the 1844 Bank Act was suspended, and bank rate started to be reduced. Meanwhile, as there were fears of an internal currency drain, plans were made to print Treasury notes. However, when the banks opened again on 7 August this fear turned out to be unfounded, and bank rate was reduced again the next day to 5 per cent. There remained problems in the bill market, and these were dealt with by direct government assistance, plans for which were announced on 13 August and 5 September. Describing the crisis, Hartley Withers (1915) wrote, 'it came upon us like a thunderbolt from a clear sky . . . no credit system could have stood up to the events'; this reflected the view of most contemporary financiers and journalists.

The unexpected and total failure of remittance had placed stockbrokers in difficulties, as they had borrowed to finance the purchase of stock for clients. These securities were often given as collateral for the loan, and as their prices fell so did the value of them as collateral. The resulting forced sales drove prices down further. Had the banks not called in their loans or demanded increased collateral, the secondary selling would not have taken place; it is on those grounds that Keynes and some other contemporaries criticized the actions of the banks.

[2] Accepting Houses guaranteed bills of exchange; discount houses lent on such bills, using both their own capital and funds borrowed from clearing banks; and clearing banks also lent on them, using their own and depositors' funds.

The banks also came under attack over their money market operations. At the end of July 1914 there were some £350m of bills outstanding in the London market. Of these, about £3m fell due each day. The failure of remittance meant that a good proportion of this—that corresponding to loans to foreigners—was irrecoverable for the foreseeable future. The accepting houses, who were liable to meet them on maturity, were immediately in difficulties. They had not expected such a sudden and large increase in defaults. The banks were concerned about the effect on their liquidity position that defaults on these bills would cause, so started to call in funds from the discount market. This in turn forced the discount market into the Bank.

The banks' behaviour was in fact perfectly comprehensible from their point of view. As Withers (1915), Morgan (1952), and Sayers (1976) have all pointed out, taking the liquidity position of the banks into account shows that they had good reason to call in loans from the stock market and the discount market and, to withdraw gold deposited at the Bank of England, another action they were criticized for at the time. For the banks were expecting heavy withdrawals by their depositors and, in addition, a good proportion of their assets had become illiquid or of uncertain value. The failure of international remittance had-rendered one of their most liquid assets, the bill of exchange (then some 9 per cent of total assets) illiquid. In addition, they had themselves accepted some £69m of such bills, and were liable to meet them on maturity. Stockbrokers were in no position to repay many of their loans from the banks, and the banks themselves had their security holdings locked up when the stock exchange closed. All in all it was neither surprising nor unreasonable, despite criticism at the time and occasionally subsequently (for example, de Cecco, 1974) that the banks sought liquidity wherever they could find it.

As is clear, the system coped well after a brief period of panic. A traditional LoLR operation, the provision of funds to the discount market, maintained liquidity in the system. That of course was insufficient, for problems of solvency loomed. Indeed, it was fear over solvency that led to the scramble for liquidity (just as in the case of Northern Rock). A large amount of debt had suddenly, to use a modern term useful in pointing up parallels, become toxic. Looking to precedent, the Bank in 1914 could have recollected the example of Barings in 1890. When that bank had been at risk of insolvency, a lifeboat (another modern term used to help point parallels) was launched and capital provided. But the scale of the 1914 problem was much greater. The Bank did not have a big enough balance sheet to help. The banks were themselves threatened. The government did not have funds immediately available, and a gilts issue was obviously impracticable. Further, supposing anyone had time to think of it as events progressed, there need be no concern over moral hazard and therefore no need to discriminate between the deserving and the undeserving. It was a common shock, one which could not have been insured against except by stopping doing business before the shock had hit the system. The moratorium dealt with the immediate consequences of this shock, and assistance to the bill markets tidied things up subsequently. Suspension of the 1844 Bank Act had always been possible in a crisis, and the issue of Treasury notes turned out to be unnecessary.

Thus the nature of the crisis influenced the solution. It was not a pure liquidity crisis, so other measures were needed. But there was a liquidity crisis, so the LoLR was not redundant, although it had to be supplemented by other policy tools.[3] Certainly at the beginning of the twentieth century, the LoLR played a crucial role in Britain. Did it continue to do so in later British episodes?

PEACE THEN WAR AGAIN

In the inter-war years, although economic performance was mixed, the banking system remained essentially robust. Even in 1931, which is sometimes misleadingly referred to as a financial crisis, the banks performed moderately well. Their profits were down a bit (the full extent was disguised at the time) but there were no grounds for concern about them. There was a currency crisis and the mistake of 1925 had to be corrected but apart from that the system was undisturbed. The Bank had imperceptibly become an overseer of the banking system. When a bank got into difficulty the Bank would suggest to another bank that it might take it over and might indeed itself provide that bank with an indemnity against loss in the process.

Although there was an immediate rise in bank rate when war broke out in 1939, in fact there was no need for it and there was no drama. After the Second World War the banking system continued to remain strong and anyone talking about financial stability in Britain would have been regarded as strange. Financial stability was taken for granted. But then as is frequently the case, after a period of increased competition in 1971–73 and of expansionary monetary policy, there was a huge growth of the fringe banking sector. This sector lay outside the banks subject to credit controls (and in many ways was a consequence of avoiding the controls), and its business model was to borrow in the short-term money markets (the interbank market) and lend on property. A great property boom developed, with all the accompanying dodgy practices that are expected. When the monetary authorities then tightened policy in the face of spiralling inflation, the market turned down, the euphoria

[3] This seems to us an early example of policy assignment, a practice that the Bank of England seems to have followed from 1866.

turned to gloom, property companies failed, and then too the fringe banks seemed in danger.

There were then fears that the difficulties might spread to other parts of the banking system and the Bank launched a rescue operation that came to be called the lifeboat. This should properly be called crisis management of the kind that was organized for Barings in 1891. The question that arises is: why not rely on that former stabilizer, the LoLR, if indeed it were needed? Any bank in difficulty that held good assets could have gone to the Bank and got the necessary liquidity. If they did not hold the appropriate assets then that might be considered poor management and they could be left to fail. If they were thought of as sufficiently good risks then a clearing bank might well have thought it worthwhile rescuing them.

Instead of which the Bank became involved in a long process (many years in some cases) of propping up or winding down a large number of institutions at considerable cost in terms of resources devoted and in some cases in substantial losses. That seems to have been the Bank's approach thereafter: quietly to bail out or otherwise arrange the affairs of banks in trouble no matter how small and insignificant they were. In the mini-crises of the early 1980s and 1990s, and from year to year across the last third of the century, that was the practice. How much moral hazard was being stoked up is hard to say.

THE FRINGE BANKS AND DIVERSIFICATION

The fringe banks got into difficulties for two reasons. They were undiversified, primarily lending on commercial property, and they relied on short-term money to finance long-term lending (just as did Northern Rock). The dangers of lack of diversified lending are highlighted by evidence from past rescues. In the course of the Great Depression over 9000 banks (roughly one-third of all banks) failed in the US. During the same period, in adjacent Canada there were no overt bank failures, although one bank, supposedly the weakest in the Canadian system, merged with another. In Britain there were no bank failures. Even after allowing for the different economic sizes of these countries (and in those days the US was not so large relative to Britain as it is now) there is still a striking discrepancy that requires explanation. It is also worth observing that in any year in the period 1950 to 2000, one could say that more banks had failed in the US in the previous year than had failed in Britain in the previous century. In good times and in bad, banks in the US seemed to be more fragile than those in the UK. Why is that the case?

SYSTEM STRUCTURE

In the US there are many small banks. There were in the 1930s, and indeed still are, unit banks—banks with only one office, concentrated in one area and doing retail banking only. These banks are very exposed to the problems of their local area—a shock, such as a major firm being in difficulties there, and the bank may well fail. These banks were the ones that pre-dominantly suffered as a consequence of the Federal Reserve's mistakes in the 1930s, and these were the banks that so regularly failed over the past century in the US.

In the Great Depression, banks which had diversified geographically to the extent US law at that time allowed, and which had gone into investment as well as retail banking, were more robust than their unbranched retail fellows. And in the UK and Canada, banks were allowed to diversify and had branched not only across the country but, particularly in the UK case, across the world.

Not surprisingly, diversification brought stability. If one line of business or activity in one geographical area of operation did not do well, another did, or at least sufficiently so to keep the bank afloat. The main cause of the wave of bank failures, and subsequent severe monetary contraction in the US, was the behaviour of the Fed, but in the banking sector the burden of the Fed's failure fell predominantly on the small undiversified retail banks. Does that mean that despite the current enthusiasm for separating 'utility banks' (retail) from 'casino banks' (investment), banks should actually be allowed to remain as they currently are, not even nudged to do something else?

The answer is not a simple yes or no. The implications of the above outline of the experiences of bank stability in different countries, and the relationship of bank stability to bank structure, are several. First, investment banking is not necessarily undesirable as an adjunct to commercial banking. It does provide a diversified income stream. But it can also be a more volatile investment stream, so there may well need to be capital requirement differences between banks which carry out investment banking as well as retail banking, and those which are purely retail.

Second, and very important, one should look below the simplistic label 'diversification'. Banks can diversify their businesses and remain different from each other. This, for example, is what British banks did in the late nineteenth and early twentieth centuries, when there was the amalgamations movement and banks diversified across Britain, thus becoming exposed to more varied industries.[4] They also diversified overseas but, quite interestingly, to somewhat different places. There were overlaps between Barclays DCO, Lloyds, Standard Chartered, and the Hong Kong and Shang Hai Banking Corporation (as it then was), but they were far from complete overlaps.

[4] See Capie and Rodrik-Bali (1982).

In other words, so long as banks can diversify and remain different from each other both the individual banks and the system gain resilience to shocks. But if they diversify and in doing so become more like each other, each individual bank may think itself more robust, and rightly so, and the regulators may agree, and rightly so, but the system has become more fragile; for since all banks are now alike, a shock to one is a shock to all. Every individual shock is also a common shock.

There can thus be bad diversification as well as good diversification. The first leads to homogeneity, the second does not. This simple observation has a policy implication of considerable importance. The FSA is committed to moving away from an almost mechanical checking of processes to an examination of banks' strategies (Lord Turner, Oral Evidence, Treasury Select Committee, 25 February 2009). That is sensible from the point of view of ensuring that each individual bank is stable, but it does not tell anything about system stability until these individual strategies are compared. If on doing so they are different, then system stability has been promoted by diversification. But if they are the same, then it has not.

Two questions of considerable difficulty then follow for the regulator. More straightforward, how will similarity be measured? And much more difficult, if similarity is found, what will be done about it? Will one bank be told to do something about it, even if the management thinks it would be to the detriment of their shareholders? These issues seem to us to be rather complex, but as they do not arise from policies which we have proposed we set them aside for others to address. We turn next to some straightforward lessons from our present troubles.

LESSONS FROM 2007–09

The regulation of banks has failed; it must be tougher; and it will be more expensive. Everyone is agreed on these propositions. Such universal agreement is unusual, and is actually easily explained. The first two statements have many possible meanings, and the third is an inevitable part of almost any government's response to a problem—more must be spent.

What should be meant by the first two remarks? What is the kind of regulation to which they lead? First, though, we define what is meant by a bank in the present context. It is a business which takes retail and wholesale deposits and makes loans. By creating deposits it contributes to the money stock, and is part of the payments system. Investment banks, whether of the traditional advisory sort or the modern type which keeps loans on its own books, are for present purposes set aside, with the remark only that when they fail it must be orderly, with due regard for the numerous types of contract and counterparty that they have.[5] When a bank which does both kinds of business fails, the traditional banking part should be handled as described below, and the investment banking part closed in an orderly manner and any remaining value used to protect the 'traditional banking' part.

Why are traditional banks regulated? All firms are regulated, but banks are regulated in a way different from any non-financial firm. There is regulation of how much capital they have, and regular testing to see if it is adequate to withstand a range of possible shocks. What is the point of this? It is undoubtedly troublesome if a bank fails; there is disruption to the businesses and lives of its customers in ways and to an extent that is not true of the failure of most kinds of firm. This does not, however, require extensive regulation, but rather a legal framework so that a bank can 'fail' while continuing to operate. That is to say, as in the US, it should be possible to take a bank away from its shareholders and management while it is still solvent, and keep it running so that all who transact with it can continue doing so. The bank can then be sold on, in an orderly way, in whole or in parts, to buyers who will keep it running and restore it to financial health. The proceeds from the sale can be used to settle the bank's debts, and anything left should go to the shareholders. For banks for which that can be done, the choice of capital ratio could be left to the management of the institutions concerned; they would simply be told that if it went below some fairly arbitrary number their assets would be expropriated. Such a facility exists in the US, was proposed in the UK by the Treasury Select Committee of the House of Commons, and is now embodied in the 2009 Banking Act. With that in place, why is any regulation different from that of non-financial firms necessary?

The answer to that question is in two parts. First, if banks are to be capable of being closed while still solvent, their capital must be monitored, and not just by their management—for in distress there would be a desire to be optimistic at the very least. Second, some banks are so big that taking them over and running them would present enormous problems. It is preferable that such large banks do not fail. In the remainder of these remarks we focus on that second reason for regulation, on the grounds that smaller banks are adequately dealt with by monitoring and prompt closure when necessary.[6] How should 'large' banks be regulated?

[5] The problem of Lehman Brothers was not that it was closed. Inside the US problems were caused by the inconsistency of treatment as compared to, for example, Bear Sterns; and outside the US problems resulted from, inter alia, the fact that normal bankruptcy procedures are intrinsically slow, so many contracts remained open much longer than expected. Indeed, many still are open at the time of writing (June 2009). In addition, only when the bank was closed did regulators discover that it had been the custom always to sweep all cash back to head office overnight.

[6] They would therefore be essentially unregulated apart from the monitoring of their capital.

A digression on liquidity is necessary at this point, for a liquidity shortage can quickly turn into a capital shortage if it forces asset sales at distressed prices. Banks must hold assets which can be readily turned into cash. These must of course include government paper, but they can extend beyond that, for in a time of general shortage of liquidity the central bank should accept a wide range of securities in exchange for cash. In doing so the central bank would be following the precedent set by the Bank of England, to such stabilizing effect, in the nineteenth century, when it started to implement the concept of LoLR. Of course, that action is intended to relieve only a general shortage of liquidity. If an institution cannot get liquidity from financial markets when these markets are not paralysed by panic then that is an institution which has run out of generally acceptable collateral, would start undertaking distress sales, and would soon collapse into the insolvency regime. These points on liquidity apply to small and to large banks alike.

And that brings us back to banks which are too big for the special insolvency regime—not too big to fail, but so big that managing an orderly failure in the sense in which small banks can fail in an orderly fashion would be hard. Such banks raise two problems. The first is how to diminish the risks of their failure, and the second is what to do about them in the long term.

Such large banks should require higher capital ratios than small banks. This is counterintuitive at first glance, because size usually brings diversification, and diversification brings stability. But that is to neglect the problems caused by the failure of such institutions. Second, the capital requirement must, for the same reason, be modelled under extreme assumptions. Extreme outcomes do sometimes occur. Hence, capital ratios should be high. What is high? A way of thinking about this would be to look back and see what capital ratios were required over a period of years, good and bad, for such banks to have the same return on equity as other types of large firms in industries where competition, in the sense of freedom of entry and exit, prevailed. We consider that would be a good starting point because it would mean that at least by that measure banks would be no more risky users of capital than other firms. But it is not a good finishing point. The reason is that it neglects incentives.

There is much concern about the bonuses bankers have received. This concern is largely on their size, and therefore manages to miss not one point but several. The first point is that there is nothing wrong with bonuses, but they must be framed so as to ensure that in a business where continuity is important, they reward not the signing of a deal but its successful conclusion. Second, there should be attention to incentive structures from top to bottom of the firm, and all the way down the firm these structures should, as at the top, encourage efforts to maintain profits rather than simply reward individual deals. Transactions-oriented reward structures should be eschewed for chief executives and loan officers alike. An illustration of the importance of this is given by the much more rapid deterioration of the mortgage books of those firms which relied on independent financial advisors for mortgage business rather than getting it through their own staff dealing, either online or in person, with the mortgagor. Bonuses, whoever they go to, should be paid on the final completion of a deal, not on its successful initiation. That would have an additional benefit—it would inevitably ensure that deals were monitored throughout their life, and perhaps even encourage banks to keep a small stake in every transaction they initiated (as was customary for them to do, as a sign of good faith, until quite recently). At the least banks would not be able to pursue a policy of 'originate and forget'. Third, management should be required to hold shares in their company. This is not foolproof—there was extensive such holding of Lehman's shares, and Andy Hornby, chief executive of HBOS when it fell, had invested all his bonuses in HBOS shares—but it should help to ensure caution, especially if the shares could not be sold until some years (five is a nice round number) after retirement or otherwise leaving the firm.[7] Who imposes these rules is considered immediately below.

Now we come to the firms' owners, the shareholders. In the UK bank shareholders appear sometimes to be a rather strange group. They are strange in that they sometimes behave differently to the banks they own than they do to other types of firm they own. With banks, they can be passive, accepting what the management does to them. With other firms they are much more active in their monitoring. This does not happen all the time, but the takeover by RBS of a foreign bank at the very peak of an asset price boom is a truly striking example of shareholder passivity.[8] It might be helpful if shareholders became at least as active with banks as they are with their other investments.[9] If they do not do so, and fail to pay adequate attention to the incentive structures in the firms they own, should regulators do it for them? That would be extraordinarily intrusive upon rights of ownership; and worse, it might not be effective. The same incentive structure is unlikely to be appropriate across all banks; the managers and owners have information about their own firms that no outsider can possibly have, and they are therefore far and away the best able to devise a sensible incentive structure. There can be no harm in regulators setting out what they see as a set of principles to guide incentive structures, but these should be for discussion, comment, and if

[7] Death would also trigger the right to sell.

[8] This comment does not apply to all shareholders. Many individual shareholders objected, as did some investment trusts and the Legal and General Insurance Company. So far as one can tell from the published correspondence, these objections received only a polite brush off (at best). This episode did also reveal a problem not noticed before. Legal and General even if it had wanted to sell its shares could not do so, as it was running index-tracking funds. How to tackle this issue is of course aside from the theme of the present chapter.

[9] One has to say 'might' because one active major shareholder in a bank targeted very aggressively HSBC, a bank which seemed to be in better shape than most.

shareholders wish, rejection. The consequences of getting it wrong fall primarily on them.

But with all that done, there is yet more. Regulators should prepare for the failure of banks. They should do that because it is almost certain that something will go wrong at some time, and because the consequence of lack of preparedness when Northern Rock got into difficulties was a nearly disastrous bank run. This preparation should have two parts. The regulators should regularly plan what they are going to do in the event of a big bank needing help, and, because each bank will be somewhat different, there should be a plan for every bank, and these plans should be regularly updated. The regulators should also plan, and announce that they have planned to sell off in parts, not as a whole, any big bank that they have to take over. This would have three benefits. It would reduce competition problems arising from the existence of large banks capable perhaps of setting up barriers to entry. While this may not be a problem worldwide, it is surely possible that it becomes so in the UK following the Lloyds Bank takeover of HBOS; after all, competition rules had formally to be waived to allow the takeover to be approved by the competition authorities. Second, it would further encourage management to be cautious. And perhaps most importantly, it would if carried out get rid of one of these troublesome big banks, and give us a few more that would not be 'too big to fail easily'.

WHY NOT JUST LoLR?

Why, having started this chapter by showing the effectiveness of classic LoLR in preserving financial stability, have we added some suggestions for bank regulation? Do not our prior arguments and evidence make such regulation unnecessary? In fact our regulatory proposal derives, as does our defence of LoLR, from examination of the Bank of England's behaviour in the nineteenth century. That examination shows that the Bank's approach to financial stability had more than one aspect.

First it developed and practised LoLR. Second, with Barings in 1890, it refined its objective of systemic stability and became concerned to ensure that any closure of a bank did not threaten the system as a whole, through reputational channels in the Barings case, but disorderly closure would also have been a source of difficulty. It therefore became concerned with individual institutions. Note, though, that the owners of Barings saw their investment in it wiped out, and the management of the institution was replaced from top to bottom.

Such drastic penalties were, very reasonably, not imposed in 1914. Perhaps with the passage of time and no longer remembering how special the crisis of

1914 was, the Bank continued to look after troubled institutions. It did not always do so; but at a minimum it always ensured such institutions a tidy end.[10] This may lie at the root of our present troubles. The idea got about that individual banks, unless actively criminal like the Bank of Credit and Commerce International (BCCI), would always be looked after by the authorities. Thus bank managements and shareholders may have become a little less cautious in both their own lending and borrowing, and in their monitoring of that of others.

Our regulatory proposal is designed to deal with this attitude. We need not go all the way back to 1866 to find an appropriate rule of conduct for the Bank.[11] The Bank should maintain its role in producing a tidy resolution, rapid or slow according to circumstances, of an individual bank problem. But it should be explicit in advance over the fates in such cases of management, shareholders, and bondholders.

The lessons the Bank had learned by 1866 are not sufficient to guide it in the twenty-first century. But the lessons it had learned by 1890, and put into practice with the failure of Barings in that year, are. Tidy failure is necessary: but the price of that tidy failure should fall as fully today on bankers and those who provide them with capital as it did in the 1890 Barings failure.

REFERENCES

Bagehot, W. (1873) *Lombard Street*, London: Henry King.

Benston, G. J. (1990) *The Separation of Commercial and Investment Banking: The Glass-Steagall Act Revisited and Reconsidered*, New York: Macmillan.

Capie, F. and G. Rodrik-Bali (1982) 'Concentration in British Banking 1870–1920', *Business History*, 6, 107–25.

De Cecco, M. (1974) *Money and Empire: The International Gold Standard*, Oxford: Basil Blackwell.

Hawtrey, R. G. (1932) *The Art of Central Banking*, London: Longmans, Green & Co.

Morgan, E. V. (1952) *Studies in British Financial Policy 1914–1925*, London: Macmillan.

Pressnel, L. (1968) 'Gold Flows, Banking Reserves and the Baring Crisis of 1890', in C. R. Whittlesey and J. S. G. Wilson (eds), *Essays in Money and Banking in Honour of R. S. Sayers*, Oxford University Press.

[10] The closure of BCCI may seem an exception to this rule, but in that case the law forced the Bank's hand.

[11] At this point we use Bank as a form of shorthand, to avoid discussion of which of Britain's Tripartite Authorities should have this responsibility. We are concerned in this chapter only to establish that there is such a responsibility.

Sayers, R. (1976) *The Bank of England 1891–1944*, Cambridge University Press.
Thornton, H. (1802) *An Enquiry in to the Effects of the Paper Crêdit of Great Britain*. Reprinted 1978 with an introduction by F. A. Hayek, Fairfield, NJ: Augustus Kelly.
Withers, H. (1915) *War and Lombard Street*, London: J. Murray.

16

Central Banking in an Age of Uncertainty

INTRODUCTION

The title of this chapter may seem a strange one. Are not all periods characterized by uncertainty, greatest of all for those who are alive and have to take decisions at the time? That is undeniably true. But it will be argued here that the present period (the 2010s) is unusually uncertain, in that there are uncertainties not just coming from what might be called 'the world outside', but also over the appropriate objective and targets for a central bank.

In a sense the central bank's mandate is unchanging. We suggest that mandate should be thought of as an instruction from a superior authority to deliver a particular outcome. In central banking terms we think of this as government entrusting the protection of the value of the currency to its bank—what usually became the central bank. So it has for a long time been, 'to protect the value of the currency' or words to that effect. The aim was to provide monetary and price stability. It has usually been implicitly understood that, at various different times and in response to various different events, the acceptable objective for achieving the mandate will change. In the early days what it meant was protection of the gold reserves. At a later point the focus became the exchange rate. It is also worth repeating here something we have always insisted on. There has been throughout central banking history a responsibility, sometimes admittedly implicit, for financial stability, since without that it would be impossible to achieve monetary stability. So while the mandate has been settled for a long time the target has changed over time. When metal coins were the sole form of money their weight and quality were all that mattered for stability. (That generally obtained in most countries prior to the eighteenth century.) When metal became the backing for a currency, albeit one that continued to have metallic coin circulating as well, the price of the currency internationally is what mattered—the exchange rate. (That had generally taken over in the nineteenth century.) And when metal disappeared as backing for currencies the focus became the price level. (That tended to be the case after the 1970s.) With each change the target became less tangible. Indeed the price level is an abstract concept, one which can be measured in a variety of defensible ways, and among which ways of measurement choice can vary and has varied. So just as it was thought the objective had been settled, it has proved on several occasions inadequate.

This has happened in the past. On three occasions in the history of central banking (which we identify largely with the history of the Bank of England, as the world's oldest central bank[1]) an apparently settled position has proved not to be so. In this paper we examine these situations so as to put the present difficulties in context and thus better to identify the present problems as well as perhaps to find solutions.

We start by summarizing briefly the current difficulties 'from the outside world', and then turn to the central bank objective.

EXTERNAL PROBLEMS

At the time of writing the world is being battered by two shocks. There is turmoil in the Middle East, and there has been a major earthquake and tsunami in Japan. The first has not merely pushed up the price of oil: it has also created uncertainty about how long the spike in the price will persist. This manifestly makes anti-inflation policy more difficult.[2] There have also been major supply shocks world wide as a result of the Japanese earthquake, as it has disrupted the supply chains of many manufacturers outside Japan. Of course there have been such disruptions before, but it seems to be the case that with increased speed of transport, specialization has increased and stocks of goods intermediate in manufacturing processes are smaller than before.

But these shocks, although perhaps unusual in their complexity, are of a kind to which central banks are accustomed. The problems—the uncertainties—with which this paper is concerned are also of a type that has occurred before, but has seldom occurred, and the last occurrence affected a generation of central bankers now largely gone from the fray.

OBJECTIVE UNCERTAINTY

The central banking objective evolved in three different settings. First there was the gold standard. (Any other commodity standard would have served the

[1] Notwithstanding the claims often made for the Sveriges Riksbank.

[2] Since this chapter is focusing primarily on the history of the Bank of England in its historical sections it is necessary to remark at this point that at the time of writing, and for some two years past, it is not clear whether the Bank of England is actually being serious in its attempts to satisfy its inflation target.

same function; but England evolved on to the gold standard.) Then there was the pegged-rate system of Bretton Woods. And then there were floating exchange rates. We examine each of these regimes in turn.

(a) The gold standard

Few countries were on the gold standard for long, and none continuously. What was this standard? Each unit of currency was freely exchangeable for a given weight of gold of a given fineness. Initially, the objective of the central bank was simple. It was to maintain that convertibility by varying its policy instrument, an interest rate, so as to maintain gold stocks at a level not only to allow, but to maintain confidence in, free convertibility. The confidence in it was of course important, as was confidence, in a different way, in the evolution of the gold standard regime rule.

Metallic coinage—gold, silver, and others—had evolved in their use over the centuries, either 'naturally' or aided by the imprimatur of the ruler, or, usually later, the state. In England silver predominated initially but gold was used for large transactions, and increasingly for settlement in international transactions. At the beginning of the eighteenth century the currency was formally defined in terms of gold, though both gold and silver coins continued to circulate. There was no announcement of the gold standard and de facto there was a bimetallic standard in place for much of the remainder of the century.

Prices remained stable and indeed almost flat across the eighteenth century in spite of the vagaries of continual war. But the pressures became too great on the outbreak of the Napoleonic Wars in the last decade of the century. At that point the promise to redeem in gold had to be suspended. There followed monetary expansion and inflation until the resumption of the gold standard at the beginning of the 1820s. The ferment of discussion on the nature of the real and nominal relationships that accompanied monetary, price, exchange-rate, and other changes, laid the foundations of monetary economics. Prominent among the contributors was Henry Thornton who spelled out the essence of central banking for not just his own times, but, as Anna Schwartz pointed out in 1981, for all times.

For our purposes the next stage is of great significance. The questions were: what was the gold standard? How should it be defined? How should it operate? The Bank from its privileged position had become the centre of the monetary system and had responsibility for protecting the reserve. But what should the relationship be? What levels of reserves should be held? Should they simply hold a large enough reserve to satisfy anticipated needs? The Bank Governor from 1830 to 1833, John Horsley Palmer, set out before the 1832 Committee of Inquiry what policy had emerged since 1827. That was that when the exchanges were 'in equilibrium' the Bank would be holding gold reserves equal to one-third of its total liabilities (these being its notes and deposits). Government securities would back the remainder of its liabilities. This specification had its critics, notably Lord Overstone, and he was instrumental in shaping the new Bank Charter Act of 1844. That Act prescribed a specified fiduciary issue and a one-to-one relationship between notes and gold stocks thereafter.

The redefinition of the gold standard did not allow for a financial crisis. Indeed its critics, of whom Palmer was prominent, claimed that it caused the crisis that arrived in 1847. The Bank was unable to respond to the demands for liquidity given the constraints imposed on it. (The appropriate responses had already been spelled out by Henry Thornton and Thomas Joplin.) The Bank needed to be able to supply liquidity without end. In order to do that it needed to be relieved of its obligation to issue only one-for-one against gold. The Bank explained its position to the Chancellor of the Exchequer who then granted the Bank freedom from the constraint. That would happen again in the crisis of 1857 and again in that of 1866. It had become clear that while the gold standard provided monetary stability in normal times, in times of crisis the standard needed to be relaxed. By 1866 that was understood, although the Bank was criticized for moving too slowly in the 1866 episode and thereby incurring all the costs of its actions without getting the benefits (Bagehot, 1873).

By the 1870s the Bank appreciated fully what its role as a lender of last resort was and in effect agreed to carry it out. In its ideal form the lender should: lend freely to all those with good collateral, but at a high rate; but it should be lending to the market as a whole and not to individual institutions—that is it should be providing liquidity anonymously; it should have no commercial rivalry that would result in conflicts of interest; it should pre-commit to its actions.

When this all became clear to the markets and each participant played his part, there followed a remarkable period of financial stability from the last third of the nineteenth century right through to the last third of the twentieth century. The government provided an environment of light regulation. The banks behaved prudently. And the Bank of England was there to provide liquidity in the event of an unforeseen shock.

From that sketch of an aspect of British monetary history, we can see aspects of the working of the British banking and monetary systems, and of the Bank's objective. The Bank adjusted its policy rate so as to maintain the gold reserve. It did so under certain operating principles. But it could deviate from that if the stability of the banking system were threatened, and could supply liquidity freely, with always in reserve but never actually used, the ability to seek a temporary suspension of the gold standard rule.[3]

Very important though, individual banks were expected to be, and were, allowed to fail. The Bank's role was to prevent individual failure contaminating

[3] In her classic 'Real and Pseudo Banking Crises' (1986) Anna Schwartz vigorously defended the distinction made by the Bank of England between the stability of an individual bank—not the Bank's concern—and the stability of the system—very much the Bank's concern.

the banking system. Failure could be and was contained. This was perhaps made easier by Britain's banks, although already large by the end of the nineteenth century, being thoroughly diversified across the country and across different economic activities.

There was a long period of growth and stability under this system, and it seemed as if it could last for ever, until it was savagely disrupted by the outbreak of the First World War.

In the summer of 1914 following the assassination of the heir to the Austrian throne alarm spread across Europe. The outbreak of war between Austria and Serbia at the end of July raised fears of a wider European war. The crisis then broke in the last week of July. For London this meant there was a failure of remittances from the continent. Brokers in London then began selling stocks and their prices collapsed. Bank Rate moved from 3 per cent on 31 July to 10 per cent on 2 August. A bank holiday was declared and a moratorium placed on bills of exchange. For London the root cause was the failure of remittance and, given that London was the major creditor, this remittance failure was on a substantial scale. The Bank behaved as it should and lent freely but, given the scale of demand, its reserves were soon under threat and the gold standard had to be suspended. There then followed a large injection of liquidity through Treasury notes, and together with other measures the crisis was resolved.

(b) The return to gold

After the war, when, why, and with what consequences did the world return to gold and thus to the old central banking objective?

The late nineteenth century had been so successful that it should not be surprising to find that when the war—the biggest upheaval ever in the world economy—was over there would be a strong desire to return to the apparent certainties of that previous era. The gold standard was part of that era and it took some time to restore it and even then it came in a different and in many respects inferior form. The old parity was aimed for by Britain partly out of the belief that a change would send the wrong signals (and perhaps carry with it implicitly the suggestion that changes could be made at any time) but partly too out of a sense of obligation to holders of sterling.

Returning to gold was difficult primarily because of the large price level adjustments that were required. Britain's price level had to fall relative to that of the US by a large amount, the actual figure ranging quite widely depending on how the calculation was carried out. But by any calculation required was a substantially larger adjustment than had occurred over any five-year (for example) period in Britain in the nineteenth century. And there were others such as it not being clear at what parities other countries would choose to return.

Be that as it may, the standard that was restored was different. There were insufficient stocks of gold to support the gold bullion standard that had operated in the nineteenth century given the changed price levels. The new standard, the gold-exchange standard, allowed the authorities to use both gold and foreign exchange in their reserves as backing for their currencies. That alone left some room for doubt. More importantly London had been at the centre of the old system—an enormously powerful centre in a leading economy. That had changed after the war when the US had become the leading/dominant economy. London was weak and New York strong, and confidence was fragile.

What happened next? The gold standard ended—not collapsed, but rather crumbled at considerable speed. Britain left it in 1931. Some other countries had abandoned gold before Britain. The US held on until 1933 and France until 1936.[4]

Thus the question of a new mandate for central banks would have arisen in the 1930s, but for the political and economic turmoil of these years resulting in policy being operated in an ad hoc way until the outbreak of the Second World War.

Throughout the inter-war years there were all kinds of turmoil as war debts, reparation payments, and political upheaval saw investors running for cover. The large-scale lending of the 1920s, mostly by the US, was followed by a wave of defaults. Capital took flight. The authorities responded with all manner of controls. After abandoning the gold standard many countries introduced exchange controls. Protectionist trade measures were not far behind in most countries, with the imposition of import tariffs and quotas, and the granting of export subsidies. Most countries were guilty, including the formerly free-trade Britain and the ever-increasingly protectionist US, and these measures reached their peak in the Schactian system of Nazi Germany.

Banking and financial crises spread across Europe following the collapse of the Creditanstalt in Austria in 1931. Separately, in the US after money was tightened in 1928 there followed a stock market collapse in 1929 and banking panic and crisis followed over the next three years. As far as central banks were concerned the target had become a managed exchange rate. In Britain this was supplemented with the Exchange Equalization Account and in the US by the Exchange Stabilization Account.

(c) Another external constraint

In the course of the Second World War, thought started to be given to the post-war economic order. The part of this planning relevant to the present discussion is the part concerned with international monetary relations.

4 An admirable review of this period is to be found in Eichengreen (1996).

It was agreed that the world should move to fixed-but-adjustable rates. There were differences in the form of arrangements proposed,[5] but the reason for the desire for fixity was clear. The inter-war years had been on continental Europe years of extraordinary turmoil. Floating exchange rates had been accompanied by very rapid inflations, in some countries by hyperinflations. Ragnar Nurkse's (1944) influential diagnosis of the period was that floating/collapsing exchange rates or competitive devaluations had pushed up prices, and accordingly there was widespread agreement that floating rates had to be avoided. Cassel's completely correct diagnosis that expectations of inflation formed on the basis of observing fiscal and monetary policies had led to exchange rates collapsing and subsequently, and from the same cause, domestic policy, to inflations, was regrettably not so influential at the time. (This is yet another example of policy-makers choosing the explanation for unfortunate events that lays the blame other than where it should be, on them.)

There is perhaps a caution that should be made here. The lessons of history are not always, indeed ever, easily discerned. The supposed lesson of the inter-war years was that floating rates were dangerous and had poor consequences and were therefore to be avoided. Nurkse had put that case powerfully; but the contrary case that was put not only by Cassel but also by for example Gottfreid Haberler (1937), who just at the end of the 1930s overviewed the economics of that turbulent decade, was ignored.

But be that as it may, the world moved to a system of fixed-but-adjustable exchange rates, all linked to the US dollar, which retained a link to gold, though without internal convertibility.

The essence of the Bretton Woods arrangements was that member countries would allow free convertibility on current account transactions while keeping capital account controls. And the 'Fund' would assist countries to manage their balance of payments in a way that was consistent with stable exchange rates. The designers envisaged a system in which each country: fixed a foreign par value for its currency; agreed to keep within 1 per cent of that value; used national monies symmetrically for foreign transactions; and drew on the 'Fund' for short-run payments imbalances. But each country was to be free to pursue its own price level and employment policies. This last meant that long-run flexibility in the exchange rate was required (see McKinnon, 1993). But it quickly became clear that the US was the only country that could behave autonomously, and the others had limited macro autonomy. So what emerged was a pegged-rate dollar standard with the US dollar as the intervention currency. Further, countries needed to subordinate long-run growth in domestic money supply to the exchange rate and the US inflation rate.

5 As found, for example, in the Keynes and White plans. See Eichengreen (1996).

A messy post-war adjustment period that involved failed attempts at restoring convertibility was followed by various devaluations and, together with other factors, meant that convertibility was delayed until the end of the 1950s.

The objective for central banks apart from the US Federal Reserve was to adjust monetary policy so as to maintain the peg. Thus it was very much like the gold standard, with life made more complicated for central banks by governments which had additional objectives and no longer ran budgets close to balance on average.[6] But on the other hand it was made easier for them by this being an age of controls. Exchange controls constrained outflows, and banking systems were regulated, sometimes by rule and sometimes by guidance, in what they could do. The regulations stifled innovation, and thus of course made the system more stable, albeit somewhat sclerotic. Problems that were to arise when significant numbers of banks failed in a world where governments claimed to look after their voters from cradle to grave, and thus felt obliged to compensate them for certain financial losses, therefore did not receive any public discussion.

In the UK individuals were protected generally by getting banks to use their profits to take over the occasional failing or failed institution. It was easy for the banks to do so, because the failures, incipient or actual, were generally modestly sized institutions. On the occasions, and these were rare, when larger banks got into difficulties, not having to mark to market, and for a time their being non-disclosing firms, saved the day. Deposit protection in the US, introduced to maintain the stability of the banking system in the face of Federal Reserve mistakes (Friedman and Schwartz, 1963), as a by-product protected individuals.[7]

The Bretton Woods system did, however, despite the difficulties both in the US and elsewhere, last for a number of years. It started to crumble in 1969, when US inflation led to one country after another breaking the link with the dollar so as to avoid importing US inflation. (Why the US inflated, and a detailed account of the end of Bretton Woods, can also be found in Meltzer, 2007.) What happened next?

(d) Freedom

Freedom eventually came in the form of a system adopted *faute de mieux*, and indeed denied by many at the time to the right of being called a system. This was a system of worldwide floating exchange rates. Under that system every

[6] As governments can finance their expenditures by taxes, borrowing, or printing money it is easy for budget deficits to lead to pressure on the central bank for monetization

[7] The US central bank nevertheless faced considerable difficulties, not least as a result of its multiple and changing objectives. See Meltzer (2007).

country has monetary autonomy (see Friedman, 1953, and McCallum, 2003). What were central banks to do in this world? Eventually they focused on inflation, and were in many cases, with the lead taken by New Zealand in 1989, given a mandate to achieve a particular rate of inflation. But that did not happen immediately.

There remained worries about stability, but not the stability of the banking system. Exchange-rate volatility—often confused with instability—was the concern of those policy-makers, and of many but not all outside those circles, who thought about financial stability. (See Allen and Wood, 2006.) Otherwise, it seemed as if risk was going away, a feeling which reached its apogee in the first decade of the twenty-first century, a decade which Charles Goodhart has characterized as one of mass delusion.

It is easy to see why many succumbed to delusion. Growth was steady throughout most of the world, and inflation low. In Britain the then Governor of the Bank of England (Mervyn King) characterized the decade as a NICE one—non-inflationary, constant expansion. And that was no exaggeration.

Low inflation, though, while very helpful to maintaining banking system stability, and indeed necessary for it, is not sufficient to achieve it. A most thorough exposition of this is given in Schwartz (1988).

There was a major banking crisis at the end of the twenty-first century's first decade. A detailed discussion of the causes of this crisis can be found in Lastra and Wood (2011). It is sufficient here to note that banking systems were, of course, bedevilled by shortages of liquidity, by low quality assets, and, very importantly, by capital ratios extremely low by historical standards.

(e) A crucial distinction

All banking crises are one of two types: liquidity crises and capital crises. One type of crisis rapidly merges with the other, so that beyond the initial stage of a crisis there are both liquidity and capital problems. But nevertheless it is useful to start with the sharp distinction.

A liquidity crisis is what might be described as the classic type of banking crisis. One bank for some reason cannot meet all its payment obligations. In consequence other banks experience runs, they too get into difficulties because, by the nature of fractional reserve banking, they cannot immediately pay out on all deposits, and in the extreme the entire banking system collapses like a row of dominoes. It is that type of crisis that the Bank of England in the nineteenth century developed lender of last resort policy to handle.

The second is when there is a sharp decline in the value of a bank's capital. This could come about, for example, if one large loan suddenly collapsed in value, or if a whole group of loans collapsed. As bank balance sheets are opaque to customers (and apparently often to management too if recent experience is anything to go by) this leads to fears about the solvency of other banks, runs take place on them, and again in the extreme the whole system fails.[8]

Liquidity crises have already been discussed in the examination of lender of last resort policy. Accordingly, pausing only to remark that it is a liquidity crisis that is modelled in the famous Diamond and Dybvig (1983) paper (it could not be otherwise, for their model of a bank is of a bank without capital), we move on to consider capital crises.

The archetypal capital crisis also occurred in England, and also in the nineteenth century. This episode, as it turned out, was confined to one bank, and thus was not a banking *system* crisis, but there were fears that it might spread to the entire system, and that it might damage the reputation of London as a financial centre. This was the 'Baring Crisis' of 1890.

Barings was then a bank of high and long-standing reputation. Driven by competition with newer banks to seek higher returns, it invested substantially in Argentina, and was caught up in difficulties there. In April 1890 the Argentinian government was unable to pay the bulk of interest then due on its debts. Next, and partly in consequence, the Argentinian national bank suspended interest payment on *its* debts. This precipitated a run on the Argentinian banking system and there was a revolution on 26 July. Barings had lent heavily in Argentina. By November it became clear to its directors that it could not survive unaided, and on 8 November it revealed its problems to the Bank of England. The Bank was horrified, fearing a run on the British banking system, and perhaps on sterling, if Barings defaulted. After a hurried inspection of the books of Barings, it was decided that the situation could be saved by a substantial injection of capital. A consortium was organized—the Bank was too small to have sufficient funds on its own—and Barings was saved. The reconstituted company continued in operation. There was some anxiety briefly in the London markets when news of the rescue leaked (as such news tends to), but no more than a tremor. The episode was contained to an individual firm (see Pressnell, 1968, and Clapham, 1970, for detailed accounts of the episode).

That is a perfect example of a capital crisis. A firm is short of capital and cannot pay its debts. If this brings down other banks, or if depositors in the original bank lose their deposits, a system-wide liquidity crisis may start. It may start because depositors are inevitably unclear about the state of the balance sheet of their bank, so fear for it when another bank previously believed to be sound appears to be in difficulties. But the injection of capital

[8] These runs may well, in modern circumstances, be what are called 'silent runs'. These are runs by relatively well-informed participants in wholesale markets, who can often 'run' simply by declining to roll over their loans. These runs can, but need not, be well founded, for a bank's balance sheet is to an extent opaque also to its banking counterparties.

can stop the crisis short. Note that central bank provision of liquidity would not suffice, for, to continue with the example of Barings, Barings did not have sufficient short-term assets to offer in exchange for the liquidity. The Bank would have had to accept some of Barings' long-term assets as collateral, and not only would this have been against a recently settled policy but the Bank's balance sheet was too small to let it assume the risk.

With the distinction between the two types of crisis clearly in mind, one can now proceed to an examination of the 2007–09 crisis. A brief initial comparison with 1929–33 is helpful.

1929–33 was manifestly a liquidity crisis at least in its origins (Friedman and Schwartz, 1963 op cit). How did it spread across the world? As the monetary approach to the balance of payments leads one to expect, the monetary squeeze in the US affected those countries pegged to the US dollar (through gold, in this case), but left countries without such a link substantially unaffected. Countries such as Sweden and the UK, which broke early from the gold standard, escaped the consequences of the US problems, while these which stayed on gold, such as France, experienced banking strains and severe recessions.[9]

The recent crisis was triggered when it was feared, or perhaps realized, that a good few banks would not be able to meet their liabilities, because many of their assets were worth less than had been paid for them. The wholesale money markets then dried up, and the crisis then became one of liquidity also. But that capital was the trigger is confirmed by how the recent crisis spread. The contrast with 1929–33 could not be sharper. It spread between countries whose exchange rates were floating—the US and the UK, for example. And it did not spread across all of an area which used a single currency, the extreme case of fixed exchange rates—for some countries in the Eurozone found their banking systems either unaffected, or affected only trivially—Finland, for example.

The first crisis of the twenty-first century was triggered by fears over capital, not by fears over liquidity.[10]

A system-wide capital shortage is rare. Indeed, the only precedent seems to be the Japanese banking crisis which started in the 1980s.

That crisis started with the bursting of an asset bubble at the end of the 1980s, and culminated in 1997 with the failure of several major financial institutions. In the latter half of the 1980s Japan had experienced above trend growth and near zero inflation. The optimism this produced led to a

[9] A brief overview of the years can be found in the introductory essay to Capie and Wood (2011).

[10] Some—notably Tim Congdon (2009)—have argued that despite this the problems were, at least in Britain, purely of liquidity. This position is considered but ultimately rejected in Wood (2010).

surge in the prices of most assets. There was also financial market deregulation. Interest-rate controls were relaxed, regulation of capital markets eased, and restrictions on the permitted activities of previously segregated institutions eased or removed. This permitted banks to take on more risk so as to offset the downward pressure on their interest margins. They did so. Credit standards for loan approvals were eased as real estate property prices rose. The stock market boomed, peaking at the end of 1989.[11] Then, to restrict rising land prices, the Ministry of Finance introduced limits on bank lending to the real estate sector. There was a slowdown in economic growth, followed by a fall in property prices and in the stock market. All these weakened Japanese banks, since the fall in property prices weakened the real estate companies to which they had lent so much; there was a fall in the value of collateral; and the decline in banks' equity holdings put pressure on their capital. The entire system was thus weakened. The system dragged on in this condition for years, impeding the growth of the Japanese economy. Then, in November 1997, Sanyo Securities declared bankruptcy. This resulted in Japan's first interbank loan default. Two weeks later Hokkaido Tokushoku found it was unable to borrow in the interbank market, and had to declare bankruptcy—this was the first failure of a major Japanese bank in the post Second World War period. Only a week later Yamaichi Securities, one of the four biggest security dealers in Japan, failed. It soon emerged that the rumours of fraud that had led to its failure were correct. Then, before the end of the month, Tokuyo City Bank (a regional bank) failed. The three-month Eurodollar Tokyo Interbank Borrowing Rate rose sharply above its London equivalent. Stress was also shown by sharply widened spreads in the domestic interbank market, and by late November some banks were finding even overnight borrowing difficult.

By the end of 1997 the government decided that 'something must be done'. They decided to inject taxpayers' funds, and also approved accounting changes which would allow banks to use either market or book value, as they wished, when valuing their share and real estate portfolios.

In February 1999, as a second capital injection was being considered, Eisuke Sakikabara, Vice Minister of Finance, declared that the banking crisis would be over within two weeks. At the end of that month the then US Deputy Treasury Secretary (Lawrence Summers) gave a speech in which he asserted that even

[11] In the aftermath of the Wall Street crash of October 1987 ('Black Monday') stock markets throughout the world followed Wall Street and fell precipitously. The one exception was Tokyo, which scarcely fell at all. The reason was that the Japanese authorities prevailed on the Japanese banks to go into the Tokyo market and buy Japanese equities, pretty indiscriminately, and property, which was the most overvalued of all sectors. Holding this poor portfolio was a major additional cause of the prolonged weakness of the Japanese banks. Further, Japanese banks were conspicuously reluctant to recognize their problems and to identify (publicly) and write down bad debts or impaired assets. This, too, hugely deepened and prolonged the Japanese crisis. We are indebted to Nigel Lawson for drawing these points to our attention.

after the proposed capital injection Japanese banks would be very weakly capitalized. And according to Kayshap (2002) a survey of six private-sector bank analysts found every analyst to estimate that the entire Japanese banking system was insolvent as of August 2002.

There is plainly much in common between the background circumstances of the Japanese crisis and the recent more widely spread one.

Why the recent crisis occurred is not discussed in detail here, as we are concerned with the problems it causes for central banks in the future. (Lastra and Wood (2011) provides a very full account of the causes, considering legal and accounting as well as strictly economic factors.) But some maintain that financial crises may well be inherent to the business cycle, or to human nature itself, and that seeking the cause or causes of an individual crisis can at best reveal only proximate causes. Minsky (1975) and Kindleberger (1978) have both argued that crises are an inevitable part of the business cycle, and result from the irrational reactions and myopia of market participants. Some banking theorists have argued, in a somewhat similar manner, that the structure of bank balance sheets makes panics inevitable (Diamond and Dybvig, 1983). In other words, persuaded by one argument or another we should expect crises always to be with us. Perhaps we should so far as financial crises are concerned; but the evidence is that we should not hold that expectation for banking crises.

Banking crises tend to occur (if they occur) around the time of cyclical downturns, and are closely associated with large declines in the value of bank loans, reflecting declines in the fortunes of the borrowers. Second, they have become more common in recent years, despite government interventions (such as government insurance of deposits) intended to achieve the opposite. Third, panics can happen without failures and failures without panics—the Panic of 1907 in the US was not associated with a rise in the bank failure rate, and the wave of agricultural bank failures in the US in the 1920s was not accompanied by a systemic panic. This suggests that uncertainty about small losses can cause panic without failure, while large losses with clear incidence cause failure without widespread panic.

But most important of all is that there are substantially different 'propensities' for crises at different times and places. The US banking system has historically been crisis prone. The US was in the forty years before the First World War unique in its high propensity for panics (Calomiris, 2009). There were nationwide bank panics in 1857, 1873, 1884, 1890, 1893, 1896, and 1907. And there were waves of bank failures in the 1830s, the 1920s, and the 1930s.

Britain, too, was crisis prone, but this changed in the middle of the nineteenth century. After 1866 there was none. On the outbreak of the First World War there were problems, but it was by no means a typical financial crisis. And finally in this overview, we look more widely. In the years 1875–1913, only four countries experienced severe waves of bank insolvency. In 1978–2009 some 140 such episodes occurred, more than 20 of which were more severe than any pre-1914 episode in terms of negative net worth of failed banks relative to GNP (Calomiris, 2009).

This diverse pattern shows clearly that there must be more to banking crises than the inevitable features of human nature or bank balance sheets. What is it?

Changes in the fragility of banking systems usually result from changes in the 'rules of the banking game.' Such changes can be stability promoting—as the Bank of England's adoption of, and commitment to, a lender of last resort role after 1866—or risk promoting, as were the Argentinian guarantees for mortgages in the 1880s or the Italian pre-1893 guarantees of the property lending of the Banca Romana. And the same story continues up to the present. Deposit insurance has reduced market discipline (Caprio and Klingbiel, 1996, or Barth, Caprio, and Levine, 2006, for example). Restrictions on structure have often proved perverse—the protection of unit banking in the US, or, again in the US, the passage of the Glass-Steagall Act despite the evidence against it (Benston, 1990). In contrast, Canada's early allowing of nationwide branch banking contributed to stability, as did the emergence of large well-diversified banks in Britain in the last quarter of the nineteenth century. Getting the rules of the banking game wrong readily makes the game go wrong.

Did that happen this time? Looking at the US, we certainly see a repetition of previous mistakes. There was pressure from the Congress on banks, on Fannie Mae, and on Freddie Mac, to promote house ownership by taking on more high-risk mortgages. There was Federal Housing Administration subsidy of high mortgage leverage; foreclosures were discouraged; and 2006 legislation encouraged rating agencies to relax standards on the rating of securitizations. Unsurprisingly, the US housing market boomed.

Banks elsewhere, some already caught up in their own housing booms, were drawn into the US boom. Then regulators were defective. Preoccupied with individual banks, they did not see, or ignored, that securitization was simply spreading risk around the system, and focused instead on the illusory reduction in individual bank risk which it produced.[12] Problems spread round the world.

Easy money and steady growth followed by ill thought-out regulatory policies were sufficient to cause the Japanese crisis. They were also present in the run—up to the present one. Whatever else contributed, these were the essential preconditions.

The system was then patched together. But what is to be done to prevent such problems in the future, or at the least to make them less likely and to handle them better when they occur?

[12] See Wood and Kabiri (2011).

THE FUTURE

When the crisis occurred various weaknesses in crisis resolution procedures were revealed, as were problems in bank management and regulation. We list the major ones of these very briefly and then turn to those which require further thought about the mandate of the central bank.

There was absence of market discipline (Haldane, 2011). Regulation of capital was so complex that it was easily circumvented and with difficulty, if at all, understood by outside observers, so market discipline was, at best, weak (Haldane, 2011). There were in most countries no procedures for orderly bank closure, and in no country were there the means to effect orderly closure of an investment bank (House of Commons Treasury Committee, 2008). Orderly resolution of a bank with substantial presence in several countries did occur, but only by the good fortune that the bank's lines of business divided more or less along country lines (Mayes and Wood, 2009).

These are by and large matters for governments to resolve, albeit with the advice of central banks (and no doubt others). There remain the following issues which require reflection on, and in all probability modification of, the central bank's mandate. These are the rules governing the provision of emergency liquidity;[13] the rules governing provision of capital in an emergency; the rules concerning the inflation mandate; the tools at the central bank's disposal; and central bank/government relations, in particular bearing on when the central bank has taken substantial losses as an inevitable consequence of satisfying its mandate.

CONCLUDING OVERVIEW

Now it is clear why we entitled this chapter as we did. There is much uncertainty facing central banks, and it is uncertainty about what must be done to central banks to make them better able than they were in this century's first decade to deal with financial crises. History is often claimed to provide lessons. These lessons are usually less clear cut than many of those who draw them claim. But we can say with confidence that we would be very surprised indeed if the world were never again to see a financial crisis. We offer a few conjectures in the introduction to this volume, drawn from the work that has gone into preparing not just this volume's chapters, but from all our work on monetary history, on how central banking may need to change to improve the crisis preventing and crisis handling abilities of central banks.

[13] In Britain the methods of liquidity provision also had to be changed. See House of Commons Treasury Committee (2008) and Milne and Wood (2009).

REFERENCES

Allen, W. A. and Wood G. E. (2006) 'Defining and Achieving Financial Stability', *Journal of Financial Stability*, 2, 156–72.

Bagehot, W. (1873) *Lombard Street; A Description of the Money Market*, London: Henry S King and Co.

Barth, J. R., Caprio, G., and Levine, R. (2006) *Rethinking Bank Regulation: Till Angels Govern*, Cambridge University Press.

Benston, G. J. (1990) *The Separation of Commercial and Investment Banking: The Glass-Steagall Act Revisited and Reconsidered*, New York: Oxford University Press.

Calomiris, C. 'Banking Crises and the Rules of the Game', NBER Working Papers 15403, National Bureau of Economic Research, Inc (2009).

Capie, F. H. and Wood, G. E. (eds) (2011) *Critical Writings on the Great Depression*, London: Routledge.

Caprio, G. and Klingbeil, D. (1996) 'Bank Insolvency: Bad Luck, Bad Policy or Bad Banking?' *Annual World Bank Conference on Development Economics*, 29–62.

Cassel, Gustav (1922) *Money and Foreign Exchange after 1914*, London: Constable & Co.

Clapham J. H. (1970) *The History of the Bank of England: 1694–1797* (reprint), Cambridge University Press.

Congdon, T. (2009) *Central Banking in a Free Society*, London: Institute of Economic Affairs.

Diamond, D. W. and Dybvig, P. H. (1983) 'Bank Runs, Deposit Insurance, and Liquidity', *The Journal of Political Economy*, 91(3).

Eichengreen, B. (1996) *Golden Fetters*, Oxford University Press.

Friedman, M (1953) 'The Case for Flexible Exchange Rates', *Essays in Positive Economics*, University of Chicago Press, pp. 157–213.

——and A. J. Schwartz (1963) *A Monetary History of the United States*, Princeton University Press for NBER.

Haldane A. (2011) 'Capital Discipline', Speech given at the American Economic Association, and published by the London: Bank of England.

Haberler G. (1937) *Prosperity and Depression: A Theoretical Analysis of Cyclical Movements*. (Reprinted) 1946 Lake Success, NY: United Nations.

House of Commons Treasury Committee (2008) 'The Run on the Rock' Fifth Report of Session 2007–08.

Kashyap, A. K. (2002) 'Sorting out Japan's Financial Crisis', *Economic Perspectives*, Federal Reserve Bank of Chicago, Issue Q IV, pp. 42–55.

Kindleberger, C. P. (1978) *Manias, Panics and Crashes: A History of Financial Crises*, London: Macmillan.

Lastra, R. M. and Wood G. E. (2011) 'The Crisis of 2007–09: Nature, Causes and Reactions', *Journal of International Economic Law*, 13(3), 531–50.

McCallum B. T. (2003) 'Theoretical Issue Pertaining to Monetary Unions', in F. H. Capie and G. E Wood (eds), *Monetary Unions: Theory, History, Public Choice*, London: Routledge.

McKinnon, Ronald I. (1993) 'Bretton Woods, the Marshall Plan, and the Post-War Dollar Standard', in Bordo and Eichengreen, eds., *A Retrospective on the Bretton Woods System*, Chicago: University of Chicago Press.

Mayes D. and Wood, G. (eds) (2009) *Designing Central Banks*, London: Routledge International Studies in Money and Banking.

Meltzer A. H. (2007) *A History of the Federal Reserve*, University of Chicago Press.

Milne, A. and Wood, G. E. (2009) 'Shattered on the Rock? British Financial Stability from 1866 to 2007', *Journal of Banking Regulation*, 10, 2.

Minsky, Hyman P. (1975) *John Maynard Keynes*, New York: Columbia University Press, 58.

——(1986) *Stability in an Unstable Economy*, New York: McGraw Hill.

Nurske, R. (1944) *International Currency Experience Economic*, Geneva: Financial and Transit Department, Series of League of Nations Publications.

Presnell L. S. (1968) 'Gold Reserves, Banking Reserves and the Baring Crisis of 1890', in C. R. Whittlesey and J. S. G. Wilson (eds), *Essays in Money and Banking in Honour of R. S. Sayers*, London: Oxford Universitiy Press.

Schwartz. A. J. (1986) 'Real and Pseudo Financial Crises', in Forrest Capie and Geoffrey Wood (eds), *Financial Crises and the World Banking System*, London: Macmillan.

——(1988) 'Financial Stability and the Federal Safety Net', *Restructuring Banking and Financial Services in America*, Washington, DC: American Institute for Public Policy Research.

——(1989) 'A Century of British Market Interest Rates, 1874–1975,' in *Monetary Economics in the 1980s*, ed. F. H. Capie and G. E. Wood, London and New York: Macmillan.

Wood, G. (2010) 'Was Tolstoy Right?' Paper prepared for a conference at European University Institute, Florence. Published in *The Politics, Economics, and History of Financial Crises*, ed. Harold James, Princeton University Press.

— with Kabiri, A. (2011) 'Firm Stability and System Stability: The Regulatory Delusion', in R. LaBrosse, R. Olivares-Caminal, and D. Singh, (ed.), *Managing Risk in the Financial System*, Cheltenham: Edward Elgar.

Index